ARCHITECTURE
NOW!

IMPRINT

PROJECT COORDINATION
Caroline Keller

COLLABORATION
Nicole Bilstein, Karl Georg
Cadenbach, Uta Hoffmann

PRODUCTION
Thomas Grell

DESIGN
Sense/Net, Andy Disl and
Birgit Reber, Cologne

GERMAN TRANSLATION
Karin Haag

FRENCH TRANSLATION
Jacques Bosser

PRINTED IN ITALY
ISBN 3–8228–6065–4

WWW.TASCHEN.COM
© 2001 TASCHEN GMBH
Hohenzollernring 53
D – 50672 Cologne

ARCHITECTURE NOW!

Architektur heute / L'architecture d'aujourd'hui

Philip Jodidio

TASCHEN

KÖLN LONDON MADRID NEW YORK PARIS TOKYO

CONTENTS

CONTENTS

INTRODUCTION

Each new building is the result of specific circumstances, ranging from function or location to cost. Trends in taste or fashion obviously play their role in determining the appearance of architecture and its deeper meanings, though some attempt to deny such influences. "Style," the French naturalist Buffon said, "is the man himself." Perhaps, but it is also a function of the times. Despite the proliferation of new means of communication, no one style has come to dominate contemporary architecture as strongly as postwar Modernism. Currents and cross-currents ripple around the globe, often delayed by the sheer amount of time it takes to design and build a large structure. Thus, architecture in the fractured Deconstructivist style, born in the 1980s, continues to be built. So too, do the neo-Minimalist designs of the 1990s. If "style is the man himself," these buildings are logically produced by architects who fought long and hard to impose their points of view against all odds. Once their ideas have taken hold, they are not likely to move quickly onto other types of design.

While aging trends play out their existence around the world, new styles are taking hold. The new century will display a return to interest in more complex buildings, born less of the disrupted Euclidean geometry seen in the late 20th century than of computer generated volumes that seek to challenge all reference to rectilinear systems. Though some architects still feel that computers are useful only for certain tasks, others have begun to explore new frontiers such as the idea of the "virtual" building – one that will exist only on screens. Asymptote in New York have been commissioned to design a "virtual museum" for the Guggenheim, just as they have created an on-line trading environment for the New York Stock Exchange. These are spaces whose primary existence will be played out on computer screens. The increasing sophistication of computer design is also permitting another form of virtual construction – that of monuments of the past that were never erected. Professor Takehiko Nagakura of MIT and his Team Unbuilt are resurrecting designs by Le Corbusier, Aalto and Tatlin. Some may see these efforts as being little more than an amusing result of the substantial means put into the creation of computer games like Myst or Riven. For the traditionally minded, the very heart of architecture is in its solidity or durability, admittedly relative qualities that are nonetheless completely obviated in the realm of the virtual. Others, like Hani Rashid of Asymptote, have a different idea of the future. "When speaking of an architecture for the next millennium," says Rashid, "there are two conditions to consider, the physical space of architecture as we have always known it where enclosure, form and permanence will undoubtedly persevere, and the realm of virtual architecture, now emerging from the digital domain of the Internet. Objects, spaces, buildings and institutions can now be constructed, navigated, comprehended, experienced, and manipulated across a global network. This is a new architecture of liquidity, flux and mutability predicated on technological advances and fueled by a basic human desire to probe the unknown. The inevitable path for both these architectures, the real and the virtual, will be one of convergence and merging."

This overview of recent contemporary architecture takes on the daunting task of collecting information from all over the world and attempting to make some sense of it in terms of trends and the evolution of what remains, in its most elevated expressions, a true art form. Even so, innovative architecture, which succeeds in reconciling the often contradictory limits of site, budget, and aesthetic ambition, is excessively rare as compared with the vast number of new buildings erected. Style, even in its varied guises, defines what makes architecture current, of our time. Driven by fashion or more profoundly perhaps, by the widening vistas of computer and Internet technology, will architecture become as fluid and changeable as a spring dress? Certainly not, but it is entering a time when flux and movement are more sought after than immutable monumentality.

VIRTUALLY YOURS

"The museum has become a tomb for art," declares Hani Rashid of Asymptote, "a repository where art is presented to a public presumed to be uninitiated, the pristine spaces of detached and privileged viewing or a space of cultural authority for the dissemination of ideas and the propagation of ideologies. Perhaps what still lingers and deserves to be maintained is an understanding of the space of the museum as a place that can incite provocation in both viewers and artists." Asymptote has been given the task of designing the first virtual museum, one that will exist essentially on the Internet. This "Guggenheim in Cyberspace" has the ambition to create nothing less than "a new architectural paradigm". More specifically, in the museum's terms, "The Guggenheim Virtual Museum will not only provide global access to all Guggenheim Museums including typical museum services, amenities, archives, and collections but will also provide a unique and compelling spatial environment to be experienced by the virtual visitor. In addition, the virtual museum is an ideal space for the deployment and experience of art and events created specifically for the interactive digital medium where simultaneous participation, as well as viewing, is made possible for an audience distributed around the globe. As envisioned by Asymptote and the Guggenheim, the Guggenheim Virtual Museum will emerge from the fusion of information space, art, commerce and architecture to become the first important virtual building of the 21st century." Beyond only creating an environment, one in which works of art can be agreeably viewed, Hani Rashid wants to make his virtual architecture interactive. Its use by visitors will modify its appearance, thus challenging the very solidity or immutability of architecture in general and museums in particular. Like the art it houses, the Virtual Guggenheim will be fluid, redefining itself according to circumstances. Such a project does redefine the architectural paradigm in the sense that it is subjected to almost none of the usual "real world" constraints that hamper buildings, from fire codes to access for the handicapped. It has neither to shelter nor to obey the mundane laws of mechanical engineering. Is this indeed architecture or rather a kind of electronic interior design? It certainly is new.

Asymptote has also created an on-line trading environment for the New York Stock Exchange (NYSE). "The 3-Dimensional Trading Floor (3DTF)," says Rashid, "is a multidimensional real-time virtual reality environment and the Advanced Trading Floor Operations Center project is a renovation and redesign of the existing operations area of the Stock Exchange." It means, the NYSE asked Asymptote to create both the on-line design for stock monitoring and sales, and for an area near the main trading floor in New York. "The 3DTF," continues Hani Rashid, "is a data-scape that brings together information flows, data, and correlation models into a single seamless 3-dimensional architectural environment. The virtual space is a real-time model displaying activity and events to users as a fully interactive navigable space with infinite possibilities of movement and viewing. The deployment of the 3DTF alongside the actual trading floor allows the operations personnel to gain a deeper and more precise understanding of the many variables and complexities that unfold during trading sessions. Asymptote utilized VRML (virtual reality markup language) and sophisticated CAD programs in the design and development of the components that make up the unprecedented 3DTF environment. In addition to the model's functional requirements, Asymptote paid special attention to the overall quality of the virtual environment through the control of light, color and texture as well as explorations and the development of various methods of navigation, movement, viewing and the overall graphic interface." Architecture or graphic design? Both, apparently.

The taste for freely flowing or a-geometrical volumes and environments is by no means limited among younger architects to such radical approaches as that of Asymptote. Another New York group, Diller + Scofidio, is challenging the concept of traditional architecture in an entirely different way. Their "Blur Building" designed for the International Expo 2002 in Yverdon on Lake Neuchâtel in Switzerland should resemble nothing so much as a cloud. Measuring just under 100 m in length, 60 m in width and 12 m in thickness, the cloud "is made of filtered lake water shot as a fine mist through a dense array of high-pressure water nozzles integrated into a large cantilevered tensegrity structure." The public will approach the immobile cloud via a ramp that becomes glass-enclosed as it enters the water mist. Within, the architects are seeking to achieve "a near absence of stimuli, an optical 'white-out' accompanied by the 'white noise' of the mist pulse…" A panoramic video image projected on a circular screen will occupy a central darkened platform for 250 people. "Since man can no longer claim to be in the center of a controllable universe, the position of the spectator continues to be an issue of critical reflection," say the architects. Diller + Scofidio make ample use of computers in their design work, but unlike Asymptote they have chosen to make physical construction their ultimate goal. They join their New York colleagues in challenging the very principles of architecture, reaching beyond form and materials to "blur" the auditory and visual perception necessary to spatial orientation. Rather than the hierarchical spatial order imposed by almost any traditional architecture, the "Blur Building" makes nothing clear, adopting a scientific and even philosophical stance in harmony with much of contemporary thinking.

Somewhat less challenging of the fundamental rules of architecture, the new restaurant of the Centre Georges Pompidou, by the young designers Jakob + MacFarlane, nonetheless does away with the distinction between floor and wall. Free-form aluminum volumes crafted in a shipyard house the kitchen, restrooms and bar on the topmost floor of the Piano and Rogers building. A consistent grid is traced on the floor panels that suddenly rise up into 3-dimensional distortions clearly inspired by computer modeling. Called "caves-nuages" (cloud caves) by the architects, these morphological volumes were built in a shipyard in France near La Rochelle. With its spectacular view on traditional Paris, this restaurant, run by the Costes family, may be more symbolic of the Centre Pompidou's commitment to contemporary creativity than much of the art housed within its walls. Though its master-grid makes a nod to Piano's more rational use of space, Jakob + MacFarlane belong to a younger generation, familiar with and attuned to the possibilities of computer-assisted design. Having come from very different horizons – Dominique Jakob grew up in the Ivory Coast, Gabon and the Niger before studying architecture in Paris, while Brendan MacFarlane is from New Zealand, and studied at Harvard's Graduate School of Design – they both worked briefly in the Santa Monica offices of Morphosis.

Takehiko Nagakura is an Assistant Professor of Design and Computation in the Department of Architecture at MIT. He studied architecture at Tokyo University under Fumihiko Maki. With funding from the Takenaka Corporation of Japan he created "Team Unbuilt," which "aims at a marriage between a serious historic research and a cutting-edge computer graphics technology." As Takehiko Nagakura explains, "the forms of the buildings are researched from the original archival drawings obtained from organizations such as the Le Corbusier Foundation in Paris. A global illumination-based visualization technology is applied to reveal the most subtle effects of interactions between light, material and geometry. The resulting computer graphics representation displays a spectacular spatial impression within the exterior and interior space, which until now have been concealed only inside the mind of the architects of these unbuilt buildings."

Takehiko Nagakura has chosen buildings such as Alvar Aalto's Church in Altstetten (Switzerland, 1967), or Le Corbusier's competition entry for the Palace of the Soviets (Moscow, Soviet Union, 1931). One of the most spectacular virtual buildings he has exhumed from archival material, however, is Vladimir Tatlin's Monument to the Third International (Petrograd, Soviet Union, 1919), one of the first buildings conceived entirely in abstract terms. Commissioned in 1919 by the Department of Fine Arts of the People's Commissariat of Enlightenment, it was shown in the form of a 6.7 m-high model at the exhibition of the 8th Congress of the Soviets in December 1920. This model was, until now, the only way to visualize this essential work of 20th-century architecture. It would have consisted of a leaning spiral iron framework supporting a glass cylinder, a glass cone, and a glass cube, each of which could be rotated at different speeds. Its interior would have contained halls for lectures, conferences, and other activities. Planned to be the world's tallest structure, almost 400 m high, it was never built because of the Soviet government's disapproval of nonfigurative art.

Insisting on the historian's work necessary in the preparation of his virtual construction projects, Takehiko Nagakura sees Team Unbuilt essentially as an educational tool. This means that a future generation of architects will be even more at ease with the concept of the virtual building. "In my opinion," says Nagakura, "this detective work coupled with virtual-practice experience is an extremely effective way of training and educating an architect. Perhaps it fits very closely to the model of traditional French education of architects, which promoted the study of architecture of antiquity. In this belief, I run a course at MIT, using the resources and materials collected for the Unbuilt project, and provide opportunities for students to learn spatial representation through the use of the cutting-edge digital technology."

TOWERING AMBITIONS

As some architects evolve toward more and more immaterial buildings, others invest themselves in designs that seem to be quintessentially related to monumentality as it was defined in the 20th century. Higher and higher towers are being proposed and actually built all over the world. The competition to build the tallest building in the world mobilizes great sums of money and talent both in Asia and in the United States. A new project in Chicago, birthplace of the skyscraper, currently seems to be the most ambitious design in the works.

Although psychological implications and height seem to be major considerations in tower design, the aesthetic aspects are often relegated to a secondary role. This, however, is true for the French architect Christian de Portzamparc, who has made a statement in favor of the aesthetics of tall buildings with his LVMH Tower in New York. Small by Shanghai or Chicago standards, his tower features an innovative glass facade and a spectacular 3-story-high room at the top. One of the world's largest luxury products groups, the French firm LVMH favored Portzamparc not because he won the 1994 Pritzker Prize, but because of his propensity to what might be termed lyrical designs. The 24-story building is clad in etched and sand-blasted glass with green, white and blue fluorescent tubes marking a "fault-line" between fractured surfaces. Made by Saint Gobain in France, the glass, at least partially, intends to avoid reflections of the massive black volume of the IBM Building located on the opposite side of 57th Street. Herbert Muschamp of the *New York Times* wrote that Portzamparc has "reimagined the idea of Art Deco", adding his voice to a chorus of praise proclaiming the tower one of the most successful new buildings in New York in many years.

At the opposite end of the world, and taking a very different approach, the American firm KPF is working on the Shanghai World Financial Center. Located in the Lujiazui Financial and Trade district in Pudong, this 95-story building is to reach a height of 460 m, making it temporarily at least, the tallest building in the world. It is a 312 152-m^2 project with a budget exceeding US$500 million. To KPF's credit, the tower, to be completed in 2004, adopts a particularly pure form that evolves from the intersection of a square prism and a cylinder. For reasons related to wind pressure, the center's most visible feature of the upper part is a 50 m circular void baptized the "moon gate." The shape of the tower's shaft brings to mind the powerful simplicity of archaic Chinese objects. Responding to the local context, termed by KPF "a visual cacophony," the void at the top of the tower corresponds in its dimensions with the sphere (or "pearl") that caps the facing Oriental Pearl TV Tower. Obviously, historical and contextual references are secondary when it comes to building the tallest building in the world, but KPF have stressed their standard of architectural quality even in this commercially driven environment. With its lower 28 m clad in rusticated stone and the upper floors with lightly reflective glass and stainless steel, the Shanghai World Financial Center (Design Principal: William Pedersen) should stand out among a number of less distinguished buildings not only because of its height. In fact, it tops Shanghai's recently completed Jin Mao Building by only 40 m.

However, even the Shanghai World Financial Center may never claim the title of "world's tallest building." Another project, slated for Chicago, is to surpass it by a mere 13 m (total height 473 m), and may be completed in 2003. On September 21, 1999, the City of Chicago Planning Commission approved plans to erect a tower designed by Adrian Smith of Skidmore, Owings & Merrill for a site located at 7 South Dearborn on the corner of Dearborn and Madison Streets. With its upper floors cantilevered from a concrete core, the building is planned to reach 108 stories, including the highest residential units in the world. Clad in aluminum, stainless steel and lightly tinted glass, the building will be topped by enormous digital television broadcasting towers.

Depending on the structural nature of buildings, their forms have a relationship to predictable types of stress. Tall buildings are particularly susceptible to such influences. After a certain height, the form of skyscrapers can be dictated by such factors as resonance, vortex shedding and flutter, all terms related to wind resistance. This means that design elements such as the large notches planned in 7 South Dearborn have little or nothing to do with aesthetics. The hole in the top of the Shanghai World Financial Center, as broad as the wingspan of a Boeing 747, is actually an elegant solution to an engineering problem. The internal design of skyscrapers is also hostage to the complex problem of efficient elevator transport.

It would be wrong to say that most very tall buildings are devoid of aesthetic merit. In fact, by their very accumulation in cities like New York, Chicago or perhaps Shanghai, they create an urban dynamic and architectural collage that is undeniably exciting. With their imposing presence, skyscrapers are difficult to ignore. Whatever may be said about trends in contemporary architecture or "styles," no overview can simply deny their existence. Responding to needs, some real and commercial, others merely psychological, tall buildings seem to be a recurrent fixture of contemporary architecture, part and parcel of its evolution, even if they seem contrary to much current theory. Skyscrapers recently proposed are approaching the 500 m-height barrier, even surpassing it in the case of the planned 574 m-tall Landmark Tower in Hong Kong.

ARTS AND CRAFTS

The arts and their exhibition continue to provide one of the most exciting areas for the development of high quality contemporary architecture. For those who are only moderately interested in the idea of "virtual" museums, art and art museums constitute one of the few areas where a certain durability and immutability are considered appropriate. Nonetheless the genre is evolving rapidly, as a few selected examples prove.

Located on a market square in the eastern Dutch city of Nijmegen, the Museum Het Valkhof is the work of UN Studio, Ben van Berkel and Caroline Bos, who also built the Erasmus Bridge in Rotterdam, in which they intended to bring together under one roof the diverse collections of the Museum Commanderie van Sint-Jan and the Provinciaal Museum G. M. Kam. A cool tonality given to the building by its greenish blue glass cladding is retained within, where the architects allow the works to speak for themselves. Indeed, rather than imposing a route through the space, as many museum designers do, van Berkel and Bos claim that there are at least 88 ways to view the Museum Het Valkhof. A long transparent gallery on one side of the building offers a view into the neighboring park. Characterized by discretion, flexibility, and openness, the Museum Het Valkhof is decidedly of its time.

Álvaro Siza's Serralves Foundation is located close to the center of Porto, Portugal, where this architect is based. The Serralves Foundation was created through a unique partnership between the Portuguese government and 50 private partners. Established in the Quinta de Serralves on a 20-hectare property including a main house built in the 1930s for the Count of Vizela, the Foundation specializes in contemporary art. Siza's structure in the park of the Foundation is both substantial in size and ambitious in scope. Using a suspended ceiling system similar to the one he devised for the Galician Center of Contemporary Art, Siza created a number of large, flexible galleries, not intended to show the permanent collection, but exclusively to facilitate temporary exhibitions. Internal courtyards and numerous windows allow the visitor to remain in contact with the very attractive park environment (3 hectares of which were created by Siza), while the interior provides all the facilities now expected of modern museums, including a gift shop, cafeteria and an auditorium. The complex is built with a visible attention to detail typical of Siza, and here he has been given the means to realize his ideas. Modernist in inspiration, the Serralves Foundation is by no means outdated in its conception. Complex despite its crisp white lines, the building is further proof that Álvaro Siza is one of the most original and powerful architects of his generation.

Born in the 1930s, like Siza, the Japanese architect Yoshio Taniguchi, recognized as a master in his own country, has emerged as a figure of international significance since he was commissioned to redesign the Museum of Modern Art in New York. His sober mastery of the Modernist vocabulary is amply demonstrated in his most recent completed work, the Gallery of Horyuji Treasures, located in the grounds of the Tokyo National Museum in Ueno Park. Since the National Museum was founded in the late 19th century as the Museum of the Imperial Household, it retains objects donated to the imperial collections in the 1870s as part of an effort to save Horyuji Temple in Nara from waves of anti-Buddhist sentiment. It was for these important items, masks, sculptures, and ritual objects made of metal that Taniguchi erected a tripartite structure. "I conceived of a building in three layers," says the architect, "an inner area walled in stone, an area outside walled in glass, and an outer area delineated by a metal canopy." The innermost box is shielded from daylight, while the entrance hall and space covered by the canopy are flooded with light. Taniguchi recalls that "the multi-layered design of the museum … is meant to symbolize the history of the precious objects it houses, which have been passed down through the ages in layers after layers of outer and inner wooden boxes that have been traditionally used to protect art treasures in Japan." Although the architect is less explicit on this point, his gallery recalls many aspects of Japanese temple design. The entry path leads the visitor toward a reflecting pool with an axial fountain, and he is required to change direction no less than four times while making his approach, thereby – typical of Japanese temples – reminding him that a significant space is being entered. He is greeted by a stone screen where he might have expected to find a door. He needs to go around this last barrier to enter the otherwise very rational exhibition space. The overall impression of extremely high quality construction is heightened by such details as the absolutely perfect alignments of every part of the building, from its innermost gallery to the outermost edges of the basin. Precise and restrained, Yoshio Taniguchi is an aristocratic master, much like his friend Fumihiko Maki. Both have found ways to blend Japanese tradition with modernity in strikingly powerful designs.

It appears that the generation of Álvaro Siza and Yoshio Taniguchi may have a more traditional view of museum architecture than do younger architects like Ben van Berkel and Caroline Bos. His flexibility and openness are contrasted with a more restrained, hierarchical type of architecture, where views are framed by Siza, and visitor approaches controlled by Taniguchi. This certainly does not mean that Siza and Taniguchi are no longer of their time; it rather reflects that in the context of the exhibition of art different approaches, perhaps linked to the age of their designers, can and do coexist.

A PASSION FOR FASHION

It would be unfair to say that an adherence to fashion is objectionable in architecture. For some applications, fashion is indeed the heart of the matter. In selling clothes or attracting people to the newest hotel, nothing succeeds so well as the very latest design, even if it entails an ephemeral approach. One of the fashion designers most committed to cutting-edge architecture and interior spaces is the Japanese businesswoman Rei Kawakubo, who heads the Comme des Garçons firm. Kawakubo has long maintained a strict control over her store interiors which usually have tended toward a minimalist purity. One of her most recent endeavors is the creation of a store on West 24th Street in the heart of Manhattan's new gallery area in Chelsea. From the outside, the store defies almost every rule of commercial logic. A plain stripped brick facade shows only the amusing "Heavenly Body Works" sign left by the previous user of the space. Only the rather futuristic glass door and the opening of an aluminum tunnel signal that this is no ordinary car repair facility. Passing through the seamless monocoque tunnel designed by the British architects Future Systems, the visitor enters a world of white enamel pods that only reluctantly reveal their secrets. Working with Studio Morsa in New York and with her long-time collaborator, the architect Takao Kawasaki, Kawakubo invites the customer to "fully enjoy the space itself first." The spare selection of items for sale contributes to what she calls "an atmosphere".

A world away and located in a modern building with a glass facade, her new Flagship Store in the Aoyama district of Tokyo has a similar atmosphere due to the recurring use of large black and white pods and her own very detailed involvement in the creation of both spaces. In Tokyo, Future Systems created an unexpected undulating glass facade, whose blue dots partially obscure the interior. Again working with

Takao Kawasaki on the interior, Kawakubo also invited Christian Astuguevieille and the artist Sophie Smallhorn to participate. She took an even more radical approach in the nearby Comme des Garçons Two shop in Tokyo. Here, only a brightly colored orange door signals the existence of a store. The rest of the cubical volume is unadorned brick veneer. As the designer says, "The door is open to all those interested in Comme des Garçons." And her approach, while seemingly anti-commercial indeed, seems to be attracting clients. As she says, "Without change nothing new can be born. Even a simple adjustment of the viewpoint can sometimes change everything dramatically. The New York and Tokyo stores are drawing many people now, and I think the reason is that people are always attracted to strong new ideas." Shop design, even the best, is ephemeral by nature. Yet Kawakubo and her talented associates have shown that good design can be commercially viable. This is of course no mass-marketing ploy – it is aimed at a rather elitist audience, but the success of the effort, in both aesthetic and marketing terms, is significant.

As Rei Kawakubo the French designer Philippe Starck has made a name in fashionable circles by designing the decors of some of the trendiest new hotels in Miami (Delano, 1995), Los Angeles (Mondrian, 1996) or New York (Royalton, 1988, and Paramount, 1990). All of these, like his most recent venture, the St. Martin's Lane Hotel in London, were carried out with the inimitable Ian Schrager, still best-known as the creator of New York's Studio 54 nightclub. Schrager is famous for his outspoken comments, such as "Design is a marketing tool… It gets us noticed," or "Hotels are not about design. Design is just one of the elements. It's part of the total equation." Perhaps it is Schrager who best defines the appeal of Starck's often outrageous inventions such as giant flower vases. "It's about an attitude," he says. "I don't think you can label what Philippe does. You can't say it's minimal. It's not Art Deco. It's not Baroque. It's not really Post-Modern. It's random. It's freeform. It's hotel as theatre!" Fitting Starck's brand of fashionable madness into a 1960s-style office building just up the street from Trafalgar Square was the task of Schrager's efficient team, also responsible for the more recent Sanderson in Berners Street in London. A bright yellow wall that Starck impishly calls "the color of the millennium" sets the tone once the visitor has passed through what is billed as the highest revolving door in Europe. This is where the "excitement" is, as Schrager says, a unique combination of Louis XIV imitation armchairs and stools that look like gold-plated teeth. This may not be a decor that will last a millennium, or even a hundred years, but Philippe Starck teamed with Ian Schrager do much to form opinion of what it means to be fashionable in architecture and design.

THE PLEASURE DOME

Tony Blair's Labor government played the Millennium Dome card for all it was worth. It was to be the symbol of all the marvelous things that New Labor was doing for the country – bringing it with a bang into the 21st century. Rather poor organization spoiled the December 31 opening prohibiting thousands from traveling to and from the structure designed by Richard Rogers. Within, visitors discovered a rather disappointing hodge-podge of pavilions, much like what one might expect to find at a World's Fair. Nonetheless, aside from Rogers, a number of the world's most talented architects participated in this initiative, and as such it deserves a mention. Millennium Dome organizers were delighted to spew out facts about the project's very dimensions before its opening. The largest roof in the world ($100\,000$ m^2); big enough to engulf Trafalgar Square; 100 times the size of Stonehenge; 80 times the volume of the Concert Hall of the Sydney Opera House; the largest dome in the world and so on. Situated in Greenwich on a peninsula opposite Christopher Wren's Royal Observatory (1675), the Dome undoubtedly surprised visitors first and foremost with its fundamental modesty. Despite its impressive statistics, not the least its phenomenal cost of £43 million, the Dome when viewed from a certain proximity appears surprisingly low and small. Because its height is relatively insignificant compared with its circumference, some even question whether it is indeed a "dome" or rather an extravagant tent.

Divided into 14 zones related to the development of contemporary life the Dome featured the work of designers like Zaha Hadid (Mind), Branson Coates (Body), Eva Jiricna (Faith), and Shigeru Ban (Shared Ground with Gumuchdjian & Spence). Hadid's Mind Zone, with its spectacular cantilevered structure, was intended to be nothing less than "the world's first intelligent building". Curiously, despite the participation of Hadid, a widely recognized architect, the Dome's public relations staff placed emphasis on the contents of her pavilion or even on the works of art by Richard Deacon, Gavin Turk and Ron Mueck, undoubtedly due to the decidedly wide public appeal for which the Dome itself was intended. From the outset, ticket sales made it clear that Millennium Dome would attract nowhere near the hoped-for million visitors per month, and unfortunately quality architecture and design do not appear here to have been viewed as a genuine selling point by the organizers. An entrepreneur like Ian Schrager, interested in far smaller, more affluent crowds, may see a designer like Starck as a selling point, but this is less obvious where mass audiences are concerned. Viewed at the end as a terrible financial fiasco, much like Hanover's Expo 2000, the Dome experience will most probably have calmed the ardor of politicians everywhere when it comes to organizing such extravagant mixtures of high and low artistic expression.

Unlike Zaha Hadid's decidedly intellectual approach, Branson Coates chose to use a readily recognizable form – that of a human body – for their pavilion, the aptly named Body Zone. The minimalist Eva Jiricna, who seemed to have insisted on a more obvious rigor, created a structure made of six arches of latticed steel. Jumbled together with far less distinguished architecture these pavilions represented quality design, but one is left wondering if the architects were right to accept their inclusion into such mixed context. One participant, Lord Richard Rogers, clearly stands above the rest, at least in a literal sense. His tensile roofed design was suspended from twelve 100 m-tall masts supported by about 60 km of steel cable. Made from durable Teflon PTFE-coated (polytetrafluoroethylene) fiberglass, the Dome was solid enough to carry the weight of a Boeing 747. It has already featured prominently in the most recent James Bond extravaganza *The World is not Enough*. Even if the Dome was principally exceptional because of its dimensions, it did represent an effort to bring together architects of the first order. It unfortunately seems clear in retrospect that they should not have participated in this circus.

YES, BUT IS IT ART?

John Ruskin made clear his feeling that architecture could claim to be the highest of the arts, allying as it does other forms of spatial expression in a unified whole. This analysis probably has more to do with buildings dating up to the 19th century than it does with modern architecture. And yet a symbiosis does exist between the most eloquent expressions of art and architecture even today. The two continue to nourish each other and when they do meet, at that point of juncture, one is likely to find architecture that does after all suit Ruskin's definition.

Tadao Ando is the undisputed master of concrete architecture in Japan. Despite the strong geometric plans of his buildings, his sensitivity to light, and to a ritual sense of space, bring an evident spirituality to his buildings. He appears to have completed his greatest work to date on the island of Awaji. Called Yumebutai or "Dream Stage," this massive complex covers a 215 000 m^2 area that provided landfill for the artificial island on which the nearby Kansai Airport was built. Although it does include a hotel, a convention center and facilities for large garden shows, the "Dream Stage" is more clearly conceived as a progression of spaces where water, architecture and light meet. Its very "uselessness" affirms this work's claim to the status of pure art. Indeed, when fettered by the need for heavy security in the convention center or loaded down with the imposed interior decor of the hotel, Ando's complex is good, but not astonishing. It is in the gentle maze of courtyards and passageways that the visitor is transported to a higher plane. Fountains cascade from the hillside above, and water flows through the astonishing succession of spaces. As Tadao Ando says, "The Alhambra in Granada provides a historical model. There, water links small patios together." A million scallop shells, selected and placed by hand, line the floors of the basins, and the visitor wonders if this is indeed a dream. Commissioned by the local authorities who were concerned that tourists would bypass Awaji on the way to more seductive destinations, the complex is located near the massive new suspension bridge linking Kobe to Awaji. Not every detail of the "Dream Stage" is perfect. A small chapel in the midst of the complex is a take-off on Ando's remarkable "Church of the Light" (Ibaraki, Osaka, 1989). Rather than placing a cruciform opening behind the altar as he did in the earlier building, here he puts it in the ceiling. One of the strengths of the "Church of the Light" was its raw energy, linked to a strictly limited budget. Could it be that here almost excessive means robbed Tadao Ando of some of that energy? But this complaint is insignificant compared with the overall success of the "Dream Stage." Due to its location on Awaji, the complex has not been published as much as it deserves. Completed late in 1999, Yumebutai represents nothing less than a final statement about the art of architecture in the 20th century. This is a masterpiece.

Like Tadao Ando (with the notable exception of Yumebutai), the Swiss-Italian architect Mario Botta may be at his best in work on a smaller scale. His mountain chapels in Mogno or on the Monte Tamaro are among the most powerful small buildings of the 1990s. Botta is deeply concerned with the art of architecture, as one of his recent projects demonstrates. A series of exhibitions relating to the architecture of the Renaissance or the Baroque have brought the magnificent models of these periods to public attention. These jewels of perfection spelled out the forms imagined by their architects on a reduced scale. Mario Botta chose to create a wooden model of part of Francesco Borromini's San Carlo alle Quattro Fontane (1641) in Rome in full scale on the shore of Lake Lugano to mark a 1999 exhibition of the Italian master's work. Anchored near the entrance to Lugano's Parco Civico, this stunning "virtual monument" allied techniques and forms of the Baroque with a decidedly ephemeral, 20th-century interpretation. Intended as a signal for the exhibition and as an hommage to Borromini's talent, this work is liberated of most of the usual functional constraints of architecture. It is in a sense the essence of architecture liberated from its weighty stone, floating freely. What remains? Art?

Born in 1959, Maya Lin, a 1986 graduate of the Yale School of Architecture, remains best known as the author of the 1981 Vietnam Veterans' Memorial in Washington, D.C. The work, which she defines as sculpture, consists of a granite wedge pressed into the ground of the Mall. The names of 50 000 American soldiers who died in the Vietnam war are engraved there, below the level of the ground, as a somber reminder. This minimalist gesture, ferociously attacked by some, has proven to be a war memorial of a different kind, attracting hundreds of visitors every day, each fascinated by the human tragedy so aptly symbolized by seemingly cold stone. Maya Lin is indeed unique in crossing the barriers that normally separate art from architecture. As she continues to work on public and private sculpture, she also is deeply involved in architecture. Her Norton Apartment (New York, 1999) is a minimalist reinterpretation of a 220 m^2-space that is partly located under ground. In the spirit of Terry Riley's 1999 "Un-Private House" exhibition at the Museum of Modern Art, Norton Apartment is a space that can be readily modified to suit one, two or more persons. Riley, head of the Architecture and Design Department at MoMA, pointed out that changing family and lifestyle patterns in America and Europe have led to substantive changes in the ways houses are organized. Architecture, in this instance, is called on to adapt to changing times, abandoning the rigid hierarchy of the living room, dining room, kitchen, and bedroom arrangements that suited previous generations. Aside from her mastery of lighting and materials, Maya Lin also makes the Norton Apartment into a fitting place of display for one of her own crushed glass sculptures further blurring the lines between just what may be called architecture, and what is indeed art.

In a more modest way, the Japanese born architect Toshiko Mori has also set out a challenge to the barriers that divide art from architecture, or perhaps architecture from the real world. Her "Woven Inhabitation", presented at the Artists Space in New York in 1999, seeks to provide a simple, elegant solution to the vast problem of providing temporary housing for refugees or victims of natural disasters. Though she lives now in New York, Mori grew up in postwar Japan. She remembers a time of deprivation in which woven fabrics provided what comfort there was. "I have always remembered the native intelligence of women during this time who helped to sustain the sense of dignity and culture. I remember their ability to create things such as clothing and meals from scraps. I'm now able to realize that this is how a culture or civilization can survive its destruction." Her concept is to make use of "the woven remnants of revolutionary industrial fabrics already utilized by the aerospace, medical and fashion industries but never before developed as architectural building products." She goes on to explain that "Originating from a single strand, the structure of a woven piece interlaces to create a warp and weft of grids; in architectural terms, these grids provide varying degrees of air flow, facilitating and regulating natural cooling or warming. An easily fabricated, effective textile-based unit like Woven Inhabitation, she concludes, "posits an approach to architecture that may become common in the future, not only as a means to create temporary shelter, but as a standard application for everyday building." From her own observation that a majority of refugees are women or children, Mori proposes an elegant solution to a growing problem. In a curiously "low-tech" kind of way, she thus moves in the same direction as the computer-gurus at Asymptote — making architecture do new things, dissolving its traditional definitions to give it the flexibility that the needs of the times require.

When asked if he feels that there is a blurring of the lines between art and architecture today the architect Richard Meier replies, "No. I'm not sure there's so much of the blurring of the lines. I think it's simply that more artists want to be architects. Maybe historically more architects have wanted to be artists, but I think that today more and more artists really would like to make architecture. I think that the beginning points are usually different for an artist than an architect. The artist has an idea of what might be, and then finds someone who wants that idea. Generally an architect waits for someone to come to him with a project and then says, I have an idea for what you can do." Meier insists nonetheless that a good piece of architecture is also a work of art. Frank O. Gehry, the most sculptural of today's major architects, cites his sources with no shame. In his 1989 acceptance speech for the Pritzker Prize he said, "My artist friends, like Jasper Johns, Bob Rauschenberg, Ed Kienholz, and Claes Oldenburg, were working with very inexpensive materials – broken wood and paper – and they were making beauty. These were not superficial details, they were direct, and raised the question in my mind of what beauty was. I chose to use the craft available, and to work with craftsmen and make a virtue out of their limitations. Painting had an immediacy that I craved for in architecture. I explored the process of new construction materials trying to give feeling and spirit to form. In trying to find the essence of my own expression, I fantasized that I was an artist standing before a white canvas deciding what the first move should be."

In any case, the fate of the architecture of the new century is no longer really in the hands of architects such as Frank O. Gehry and Richard Meier. Rather it is in those of a younger generation like Toshiko Mori or Hani Rashid of Asymptote. Trailblazers like Kawakubo or even the designer Philippe Starck and many others have shown that fashion need not be a "dirty" word in architectural design. Movement and change are indeed the key to the new forms, an espousal of flux, a readiness to meet needs. This may often rule out rigid, hierarchical spaces, although the demand for the most wind-resistant of buildings, the skyscraper, defies this logic. From neo-Minimalism to a kind of messy confrontation with everyday reality and computer-generated volumes, architecture is probably changing faster today than ever before.

EINLEITUNG

Jedes neue Bauwerk ist das Ergebnis von Funktion, Standort und Kosten. Der Wandel von Geschmack oder Mode hat offenbar nicht nur Auswirkungen auf die äußere Gestaltung von Architektur, sondern auch auf ihre Bewertung und Interpretation – auch wenn dies oft geleugnet wird. »Der Stil«, sagte Buffon, »ist der Mensch selbst«. Das mag sein, aber Stil ist auch eine Zeiterscheinung. Trotz moderner Kommunikationsmittel hat keine Stilrichtung die Gegenwartsarchitektur so nachhaltig geprägt wie die Nachkriegs-Moderne. Vielmehr breiten sich unterschiedliche Strömungen und Gegenströmungen weltweit aus, oft verzögert durch lange Planungs- und Bauzeiten. So entwerfen Architekten noch heute Bauten in den gebrochenen, dekonstruktivistischen Formen der 80er oder im neo-minimalistischen Stil der 90er-Jahre. Wenn es stimmt, dass der »Stil der Mensch selbst« ist, dann bedeutet das, dass diese Gebäude von Architekten geschaffen wurden, die lange und hart kämpfen mussten, um ihre Ideen durchzusetzen und deshalb wahrscheinlich nicht so rasch den Baustil wechseln.

Während sich die Legitimation älterer Stile erschöpft, gewinnen neue an Gültigkeit. Im gerade angebrochenen Jahrhundert wird sich das Interesse vermutlich wieder zu komplexeren Bauten verlagern. Das ist jedoch weniger auf die Verwerfung der euklidischen Geometrie zurückzuführen als vielmehr auf computergenerierte Räume, die das orthogonale System hinter sich lassen. Sehen einige Architekten den Nutzen des Computers immer noch auf gewisse Aufgaben begrenzt, so haben andere begonnen, mit seiner Hilfe neues Terrain zu erkunden – etwa das Konzept des »virtuellen« Gebäudes. Die New Yorker Gruppe Asymptote etwa erhielt den Auftrag, ein »virtuelles Museum« für das Guggenheim Museum zu entwerfen, dessen Räume praktisch nur auf Computerbildschirmen existieren werden. Die zunehmende Rafinesse von CAD-Entwürfen indes erlaubt noch andere Formen virtuellen Gestaltens: die etwa von Architekturdenkmälern der Vergangenheit, die nie gebaut wurden. Professor Takehiko Nagakura vom Massachusetts Institute of Technology (MIT) und sein »Team Unbuilt« lassen Entwürfe von Le Corbusier, Aalto und Tatlin im Computer wieder auferstehen. Manch einer mag diese Arbeit als amüsante Variante von Computerspielen wie Myst oder Riven sehen. Traditionalisten sehen das Wesen der Architektur in ihrer Solidität, Stofflichkeit und Dauerhaftigkeit – relativen Eigenschaften, die im Reich des Virtuellen überflüssig werden. Andere, wie Hani Rashid von Asymptote, denken anders über die Zukunft: »Wenn wir über Architektur im neuen Jahrtausend sprechen, müssen wir zwei Bedingungen berücksichtigen. Einmal den vertrauten physischen Aspekt von Architektur, in dem es auch weiterhin räumliche Begrenzung, Form und Dauerhaftigkeit geben wird, und dann den Bereich der virtuellen Architektur, der sich im digitalen Raum des Internet entwickelt. Objekte, Räume, Gebäude und Institutionen können heute in einem weltumspannenden Netzwerk konstruiert, gesteuert, verstanden, erfahren und gestaltet werden. Dies ist eine neue Architektur der fließenden Grenzen, des beständigen Wechsels und der dauernden Veränderlichkeit. Sie basiert auf dem technischen Fortschritt und wird getrieben von dem menschlichen Grundbedürfnis, ins Unbekannte vorzustoßen. Der einzig gangbare Weg für diese beiden Architekturformen, die reale und die virtuelle, liegt darin, sich einander anzunähern und zu ergänzen.«

Der vorliegende Überblick über Architektur der Gegenwart fasst Informationen aus der ganzen Welt zusammen und bewertet sie im Hinblick auf Trends und entwicklungsgeschichtliche Perspektiven. Dabei zeigt sich: Unter den zahllosen Bauten weltweit ist innovative Architektur, die die häufig widerstreitenden Vorgaben von Standort, Budget und ästhetischem Anspruch erfolgreich miteinander in Einklang bringt, äußerst selten. Stil bestimmt die Aktualität von Architektur. Wird Architektur damit so unbeständig wie eine Frühlingsmode? Das sicher nicht. Sie tritt jedoch in ein Zeitalter ein, in dem Veränderbarkeit und Lebendigkeit wichtiger geworden sind als Unvergänglichkeit und Monumentalität.

VIRTUELLE WIRKLICHKEITEN

»Das Museum ist zu einer Art Mausoleum für die Kunst geworden«, erklärt Hani Rashid von Asymptote. »Museen sind unbelebte Orte, wo Kunst einer für unwissend gehaltenen Öffentlichkeit präsentiert wird. Es sind Tempel der distanzierten und privilegierten Betrachtung oder Domänen kultureller Autorität zur Verbreitung von Ideen und Ideologien. Daneben wird das Museum vielleicht noch – und das ist auch erhaltenswert – als Ort verstanden, der auf Besucher wie Künstler provozierend wirken kann.« Asymptote hat den Auftrag für die Gestaltung des ersten virtuellen Museums erhalten, eines Kunstraums, der nur im Internet existiert. Dieses »Guggenheim in Cyberspace« hat den Ehrgeiz, »ein neues Paradigma für die Architektur« zu schaffen. Oder, wie die Leitung des Museums konkretisiert: »Das Guggenheim Virtual Museum wird nicht nur einen weltweiten Zugang auf alle Guggenheim Museen einschließlich deren individueller Serviceleistungen, Archive und Sammlungen bieten, sondern dem virtuellen Besucher auch das Erlebnis einer einzigartigen und faszinierenden räumlichen Umgebung vermitteln. Darüber hinaus ist das virtuelle Museum der ideale Ort für das Betrachten und Erleben von Kunst und künstlerischen Events, die eigens für das interaktive digitale Medium konzipiert werden. Hier wird einem globalen Publikum die gleichzeitige Teilnahme an und Betrachtung von Kunst ermöglicht. Wie von Asymptote und dem Guggenheim konzipiert, entsteht das »Guggenheim Virtual Museum aus der Verbindung von Information, Kunst, Handel und Architektur und wird damit zum ersten bedeutenden virtuellen Gebäude des 21. Jahrhunderts.« Hani Rashid will nicht nur eine besonders angenehme künstliche Umgebung für die Betrachtung von Kunstwerken schaffen. Ihm geht es um eine interaktive virtuelle Architektur, die sich durch die Nutzung der Besucher verändert, womit genau jene Solidität und Unvergänglichkeit unterlaufen wird, die Architektur im Allgemeinen und Museen im Besonderen zugeschrieben wird. Ebenso wie die Kunst, die es ausstellt, wird das Guggenheim Virtual Museum also ständig im Fluss sein und sich, den jeweiligen Umständen entsprechend, neu definieren. Ein solches Projekt bedeutet insofern einen Paradigmawechsel, als es keine jener Beschränkungen kennt – z. B. Feuerschutzbestimmungen –, denen die »reale« Architektur üblicherweise unterworfen ist. Ist es dann überhaupt Architektur oder eher eine Art elektronische Innenraumgestaltung? Auf jeden Fall ist es etwas Neues.

Asymptote hat auch ein Online-Börsenparkett für die New York Stock Exchange (NYSE) entworfen. Laut Hani Rashid ist der sogenannte »Three Dimensional Trading Floor (3DTF)« ein mehrdimensionales und interaktives Environment. Das ganze »Advanced Trading Floor Operations Center«-Projekt ist eine Neugestaltung des bestehenden Börsengeschäfts. NYSE hat Asymptote sowohl mit dem Online-Design der Bereiche Kurskontrolle und Wertpapierverkauf als auch mit der Gestaltung eines Raums neben dem Hauptbörsenparkett in New York beauftragt. »Das 3DTF«, führt Rashid weiter aus, »ist eine Daten-Landschaft, die Informationen, Datenübertragungen und Korrelationsmodelle in einem einzigen nahtlosen, dreidimensionalen Environment zusammenführt. Dieser virtuelle Raum ist ein Echtzeit-Modell, das den Benutzern alle Aktivitäten und Ereignisse als voll-interaktive steuerbare Realität mit unbegrenzten Bewegungs- und Betrachtungsmöglichkeiten darstellt. Der 3DTF neben dem realen Börsenparkett ermöglicht den Mitarbeitern ein tieferes Verständnis der vielen Variablen und komplexen Beziehungen, die sich während des Handels ergeben. Asymptote setzte VRML (Virtual Reality Markup Language) und raffinierte CAD-Programme für die Konzeption und Entwicklung der einzelnen 3DTF-Komponenten ein. Zusätzlich zu den funktionalen Anforderungen des Modells war für uns von Asymptote besonders die Gesamtqualität der virtuellen Umgebung wichtig, was sich im Einsatz von Licht, Farbe und Oberfläche sowie in der Erforschung und Entwicklung verschiedener Methoden zur Steuerung, Bewegung, Betrachtung und allgemeinen grafischen Aufbereitung ausdrückt.« Architektur oder Grafikdesign? Offenbar beides.

Die Vorliebe junger Architekten für freie oder nicht-euklidische Formen und Räume beschränkt sich jedoch nicht auf so radikale Lösungen wie die von Asymptote. So geht die ebenfalls in New York ansässige Gruppe Diller + Scofidio andere Wege, um die traditionelle Auffassung von Architektur zu hinterfragen. Ihr »Blur Building« (blur = verwischen, nebelhaft machen), das sie für die Expo 2002 im schweizerischen Yverdon am Neuburger See entworfen haben, soll einer Wolke ähneln. Knapp 100 m lang, 60 m breit 12 m tief, besteht diese Wolke »aus gefiltertem Seewasser, das als feiner, feuchter Nebel aus dicht angeordneten Hochdruckdüsen versprüht wird, die in eine große, freitragende Seilnetz-Konstruktion eingebettet sind.« Die Besucher betreten die unbewegliche Wolke über eine Rampe, die im Bereich des Wasserdunstes verglast ist. Im Innern streben die Architekten nach »der möglichst vollständigen Abwesenheit aller Sinnesreize; ein optisches weißes Nichts, begleitet vom weißen Rauschen der Nebeldüsen...« Ein auf eine kreisförmige Leinwand projiziertes Panoramabild umschließt eine abgedunkelte Plattform für 250 Besucher. »Da der Mensch nicht länger beanspruchen kann, der Mittelpunkt eines kontrollierbaren Universums zu sein, bleibt die Position des Betrachters Gegenstand kritischer Reflexion«, erläutern die Architekten. Diller + Scofidio machen zwar ausgiebig Gebrauch von CAD, anders als Asymptote ist ihr Ziel jedoch der Entwurf physisch-realer Konstruktionen. Einig sind sich beide Gruppen jedoch in der Herausforderung tradierter architektonischer Prinzipien, indem sie über die Gestaltung von Form und Material hinaus die akustischen und visuellen Bedingungen für die räumliche Orientierung »verwischen«. Im Gegensatz zur hierarchischen Raumfolge traditioneller Architektur macht das »Blur Building« nichts klar oder eindeutig und nimmt damit eine Position ein, die sich in Einklang mit weiten Bereichen des zeitgenössischen Denkens befindet.

Etwas weniger kühn verzichten auch die jungen Designer Jakob + MacFarlane in ihrem neuen Restaurant im Pariser Centre Georges Pompidou auf so konventionelle Annehmlichkeiten wie die Unterscheidung zwischen Fußboden und Wand. Im obersten Stockwerk des Baus von Piano und Rogers sind Küche, Bar und Toiletten in frei geformten Hohlkörpern aus Aluminium untergebracht. Das geordnete Raster des Bodenbelags wird unvermittelt von Platten unterbrochen, die sich zu dreidimensionalen Formen in die Höhe biegen. Diese Gebilde, von den Architekten »caves-nuages« (Wolkenhöhlen) genannt, wurden in einer französischen Schiffswerft in der Nähe von La Rochelle gefertigt. Mit seinem phantastischen Ausblick auf das alte Paris steht das von der Costes-Familie geführte Restaurant dem Geist der zeitgenössischen Kreativität vielleicht näher als viele der im Centre Pompidou ausgestellten Kunstwerke. Das Raster ihres Restaurants ist zwar eine Referenz an Pianos eher rationale Raumauffassung, aber Jakob + MacFarlane gehören zu einer jüngeren Generation, die mit den Möglichkeiten des computergestützten Gestaltens vertraut ist. Aus grundverschiedenen Welten kommend – Dominique Jakob wuchs an der Elfenbeinküste und in Gabun und Niger auf, bevor sie in Paris Architektur studierte; Brendan MacFarlane kommt aus Neuseeland und studierte an der Harvard Graduate School of Design (GSD) – haben beide zeitweilig im Architekturbüro Morphosis in Santa Monica gearbeitet.

Takehiko Nagakura, der bei Fumihiko Maki an der Universität Tokio studierte, ist gegenwärtig außerordentlicher Professor für Design und Computerisierung am Fachbereich Architektur des MIT. Mit finanzieller Unterstützung der japanischen Takenaka Corporation gründete er »Team Unbuilt«, eine Gruppe, die sich die Verknüpfung von kunsthistorischer Forschung und modernster Computertechnologie zum Ziel gesetzt hat. Nagakura über dieses Projekt: »Die Gebäudeformen werden anhand der Originalentwürfe erarbeitet, die wir aus den Archiven von Institutionen wie der Fondation Le Corbusier in Paris erhalten. Dann wird eine Visualisierungstechnologie auf der Basis von Globalillumination verwendet, um auch noch die feinsten Nuancen des Zusammenspiels von Licht, Material und Geometrie herauszuarbeiten. Die daraus resultierende computergrafische Darstellung vermittelt einen aufregenden dreidimensionalen Eindruck von Außen- und Innenraum, wie er bislang nur in den Köpfen der Architekten dieser nicht realisierten Bauten existierte.«

Takehiko Nagakura hat für seine Arbeit Bauten wie Alvar Aaltos Kirche im schweizerischen Altstetten (1967) oder Le Corbusiers Wettbewerbsbeitrag für den Moskauer Sowjetpalast (1931) ausgewählt. Einer der spektakulärsten Entwürfe, die er zu neuem Leben erweckt hat, ist Vladimir Tatlins Denkmal für die Dritte Internationale (Petrograd, Sowjetunion, 1919), eins der ersten Bauwerke in vollkommen abstrakter Formensprache. Es wurde 1919 von der Abteilung für bildende Künste des Volkskommissariats für Volksaufklärung der Sowjetunion in Auftrag gegeben und in Form eines 6,70 m hohen Modells auf der Ausstellung des achten Sowjetkongresses im Dezember 1920 gezeigt. Der Bau sollte aus einem geneigten, spiralförmigen Eisenskelett bestehen, das einen Glaszylinder, einen Glaskegel und einen Glaskubus trägt. Diese sollten sich mit jeweils unterschiedlicher Geschwindigkeit drehen lassen. Im Innern sollten sich unter anderem Hörsäle und Versammlungsräume befinden. Mit einer Höhe von fast 400 m wäre es das größte Bauwerk der damaligen Welt gewesen. Es wurde jedoch nie realisiert, da die Sowjetregierung jede Form abstrakter Kunst ablehnte.

Takehiko Nagakura betont die Wichtigkeit der kunsthistorischen Vorarbeiten für seine virtuellen Konstruktionen und sieht sein »Team Unbuilt« in erster Linie als pädagogisches Hilfsmittel, wobei er überzeugt ist, dass die nachfolgende Architektengeneration noch unbefangener mit dem Konzept des virtuellen Bauens umgehen wird als die heutige. Er sagt: »Ich halte diese Art Detektivarbeit in Verbindung mit der praktischen virtuellen Arbeit für eine äußerst effiziente Ausbildungsmethode für Architekten. Ich sehe in ihr eine gewisse Nähe zum traditionellen französischen Architekturstudium, bei dem großer Wert auf das Studium der antiken Baukunst gelegt wurde. In dem von mir geleiteten Kurs am MIT verwende ich Quellen und Materialien, die wir für das Unbuilt-Projekt gesammelt haben, und gebe damit den Studenten die Möglichkeit, die räumliche Darstellung mit Hilfe modernster Computertechnik zu erlernen.«

TURMHOHE AMBITIONEN

Während die Entwürfe einiger Architekten zunehmend immaterieller werden, haben sich andere einer Richtung verschrieben, deren Kern eine noch im 20. Jahrhundert wurzelnde Monumentalität zu sein scheint. Immer höhere Wolkenkratzer werden entworfen und weltweit gebaut. Besonders in Asien und den Vereinigten Staaten mobilisiert der Wettstreit um den Anspruch auf das höchste Gebäude der Welt große Mengen an Geld und Talent. Ein neues Projekt in Chicago, dem Geburtsort des Wolkenkratzers, ist zur Zeit das ambitionierteste seiner Art.

Scheinen psychologische Implikationen und Höhenmeter die wichtigsten Faktoren bei der Planung von Hochhäusern zu sein, so geraten ästhetische Aspekte häufig in den Hintergrund. Der französische Architekt Christian de Portzamparc hat sich mit seinem LVMH Tower in New York für die Kategorie des Ästhetischen entschieden. Sein nach Shanghaier oder Chigagoer Standards eher kleines Gebäude weist eine innovative Glasfassade und einen spektakulären dreigeschossigen Raum an der Spitze auf. Die Wahl der französischen Louis Vuitton Moët Hennessy-Konzerns fiel zweifellos nicht nur auf Portzamparc, weil er 1994 den Pritzker Prize gewonnen hatte. Seine Auftraggeber fühlten sich sicher von seinem Hang zu einer lyrischen Gestaltungsweise angesprochen. Das 24-geschossige Gebäude ist mit geätztem, sandgestrahltem

Glas von Saint-Gobain in Frankreich sowie grün-, weiß- und blau-fluoreszierenden Röhren verkleidet, die eine »Bruchlinie« zwischen den gebrochenen Oberflächen markieren. Die Verkleidung verhindert störende Spiegelungen des IBM-Gebäudes auf der gegenüberliegenden Seite der 57. Straße. Herbert Muschamp von der »New York Times« schrieb in seiner Kritik, Portzamparc habe »den Begriff des Art déco neu erfunden«, womit er sich in den Chor der Lobgesänge auf einen der gelungensten Bauten der letzten Jahre in New York einreihte.

Am anderen Ende der Welt und mit einem gegensätzlichen Ansatz errichtet das amerikanische Büro Kohn Pedersen Fox (KPF) das Shanghai World Financial Center. Im Finanz- und Handelsdistrikt Lujiazui von Pudong wird dieses 95-stöckige Bauwerk eine Höhe von 460 m erreichen, was es, zumindest vorläufig, zum höchsten Gebäude der Welt macht. Das Projekt wurde mit einer Geschossfläche von 312 152 m^2 und einem Budget von mehr als 500 Millionen Dollar konzipiert. Es ist KPF als Verdienst anzurechnen, dass der Bau, der 2004 fertiggestellt sein soll, geradezu puristische Formen hat, die sich aus der Durchdringung eines quadratischen Prismas und eines Zylinders ergeben. In seiner Spitze besitzt das Shanghai World Financial Center eine kreisrunde Öffnung von 50 m Durchmesser, das so genannte »moon gate« (Tor des Monds), das den Winddruck auf den Bau reduzieren soll. Ohne krampfhaft nach historischen oder künstlerischen Analogien zu suchen, kann man sagen, dass die Form dieses Turms einige Ähnlichkeit mit der kraftvollen Schlichtheit archaischer chinesischer Objekte aufweist. Indem er sich auch auf seine Umgebung bezieht, hat der Hohlraum auf der Turmspitze ähnliche Ausmaße wie die Kugel (oder »Pearl«), die den gegenüberliegenden Oriental Pearl TV Tower krönt. Obwohl historische und kontextuelle Bezüge eher zweitrangig sind, wenn es darum geht, das höchste Gebäude der Welt zu errichten, haben KPF in bei einem so kommerziell orientierten Projekt lobenswerter Weise den Akzent auf architektonische Qualität gelegt. Mit seiner Verkleidung aus roh behauenem Naturstein für die unteren 28 m und zart spiegelndem Glas und Edelstahl für die oberen Stockwerke gebührt dem Shanghai World Financial Center (Planungsschef: William Pedersen) nicht nur wegen seiner Höhe – es ist 40 m höher als das kürzlich in Shanghai vollendete Jin Mao Gebäude – ein besonderer Rang unter einer Reihe architektonisch weniger bemerkenswerter Bauwerke.

Wahrscheinlich wird das Shanghai World Financial Center den Titel »höchstes Gebäude der Welt« trotzdem nicht für sich in Anspruch nehmen dürfen. Ein Projekt für Chicago, das 2003 fertiggestellt sein soll, wird es um knappe 13 m überragen. Am 21. September 1999 genehmigte die städtische Planungskommission den Bau eines von Adrian Smith von Skidmore, Owings & Merrill entworfenen Wolkenkratzers an der Ecke von Dearborn und Madison Street. Mit seinen von einem Betonkern auskragenden oberen Etagen, in denen die höchsten Wohnungen der Welt liegen werden, wird das Gebäude eine Höhe von 108 Stockwerken erreichen. Der Wolkenkratzer soll mit Aluminium, Edelstahl und leicht getöntem Glas verkleidet werden und auf der Spitze zwei riesige Digitalfernsehsendemasten tragen.

Die Form von Bauwerken hängt häufig mit den zu erwartenden Belastungsfaktoren zusammen. Die Konstruktion hoher Gebäude ist besonders anfällig für solche Einflüsse. Ab einer bestimmten Höhe kann die äußere Form eines Wolkenkratzers von so ausgefallenen Faktoren wie Resonanz, Wirbelablösung und Flatterschwingung diktiert werden, die alle mit dem Windwiderstand zusammenhängen. Das bedeutet, dass Gestaltungselemente wie die tiefen Kerben des Chicagoer Wolkenkratzers kaum oder gar nicht von ästhetischen Kriterien bestimmt sind. Dabei ist die Öffnung an der Spitze des Shanghai World Financial Center mit der Spannweite einer Boeing 747 eine wirklich elegante Lösung für ein bautechnisches Problem.

Es wäre allerdings übertrieben zu sagen, die meisten Hochhäuser hätten keinerlei ästhetischen Reiz. Schon ihre schiere Ballung in Städten wie New York, Chicago oder Shanghai erzeugt dynamische Urbanität. Außerdem sind Wolkenkratzer mit ihrer imposanten Präsenz kaum zu ignorieren. Was immer man über Trends oder »Stile« in der zeitgenössischen Architektur zu sagen hat: Kein Überblick kann ihre Existenz einfach übergehen. In Reaktion auf bestimmte Bedürfnisse – seien sie »realer« und kommerzieller oder psychologischer Art – scheinen Hochhäuser zum Kernbestand zeitgenössischer Architektur zu gehören. Und damit sind sie ein wesentlicher Bestandteil ihrer Entwicklung, auch wenn sie aktuellen Architektur-Theorien in weiten Teilen zu widersprechen scheinen. Derzeit geplante Wolkenkratzer nähern sich der 500 m-Grenze oder werden sie sogar überschreiten, wie der 574 m hohe Landmark Tower in Hong Kong.

KUNSTRÄUME – RÄUME FÜR KUNST

Die bildenden Künste und ihre öffentliche Präsentation bieten weiterhin eines der dankbarsten Tätigkeitsfelder für anspruchsvolle Gegenwartsarchitektur. Für jene, die nur ein begrenztes Interesse am Konzept des »virtuellen« Museums aufbringen, bilden Kunst und Ausstellungsräume einen der wenigen Bereiche, in denen eine gewisse Dauerhaftigkeit und Unveränderlichkeit nach wie vor als angemessen gelten. Dennoch hat sich auch dieses Genre rapide verändert, wie einige Beispiele belegen.

Das Museum Het Valkhof an einem Marktplatz in der ostniederländischen Stadt Nijmegen ist das Werk von UN Studio/ Van Berkel & Bos, das auch die Erasmus-Brücke in Rotterdam ausgeführt hat. Es sollte die Kunstsammlungen des Museums Commanderie van Sint Jan und des Provinciaal Museum G. M. Kam unter einem Dach vereinen. Der kühle Farbton, den das Bauwerk durch seine grünlich-blaue Glasverkleidung erhält, wird auch in den Innenräumen beibehalten, wo die Architekten die Kunstwerke für sich selbst sprechen lassen. Anstatt einen bestimmten Weg durch die Sammlung vorzugeben, wie es viele Museumsarchitekten tun, gibt es laut van Berkel mindestens 88 Wege für eine Besichtigung des Museums Het Valkhof. Auf einer Seite des Gebäudes gestattet eine langgestreckte, transparente Galerie den Ausblick auf das benachbarte Parkgelände. In seiner Zurückhaltung, Flexibilität und Offenheit ist dieses Museum sicher ein Beispiel für zeitgemäße Architektur.

Die von Álvaro Siza entworfene Stiftung Serralves im portugiesischen Porto liegt in der Nähe des Stadtzentrums, wo auch Siza sein Büro hat. Die auf zeitgenössische Kunst konzentrierte Stiftung wurde durch eine einzigartige Zusammenarbeit der portugiesischen Regierung mit 50 Partnern aus der Wirtschaft ins Leben gerufen. Ihr Sitz in der Quinta de Serralves erstreckt sich über ein Gelände von 20 ha, einschließlich eines in den 1930er-Jahren für den Grafen von Vizela erbauten Haupthauses. Sizas Bau im Park der Stiftung ist in Ausmaß und Anspruch ein groß angelegtes Unternehmen. Unter Verwendung einer Hängedeckenkonstruktion, ähnlich jener, die er für das Galicische Zentrum für Zeitgenössische Kunst entworfen hat, gestaltete Siza eine Reihe großer, flexibler Galerien für Wechselausstellungen. Innenhöfe und Fenster bieten dem Besucher ständigen Ausblick auf den Park (von dem Siza 3 ha gestaltete); im Innern befinden sich zudem ein Museumsshop, ein Café und ein Vortragssaal. Der ganze Bau ist von einem augenfälligen Gespür für Details geprägt, das typisch für Siza ist. Hierfür hat man ihm alle erdenklichen Mittel zur Verfügung gestellt. Von der klassischen Moderne inspiriert, ist die Stiftung Serralves in ihrer Anlage keineswegs überholt. Trotz ihrer klaren weißen Linien eher komplex in der Formensprache, beweist sie ein weiteres Mal, dass Álvaro Siza einer der kreativsten und kraftvollsten Architekten seiner Generation ist.

Der japanische Architekt Yoshio Taniguchi wurde ebenso wie Siza in den 30er-Jahren geboren. Im eigenen Land ist er seit langem ein anerkannter Meister, und mit dem Auftrag für den Umbau des Museum of Modern Art in New York hat er auch internationale Bedeutung erlangt. Seine souveräne Beherrschung des Stilvokabulars der Moderne zeigt sich besonders deutlich in seinem letzten Bau, den Räumen der Horyuji-Schatzkammern im Untergeschoss des Tokioter Nationalmuseums im Ueno Park. Diese Institution wurde im späten 19. Jahrhundert als Museum des kaiserlichen Hofs gegründet und enthält Kunstobjekte, die der kaiserlichen Sammlung in den 1870er-Jahren als Schenkung überlassen wurden, um den Bestand des Horyuji-Tempels in Nara vor der damals aufflackernden anti-buddhistischen Stimmung zu retten. Für diese bedeutenden Ausstellungsstücke wie Masken, Skulpturen und rituelle Gegenstände aus Metall hat Taniguchi eine dreiteilige Konstruktion errichtet. Der Architekt über seinen Entwurf: »Ich hatte die Vorstellung eines Gebäudes, das aus drei Schichten besteht: einem von einer Steinmauer umgebenen inneren, einem von einer Glaswand umschlossenen mittleren und einem durch ein überhängendes Schutzdach aus Metall definierten äußeren Bereich.« Der innere Raum ist vom Tageslicht abgeschirmt, während die Eingangshalle und der von dem Schutzdach überdeckte Bereich von Licht durchflutet werden. Taniguchi führt weiter aus, dass die mehrschichtige Konzeption des Museums »die Geschichte seiner kostbaren Ausstellungsstücke symbolisieren soll, die Jahrhunderte lang in den zahllosen Fächern hölzerner Kisten, die im alten Japan zur Aufbewahrung von Kunstschätzen verwendet wurden, auf uns gekommen sind«. Obgleich der Architekt weniger ausführlich auf diesen Punkt eingeht, erinnert seine Museumsgestaltung auch an viele Aspekte der japanischen Tempelarchitektur. Der Zugangsweg führt die Besucher auf ein spiegelndes Wasserbecken mit einem symmetrisch angeordneten Springbrunnen hin, dabei muss man nicht weniger als viermal die Richtung wechseln. Diese Gestaltung stellt einen für japanische Tempel typischen Zugang dar, der die Besucher daran erinnert, dass sie einen bedeutungsvollen Ort betreten. Anstelle einer Eingangstür passiert der Besucher dann einen steinernen Wandschirm, bevor er das sonst sehr zweckmäßig angelegte Gebäude betritt. Der allgemeine Eindruck eines qualitativ äußerst anspruchsvollen Bauwerks wird noch verstärkt durch Details wie eine absolut perfekte Übereinstimmung sämtlicher Gebäudeteile, von der innersten Galerie bis zum äußersten Rand des Wasserbeckens. Mit seiner präzisen und beherrschten Formensprache ist Taniguchi ein aristokratischer Meister seiner Kunst, ganz ähnlich wie sein Freund Fumihiko Maki. Beide haben in ihren eindrucksvollen, inhaltsreichen Entwürfen ganz eigene Wege gefunden, um die japanische Tradition harmonisch mit der Moderne zu verbinden.

Insgesamt lässt sich sagen, dass die Generation von Álvaro Siza und Yoshio Taniguchi eine traditionellere Auffassung von Museumsarchitektur hat als ein jüngerer Architekt wie Ben van Berkel. Während van Berkels Architektur für Flexibilität und Offenheit steht, verkörpern die Werke Sizas und Taniguchis eine kontrolliertere und hierarchischere Bauweise, in der wie bei Siza Ausblicke gerahmt und wie bei Taniguchi die Besucher in bestimmte Bahnen gelenkt werden. Das soll keineswegs heißen, Siza und Taniguchi befänden sich nicht mehr auf der Höhe ihrer Zeit. Es bedeutet vielmehr, dass bei der öffentlichen Präsentation von Kunst unterschiedliche Zugangsweisen, die möglicherweise vom Alter der Architekten beeinflusst sind, durchaus nebeneinander existieren können.

MIT DER MODE BAUEN

Es wäre unfair zu behaupten, es sei anstößig, wenn Architekten mit der Mode gehen. Tatsächlich trifft Mode bei einigen Bauaufgaben sogar den Kern der Sache. Um Bekleidung zu verkaufen oder um das Publikum auf ein neues Hotel aufmerksam zu machen, ist nichts so

Erfolg versprechend wie das allerneueste Design, selbst wenn das eine eher kurzlebige Stilgebung mit sich bringt. Die Japanerin Rei Kawakubo gehört zu den Modedesignern, die sich am stärksten mit avantgardistischer Architektur und Innenraumgestaltung auseinandersetzen. Als Chefin der Firma Comme des Garçons achtet sie seit langem genau auf die meist zu minimalistischer Strenge neigenden Interieurs ihrer Läden. Eines ihrer jüngsten Projekte ist die Gestaltung einer Boutique in der 24. Straße West in Manhattan, mitten im neuen Galerienviertel Chelsea. Äußerlich widerspricht das Geschäftsgebäude beinahe jeder Marketing-Regel und kommerziellen Logik. Eine schmucklose Fassade aus unverputztem Backstein fällt nur durch das ironische »Heavenly Body Works« Schild auf, das von der vorher dort ansässigen Autowerkstatt übriggeblieben ist. Lediglich eine futuristisch anmutende Tür und die Öffnung eines Aluminiumtunnels weisen darauf hin, dass es sich hier nicht um einen gewöhnlichen Laden handelt. Durch den von den britischen Architekten Future Systems entworfenen Tunnel gelangt der Kunde in eine Welt aus weiß emaillierten kokonartigen Gebilden, die nur widerstrebend ihr Inneres preisgeben. In Zusammenarbeit mit Studio Morsa in New York und ihrem langjährigen Lieblingsarchitekten Takao Kawasaki wollte Kawakubo erreichen, dass der Kunde »zuerst den Raum selbst ausgiebig genießt«. Die sparsame Auswahl an Kleidungsstücken trägt zu dem bei, was sie »eine Atmosphäre« nennt.

Auch der neue Comme des Garçons Flagship Store im Tokioter Distrikt Aoyama strahlt, obwohl es sich in einem modernen Gebäude mit Glasfassade befindet, eine ähnliche Atmosphäre wie die Boutique in Manhattan aus. Das rührt zweifellos von der wiederholten Verwendung weißer Emaille-Kokons und Kawakubos ins Detail gehender Beteiligung an der Gestaltung der beiden Ladenlokale. Für Tokio haben Future Systems eine ungewöhnliche gewellte Glasfassade entworfen, hinter deren blauen Tupfen das Ladeninnere teilweise verborgen bleibt. Kawakubo hat auch hier bei der Innenraumgestaltung mit Takao Kawasaki zusammengearbeitet und daneben Christian Astuguevieille und die Künstlerin Sophie Smallhorn hinzugezogen. Eine noch radikalere Eingangslösung hat sie für die nahegelegene zweite Tokioter Boutique von Comme des Garçons gewählt. Hier weist nur eine hellorange Tür auf die Existenz eines Geschäfts hin. Der Rest des kubischen Raums besteht aus einer schlichten Backsteinverkleidung. Die Designerin erklärt dazu: »Die Tür steht allen offen, die sich für Comme des Garçons interessieren.« Und ihre Ladengestaltungen, obwohl eher anti-kommerziell, scheinen bei den Kunden tatsächlich gut anzukommen. Rei Kawakubo: »Ohne Veränderung kann nichts Neues entstehen. Manchmal kann sogar eine leichte Abwandlung des Blickwinkels alles dramatisch verändern. Die Geschäfte in New York und Tokio werden nun stark frequentiert, und ich denke, das kommt daher, dass überzeugende neue Ideen immer eine große Anziehungskraft auf die Leute haben.« Obwohl die Gestaltung von Ladeninterieurs von Natur aus kurzlebig ist, haben Kawakubo und ihre Mitarbeiter gezeigt, dass gutes Design von kommerziellem Nutzen sein kann. Das ist natürlich keine Strategie für den Massenkonsum – schließlich geht es um eine eher elitäre Zielgruppe. Aber der Erfolg ihrer Bemühungen ist sowohl in ästhetischer als auch in kommerzieller Hinsicht bemerkenswert.

Der französische Designer Philippe Starck hat sich einen Namen mit der Innenausstattung für einige der trendigsten Hotels in Miami (Delano, 1995), Los Angeles (Mondrian, 1996) oder New York (Royalton, 1988 und Paramount, 1990) gemacht. Diese wie auch sein jüngstes Projekt, das St. Martin's Lane Hotel in London, wurden in Zusammenarbeit mit Ian Schrager ausgeführt, der vor allem als Schöpfer des New Yorker Nachtclubs Studio 54 bekannt ist. Schrager erklärt die Attraktivität von Starcks gelegentlich extremen Entwürfen wie gigantischen Blumenvasen immer noch am besten, wenn er sagt: »Es geht um eine bestimmte Haltung. Ich glaube nicht, dass man das, was Philippe tut, mit einem Etikett versehen kann. Man kann nicht sagen, es sei minimalistisch. Es ist kein Art déco. Es ist kein Barock. Und es ist nicht wirklich postmodern. Es ist zufällig, spontan und frei fließend. Es ist das Hotel als Theaterbühne!« Starcks modisch-elegante und verrückte Details in ein Bürogebäude im Stil der 1960er Jahre in der Nähe des Trafalgar Square einzufügen, war die Aufgabe für Schragers effizientes Team, das auch für das jüngere Sanderson-Projekt in Londons Berners Street verantwortlich zeichnet. Eine Wand in hellem Gelb, von Starck schelmisch als »die Farbe des Jahrtausends« bezeichnet, macht den Auftakt, nachdem man die (nach eigenen Angaben) höchste Drehtür Europas passiert hat. Laut Schrager liegt »das Aufregende« in der einzigartigen Kombination aus Armsesseln in Louis XIV-Imitation und Stühlen, die aussehen wie vergoldete Backenzähne. Das mag kein Dekor sein, das ein Jahrhundert oder gar ein Jahrtausend überdauert, aber Philippe Starck und Ian Schrager sind maßgebend, wenn es darum geht, in Architektur und Design den Zeitgeschmack zu treffen.

DER MILLENNIUM DOME

Tony Blairs britische Labour-Regierung hatte alles auf die Millennium-Dome-Karte gesetzt. Er sollte das Symbol sein für alle die fabelhaften Dinge, die New Labour für das Land tut – und es mit einem Paukenschlag ins 21. Jahrhundert katapultieren. Statt dessen machte schlechte Organisation die Eröffnungsfeier am 31. Dezember 1999 zu einem Flop: Tausende wurden an der Zu- oder Abfahrt gehindert. Wer trotz allem ins Innere des von Lord Richard Rogers entworfenen Bauwerks gelangte, dem bot sich ein planloses Durcheinander von Pavillons. Neben Rogers haben eine Reihe der talentiertesten Architekten der Welt an diesem Projekt mitgewirkt, weshalb es hier erwähnt werden soll. Vor der Eröffnung waren die Organisatoren des Millennium Dome nur zu gerne bereit, Informationen über seine genauen Dimensionen bekanntzugeben: die größte Dachkonstruktion der Welt (100 000 m^2); eine Fläche, groß genug, um den Trafalgar Square unterzubringen; 100mal größer als Stonehenge; der 80fache Umfang vom Konzertsaal des Opernhauses in Sydney; der größte Kuppelbau der Welt und so weiter. Auf einer Halbinsel in Greenwich, gegenüber Christopher Wrens Royal Observatory (1675) gelegen, überraschte der Millennium Dome die Besucher vor allem durch eine gewisse Bescheidenheit. Trotz seiner beeindruckenden statistischen Daten, nicht zuletzt seiner phänomenalen Kosten von 43 Millionen Pfund, erscheint der Bau aus der Nähe betrachtet überraschend niedrig und klein. Da seine Höhe im Verhältnis zum Umfang relativ gering ist, stellten manche sogar die Frage, ob es sich tatsächlich um eine Kuppel handelt oder nicht eher um ein überdimensionales Zelt.

In 14 Zonen unterteilt, die verschiedenen Themenbereichen des modernen menschlichen Lebens gewidmet sind, präsentiert der Millennium Dome Arbeiten von Architekten und Designern wie Zaha Hadid (Geist), Branson Coates (Körper), Eva Jiricna (Glaube) oder Shigeru Ban (Gemeinsames Territorium, in Kooperation mit Gumuchdijian & Spence). Die von Hadid gestaltete »Mind Zone« mit ihrer spektakulären freitragenden Konstruktion beansprucht, »das erste intelligente Gebäude der Welt« zu sein. Obwohl Zaha Hadid eine anerkannte Architektin ist, scheinen die Angestellten der PR-Abteilung lieber den Inhalt des Pavillons oder die Kunstwerke von Richard Deacon, Gavin Turk und Ron Mueck hervorzuheben als Hadids Architektur. Das hängt zweifellos damit zusammen, dass der Millennium Dome ein möglichst breites Publikum ansprechen sollte. Frühzeitig durchgeführte Statistiken machten zwar deutlich, dass er nicht annähernd die erhofften vier Millionen Besucher pro Monat anziehen würde. Aber anspruchsvolle Architektur und hochwertiges Design wurden offenbar nicht als Anreiz betrachtet. Ein Unternehmer wie Ian Schrager, der an einer wesentlich kleineren, aber dafür wohlhabenderen Zielgruppe interessiert ist, mag einen Designer wie Starck als gewinnbringendes Verkaufsargument einsetzen. Das ist jedoch weniger naheliegend, wenn ein Massenpublikum angesprochen werden soll.

Im Gegensatz zum entschieden intellektuellen Konzept Zaha Hadids hat das Londoner Büro Branson Coates eine leichter zugängliche Form für ihren Pavillon »Body Zone« gewählt – die des menschlichen Körpers. Andere wiederum, wie die Minimalistin Eva Jiricna, die eine aus sechs Gewölben bestehende Stahlgitter-Konstruktion entworfen hat, scheinen das Gewicht auf eine eher vordergründige Strenge zu legen. Richard Rogers hebt sich zumindest im übertragenen Sinne deutlich von den anderen ab. Seine Konstruktion mit ihrem dehnbaren Schutzdach ist mit fast 60 km Stahlseilen an zwölf 100 m hohen Masten aufgehängt. Aus Glasfaser gefertigt, die mit abnutzungsfestem Teflon-PTFE (Polytetrafluorethylen) beschichtet wurde, soll die Kuppel das Gewicht eines Jumbojets tragen können. Sie wurde bereits im letzten James Bond-Abenteuer »The World is not Enough« effektvoll in Szene gesetzt. Auch wenn dieser Bau in erster Linie aufgrund seiner Dimensionen außergewöhnlich genannt werden kann, ist es der Versuch, erstklassige Architekten in die Öffentlichkeit zu bringen. Ob sie gut beraten waren, an diesem Zirkus teilzunehmen, ist indes ein Punkt, über den sich streiten lässt.

ARCHITEKTUR ALS KUNST?

John Ruskin vertrat die Ansicht, die Architektur könne beanspruchen, die höchste Kunstform zu sein, da sie andere räumliche Ausdrucksformen zu einem einheitlichen Ganzen verbindet. Diese Einschätzung lässt sich wahrscheinlich eher auf Bauwerke beziehen, die vor dem Ende des 19. Jahrhunderts entstanden sind als auf die moderne Architektur. Und dennoch existiert sogar heute noch eine Symbiose zwischen den überzeugendsten Werken der Kunst und der Architektur. Weiterhin befruchten beide Bereiche einander, und an dem Punkt, an dem sie sich treffen, kann man auf eine Form von Architektur stoßen, die der Definition von Ruskin durchaus entspricht.

Tadao Ando ist der unbestrittene Meister der Betonarchitektur in Japan. Sein sensibler Umgang mit Licht und sein rituelles Raumgefühl geben Andos geometrisch-strengen Bauten eine spürbare Spiritualität. Auf der Insel Awaji scheint er sein bislang größtes Werk vollendet zu haben. Der umfangreiche Komplex mit dem Namen Yumebutai oder »Dream Stage« (Traumbühne) nimmt eine Fläche von 215 000m^2 ein, die Schüttmaterial für die künstliche Insel lieferte, auf welcher der nahegelegene Flughafen Kansai erbaut wurde. Obwohl es ein Hotel, ein Kongresszentrum und Anlagen für Gartenbauausstellungen umfasst, ist »Dream Stage« eher eine Abfolge von Räumen, in denen sich Wasser, Architektur und Licht begegnen. Gerade in seinen scheinbar zweckfreien Elementen bestätigt die Anlage ihren Anspruch auf den Status eines reinen Kunstwerks. In Bereichen wie dem Kongresszentrum und dem Hotel dagegen wirkt Yumebutai zwar gelungen, aber keineswegs verblüffend. Es ist vielmehr das sanft verwirrende Labyrinth aus Innenhöfen und Durchgängen, das den Besucher seiner Alltagswelt enthebt. Wasserfälle stürzen von Hängen und Wasserläufe strömen durch eine erstaunliche Vielzahl von Räumen. Tadao Ando meint dazu: »Die Alhambra in Granada, wo das Wasser kleine Patios miteinander verbindet, lieferte ein historisches Vorbild.« Eine Million Muschelschalen bedecken die Böden der Wasserbecken, und der Besucher fragt sich, ob das alles nicht eigentlich ein Traum sei. In Auftrag gegeben wurde der Komplex von den örtlichen Behörden, die besorgt waren, dass die Touristen Awaji auf ihrem Weg zu verlockenderen Reisezielen übersehen könnten. Er liegt zudem nicht weit von der eindrucksvollen neuen Hängebrücke entfernt, die Kobe mit Awaji verbindet. Allerdings ist nicht jedes Detail von »Dream Stage« perfekt. Eine kleine Kapelle in der Mitte der Anlage ist ein Abklatsch von Andos außergewöhnlicher »Church of the Light« (Kirche des Lichts) in Ibaraki, Osaka (1989). Statt wie hier eine kreuzförmige Öffnung hinter den Altarraum zu platzieren, verlegt Ando sie nun an die Decke. Eine der Stärken seiner »Church of the Light« ist ihre kraftvolle Energie; und dabei hatte Ando für dieses Projekt nur ein relativ geringes Budget. Könnte es sein, dass Ando wegen der fast grenzenlosen Mittel, die ihm für »Dream Stage« zur Verfügung standen, etwas von dieser Energie eingebüßt hat? Dieser Einwand scheint jedoch nebensächlich angesichts des erfolgreichen Konzepts von »Dream Stage«. Aufgrund seiner Lage auf Awaji hat der Komplex nicht die Publizität erlangt, die er verdient. Yumebutai wurde Ende 1999 vollendet und ist nichts Geringeres als ein abschließendes Statement zur Kunst der Architektur im 20. Jahrhundert. Es ist in der Tat ein Meisterwerk.

Wie Tadao Ando (mit der rühmlichen Ausnahme von Yumebutai) zeigt sich auch Mario Botta aus dem Tessin in kleineren Projekten von seiner besten Seite. Seine Bergkapellen in Mogno und auf dem Monte Tamaro gehören zu den kraftvollsten kleineren Bauten der 1990er-Jahre. Für Botta ist der künstlerische Aspekt von Architektur sehr wichtig, wie eines seiner jüngsten Projekte demonstriert. Aus Anlass der Francesco Borromini-Ausstellung 1999 errichtete Botta am Ufer des Luganer Sees das originalgroße Holzmodell eines Teils von Borrominis Kirche San Carlo alle Quattro Fontane (1641) in Rom. Dieses großartige »virtuelle Denkmal« verband Bautechniken und -formen des Barock mit einer bewusst flüchtigen Interpretation des 20. Jahrhunderts. Zugleich ist Bottas Hommage an den großen Barockarchitekten von den funktionalen Beschränkungen befreit, denen Architektur meist unterliegt.

Maya Lin, geboren 1959, schloß 1986 ihr Studium an der School of Architecture in Yale ab. Ihr bekanntestes Werk ist das 1981 fertiggestellte Vietnam Veterans' Memorial in Washington, D. C. Von ihr selbst als »Skulptur« bezeichnet, besteht es aus Granit, der keilförmig in den Erdboden gepresst wurde. Die Namen von 50 000 im Vietnamkrieg gefallenen amerikanischen Soldaten sind in diesen Stein eingraviert. Diese »minimalistische Geste«, die von einigen heftig attackiert wurde, hat sich als besonderes Kriegsdenkmal erwiesen. Tatsächlich gelingt es Maya Lin auf einzigartige Weise, die Schranken zwischen Kunst und Architektur zu öffnen. Während sie ihre bildhauerische Arbeit im öffentlichen und privaten Raum weiterführt, setzt sie sich intensiv mit Architektur auseinander. Ihr Norton Apartment in New York (1999) ist die minimalistische Gestaltung eines 220 m² großen, teilweise unterirdisch gelegenen Raums. Im Geist von Terry Rileys Ausstellung »The Un-Private House« im Museum of Modern Art 1999 lässt sich dieser Raum leicht so verändern, dass er für eine, zwei oder mehr Personen nutzbar ist. Riley, Leiter der Abteilung für Architektur und Design am New Yorker MoMA, hat betont, dass der Wandel im familiären und individuellen Lebensstil in den USA und Europa zu einer tiefgreifenden Veränderungen in der Organisation von Wohnräumen geführt hat. Architektur ist dazu aufgerufen, sich einer gewandelten Zeit anzupassen und die strenge Ordnung von Wohn-, Ess-, Schlafzimmer und Küche aufzuheben. Abgesehen von ihrer meisterhaften Beherrschung von Licht und Materialien macht Maya Lin das Norton Apartment auch zu einem Ausstellungsraum für eine ihrer Glasskulpturen. So verwischt sie die Unterschiede zwischen Architektur und Kunst noch weiter.

Auch die New Yorker Architektin Toshiko Mori versucht, die Trennung zwischen Architektur und Kunst (oder zwischen Architektur und dem wirklichen Leben) zu überwinden. Mit ihrer »Woven Inhabitation«, 1999 im Artists Space in New York präsentiert, versucht sie, eine einfache und elegante Lösung für das drängende Problem zu finden, Flüchtlingen oder Opfern von Naturkatastrophen eine vorübergehende Unterkunft zu bieten. Mori wuchs im Japan der Nachkriegszeit auf und erinnert sich an eine Zeit der Entbehrungen, in der gewebte Stoffe die einzige Annehmlichkeit darstellten. »Ich habe nie die Lebensklugheit der japanischen Frauen vergessen, die ihnen half, sich auch in diesen Zeiten einen Sinn für Würde und Kultur zu bewahren. Ich erinnere mich an ihre Fertigkeit, aus Fetzen Kleidung und aus Nahrungsresten Mahlzeiten herzustellen. Heute weiß ich, dass eine Kultur so auch ihre Zerstörung überleben kann.« Moris Konzept besteht in der »Resteverwertung neuartiger Industriegewebe, die bereits in der Raumfahrt und von Pharma- und Modeindustrie verwendet, aber noch nie als Baumaterial eingesetzt wurden.« Sie erklärt weiter: »Ausgehend von einem einzigen Faden fügt sich die Struktur eines Gewebes zu einem Gitter aus Kette und Schuss zusammen. In architektonischen Begriffen ausgedrückt: Diese Gitter ermöglichen unterschiedlich starke Luftzirkulation, die den Kälte- und Wärmeaustausch erleichtert und reguliert.« Eine leicht herzustellende Bauform auf Textilbasis wie »Woven Inhabitation« schafft »einen Zugang zur Architektur, der in Zukunft allgemein gebräuchlich werden könnte – nicht nur für Behelfskonstruktionen, sondern als genormter Bestandteil für die Alltagsarchitektur.« Da es sich bei der Mehrheit der Flüchtlinge um Frauen und Kinder handelt, schlägt Mori eine elegante Lösung für ein wachsendes Problem vor. Mit völlig anderen Mitteln bewegt sie sich damit in die gleiche Richtung wie Asymptote: Sie weist der Architektur neue Aufgaben zu und löst ihre tradierten Begriffe auf, um ihr eine angesichts der gegenwärtigen Bedürfnisse erforderliche Flexibilität zu geben.

Auf die Frage, ob er der Meinung sei, dass sich die Grenzen zwischen Kunst und Architektur gegenwärtig verwischen, antwortete der amerikanische Architekt Richard Meier: »Nein, ich glaube nicht, dass die Grenzen sich so sehr verwischen. Eher denke ich, dass es einfach mehr Künstler gibt, die auch Architekten sein wollen. Vielleicht wollten in der Vergangenheit mehr Architekten Künstler sein. Aber ich glaube, heute würden sich immer mehr Künstler wirklich gerne als Architekten betätigen… Die Ausgangspunkte sind meiner Meinung nach für Künstler und Architekten unterschiedlich. Der Künstler hat eine Idee von dem, was sein könnte, und dann findet er jemanden, der diese Idee verwirklicht haben will. Ein Architekt dagegen wartet in der Regel darauf, dass jemand mit einem Projekt auf ihn zukommt, und dann entwickelt er eine Idee für dieses Projekt.« Dennoch betont Meier, dass ein gelungenes Bauwerk immer auch ein Kunstwerk ist. Frank O. Gehry, der am stärksten plastisch gestaltende unter den bedeutenden zeitgenössischen Architekten, zitiert ohne Scheu die Quellen seiner künstlerischen Inspiration. 1989 sagte er in seiner Dankesrede zur Verleihung des Pritzker Prize: »Meine Künstlerfreunde wie Jasper Johns, Bob Rauschenberg, Ed Kienholz und Claes Oldenburg arbeiteten mit sehr billigen Materialen – Holzstücken und Papier –, und sie schufen Schönheit. Diese Materialien waren keine oberflächlichen Details, sie waren bewusst eingesetzt und weckten in mir die Frage, was Schönheit sei. Ich entschied mich für das Handwerk, das mir zur Verfügung stand, und dafür, aus dessen Begrenzungen eine Tugend zu machen. Malerei hat eine Unmittelbarkeit, nach der ich mich in der Architektur sehnte. Ich erforschte die Entwicklung neuer Baustoffe und versuchte, die Form mit Gefühl und Geist zu füllen. In dem Bemühen, den wahren Kern meines eigenen Ausdrucks zu finden, stellte ich mir vor, ich sei ein Maler, der vor einer weißen Leinwand steht und sich den ersten Arbeitsschritt überlegt.«

Letztlich liegt das Schicksal der Architektur des neuen Jahrhunderts jedoch nicht in den Händen von Architekten wie Frank O. Gehry und Richard Meier. Ihr Weg wird vielmehr von den Vertretern einer jüngeren Generation wie Toshiko Mori oder Hani Rashid von Asymptote bestimmt. Bahnbrechende Pioniere wie Rei Kawakubo oder Philippe Starck und viele andere haben gezeigt, dass Mode im Kontext architektonischer Gestaltung kein Schimpfwort sein muss. Lebendigkeit und Veränderung sind Kernbegriffe für die neuen Bauformen, ebenso wie das Zulassen eines beständigen Wechsels und die Bereitschaft, wechselnden Bedürfnissen zu entsprechen. Oft mag das streng gegliederte Räume ausschließen, obgleich die anhaltende Nachfrage nach dem wohl am stärksten hierarchisierten Gebäude, dem Wolkenkratzer, dieser Logik widerspricht. Vom Neo-Minimalismus über die ungeordnete Konfrontation mit der alltäglichen Lebenswirklichkeit bis zu virtuellen Bauwerken: Die Architektur verändert sich gegenwärtig wohl so rasch wie nie zuvor.

INTRODUCTION

Chaque réalisation architecturale naît de circonstances spécifiques liées à sa fonction, à son site, à son budget. Le goût, voire la mode jouent évidemment leur rôle dans la détermination de l'aspect du bâti et même dans sa signification profonde, même si certains tentent de nier ce type d'influences. Buffon disait « Le style, c'est l'homme. » C'est peut-être exact, mais le style est aussi fonction du temps. Malgré la prolifération des nouveaux moyens de communication, aucun mouvement stylistique n'a réussi à s'imposer en architecture contemporaine avec autant de force que le modernisme dans la période de l'après-guerre. Des courants et sous-tendances se répandent sur le globe, souvent ralentis par la durée nécessaire à la conception et à la réalisation d'une œuvre importante. Ainsi, des projets de style déconstructiviste apparus dans les années 1980 continuent à être réalisés. Il en va de même pour le néo-minimalisme des années 1990. Si le style est l'homme, ces bâtiments sont les produits d'architectes qui se sont longtemps battus pour imposer leur point de vue dans le passé. Une fois que leurs idées semblent triompher, on ne peut attendre d'eux qu'ils s'orientent immédiatement vers une démarche différente.

Alors que des tendances surannées terminent leur existence par un tour du monde, d'autres styles apparaissent. Le XXIe siècle assistera à un renouveau de l'intérêt pour des constructions plus complexes, moins liées à la géométrie euclidienne – passablement bousculés à la fin du siècle précédent – qu'aux recherches par ordinateur qui s'efforcent de remettre en question les références aux systèmes rectilignes. Bien que certains architectes pensent encore que l'ordinateur n'est utile qu'à certaines tâches, d'autres ont commencé à explorer de nouvelles frontières comme ce concept de « bâtiment virtuel » qui n'existerait que sur écran. A New York, l'agence Asymptote, qui a été retenue pour concevoir un musée virtuel pour Guggenheim, vient de créer un environnement de marchés en ligne pour le New York Stock Exchange. Il s'agit d'espaces dont l'existence première se déroulera sur l'écran de l'ordinateur. La sophistication grandissante de la conception informatisée permet aussi une autre forme de construction virtuelle, celle de monuments du passé jamais édifiés. Le professeur Takehiko Nagakura du MIT et sa Team Unbuilt ont ainsi donné vie à des projets du Corbusier, d'Aalto ou de Tatline. On peut penser que ces efforts ne vont guère plus loin que les importants moyens investis dans la création de jeux vidéo comme « Myst » ou « Riven ». Pour un esprit traditionaliste, l'essence même de l'architecture réside dans sa solidité ou sa permanence, qualités assez relatives faut-il le préciser, mais qui n'en sont pas moins entièrement éliminées de l'univers virtuel. D'autres, comme Hani Rashid d'Asymptote ont une vision différente du futur. « Lorsque l'on parle de l'architecture du millénaire à venir, » explique Rashid, « il faut prendre en compte deux conditions, l'espace physique de l'architecture tel que nous l'avons toujours connu, dont l'enveloppe, la forme et la permanence subsisteront sans aucun doute, et le domaine de l'architecture virtuelle qui émerge aujourd'hui de l'espace numérique de l'Internet. Objets, volumes, espaces, immeubles et institutions peuvent désormais être édifiés, transmis, appréhendés, expérimentés et manipulés sur le réseau global. C'est une nouvelle architecture de fluidité, de flux et de mutabilité qui repose sur des avances technologiques, nourrie d'un désir humain fondamental d'affronter l'inconnu. La voie inévitable de ces deux architectures, la réelle et la virtuelle, sera la convergence et la fusion. »

Ce survol de l'architecture contemporaine récente s'efforce de remplir une tâche audacieuse : réunir des informations venues du monde entier et tenter de trouver quelque sens en termes de tendances et d'évolution dans ce qui reste, à travers ses expressions les plus élevées, une authentique forme d'art. Même ainsi, l'architecture novatrice, celle qui réussit à réconcilier les limites souvent contradictoires d'un site, d'un budget et d'une ambition esthétique, reste excessivement rare comparée à l'énorme masse de ce qui se construit à chaque instant. Le style, même sous ses différents atours, fait l'architecture du moment, de notre temps. Animée par la mode ou plus profondément peut-être, par les perspectives plus vastes qu'ouvrent l'ordinateur et l'Internet, l'architecture deviendra-t-elle aussi fluide et changeante qu'une petite robe de printemps ? Certainement pas, mais elle fait néanmoins son entrée dans une époque où le flux et le mouvement seront des valeurs plus recherchées que la monumentalité et l'immuabilité.

VIRTUELLEMENT VOTRE

« Le musée est devenu le tombeau de l'art, » affirme Hani Rashid d'Asymptote « une châsse dans lequel l'art est présenté à un public présumé non initié, dans les espaces splendides d'une vision détachée et privilégiée d'un lieu d'autorité culturelle au service de la diffusion d'idées et de la propagation d'idéologies. Ce qui subsiste encore et mérite d'être maintenu est peut-être la compréhension de l'espace du musée, lieu qui peut inciter à la provocation, chez les spectateurs comme chez les artistes. » Asymptote s'est vu confier la tâche de concevoir le premier musée virtuel qui existera essentiellement sur Internet. Ce « Guggenheim du cyberespace » possède l'ambition de créer rien de moins qu'un « nouveau paradigme architectural. » Plus spécifiquement, « le Guggenheim Virtual Museum, donnera non seulement accès à tous les musées Guggenheim, y compris aux services, archives et collections caractéristiques d'un musée, mais offrira également un environnement exclusif et convaincant que pourra expérimenter le visiteur virtuel. Par ailleurs, le musée virtuel est l'espace idéal pour le déploiement et la connaissance de l'art et d'événements spécifiquement créés pour un médium numérique qui permet en même temps à un public dispersé dans le monde entier de visiter et d'intervenir sur le site. Pour Asymptote et le Guggenheim, le Guggenheim Virtual Museum, né de la fusion d'un espace d'information, de l'art, du commerce et de l'architecture, deviendra le premier bâtiment virtuel important du XXIe siècle. » En plus de créer un environnement, dans lequel les œuvres d'art pourront être facilement regardées, Hani Rashid veut que son architecture virtuelle soit interactive. Son utilisation par les visiteurs modifiera son apparence, et remettra en cause la solidité ou l'immuabilité même de l'architecture en général et des musées en particulier. Comme l'art qu'il accueillera, le Guggenheim virtuel sera fluide, se redéfinissant de lui-même en fonction des circonstances. Un tel projet remet en question le paradigme architectural dans le sens où il n'est soumis pratiquement à aucune des contraintes du « monde réel » qui entravent la construction, comme les réglementations de sécurité ou l'accès des handicapés. Il ne doit ni protéger ni obéir aux lois communes de l'ingénierie. Architecture ou aménagement intérieur électronique ? En tous cas, cette orientation est la dernière nouveauté.

Asymptote a également créé un environnement de salle de marchés pour le New York Stock Exchange (NYSE). « La salle des marchés en trois dimensions, » explique Rashid, « est un environnement multidimensionnel fait de réalité virtuelle en temps réel, et le projet de l'Advanced Trading Floor Operations Centre est la rénovation et la re-conception d'espaces existants du Stock Exchange. » Plus clairement, le NYSE a demandé à Asymptote de créer à la fois le projet en ligne de contrôle et de vente de titres, ainsi qu'un espace près de la principale salle des marchés à New York. « Le 3DTF, » poursuit Hani Rashid, « est un *datascape* (paysage de données) qui rapproche des flux d'informations, des données et des modèles de corrélation en un environnement architectural tridimensionnel unique. L'espace virtuel est un modèle en temps réel qui montre aux utilisateurs l'activité et les événements sous la forme d'un espace interactif dans lequel ils peuvent naviguer avec des possibilités infinies de déplacements et de perspectives. Le déploiement du 3DTF parallèlement aux salles de marchés actuelles permet au personnel traitant les ‹ Operations › d'accéder à une compréhension plus approfondie et plus précise des multiples variables et événements complexes qui interviennent au cours des séances. Asymptote s'est servi du VRML (Virtual Reality Markup Language) et de programmes de CAO sophistiqués pour concevoir et mettre au point les divers éléments nécessaires. Parallèlement aux exigences fonctionnelles du modèle, Asymptote a porté une attention particulière à la qualité générale de l'environnement virtuel : lumière, couleur, textures aussi bien qu'exploration et développement de diverses méthodes de navigation, de mouvement, de vision et d'interface graphique. » Architecture ou design graphique ? Les deux, semble-t-il.

Dans la jeune génération d'architectes, le goût pour les volumes ou environnements libres et fluides, voire non géométriques, ne se limite pas à l'approche radicale d'Asymptote. Une autre agence new-yorkaise, Diller + Scofidio remet ainsi en question le concept d'architecture traditionnelle de façon entièrement différente. Leur « Blur Building » (bâtiment flou) conçu pour l'International Expo 2002 d'Yverdon-les-Bains (au bord du lac de Neuchâtel, Suisse) devrait ressembler à rien de plus qu'à un nuage. Avec près de 100 m de long, 60 de large et 12 d'épaisseur, ce nuage « se matérialisera grâce à l'eau du lac filtrée et projetée en brouillard par un réseau serré de jets sous haute-pression dans une vaste sculpture en porte-à-faux. Le public s'approchera de cette masse gazeuse immobile par une rampe prise dans une structure de verre à l'endroit où elle pénètre dans le brouillard. A l'intérieur, les architectes cherchent à obtenir une quasi absence de stimuli, une sorte de ‹ blanc › optique accompagné du seul bruit — tout aussi blanc — de la brume. Une image vidéopanoramique projetée sur écran circulaire occupera la plate-forme centrale conçue pour 250 personnes. Comme l'homme ne peut plus prétendre être au centre d'un univers qu'il maîtriserait, la position du spectateur est l'enjeu de réflexions critiques, » expliquent les architectes. Diller + Scofidio utilisent abondamment les ordinateurs dans leur travail de conception, mais à la différence d'Asymptote, leur objectif final est toujours de construire. Il se rapprochent de leurs collègues new-yorkais dans la remise en cause des principes mêmes de l'architecture, allant au-delà de la forme et des matériaux pour « rendre flous » les repères visuels et auditifs nécessaires à l'orientation spatiale. Plutôt que l'ordre spatial hiérarchique imposé par presque toutes les architectures traditionnelles, le Blur Building n'apporte aucune solution claire, mais adopte une attitude scientifique et même philosophique en harmonie avec une bonne partie de la pensée contemporaine.

Moins provocant et plus respectueux des règles fondamentales de l'architecture, le nouveau restaurant du Centre Georges Pompidou, œuvre des jeunes architectes Jakob + MacFarlane, ne se débarrasse pas moins de notions accessoires comme la distinction sol et mur. Des volumes libres en aluminium, élaborés dans un chantier naval, abritent la cuisine, les toilettes et un bar au sommet du Centre réalisé par Piano et Rogers. La trame tracée sur les panneaux qui constituent le sol s'élève brusquement pour former des distorsions tridimensionnelles inspirées des modélisations par ordinateur. Bénéficiant toujours d'une vue spectaculaire sur le Paris ancien, ce restaurant de la famille Costes s'avère peut-être plus symbolique de l'engagement du Centre envers la créativité contemporaine que beaucoup des œuvres d'art exposées en ses murs. Si la trame salue l'utilisation plus rationnelle de l'espace par Piano, Jakob + MacFarlane sont les produits d'une génération plus jeune, familiarisée avec les possibilités de la CAO.

Takehiko Nagakura est professeur assistant de design et d'informatique au département d'architecture du MIT. Il a étudié l'architecture à l'Université de Tokyo auprès de Fumihiko Maki. Grâce aux fonds de la Takenaka Corporation, il a créé « Team Unbuilt » qui se propose de marier la recherche historique approfondie aux technologies d'imagerie de synthèse d'avant-garde. « Les formes des bâtiments ont été travaillées à partir de dessins d'archives originaux obtenus auprès d'organismes comme la Fondation Le Corbusier à Paris. » explique-t-il. «Une technologie de visualisation basée sur des principes d'éclairage révèle les plus subtils effets d'interaction entre la lumière, les matériaux et la géométrie. La représentation en images de synthèse qui en résulte donne une spectaculaire impression de volumes dans l'espace, aussi bien intérieur qu'extérieur, qui jusqu'à présent étaient restés enfouis dans l'imaginaire des architectes de ces œuvres jamais réalisées. »

Takehiko Nagakura a choisi des bâtiments comme l'église d'Altstetten d'Alvar Aalto (Suisse, 1967) ou le projet de concours pour le Palais des Soviets du Corbusier (Moscou, 1931). L'une de ses réalisations virtuelles les plus spectaculaires est le monument à la IIIe Internationale de Vladimir Tatline (Pétrograde, aujourd'hui Saint-Pétersbourg, 1919), l'un des premiers bâtiments entièrement abstraits jamais conçu. Commandé en 1919 par le département des Beaux-Arts, il fut exposé sous forme d'une maquette de 6,7 m de haut lors du huitième Congrès des Soviets en décembre 1920. Cette présentation était jusqu'alors la seule façon de visualiser cette œuvre essentielle de l'architecture du XXe siècle. La version définitive aurait consisté en une structure de fer inclinée et en spirale, supportant un cylindre, un cône et un cube de verre, chacun tournant sur lui-même à une vitesse différente. L'intérieur aurait abrité des salles de conférences et divers locaux pour d'autres activités. Avec ses 400 m de haut, ce devait être la construction la plus élevée du monde. Elle ne fut jamais édifiée car le gouvernement soviétique proscrivait l'art non figuratif.

Insistant sur le travail d'historien nécessaire à la préparation de ses constructions virtuelles, Takehiko Nagakura présente avant tout « Team Unbuilt » comme un outil d'enseignement. Pour lui, les futures générations d'architectes seront bien plus à l'aise avec le concept de construction virtuelle. «A mon avis, » dit-il, « ce travail de détective couplé à la pratique du virtuel est une manière extrêmement efficace de former et d'éduquer un architecte. Peut-être est-elle même très proche du modèle de la formation traditionnelle à la française des architectes, qui préconisait l'étude de l'architecture de l'antiquité. C'est pourquoi mon cours au MIT utilise les informations et les matériaux réunis pour le projet Unbuilt et donne aux étudiants la chance d'apprendre la représentation spatiale en se servant de technologies numériques d'avant-garde. »

DES AMBITIONS MONTANTES

Même si certains architectes évoluent vers des concepts de plus en plus immatériels, d'autres préfèrent s'investir dans des projets tendant vers la quintessence de la monumentalité du XXe siècle. Des tours de plus en plus hautes sont projetées et édifiées partout dans le monde. Les concours pour le plus haut immeuble de la planète mobilisent d'énormes sommes d'argent et de talent en Asie et aux Etats-Unis. Le projet le plus ambitieux du moment concerne Chicago, par ailleurs ville natale du gratte-ciel.

Si la psychologie des commanditaires et le gigantisme semblent être les considérations majeures qui président à la conception de ces tours, leur aspect esthétique est souvent relégué à un rôle secondaire. L'architecte français Christian de Portzamparc a porté un regard nouveau sur l'esthétique des immeubles de grande hauteur à l'occasion du projet de la tour LVMH à New York. Petit, selon les standards de Shanghai ou de Chicago, cet immeuble se pare d'une façade de verre novatrice et se termine par une spectaculaire salle de trois étages de haut.

L'un des premiers groupes mondiaux de produits de luxe, le groupe français LVMH, a sans aucun doute été sensibilisé au travail de Portzamparc par le Prix Pritzker qui lui a été attribué en 1994, mais également par son goût pour ce que l'on pourrait qualifier de lyrisme. Sa tour de 24 niveaux est recouverte de panneaux de verre sablé ou décapé à l'acide, derrière lesquels des tubes fluorescents vert, blanc et bleu créent une « ligne de fracture » entre les divers plans, eux-mêmes brisés. Fabriqué en France par Saint-Gobain, ce verre est en partie conçu pour éviter les reflets de la masse sombre de l'imposant IBM Building qui lui fait face. Herbert Muschamp du *New York Times* a écrit que Portzamparc avait « réinventé l'esprit de l'Art Déco » ajoutant ainsi sa voix au concert de louanges qui accueillit cet immeuble considéré comme l'un des plus réussis édifiés à New York au cours de ces dernières années.

A l'autre bout du monde, dans une approche très différente, l'agence américaine KPF travaille au projet du Shanghai World Financial Center. Situé dans le quartier d'affaires de Lujiazui à Pudong, cet immeuble de 95 étages devrait atteindre 460 m de haut, en 2004, ce qui en fera provisoirement sans doute le plus haut du monde. Ses 317 000 m^2 coûteront $500 millions. KPF a imaginé une forme particulièrement pure qui se déploie à partir de l'intersection d'un prisme carré et d'un cylindre. Pour des raisons qui tiennent à la pression exercée par les vents, la partie supérieure comporte une ouverture de 50 m de circonférence appelé « porte de la lune. » Sans vouloir trop jouer des analogies historiques ou artistiques, on peut noter que la forme de cette tour n'est pas sans rappeler la puissante simplicité des objets archaïques chinois. Par ailleurs, pour répondre au contexte, qualifié par KPF de « cacophonie visuelle, » les dimensions du vide ménagé au sommet de la tour sont similaires à celles de la sphère ou « pearl » (perle) qui surmonte la tour Pearl TV qui lui fait face. Il est évident que les références contextuelles et historiques sont secondaires lorsque l'on parle du plus haut bâtiment jamais construit, mais KPF a su mettre en valeur l'intérêt de la qualité architecturale même dans un environnement aussi commercial. Avec sa base revêtue de grès sur une hauteur de 28 m et ses étages supérieurs bardés d'acier inoxydable et d'un verre légèrement réfléchissant, le Shanghai World Financial Center (architecte principal William Pedersen) devrait se faire une place à part parmi quelques réalisations de moindre importance, sa hauteur n'étant pas le seul critère de jugement. En fait, il n'a que 40 m de plus que le Jin Mao Building récemment achevé, toujours à Shanghai.

Or, le Shanghai World Financial Center risque de ne jamais pouvoir arborer le titre de « plus haut gratte-ciel du monde. » En effet, un autre projet, à Chicago cette fois, est en bonne voie de le surpasser de 13 m (473 m). Il devrait être achevé en 2003. Le 21 septembre 1999, la commission d'urbanisme de la ville de Chicago a approuvé les plans d'une tour dessinée par Adrian Smith (Skidmore, Owings & Merrill) pour un terrain situé 7 South Dearborn, à l'angle de Dearborn et Madison Streets. Avec ses étages supérieurs en porte-à-faux à partir d'un noyau de béton, l'immeuble devrait compter 108 étages, dont ceux des plus hauts appartements du monde. Recouvert d'aluminium, d'acier inoxydable et de verre légèrement teinté, il sera surmonté d'énormes antennes de télévision.

La structure et la forme des immeubles de grande hauteur dépendent souvent de contraintes prévisibles, et de facteurs locaux exigeant qu'ils résistent aux vents, aux résonances, aux tourbillons et aux oscillations. Ceci explique, entre autres, que des éléments comme les grandes encoches prévues 7 South Dearborn n'aient rien ou pas grand chose à voir avec l'esthétique. L'ouverture sommitale du Shanghai World Financial Center, de la taille d'une aile d'un 747, est en réalité une élégante solution à un problème d'ingénierie. L'aménagement interne des gratte-ciel est également tributaire de la problématique complexe de la capacité des ascenseurs.

Il serait exagéré de dire que la plupart des immeubles de très grande hauteur sont dénués de tout qualité esthétique. En fait, par leur multiplication dans des villes comme New York, Chicago ou Shanghai, ils créent une dynamique urbaine indéniablement stimulante. Leurs connotations freudiennes et leur imposante présence les rendent difficiles à ignorer, et, quelles que soient les tendances de l'architecture ou du style, on ne peut tout simplement pas dénier leur existence. Répondant à des besoins, certains réels et commerciaux d'autres surtout psychologiques, les tours semblent une composante récurrente de l'architecture contemporaine, intrinsèquement liée à l'évolution de celle-ci, même si elle paraît contraire à une bonne partie des théories actuelles. Les gratte-ciel actuellement en projet approchent la barrière des 500 m, et la dépassent même dans le cas de la Landmark Tower (574 m) prévue à Hongkong.

ARTS AND CRAFTS

Les arts, et leur exposition, restent l'un des champs d'élection de l'architecture contemporaine de haute qualité. Pour tous ceux qui ne s'intéressent que modérément aux musées virtuels, l'art et les musées d'art constituent l'un des domaines dans lesquels une certaine immuabilité et durabilité semblent appropriées. Le genre évolue néanmoins rapidement comme le montrent les quelques exemples choisis ici.

Situé sur la place du marché de la ville néerlandaise de Nimègue, le Museum Het Valkhof est l'œuvre de UN Studio/Van Berkel & Bos, auteur du pont Erasmus de Rotterdam. Il réunit sous un même toit diverses collections du monastère Saint Jean et du Musée provincial G. M. Kam. La tonalité froide que donne au bâtiment son parement de verre bleu-vert s'atténue à l'intérieur où l'architecte laisse les œuvres s'exprimer. Loin d'imposer un cheminement, comme le font beaucoup de concepteurs de musées, van Berkel affirme que l'on peut visiter son musée en empruntant 88 itinéraires différents. Une longue galerie latérale transparente offre une vue sur un parc voisin. Caractérisé par sa discrétion, sa souplesse et son ouverture, le Museum Het Valkhof est résolument de son temps.

La Fondation Serralves d'Alvaro Siza (Porto, Portugal) se situe non loin du centre de la ville de Porto, base de son agence. La Fondation a été créée grâce à un partenariat d'un type unique entre le gouvernement portugais et 50 entreprises du secteur privé. Edifiée dans le parc de la Quinta de Serralves – propriété de 20 ha, comprenant une résidence construite dans les années 1930 pour le comte de Vizela – elle se consacre à l'art contemporain. Le projet de Siza est très ambitieux. A partir d'un principe de plafonds suspendus similaires à ceux mis au point pour le Centre d'Art Contemporain de Galice, l'architecte a créé un certain nombre de grandes galeries aux aménagements souples, non pas destinées à une collection permanente, mais à des expositions temporaires. Des cours intérieures et de nombreuses baies permettent au visiteur de rester en contact avec le merveilleux parc aménagé sur 3 ha par Siza lui-même. L'intérieur offre toutes les facilités que l'on attend aujourd'hui d'un musée, entre autres une boutique, une cafétéria et un auditorium. L'ensemble est réalisé avec un soin visible du détail, attitude typique de l'architecte mais qui, pour une fois, a disposé d'un budget conséquent. D'inspiration moderniste, la Fondation Serralves n'en est pas pour autant de conception dépassée. Complexe en dépit de ses lignes nettes et tendues, elle démontre une fois encore qu'Alvaro Siza est l'un des architectes les plus originaux et les plus créatifs de sa génération.

Né dans les années 1930, comme Siza, l'architecte japonais Yoshio Taniguchi, considéré comme un maître dans son propre pays, a accédé à la réputation internationale lorsqu'il a été choisi pour rénover le Museum of Modern Art de New York. La sobriété majestueuse de son vocabulaire moderniste se retrouve dans son œuvre la plus récente, la Galerie des Trésors Horyuji, située dans l'enceinte du Musée National de Tokyo au parc Ueno. Depuis sa fondation à la fin du XIXᵉ siècle, comme Musée de la maison impériale, cette institution conserve les objets offerts aux collections de l'Empereur dans les années 1870. Elle visait à préserver le contenu du temple Horyuji de Nara des agissements d'un mouvement anti-bouddhiste. C'est pour exposer ces importantes œuvres d'art en métal que Taniguchi a érigé un bâtiment en trois parties. « J'ai conçu un bâtiment en trois strates : une zone intérieure aux murs de pierre, une aire périphérique aux murs de verre et une zone extérieure délimitée par un auvent métallique. » La boîte centrale est protégée de la lumière naturelle, tandis que le hall d'entrée et l'espace sous auvent sont baignés de lumière. Taniguchi se rappelle que « cette conception symbolise l'histoire des précieux objets que le bâtiment abrite, objets transmis au cours des âges dans ces boîtes gigognes en bois qui, au Japon, servent traditionnellement à protéger les trésors. » Bien que l'architecte soit moins explicite sur ce point, sa galerie évoque également de multiples aspects des temples japonais. Le visiteur qui suit le cheminement prévu tombe d'abord sur un bassin à fontaine axiale ; ensuite, il doit changer au moins quatre fois de direction avant d'atteindre l'entrée. Ce parcours typique des temples japonais rappelle au passant qu'il pénètre dans un espace chargé de sens. Un écran de pierre l'accueille là ou il s'attendait à trouver une porte. Il faut contourner cette ultime barrière pour pénétrer dans le musée lui-même, d'organisation par ailleurs très rationnelle. L'impression générale est celle d'une construction de grande qualité, mise en valeur par des détails de finition comme l'alignement absolument parfait de chaque partie du bâtiment et de la galerie intérieure en fonction des contours extérieurs du bassin. La précision et la rigueur de Yoshio Taniguchi font de lui un maître possédant la même noblesse que son ami Fumihiko Maki. Tous deux savent comment unir la tradition japonaise à la modernité dans des créations d'une grande force.

Sans vouloir généraliser, la génération de Siza et de Taniguchi semble avoir une vision plus traditionnelle de l'architecture muséale que celle d'architectes plus jeunes comme Ben van Berkel. La souplesse et l'ouverture contrastent avec l'architecture plus retenue et plus hiérarchisée qui caractérise les perspectives cadrées de Siza, par exemple, ou l'approche contrôlée des visiteurs chez Taniguchi. Ceci ne signifie certainement pas que ces deux créateurs ne soient plus de leur temps, mais plutôt que, dans le contexte de l'art et de sa présentation, des orientations différentes, éventuellement liées à l'âge de leur concepteur, peuvent et doivent coexister.

UNE PASSION POUR LA MODE

Il serait injuste de dire que la mode n'a rien à faire en architecture. Dans certains cas, elle se trouve même au cœur du sujet. Pour vendre des vêtements, attirer des clients dans un nouvel hôtel, rien n'est plus efficace que les dernières tendances du design, même au prix de l'éphémère. L'une des créatrices de mode les plus engagées en faveur de l'architecture et de l'aménagement des espaces intérieurs d'avant-garde est la Japonaise Rei Kawakubo, de Comme des Garçons. Elle a longtemps surveillé de très près la décoration intérieure de ses boutiques qui tendent d'habitude à une pureté minimaliste des plus austères. L'une de ses entreprises les plus récentes est une boutique située West 24th Street à Manhattan, au cœur du nouveau quartier des galeries de Chelsea. Vu de l'extérieur, le magasin défie pratiquement toutes les règles commerciales. La façade aveugle, en brique, porte simplement l'amusante enseigne « Heavenly Body Works » abandonnée là par le précédent occupant du local. Seule, une étrange porte de verre assez futuriste et l'ouverture d'un tunnel d'aluminium signalent qu'il ne s'agit pas d'un atelier de carrosserie comme l'enseigne pourrait le laisser entendre. En franchissant ce tunnel monocoque dessiné par les architectes britanniques de Future Systems, le visiteur se retrouve dans un univers peuplé de cocons émaillés blancs qui semblent ne révéler qu'à regret leurs secrets. En collaboration avec le Studio Morsa, New York, et son collaborateur de longue date, l'architecte Takao Kawasaki, Rei Kawakubo voulait que le client «ressente d'abord pleinement l'espace en lui-même.» La sélection parcimonieuse d'articles en vente contribue à créer ce qu'elle appelle : «une atmosphère».

Un univers plus loin, dans un immeuble moderne à façade de verre, le nouveau vaisseau-amiral de Comme des garçons, qui vient de s'ouvrir dans le quartier d'Aoyama à Tokyo, semble recréer une ambiance similaire. L'effet est certainement dû aux cocons blancs que l'on y retrouve et à l'implication attentive de Kawakubo dans la création des ces deux espaces. Ici, Future Systems a mis au point une surprenante façade en verre ondulé parsemée de taches bleues qui obscurcissent en partie l'intérieur. Travaillant là encore en collaboration avec Takao Kawasaki pour l'intérieur, Kawakubo a également fait appel à Christian Astuguevieille et à l'artiste Sophie Smallhorn. Elle s'est engagée dans une approche encore plus radicale dans l'autre boutique voisine de Comme des Garçons. Là, seule une porte orange vif signale l'existence du magasin. Le reste du volume cubique est recouvert de briques sans le moindre ornement. Comme elle le précise : «La porte est ouverte à tous ceux qui s'intéressent à Comme des Garçons.» Sa démarche aussi anti-commerciale puisse-t-elle paraître, attire en fait beaucoup de clients. «Sans changement, rien de neuf ne peut se produire. Une simple modification de point de vue peut parfois tout changer. Les boutiques de New York et de Tokyo drainent beaucoup de gens maintenant, et je pense qu'ils sont toujours attirés par des idées nouvelles et fortes.» La conception de magasins, même dans le meilleur des cas, est de nature éphémère. Pourtant, Kawakubo et ses talentueux associés ont montré que le «Good design» pouvait être parfaitement viable. Il ne s'agit évidemment pas ici marketing de grande consommation. Ces projets sont destinés à un public plutôt élitiste, mais le succès de ces efforts, tant en termes d'esthétique que de marketing, est significatif.

Plus connu encore que Rei Kawakubo dans les cercles à la mode, le designer français Philippe Starck s'est fait un nom en signant les décors d'hôtels très branchés comme le Delano (Miami, 1995), le Mondrian (Los Angeles, 1996), le Royalton et le Paramount (New York, 1988 et 1990). Tous, comme son dernier né, le St Martin's Lane Hotel à Londres, ont été financés par l'inimitable Ian Schrager, plus connu pour avoir créé le club Studio 54 à New York. Schrager est réputé pour des commentaires tels que : «Le design est un outil de marketing… il nous fait remarquer,» ou «les hôtels ne sont pas du design. Le design n'est qu'un élément parmi d'autres. Il fait partie d'une équation plus vaste.» Peut-être est-ce Schrager qui définit encore le mieux la séduction des interventions parfois provocantes de Starck, comme ses vases de fleurs géants. «C'est une question d'attitude,» dit-il, «Je ne pense pas que l'on puisse mettre une étiquette sur ce que fait Philippe. On ne peut pas dire que ce soit minimal ; ce n'est pas Art Déco ; ce n'est pas baroque ; ce n'est pas vraiment post-moderne. C'est le hasard. Une forme libre. C'est l'hôtel, considéré comme un théâtre !» Appliquer la mode Starck à un immeuble de bureaux des années 1960 transformé en hôtel non loin de Trafalgar Square est la dernière aventure de l'équipe de Schrager, également responsable du plus récent Sanderson Hotel, Berner Street, toujours à Londres. Un mur jaune vif, que Starck appelle espièglement «la couleur du millénaire», donne le ton dès que le visiteur a franchi ce qui serait la plus haute porte pivotante d'Europe. C'est cela «the excitement» dont parle Schrager, une combinaison unique de fauteuils imitation Louis XIV et de tabourets qui ressemblent à des dents plaquées or. Ce décor ne durera peut-être pas un millénaire, ni même cent ans, mais Philippe Starck, soutenu sur Ian Schrager, fait beaucoup pour former l'opinion à ce qui est élégant en architecture comme en design.

UN NOUVEAU TEMPLE

Le gouvernement travailliste de Tony Blair a joué la carte du Millennium Dome, symbole de toutes les merveilles que le New Labour apportait à un pays qu'il aidait à entrer avec panache dans le XXIe siècle. Une organisation médiocre a gâché l'inauguration du 31 décembre, empêchant des dizaines de milliers de personnes d'aller et de venir entre Londres et la structure conçue par Richard Rogers. A l'intérieur, les visiteurs ont découvert un bric-à-brac irréel de pavillons, assez comparable à ce que l'on peut trouver dans une exposition universelle. Cependant, outre Rogers, un certain nombre des plus talentueux architectes du moment ont participé à cette initiative qui mérite à ce titre d'être mentionnée. Les organisateurs du Millennium Dome étaient ravis de communiquer les chiffres impressionnants du projet avant son inauguration : le plus vaste toit du monde (100 000 m^2), assez grand pour recouvrir Trafalgar Square, 100 fois la taille de Stonehenge, 80 fois le volume de la salle de concert de l'opéra de Sydney, la plus grande coupole du monde, etc. Situé à Greenwich sur une avancée de terre face à l'Observatoire royal de Christopher Wren (1675), il a sans aucun doute surpris ses visiteurs, d'abord et avant tout, par sa... son aspect plutôt modeste. Malgré ces chiffres, dont le moindre n'est pas son coût phénoménal de £758 millions, il semble étonnement bas et petit, sans doute parce sa hauteur est relativement insignifiante par rapport à sa circonférence. Certains se sont demandé s'il s'agissait bien d'un « dôme » et non pas seulement d'une tente de dimensions extravagantes.

Divisé en 14 zones consacrées à la vie contemporaine, il contient des réalisations de créateurs comme Zaha Hadid (l'Esprit), Branson Coates (le Corps), Eva Jiricna (La Foi) ou Shigeru Ban (Le territoire commun, avec Gumuchdjian & Spence). La section « Esprit » de Hadid et sa structure spectaculaire en porte-à-faux ne prétend à rien moins que d'être « le premier bâtiment intelligent au monde. » Conséquence de l'approche volontairement « grand public » choisie par les initiateurs du projet, le service des relations publiques du dôme a préféré mettre davantage l'accent sur le contenu du pavillon et même sur les œuvres d'art de Richard Deacon, Gavin Turk ou Ron Mueck que sur la participation de la célèbre architecte. Très vite, on sut que le dôme n'attirerait pas le million de visiteurs mensuels attendus au départ. La qualité de l'architecture et du design n'a donc pas été considérée comme un argument de vente suffisant. Un homme d'affaires comme Ian Schrager, qui s'intéresse à des cibles bien définies mais beaucoup plus aisées, peut voir en Starck un argument de vente, mais le raisonnement semble moins évident dès qu'il s'agit de foules.

A la différence de l'approche très intellectuelle de Zaha Hadid, Branson Coates ont préféré se référer à une forme facilement identifiable – un corps humain – pour leur pavillon, le bien nommé « Body Zone ». D'autres comme la minimaliste Eva Jiricna, qui a dessiné une structure soutenue par six arcs en lattes d'acier, semblent avoir opté pour davantage de rigueur. Dans l'esprit d'œuvres d'architectes moins célèbres, ces pavillons défendent les couleurs d'une conception de qualité, mais on peut se demander si ces architectes ont eu raison de s'afficher dans un ensemble aussi disparate. Richard Rogers se détache clairement, du moins au sens littéral. Son toit tendu est suspendu à 12 mâts de 100 m de haut au moyen de 60 km de câbles d'acier. Réalisé en fibre de verre enduite de Teflon-PTFE (polytétrafluoroéthylène), le dôme est assez solide pour résister au poids d'un 747. Il a déjà tenu un rôle dans un film, le dernier James Bond : « The World is not Enough ». Même si son caractère exceptionnel est surtout dû à ses dimensions, le but de ses concepteurs était de promouvoir des architectes de haut niveau. Qu'ils aient mérité de participer à ce cirque ou non est un autre débat.

OUI, MAIS EST-CE BIEN DE L'ART ?

Pour John Ruskin, il était évident que l'architecture pouvait prétendre au titre d'art suprême, puisqu'elle associait de multiples formes d'expression et de conceptions spatiales en un tout unifié. Cette analyse concernait sans doute davantage les constructions de son époque que l'architecture moderne. Une symbiose existe cependant entre l'architecture contemporaine et les expressions artistiques les plus éloquentes. Elles continuent à se nourrir mutuellement et lorsqu'elles se rencontrent, il est permis de penser qu'après tout, l'architecture répond bien à la définition qu'en donnait Ruskin.

Tadao Ando est sans conteste le grand maître de l'architecture en béton au Japon. Aussi puissante l'articulation géométrique de ses plans puisse-t-elle être, sa sensibilité à la lumière et à la ritualisation de l'espace, enrichit ses réalisations d'une indéniable spiritualité. C'est sur l'île d'Awaji, qu'il vient de mettre la dernière main à son chef d'œuvre. Appelée Yumebutai ou « Scène de rêve » ce complexe imposant recouvre 215 000m² d'un terrain dont la terre a servi à créer l'île artificielle de l'aéroport voisin de Kansai. Bien qu'il comprenne un hôtel, un centre de congrès et des installations pour de grandes expositions horticoles, cette « Scène » est essentiellement un cheminement d'un espace à l'autre, l'eau, l'architecture et la lumière jouent de concert. Son « inutilité » lui permet de revendiquer le statut d'œuvre d'art. En fait, entravé par les exigences de sécurité du centre de congrès et gêné par le décor imposé de l'hôtel, le complexe d'Ando est intéressant, sans être bouleversant. C'est dans le délicat labyrinthe de cours et d'allées que le visiteur se sent transporté à un niveau plus élevé. Des cascades descendent de la colline et l'eau court à travers une étonnante succession d'espaces. Ando s'explique : « L'Alhambra de Grenade m'a fournit un modèle historique. Là-bas, l'eau relie les petits patios. » Un million de coquilles Saint-Jacques, choisies et disposées à la main, bordent les bassins et le visiteur peut se demander s'il ne rêve pas. Commandé par les autorités locales qui craignaient que les touristes ne sautent Awaji en se rendant vers des destinations plus séduisantes, le complexe est situé près de l'énorme pont suspendu qui relie l'île à Kobe. Tous les détails ne sont pas parfaits. La petite chapelle centrale est une reprise de la remarquable « Eglise de lumière » (Ibaraki, Osaka, 1989) d'Ando. L'ouverture cruciforme est ici découpée dans le plafond et non dans le mur derrière l'autel. L'un des intérêts de l'église d'Ibaraki résidait dans son énergie brute, due en partie à son budget limité. L'excès de moyens a-t-il privé Ando de cette énergie ? Néanmoins cette critique est mineure face à la réussite de cette « Scène de rêve », qui du fait de sa localisation n'a pas bénéficié des publications qu'elle mérite. Achevé fin 1999, Yumebutai ne représente rien moins qu'une date marquante de l'art architectural du XXe siècle. C'est un chef d'œuvre.

Comme Tadao Ando, l'architecte suisse Mario Botta se sent particulièrement à l'aise dans les réalisations de dimensions plus intimes. Ses chapelles de montagne à Mogno ou au sommet du Monte Tamaro comptent parmi les plus impressionnantes constructions de dimensions réduites des années 1990. La profonde sensibilité architecturale de Botta transparaît dans un de ses plus récents projets. Une série d'expositions sur l'architecture de la Renaissance et de la période baroque ont attiré l'attention sur les superbes maquettes datant de cette période. Mario Botta a choisi de recréer en maquette grandeur nature et en bois une partie de l'église romaine de Francesco Borromini, San Carlo alle Quattro Fontane (1641), sur les rives du lac de Lugano pour annoncer une exposition sur l'œuvre du maître italien. Ancré près de l'entrée du Parco Civico de Lugano, cette étonnant «monument virtuel» allie les techniques et les formes du baroque à une interprétation éphémère du XXᵉ siècle. L'œuvre est affranchie de la plupart des contraintes fonctionnelles de l'architecture. Elle représente l'essence de celle-ci, libérée de son carcan de pierre, flottant librement. Qu'en reste-t-il? L'art?

Née en 1959, Maya Lin, diplômée en 1986 de la Yale School of Architecture, est surtout connue pour son Mémorial des vétérans du Vietnam à Washington (1981). Cette œuvre, qui se définit comme une sculpture, consiste en dalles de granit enfoncées dans le sol du Mall sur lesquelles sont gravés les noms de 50 000 soldats américains morts pendant la guerre. Ce geste minimaliste, objet de vives attaques de la part de certains, est un mémorial de guerre d'un type différent qui attire chaque jour des centaines de visiteurs fascinés par une tragédie humaine symbolisée par une pierre apparemment froide. Parce qu'elle ignore les barrières qui séparent habituellement l'art de l'architecture, la démarche de Maya Lin est unique. Tout en travaillant à des projets de monuments publics ou de sculptures, elle se consacre également à des recherches architecturales personnelles. L'appartement Norton (New York, 1999) est la réinterprétation minimaliste d'un espace de 220 m² en partie souterrain. Dans l'esprit de la «Un-Private House» (exposition de Terry Riley de 1999 au Museum of Modern Art), ce volume peut être modifié en fonction du nombre de ses occupants. Riley, responsable du département d'architecture et de design du MoMA a fait remarquer que les changements de style de vie et de la structure familiale en Amérique et en Europe conduisaient à des modifications substantielles de la façon dont s'organisaient les maisons. L'architecture est appelée à s'adapter à cette évolution et à abandonner la hiérarchie rigide entre salle-de-séjour, salle-à-manger, cuisine, chambres qui convenait aux générations précédentes. Prouvant une fois encore sa maîtrise de l'éclairage et des matériaux, Maya Lin a également fait de cet appartement un lieu d'exposition pour ses propres sculptures en verre brisé, rendant encore plus floues les frontières entre ce que l'on peut appeler architecture, et ce qui est bien de l'art.

D'une façon plus modeste, l'architecte japonaise Toshiko Mori s'est elle aussi attaquée aux barrières qui séparent l'art de l'architecture, ou peut-être l'architecture du monde réel. Son «Woven Inhabitation»(in-habitation tissée), présentée à l'Artists Space à New York en 1999, cherche à apporter une solution simple et élégante au vaste problème de l'habitat provisoire des réfugiés et victimes de catastrophes naturelles. Bien qu'elle vive aujourd'hui à New York, Mori a grandi dans le Japon de l'après-guerre. Elle se souvient d'une période de privations pendant laquelle les tissus étaient le seul élément de confort. «Je me suis toujours rappelé l'intelligence innée de femmes qui arrivaient à maintenir le sens de la dignité et de la culture. Je me souviens de leur talent à créer des vêtements ou des repas à partir de rien. Je sais maintenant que c'est ainsi qu'une culture ou une civilisation peuvent survivre à leur destruction.» Son concept est d'utiliser «les déchets de textiles industriels révolutionnaires déjà utilisés en aéronautique, dans la mode ou dans le secteur de la santé, que personne n'a jamais pensé employer comme matériaux dans une conception architecturale... un seul brin suffit à créer la structure d'une pièce tissée, l'entrelacs de la chaîne et de la trame; en termes architecturaux, ces trames offrent diverses possibilités de circulation de l'air, facilitant et régulant la chaleur et le rafraîchissement naturels.» Un logement efficace, facile à fabriquer à partir de textiles comme la «Woven Inhabitation», conclut-elle «positionne une approche de l'architecture qui peut devenir courante dans le futur, non seulement pour des abris temporaires, mais également-ment comme application standard dans la construction de tous les jours. » Observant que la majorité des réfugiés est composée de femmes et d'enfants, elle propose une solution élégante à un problème de plus en plus pressant. Elle opte pour le « low-tech » et va dans la même direction que les gourous informaticiens d'Asymptote : pousser l'architecture vers de nouveaux enjeux, dissoudre ses définitions traditionnelles pour lui apporter la souplesse que les besoins du moment exigent.

Lorsqu'on lui demande si les barrières entre l'art et l'architecture s'estompent, l'architecte Richard Meier réplique : « Non. Je ne pense pas que le problème se pose ainsi. Je crois simplement que davantage d'artistes veulent être architectes. Mais peut-être qu'il y a eu dans l'histoire encore plus d'architectes ayant voulu être artistes. Je pense qu'aujourd'hui de plus en plus d'artistes souhaiteraient faire de l'architecture. Les points de départ de l'artiste et de l'architecte sont généralement différents. L'artiste a une idée de ce qui pourrait être, puis il trouve une personne intéressée par cette idée. Généralement, un architecte attend que quelqu'un vienne vers lui avec un projet avant de dire : j'ai une idée de ce que vous pourriez faire. » Meier insiste néanmoins sur le fait qu'une grande réalisation architecturale est aussi une œuvre d'art. Frank O. Gehry, le plus sculptural des grands architectes contemporains cite ses sources sans honte. Dans son discours prononcé lors de la remise du Prix Pritzker en 1989, il déclarait : « Mes amis artistes, comme Jasper Johns, Bob Rauschenberg, Ed Kienholz et Claes Oldenburg travaillaient à partir de matériaux très bon marché – morceaux de bois et papier – et ils en faisaient naître la beauté. Il ne s'agissait pas de détails superficiels, leur approche était directe et soulevait en moi la question même de la beauté. Je choisis d'utiliser ce qui était alors disponible, de travailler avec des artisans, et de faire de leurs limites une vertu. La peinture offrait ce caractère immédiat que j'enviais pour l'architecture. J'explorais les nouveaux matériaux de construction pour essayer de donner un esprit et un sentiment à la forme. En tentant de trouver l'essence de ma propre expression, je m'imaginais comme un artiste devant sa toile blanche, et qui va décider de ce que sera son premier mouvement. »

De toutes façons, le destin de l'architecture du siècle qui commence n'est plus vraiment entre les mains d'architectes comme Frank O. Gehry ou Richard Meier. Il est plutôt entre celles d'une génération plus jeune, celle de Toshiko Mori ou d'Hani Rashid d'Asymptote. Trail Balzer comme Kawakubo ou même le designer Philippe Starck et tant d'autres ont montré que la mode n'est pas forcément un mot « vulgaire » en matière de conception architecturale. Le mouvement et le changement sont bien la clé des formes nouvelles, le mariage des tendances, une disponibilité à répondre aux besoins. Ceci peut souvent rendre obsolète les espaces rigides et hiérarchisés, bien que la demande pour le type d'immeuble le plus résistant au vent, le gratte-ciel, défie cette logique. Entre le minimalisme et une sorte de confrontation brouillonne avec la réalité de tous les jours et les volumes créés par ordinateurs, l'architecture change probablement aujourd'hui plus vite qu'elle ne l'a jamais fait.

TADAO ANDO

Tadao Ando Architect & Associates
5-23, Toyosaki 2-chome
Kita-ku, Osaka 531-0072
Japan

Chicago House ▶

Born in Osaka in 1941, **TADAO ANDO** is self-educated as an architect, largely through his travels in the United States, Europe and Africa (1962-69). He founded Tadao Ando Architect & Associates in Osaka in 1969. He has received the Alvar Aalto Medal, Finnish Association of Architects (1985), Medaille d'or, French Academy of Architecture (1989), the 1992 Carlsberg Prize and the 1995 Pritzker Prize. He has taught at Yale (1987), Columbia (1988) and Harvard (1990). Notable buildings include: Rokko Housing (Kobe, 1981-93), Church on the Water, Hokkaido (1988), Japan Pavilion Expo '92 (Seville, Spain, 1992), Forest of Tombs Museum (Kumamoto, Japan, 1992), and the Suntory Museum (Osaka, 1994). Recent work includes the Awaji Yumebutai (Awajishima, Hyogo, Japan, 1997-2000), Modern Art Museum of Fort Worth, Texas (1999-2002), and Pulitzer Foundation for the Arts (St. Louis, Missouri, 1999-2001).

TADAO ANDO, geboren 1941 in Osaka, erlernte den Beruf des Architekten als Autodidakt, vorwiegend auf Reisen durch Nordamerika, Europa und Afrika (1962-69). 1969 gründete er das Büro Tadao Ando Architect & Associates in Osaka. Er wurde mit der Alvar-Aalto-Medaille des Finnischen Architektenverbands (1985), der Medaille d'or der Académie Française d'Architecture (1989), dem Carlsberg-Preis (1992) und dem Pritzker Prize (1995) ausgezeichnet. Ando lehrte an den Universitäten Yale (1987), Columbia (1988) und Harvard (1990). Zu seinen bekanntesten Bauten zählen die Rokko Wohnanlage in Kobe, Japan (1981-93), die Kirche auf dem Wasser in Hokkaido (1988), der Japanische Pavillon für die Expo '92 in Sevilla (1992), das Forest of Tombs Museum in Kumamoto, Japan (1992) und das Suntory Museum in Osaka (1994). Neuere Projekte sind das Modern Art Museum of Fort Worth, Texas (1999-2002) und die Pulitzer Foundation for the Arts in St. Louis, Missouri (1999-2001).

Né à Osaka en 1941, **TADAO ANDO** est un architecte autodidacte, formé en grande partie lors de ses voyages aux U.S.A., en Europe et en Afrique (1962-69). Il fonde Tadao Ando Architects & Associates à Osaka en 1969. Titulaire de la Médaille Alvar Aalto de l'Association finlandaise des architectes (1985), de la Médaille d'or de l'Académie Française d'Architecture (1989), du Prix Carlsberg 1992, et du Pritzker Prize 1995. Il a enseigné à Yale (1987), Columbia (1988) et Harvard (1990). Parmi ses réalisations les plus notoires : immeuble d'habitation Rokko, Kobé (1982-83) ; église sur l'eau, Hokkaido (1988) ; pavillon japonais pour Expo '92, Séville, Espagne (1992) ; Musée de la forêt des tombes, Kumamoto (1992) ; Musée Suntory, Osaka (1994). Parmi ses réalisations récentes : le Awaji Jumebutai, Awajishima, Hyogo, Japon (1997-2000), le Modern Art Museum of Fort Worth, Texas (1999-2002) et le Pulitzer Foundation for the Arts, St. Louis, Missouri (1999-2001).

CHICAGO HOUSE

Chicago, Illinois, USA, 1992-97

Planning: 5/92-12/94. Construction: 12/93-12/97.
Client: withheld. Floor area: 835 m².

Located in a quiet residential area near Lincoln Park, the **CHICAGO HOUSE** (total floor area 835 m²) consists of a 12 x 12 m – unit on the south side containing the private family quarters, while a rectangular unit half its size on the north side includes more public areas for receiving guests. A long, narrow living room links these two basic forms. A terrace and lower-level pool create a spectacular reception space that brings to mind the concept of some of Ando's smaller museums in Japan. The design takes into account the natural setting in particular one poplar tree that the owners are fond of. This is Tadao Ando's first residential project in the United States. It is, in fact, his first completed building in North America.

Das **CHICAGO HOUSE,** ein Privathaus mit einer Gesamtnutzfläche von 835 m², liegt in einer ruhigen Wohngegend unweit des Lincoln Park. Es besteht aus einem 12 x 12 m großen Bauteil auf der Südseite, in dem sich die Privaträume der Familie befinden und einem halb so großen rechteckigen Bauteil, der mehrere Räume für den Empfang und die Unterbringung von Gästen besitzt. Ein langgestreckter, schmaler Wohnraum verbindet diese beiden Bereiche. Die Terrasse und der unterhalb davon angelegte Swimmingpool bilden einen spektakulären Eingangsbereich, der an das Baukonzept einiger von Ando ausgeführter kleinerer Museen in Japan erinnert. Der Entwurf bezieht die natürliche Umgebung mit ein, speziell eine Pappel, die den Eigentümern besonders am Herzen liegt. Bei diesem Projekt handelt es sich um Tadao Andos erstes fertiggestelltes Bauwerk in Nordamerika.

Située dans un tranquille quartier résidentiel, près de Lincoln Park, la **MAISON CHICAGO** de 835 m² se compose d'un élément de 12 x 12m au sud contenant les pièces privées tandis que le volume rectangulaire de moitié moins important au nord est réservé à la réception. Ces deux formes géométriques élémentaires sont reliées par une longue et étroite salle-de-séjour. Une terrasse et une piscine en contrebas déterminent un vaste espace de réception qui rappelle certains petits musées édifiés par Ando au Japon. Le projet tient compte du cadre naturel, en particulier d'un peuplier qu'aimaient les propriétaires. C'est la première maison signée par l'architecte aux Etats-Unis, et en fait sa première réalisation achevée dans ce pays.

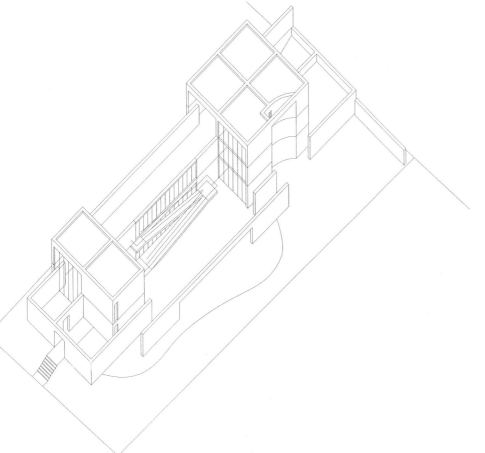

With its large pond and inclined stairway, the Chicago House brings to
mind certain Japanese buildings of
Ando such as the Nariwa Municipal
Museum (Nariwa-cho, Okayama,
1993-94).

Mit seinem großen Wasserbecken
und der geneigten Treppe erinnert
dieses Wohnhaus an andere in Japan
entstandene Bauten des Architekten,
wie etwa sein 1994 fertiggestelltes
Nariwa Municipal Museum in Nariwa-
cho, Okayama.

Par son grand plan d'eau et sa
rampe inclinée, la Maison Chicago
rappelle certaines créations de Ando
au Japon, dont le Musée municipal
de Nariwa (Nariwa-cho, Okayama,
1993-94).

AWAJI YUMEBUTAI

Awajishima, Hyogo, Japan, 1992-2000/03

Planning: 1992-94/94-97. Construction: 10/97-2000/03.
Client: Hyogo Prefecture. Floor area: 93 500 m².

AWAJI YUMEBUTAI, in many ways Tadao Ando's most ambitious project, covers a site area of 215 000 m² that had been used to obtain landfill for the Kansai International Airport, built on an artificial island. Named Yumebutai or "A Stage for Dreams," the complex includes a hotel and a conference center, but its most striking feature is a succession of fountains and internal courtyards. Tadao Ando has said, "The basic framework of this project is round universes and square universes, which are connected by walkways. Rather than depending solely on geometry, I experimented with using the spaces created by the irregular topography that remained. In addition, I tried to create a new style of garden combining the traditional Japanese tour garden with Western tour gardens, whose framework is much less ambiguous."

AWAJI YUMEBUTAI ist in vielerlei Hinsicht Tadao Andos ehrgeizigstes Werk. Es bedeckt eine Fläche von 215 000 m² und liegt in der Nähe des auf einer künstlichen Insel erbauten internationalen Flughafens Kansai. »Yumebutai« oder »Eine Bühne für Träume« getauft, umfaßt der Komplex ein Hotel und ein Konferenzzentrum, sein auffälligstes Merkmal ist aber wohl eine Abfolge von Brunnen und offenen Innenhöfen. Tadao Ando erklärte dazu: »Die Grundidee für dieses Projekt ist die Verbindung von runden und quadratischen Einheiten durch Gehwege. Statt mich ausschließlich von der Geometrie bestimmen zu lassen, experimentierte ich mit der Gestaltung von Räumen, die sich durch die unregelmäßige topografische Beschaffenheit des Standorts ergaben. Darüber hinaus wollte ich einen Garten neuen Stils kreieren, indem ich den traditionellen japanischen Garten mit westlichen Gärten kombinierte, deren Anlage wesentlich klarer ist.«

A de nombreux égards projet le plus ambitieux de Tadao Ando, le complexe **AWAJI YUMEBUTAI** s'étend sur un terrain de 215 000 m² dont la terre a été prélevée pour créer l'île artificielle de l'aéroport international de Kansai. Appelé « Yumebutai » ou « Une scène pour les rêves », l'ensemble comprend un hôtel et un centre de conférence. Son intérêt tient cependant surtout à une succession de fontaines et de cours intérieures. Tadao Ando précise que : « La base de ce projet repose sur des univers ronds et des univers carrés, reliés par des allées. Plutôt que de m'appuyer exclusivement sur la géométrie, je me suis servi des espaces générés par les irrégularités de la topographie. J'ai essayé de créer un nouveau style de jardin qui combine le traditionnel jardin de promenade japonais et les modèles occidentaux, dont la trame est beaucoup moins ambiguë. »

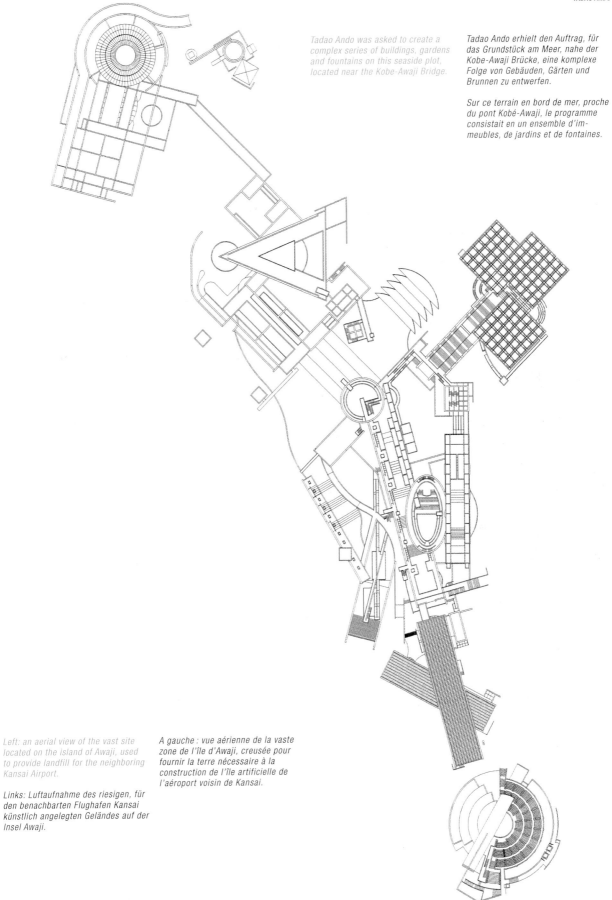

Tadao Ando was asked to create a complex series of buildings, gardens and fountains on this seaside plot, located near the Kobe-Awaji Bridge.

Tadao Ando erhielt den Auftrag, für das Grundstück am Meer, nahe der Kobe-Awaji Brücke, eine komplexe Folge von Gebäuden, Gärten und Brunnen zu entwerfen.

Sur ce terrain en bord de mer, proche du pont Kobé-Awaji, le programme consistait en un ensemble d'immeubles, de jardins et de fontaines.

Left: an aerial view of the vast site located on the island of Awaji, used to provide landfill for the neighboring Kansai Airport.

Links: Luftaufnahme des riesigen, für den benachbarten Flughafen Kansai künstlich angelegten Geländes auf der Insel Awaji.

A gauche : vue aérienne de la vaste zone de l'île d'Awaji, creusée pour fournir la terre nécessaire à la construction de l'île artificielle de l'aéroport voisin de Kansai.

Hundreds of thousands of scallop shells recovered from a canning facility in Northern Japan were placed by hand in the concrete of the ponds and waterfalls of the complex.

Hunderttausende von Muschelschalen aus einer nordjapanischen Konservenfabrik wurden von Hand in den Beton der Brunnen und Wasserfälle eingesetzt.

Des centaines de milliers de coquilles saint-jacques récupérées dans une conserverie du Nord du Japon furent pressées à la main dans le béton des bassins et des cascades du complexe.

Both visually and in terms of the sound of falling water, the Awaji Yumebutai complex is based on a series of cascades. Stairs, fountains and flowers are arranged in a geometric progression not unlike a musical composition.

Stufen, Brunnen und Pflanzen bilden, ähnlich einer musikalischen Komposition, in Kaskaden angeordnet, sowohl optisch als auch akustisch den zentralen Aspekt des Awaji Yumebutai-Komplexes.

La conception visuelle et sonore du complexe d'Awaji Yumebutai repose sur une série de cascades. Des escaliers, des fontaines et des fleurs sont disposés en une progression géométrique qui évoque une composition musicale.

Ando's powerful sense of architectural drama finds expression in these images. Vast areas of the Awaji Yumebutai complex serve no specific purpose, but lead visitors to a heightened awareness of space, light, sound and architecture.

Andos ausgeprägtes Gefühl für architektonische Dramatik wird an diesen Bauten spürbar. Große Teile des Awaji Yumebutai-Komplexes dienen allein dazu, den Besuchern ein höheres Bewusstsein für Architektur, Raum, Licht und Akustik zu vermitteln.

Le sens du spectacle architectural dont fait souvent preuve Ando s'exprime dans ces images. Si de vastes parties du Awaji Yumebutai ne répondent à aucune fonction précise, elles suscitent chez le visiteur une conscience aiguë de l'espace, de la lumière, du son et de l'architecture.

ANDRESEN O'GORMAN

Andresen O'Gorman Architects
The Studio, 9 Ormond Terrace
Indooroopilly
Queensland 4068
Australia

Tel: +61 7 3878 5855
Fax: +61 7 3878 4900
e-mail: B.Andresen@mailbox.uq.edu.au

BRIT ANDRESEN received her degree in architecture at the Norges Tekniske Høgskole in Trondheim, Norway. She had her own firm, Brit Andresen Architect (1970-76), and worked in association with Barry Gasson and John Meunier for the Burrell Museum in Glasgow (1971-76) before her association with **PETER O'GORMAN**. O'Gorman received his B.Arch. degree from Queensland University. He had his own practice, Peter O'Gorman Architect, from 1965 to 1980. He taught at Queensland University from 1968 to 1998. Brit Andresen has taught at Cambridge (1970-76), the Architectural Association in London (1971-76), Queensland University (1977-2000), and at the University of California, Los Angeles (1981-83). Together, they have worked on private residences in Australia, such as the Mooloomba House (North Stradbroke Island, 1995-99), the Ocean View House (Mount Mee, 1993-95), and the Tomsgate Way House (Mount Nebo, 1988-90).

BRIT ANDRESEN schloss ihr Architekturstudium an der Norges Tekniske Høgskole im norwegischen Trondheim ab. Bevor sie sich mit **PETER O'GORMAN** zusammenschloss, war sie von 1970 bis 1976 in ihrem eigenen Büro tätig und arbeitete zusammen mit Barry Gasson und John Meunier für das Burrell Museum in Glasgow (1971-76). Sie lehrte in Cambridge (1970-76), an der Architectural Association in London (1971-76), der Queensland University (1977-2000) und der University of California, Los Angeles (1981-83). Peter O'Gorman erwarb seinen Bachelor of Architecture an der Queensland University und arbeitete von 1965 bis 1980 in seinem eigenen Büro Peter O'Gorman Architect. Von 1968 bis 1998 lehrte er an der Queensland University. Zu den von Andresen und O'Gorman gemeinsam ausgeführten Wohnbau-Projekten in Australien gehören das Mooloomba House auf North Stradbroke Island (1995-99), das Ocean View House, Mount Mee (1993-95) und das Tomsgate Way House, Mount Nebo (1988-90).

BRIT ANDRESEN est diplômée d'architecture du Norges Teknikse Nøgskole norvégien. Elle crée sa propre agence, Brit Andresen Architect (1970-76) et travaille en association avec Barry Gasson et John Meunier pour le Burrell Museum de Glasgow (1971-76) avant de s'associer à **PETER O'GORMAN**. Elle a enseigné à Cambridge (1970-76), à l'Architectural Association de Londres (1971-76), à Queensland University (1977-2000) et à l'UCLA (1981-83). Peter O'Gorman est diplômé d'architecture de Queensland University. Il dirige son agence, Peter O'Gorman Architect, de 1965 à 1980. Il enseigne à Queensland University de 1968 à 1988. Ils ont travaillé ensemble sur des résidences privées en Australie entre autres pour Mooloomba House (North Stradbroke Island, 1995-99), Ocean View House (Mount Mee, 1993-95) et Tomsgate Way House (Mount Nebo, 1988-90).

ROSEBERY HOUSE

Highgate Hill, Queensland, Australia, 1995-97

Planning: 1995-96. Construction: 1997. Client: withheld.
Floor area: c. 280 m². Costs: US$132 000.

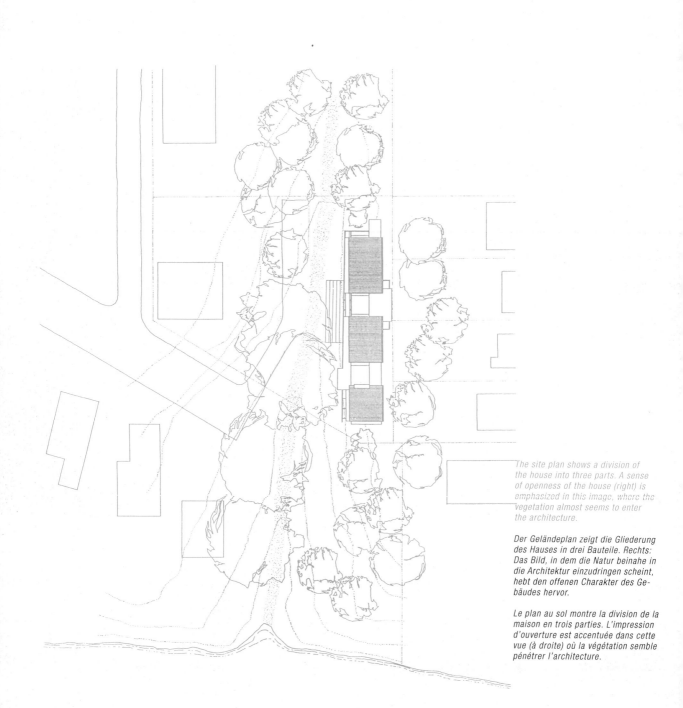

The site plan shows a division of
the house into three parts. A sense
of openness of the house (right) is
emphasized in this image, where the
vegetation almost seems to enter
the architecture.

Der Geländeplan zeigt die Gliederung
des Hauses in drei Bauteile. Rechts:
Das Bild, in dem die Natur beinahe in
die Architektur einzudringen scheint,
hebt den offenen Charakter des Gebäudes hervor.

Le plan au sol montre la division de la
maison en trois parties. L'impression
d'ouverture est accentuée dans cette
vue (à droite) où la végétation semble
pénétrer l'architecture.

Seen from certain angles (below, left) the house seems to constitute a linear whole. It is the timber-battened screen on the western side that gives this feeling of unity.

Aus bestimmten Blickwinkeln scheint das Haus eine geradlinige Einheit zu bilden (unten links). Auf der Westseite des Gebäudes wird dieser Eindruck durch die mit Holz verschalte Schutzwand erzeugt.

Sous certains angles (ci-dessous à gauche) la maison donne l'impression de se développer en ligne droite. Côté Ouest, un écran de bois à claire-voie confirme ce sentiment d'unité.

Situated in a hilly, overgrown gully in Brisbane, the US$132 000 **ROSEBERY HOUSE** is essentially composed of three pavilions connected by decks. Because of the subtropical climate, the decks are neither exclusively interior nor exterior elements, an impression heightened by the use of corrugated polycarbonate for the roofs of the eastern deck area. The division of the house into three parts (bedrooms, kitchen/dining room, and printmaking studio/laundry) was at least partially intended to bring light into the different areas. A timber-battened screen on the western side brings together the entire composition. Built of Australian eucalyptus, the house is not atypical in an area that favors light wooden houses. With its relaxed style and sensitivity to its natural environment, the house fits into the local traditions, even though it improves them technically by several steps.

Das in einer überwachsenen Geländefurche in Brisbane gelegene, für 132 000 US$ erbaute **ROSEBERY HOUSE** besteht im Wesentlichen aus drei Pavillons, die durch Plattformen miteinander verbunden sind. Wegen des subtropischen Klimas sind diese Plattformen weder reine Innen- noch reine Außenräume, was optisch durch die Verwendung von gewelltem Polycarbonat für die Dächer des östlichen Bereichs unterstrichen wird. Die Aufteilung des Hauses in drei Teile (Schlafzimmer, Küche/Esszimmer, Grafikatelier/Waschküche) entspricht den unterschiedlichen Lichtanforderungen der verschiedenen Wohnbereiche. Eine holzverschalte Wand auf der Westseite fügt die Komposition zu einem Ganzen zusammen. Das aus australischem Eukalyptus gebaute Haus ist nicht untypisch für diese Gegend, in der leichte Holzhäuser bevorzugt werden. Mit seiner schlichten Architektur, die Rücksicht auf die umgebende Natur nimmt, fügt sich der Bau in lokale Traditionen ein, auch wenn er diese in technischer Hinsicht um ein Vielfaches übertrifft.

Située dans un ravin à la végétation luxuriante au milieu des collines de Brisbane, le **ROSEBERY HOUSE** dont le budget s'est élevé à US$ 132 000 se compose de trois pavillons réunis par des terrasses. Sous ce climat subtropical, les terrasses n'appartiennent vraiment ni au dedans ni au dehors, impression renforcée par l'emploi de polycarbonate ondulé pour les toits qui protègent la terrasse ouest. La division de la maison en trois parties (chambres, cuisine/salle-à-manger et atelier d'impression/buanderie) devait permettre de profiter au mieux de la lumière naturelle. L'écran en lattis de bois sur la façade ouest unifie la composition. Construite en eucalyptus d'Australie, cette maison n'est pas atypique dans une région qui apprécie les constructions légères en bois. Son style décontracté et sa sensibilité à l'environnement naturel, renvoient aux traditions locales qu'elle fait techniquement progresser de plusieurs pas.

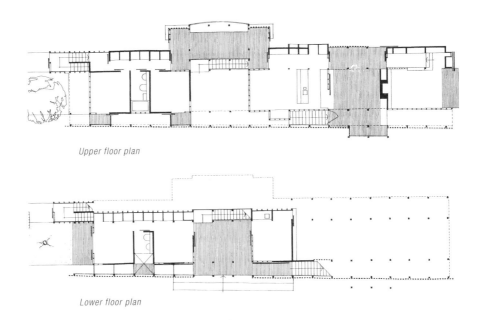

Upper floor plan

Lower floor plan

The penetration of the natural surroundings and light into the interior
of the house is clear in these images.

*Natur und Licht scheinen fließend
in die Innenbereiche des Hauses
überzugehen.*

*La pénétration de l'environnement
naturel et de la lumière est évident
dans l'intérieur de la maison.*

PAUL ANDREU

Paul Andreu
Architect
Orly Sud 103
94396 Orly Aérogare cedex
France

Tel: +33 1 4975 1200
Fax: +33 1 4975 3938
e-mail: patricia.casse@adp.fr

PAUL ANDREU was born on July 10, 1938 in Caudéran in the Gironde region of France. He obtained diplomas from the École Polytechnique (1961), the École Nationale des Ponts et Chaussées (1963) as an engineer, and as an architect from the École des Beaux-Arts in Paris (1968). As the Chief Architect of the Aéroports de Paris he has been responsible not only for the development of Charles de Gaulle (Roissy) Airport, but also for the development of approximately 50 airports around the world, among them Jakarta (1986), Teheran (1996), Manila (1999) or, more recently still, Shanghai-Pudong. Andreu has also worked on other large-scale projects such as the French terminal for the Eurotunnel project (1987) and currently the National Grand Theater of China in Beijing, published here. Other current work includes the Maritime Museum in Osaka, Japan.

PAUL ANDREU wurde am 10. Juli 1938 in Caudéran in der französischen Gironde geboren. Er erwarb seine Ingenieurdiplome an der École Polytechnique (1961) und der École Nationale des Ponts et Chaussées (1963) sowie als Architekt an der École des Beaux-Arts in Paris (1968). Als leitender Architekt der Aéroports de Paris war er nicht nur für die Planung des Flughafens Charles de Gaulle (Roissy) verantwortlich, sondern erarbeitete auch die Planung von ca. 50 weiteren Flughäfen in der ganzen Welt, so z. B. für Jakarta (1986), Teheran (1996), Manila (1999) oder den kürzlich fertig gestellten Flughafen Shanghai-Pudong. Zu Andreus Großprojekten gehören der französische Terminal des Eurotunnel (1987) und das hier vorgestellte Opernhaus in Peking. Gegenwärtig arbeitet er unter anderem am Osaka Maritime Museum in Japan.

PAUL ANDREU est né le 10 juillet 1938 à Caudéran (Gironde, France). Il est diplômé de l'Ecole Polytechnique (1961), ingénieur de l'Ecole Nationale des Ponts et Chaussées (1963) et architecte diplômé de l'Ecole des Beaux-Arts (Paris, 1968). Architecte-en-chef des Aéroports de Paris, il a été responsable non seulement du développement de l'aéroport de Roissy-Charles de Gaulle, mais également de la conception d'une cinquantaine d'aéroports dans le monde : Djakarta (1986), Téhéran (1996), Manila (1999) et plus récemment de celui de Shanghai-Pudong. Andreu a également travaillé sur d'autres grands projets comme le terminal d'Eurotunnel (côté français) et a reçu la commande du futur opéra de Pékin, publié ici. Parmi ses autres chantiers actuels : le Musée maritime d'Osaka au Japon.

ROISSY 2F

Paris, France, 1990-98

Planning: 1990 fixed. Construction: 2/94-12/98. Client: Aéroports de Paris. Floor area: 130 000 m².
Costs: FF 2.2 billion. Capacity: 10 million passengers p. a.

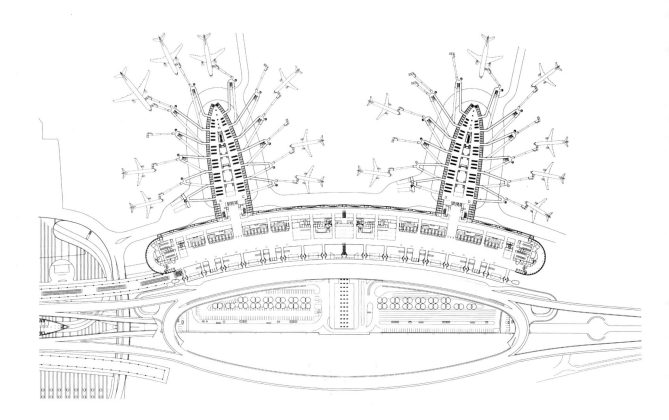

Best known as the architect of the Paris airports, Paul Andreu recently completed a new terminal building. The complex is 400 m long and, has a floor area of 130 000 m² and a parking lot. Divided into four levels, the terminal is equipped to process 10 million passengers per year who are traveling from and to "Schengen" countries (i. e. European countries with which France no longer has customs checks). More open than other Roissy terminals, **ROISSY 2F** features extensive glazing. Its close proximity to a hotel and TGV station and easy access for cars and buses make the complex very convenient to use for travelers. The budget for the building itself was 2.2 billion FF.

Der vor allem als Architekt des Pariser Flughafens Roissy bekannte Paul Andreu hat 1998 dort ein neues Terminalgebäude fertiggestellt. Der 400 m lange Bau hat eine Nutzfläche von 130 000 m² und ist mit einem Parkdeck ausgestattet. In vier Ebenen aufgeteilt, soll die Abfertigungshalle jährlich 10 Millionen Reisende aus und in die Schengen-Länder bewältigen. **ROISSY 2F** ist rundherum verglast und damit offener angelegt als die anderen Terminals. Praktisch für Reisende sind die direkte Anbindung an ein Hotel, einen TGV-Bahnhof und die guten Parkmöglichkeiten für Autos und Busse. Die Baukosten für dieses Projekt lagen bei 2,2 Milliarden FF.

Surtout connu pour ses responsabilités d'architecte-en-chef des Aéroports de Paris, Paul Andreu a récemment achevé ce nouveau terminal de 400 m de long et 130 000 m² de surface sur quatre niveaux, complétés par un parking. Il est prévu pour accueillir 10 millions de passagers par an voyageant dans le cadre de l'espace « Schengen » (pays européens, dont la France, sans contrôles douaniers). Plus ouvert que d'autres terminaux de **ROISSY 2F** fait abondamment appel au verre. La proximité d'un hôtel et de la gare du T. G. V. ainsi qu'un accès facile aux cars et bus en fait un équipement très pratique pour les voyageurs. Le budget du seul bâtiment s'est élevé à 2,2 milliards de F.

Passenger transition to the gates is handled through large, bright pods that radiate out toward the actual gates for the aircraft.

Die Passagiere werden durch zwei weite, helle tragflächenartige Konstruktionen, die strahlenförmig vom Hauptgebäude ausgehen, zu den Gates geleitet.

La passagers accèdent aux points d'embarquement par deux constructions lumineuses en forme d'ailes d'avion qui ertent du bâtiment principal.

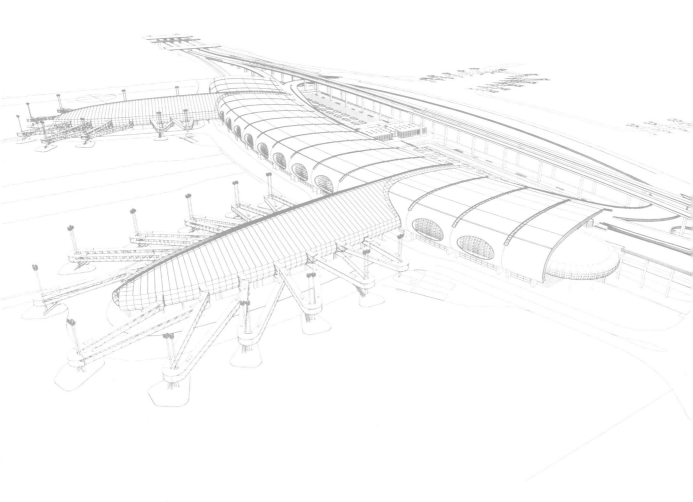

Roissy 2F is directly connected to
a hotel and to a TGV rapid train line
station, designed in collaboration
between Andreu and Jean-Marie
Duthilleul (below right).

Roissy 2F ist unmittelbar mit einem
Hotel und einem TGV-Bahnhof ver-
bunden, die von Paul Andreu und
Jean-Marie Duthilleul gemeinsam
entworfen wurden (unten rechts).

Roissy 2F est directement relié à
un hôtel et à une gare T. G. V., conçue
en collaboration par Andreu et
Jean-Marie Duthilleul (en bas à
droite).

Large glazed surfaces (right) and
substantial, high, free-span spaces
within the terminal (above) give it
an unusual degree of openness, unlike many transport facilities built
in preceding decades.

Die nahezu komplett verglasten
Außenflächen (rechts) und die
hohen, freitragenden Innenräume
(oben) verleihen dem Gebäude ein
ungewöhnliches Maß an Offenheit.

De vastes surfaces vitrées (à droite)
et d'énormes espaces sans piliers
(ci-dessus) confèrent à ce terminal
un degré d'ouverture rare, qui le
différencie de nombreux aéroports
des décennies précédentes.

NATIONAL GRAND
THEATER OF CHINA

Beijing, China, 1999-2002

Competition: 7/99 (1st prize). Completion: 2002 (scheduled).
Client: The Grand National Theater Committee. Floor area: 140 000 m².

Awarded in August 1999 to Paul Andreu, the winner (in the final phase, over Carlos Ott, author of the Paris Bastille Opera and the English architect Terry Farrell) of an international design competition, the **PEKING OPERA**, a 140 000-m² structure will be erected just beside the Great Hall of the People, near Tienanmen Square. A 212 m-long ellipsoidal titanium shell will house the opera, a concert hall, and two theaters, ranging in capacity from 520 to 2 500 seats. In order to leave the external shell intact, the architect has chosen to provide public access through a 60 m-long tunnel that will pass beneath a basin surrounding the building. Extensive urban renewal efforts are making way for a large park around the opera, scheduled for rapid construction with a planned opening in 2002, or somewhat later because of administrative delays.

Nach einem internationalen Wettbewerb wurde im August 1999 Paul Andreu als Gewinner (vor den anderen Finalisten Carlos Ott, Architekt der Pariser Bastille Oper, und dem englischen Architekten Terry Farrell) mit der Planung dieses 140 000 m² großen **PEKINGER OPERNHAUSES** beauftragt, das unmittelbar hinter der Großen Halle des Volkes nahe dem Tiananmen-Platz errichtet werden soll. Das 212 m lange elliptische Titangehäuse wird vier Säle mit jeweils 520 bis 2 500 Sitzen beherbergen. Um die äußere, muschelförmige Gestalt nicht zu beeinträchtigen, hat der Architekt den Zugangsweg in einen 60 m langen Tunnel verlegt, der unter einem das Gebäude umgebenden Wasserbecken verlaufen wird. Umfangreiche Stadterneuerungsarbeiten machen den Weg frei für einen ausgedehnten Park um das Opernhaus, das zügig fertiggestellt und im Jahr 2002 oder etwas später (aus verwaltungstechnischen Gründen) eröffnet werden soll.

C'est en août 1999 que Paul Andreu a remporté (en phase finale devant Carlos Ott, auteur de l'Opéra de Paris Bastille, et le Britannique Terry Farrell) le concours international pour l'**OPÉRA DE PÉKIN** de 140 000 m² qui sera édifié juste derrière le Palais du Peuple, près de la place Tienanmen. Une coque ellipsoïdale en titane de 212 m de long abritera quatre salles de concert de 520 à 2 500 places. Pour préserver son aspect extérieur, Andreu a imaginé un accès par un tunnel de 60 m de long passant sous le bassin qui entourera l'ensemble du bâtiment. Des travaux importants sont en cours pour créer un vaste parc autour de cet opéra qui devrait ouvrir, d'après un calendrier serré, en 2002, ou, un peu plus tard en cas de délais dus à l'administration.

These computer perspectives give some idea of the finished volumes, although they carefully avoid showing any of the neighboring structures.

Die Computergrafiken geben eine Vorstellung von der Wirkung des fertigen Bauwerks, auch wenn die benachbarten Gebäude ausgeblendet sind.

Ces perspectives par ordinateur donnent une idée globale des volumes achevés, même si elles évitent de montrer les constructions voisines.

An aerial computer perspective (above) shows the basin around the structure and the back of the Great Hall of the People (in the picture left).

Die Vogelperspektive (oben) zeigt das den Bau umgebende Wasserbecken und (links im Bild) die Rückseite der Großen Halle des Volkes.

Perspective par ordinateur (ci-dessus) montrant le bassin au milieu duquel se dresse la construction et l'arrière du Palais du Peuple (du côté gauche de l'image).

The foyer areas that greet the visitors who come up from the underground entrance are spectacular in their height and volume. It is hoped that a number of large works of art will be created for the space.

Die Eingangshalle, die die vom unterirdischen Zugang heraufkommenden Besucher empfängt, beeindruckt in ihren Ausmaßen. Für diesen Bereich sollen etliche großformatige Kunstwerke geschaffen werden.

Le foyer auquel le visiteur accède par une entrée souterraine a des proportions impressionnantes. On espère qu'un certain nombre d'œuvres d'art de grand format seront créées pour ce volume.

ANGÉLIL/GRAHAM/
PFENNINGER/SCHOLL

Angélil/Graham/Pfenninger/Scholl Architecture
Zypressenstrasse 71
8004 Zurich
Switzerland

Tel: +41 1 298 2020
Fax: +41 1 298 2021
e-mail: architektur@agps.ch

MARC ANGÉLIL studied at the Eidgenössische Technische Hochschule (ETH) in Zurich (1973-79) before obtaining a doctorate from the same institution in 1987. He has been a professor at Harvard (1982-87), University of Southern California (1987-94), and at the ETH since 1994. **SARAH GRAHAM** received her B.A. degree from Stanford University, Palo Alto, California (1970-74), and her M.A. degree from Harvard (1979-82). She was a Professor at the University of Southern California from 1987 to 1996. **RETO PFENNINGER** studied at the Technikum Winterthur (1984-87), at the Akademie der Bildenden Künste in Munich (1992-94) and at the ETH (1994-98). **MANUEL SCHOLL** studied at the ETH Zurich (1982-88) and taught architecture and design at the ETH (1994-97). Angélil/Graham was founded in 1982 in Boston. AGPS was established in 1990 in Zurich. The firm's projects include the Midfield Airport Terminal (Zurich-Kloten, 2000-02), the renovation and new construction of apartments, offices and shops at Waschanstalt Zurich-Wollishofen (1999-2000), and the Herzo Base with Adidas "World of Sports" at Herzogenaurach near Nuremberg (Germany) masterplan 2000.

MARC ANGÉLIL studierte von 1973 bis 1979 an der Eidgenössischen Technischen Hochschule (ETH) in Zürich, bevor er dort 1987 den Doktorgrad erwarb. Von 1982 bis 1987 war er Professor in Harvard, von 1987 bis 1994 an der University of South California (USC), und seit 1994 lehrt er als Professor an der ETH. **SARAH GRAHAM** schloß ihr Studium in Stanford 1974 mit dem B. A. und in Harvard 1982 mit dem M. A. ab. Von 1987 bis 1996 lehrte sie an der USC. **RETO PFENNINGER** studierte am Technikum Winterthur (1984-87), an der Akademie der Bildenden Künste in München (1992-94) und an der ETH (1994-98). **MANUEL SCHOLL** studierte an der ETH in Zürich (1982-88) und lehrte Architektur und Design an der ETH (1994-97). Das Büro Angélil/Graham wurde 1982 in Boston gegründet, und 1990 wurde AGPS in Zürich eröffnet. Zu den von AGPS durchgeführten Projekten gehören der Midfield Airport Terminal in Zürich-Kloten (2000-02), Renovierung und Umbau von Wohnungen, Büros und Geschäften der Waschanstalt Zürich-Wollishofen (1999-2000) und der Masterplan 2000 für Adidas' »World of Sports« in Herzogenaurach.

MARC ANGÉLIL a enseigné à l'ETH de Zurich (1973-79), dont il sera docteur en 1987. Il enseigne à Harvard (1982-87) et à l'ETH depuis 1994. **SARAH GRA-HAM** est diplômée d'architecture de la Stanford University (1970-74) et titulaire d'un master de Harvard (1979-82). Elle a enseigné à l'University of Southern California de 1987 à 1996. **RETO PFENNINGER** a étudié au Technikum Winterthur (1984-87), à l'Akademie der Bildenden Künste de Munich (1992-94) et à l'ETH (1994-98). **MANUEL SCHOLL** a étudié à l'ETH à Zurich (1982-88), et a enseigné à l'ETH (1994-97). L'agence Angélil/Graham a été fondé à Boston en 1982, et AGPS en 1990 à Zurich. Parmi les projets de l'agence : le terminal de l'aéroport de Midfield (Zurich-Kloten, 2000-02), la rénovation et la construction d'appartements, de bureaux et de magasins Waschanstalt (Zurich-Wollishofen, 1999-2000) et le plan de masse du « World of Sports » d'Adidas (2000) a Herzogenaurach, près de Nuremberg (Allemagne).

TRÜB HOUSE

HT 96.4, Horgen, Switzerland, 1996-98

Planning: 11/96-8/97. Construction: 9/97-4/98. Client: Patrik and Karin Trüb.
Floor area: 400 m². Costs: 450 SFr/m³ (total: SF 1 800 000)

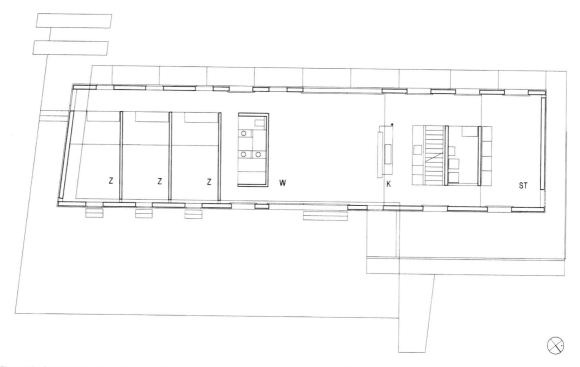

The result of an unusual collaboration of architects based in Los Angeles and in Zurich, the **TRÜB HOUSE** is in fact a double residence, with a visible part constructed of 30 larch-clad prefabricated wood panels containing recycled paper insulation that rests on a concrete multifunctional space. Some of the panels are mounted on sliding tracks and serve as "movable sun protection and security gates for the vertical windows." Set half into the sloping site, the concrete volume is intended to be entirely flexible in its use, echoing the high flexibility of the above-ground wooden facade. The architects have also designed the sober interior, coloring the entry space in black and circulation zones in mustard yellow, leaving the rest "relatively colorless." Spartan and minimalist, the house has numerous spatial surprises, such as a mezzanine supported by a column on one side and suspended on the other by a tension rod from the roof.

HAUS TRÜB ist das Resultat einer ungewöhnlichen Zusammenarbeit von Architekten, die in Los Angeles und in Zürich ansässig sind. Es handelt sich um ein Doppelhaus: Auf einem in die Erde eingebetteten Mehrzweckraum aus Beton ruht der sichtbare Bauteil aus 30 vorgefertigten Platten, die mit Lärchenholz ummantelt sind und eine Isolierung aus Recyclingpapier haben. Einige dieser Platten sind auf Gleitschienen montiert und dienen als »beweglicher Sonnenschutz oder Sicherheitstore für die senkrecht gestellten Fenster«. Der halb in den Hang gesetzte Baukörper ist für eine vollkommen flexible Nutzung ausgelegt und greift damit die hohe Flexibilität der oberhalb liegenden Holzfassade auf. Die Architekten entwarfen auch die nüchterne Innenausstattung, wobei sie den Eingangsbereich schwarz, die Verbindungsräume senfgelb und den Rest nahezu farblos gestalteten. Obwohl eher spartanisch und minimalistisch in der Formgebung, birgt das Haus zahlreiche Überraschungen, wie etwa ein Zwischengeschoss, das auf einer Seite von einer Säule getragen wird und auf der anderen Seite an einem vom Dach herabhängenden Spannbolzen aufgehängt ist.

Née d'une collaboration originale entre des architectes basés à Los Angeles et à Zurich, la **MAISON TRÜB** est en fait une double résidence, dont la partie visible en panneaux de bois préfabriqués plaqués de mélèze et remplis de papier recyclé isolant, repose sur une salle multifonctional en béton. Certains panneaux sont montés sur rails coulissants et servent de «pare-soleil mobiles ou de volets de sécurité masquant des fenêtres verticales». A moitié inscrit dans la pente du terrain, le volume en béton se veut d'utilisation totalement souple, en écho avec la flexibilité de la façade de bois qui le surmonte. Les architectes ont également conçu les sobres aménagements intérieurs, colorant l'espace d'entrée en noir, les circulations en jaune moutarde, et laissant le reste pratiquement incolore. Minimaliste, la maison réserve néanmoins de nombreuses surprises comme une mezzanine soutenue d'un côté par une colonne et suspendue de l'autre à une tige en tension accrochée à la charpente.

Above right: The wood panel cladding is laid in a vertical pattern, corresponding to the full-height openings on the rear facade, yet it is the horizontal design that stands out.

Oben rechts: Die vertikale Verkleidung aus Lärchenholzplatten korrespondiert mit den teilweise über die gesamte Gebäudehöhe reichenden Fensteröffnungen. Insgesamt ist die Gestaltung des Hauses jedoch horizontal bestimmt.

En haut à droite : Les panneaux de bois sont posés verticalement, parallèlement aux ouvertures toute hauteur de la façade arrière. Pourtant, ce sont les lignes horizontales qui dominent.

WIEL ARETS

ir Wiel Arets Architect & Associates bv
d'Artagnanlaan 29
6213 CH Maastricht
Netherlands

Tel: +31 43 351 2200
Fax: +31 43 321 2192
e-mail: arets@wxs.nl

Born in Heerlen, Netherlands, in 1955, **WIEL ARETS** graduated from the Technical University in Eindhoven in 1983. He established Wiel Arets Architect & Associates in Heerlen in 1984. He traveled extensively in Russia, Japan, America, and Europe (1984-85), and taught at the Academy of Architecture, Amsterdam and Rotterdam (1986). His interest in architectural theory led him to create the publishing house Wiederhall in 1986. Arets was a Diploma Unit Master at the Architectural Association (London, 1988-92), and a Visiting Professor at Columbia University (New York, 1991-92). He is Dean of the Berlage Institute, Postgraduate Laboratory of Architecture in Amsterdam (1995-2001), where he was the successor to Herman Hertzberger. His built work includes a House & Pharmacy (Schoonbroodt, Brunssum, 1985-86), Barbershop and House (Mayntz, Heerlen, 1986-87), Fashionshop Beltgens (Maastricht, 1987-88), Academy of Art and Architecture (Maastricht, 1989-93), 67 apartments (Tilburg, 1992-94), the Headquarters of the AZL Pensionfund (Heerlen, 1990-95), a Police Station (Vaals, 1993-94), 104 apartments at Jacobsplaats (Rotterdam, 1995-97), and the Lensvelt Factory and Offices (Breda, 1995-2000), all in the Netherlands.

WIEL ARETS, 1955 im niederländischen Heerlen geboren, schloß 1983 sein Studium an der Technischen Universität in Eindhoven ab und gründete im Jahr darauf Wiel Arets Architect & Associates in Heerlen. Von 1984 bis 1985 unternahm er ausgedehnte Reisen durch Russland, Japan, Amerika und Europa und 1986 lehrte er an den Akademien für Architektur in Amsterdam und Rotterdam. Sein Interesse an Architekturtheorie veranlaßte ihn 1986 zur Gründung des Verlagshauses Wiederhall. Von 1988 bis 1992 war er Diploma Unit Master an der Architectural Association (AA) in London und von 1991 bis 1992 Gastprofessor an der Columbia University in New York. Als Nachfolger von Hermann Hertzberger wurde Arets 1995 bis 2001 Dekan am Postgraduate Laboratory of Architecture des Institut Berlage in Amsterdam. Zu seinen ausgeführten Projekten gehören das Wohnhaus mit Apotheke Schoonbroodt in Brunssum (1985-86), Haus und Friseursalon Mayntz in Heerlen (1986-87), das Modegeschäft Beltgens in Maastricht (1987-88), 67 Wohnungen in Tilburg (1992-94), die Zentrale der Rentenversicherungsanstalt AZL in Heerlen (1990-95), eine Polizeiwache in Vaals (1993-94), 104 Wohnungen am Jacobsplaats in Rotterdam (1995-97) sowie das hier vorgestellte Lensvelt Fabrik- und Bürogebäude in Breda (1995-2000), alle in den Niederlanden.

Né en 1955 à Heerlen, Pays-Bas, **WIEL ARETS** est diplômé de l'Université technique de Eindhoven en 1983, il fonde Wiels Arets Architect & Associates à Heerlen en 1984. Il voyage en Russie, au Japon, en Amérique et en Europe (1984-85) et enseigne aux Académies d'architecture d'Amsterdam et de Rotterdam (1986). L'intérêt qu'il porte à la théorie architecturale le conduit à créer une maison d'édition, Wiederhall, en 1986. Il est Diploma Unit Master de l'Architectural Association (Londres, 1988-92), et professeur invité à Columbia University (New York, 1991-92). Doyen du Laboratoire Supérieur d'architecture de l'Institut Berlage (Amsterdam, 1995-2001), il succède à ce poste à Herman Hertzberger. Parmi ses réalisations, toutes aux Pays-Bas : une maison et une pharmacie (Schoonbroodt, Brunssum, 1985-86), une maison et un salon de coiffure (Mayntz, Heerlen, 1986-87), la boutique de mode Beltgens (1987-88) et l'Académie d'art et d'architecture (1989-93) à Maastricht, un immeuble de 67 appartements (Tilburg, 1992-94), le siège social du fond de pensions AZL (Heerlen, 1990-95), un poste de police (Vaals, 1993-94), un immeuble de 104 appartements, Jacobsplaats (Rotterdam, 1995-97), et l'usine et les bureaux de la société Lensvelt (Breda, 1995-2000).

LENSVELT FACTORY AND OFFICES

Breda, Netherlands, 1995-2000

Planning: 1995. Construction: 1999-2000.
Client: Lensvelt B.V. Floor area: 6 200 m². Costs: DM 9 200 000.

Consisting of a warehouse, office, showroom and assembly area, **LENSVELT FACTORY AND OFFICES** built for a furniture manufacturer is set in an industrial park. With a floor area of about 6 200 m², and a height of 8 m, the double-glazed structure is intended to glow from within after nightfall. The vertical glass panels are attached to the steel frame only at mid-height, giving to the building an impression of simplicity and transparency. A cantilevered opaque metal box, set 2 m above ground on the east side of the building, houses a conference room. A similar box on the west side, set much closer to the ground, marks the main entrance and employees' lounge. Between these two opaque volumes, an interior courtyard offers access to two symmetrical showrooms. Corrugated metal roofing material forms the interior ceiling of the warehouse, while a simple concrete floor accentuates the intelligent, minimalist design.

Die für den Möbelhersteller Lensvelt auf einem Industriegelände erbaute **LENSVELT FACTORY AND OFFICES** umfaßt bei einer Nutzfläche von circa 6 200 m² eine Lagerhalle, Büros, Ausstellungsräume und einen Montagebereich. Die aus vertikalen Glastafeln bestehende Außenverkleidung des Hauptbaus, der als Stahlskelettkonstruktion konzipiert ist, läßt das Gebäude nach Anbruch der Dunkelheit von innen leuchten und vermittelt den Eindruck von Schlichtheit und Transparenz. Aus diesem langgestreckten Bauteil ragt auf der Ostseite ein lichtundurchlässiger, 2,5 m über dem Boden schwebender Metallkasten hervor, der einen Konferenzraum beherbergt. Auf der Westseite markiert ein ähnlicher, aber näher am Boden angebrachter Kasten den Haupteingang und Aufenthaltsraum für die Angestellten. Zwischen diesen beiden undurchsichtigen Baukörpern liegt ein Innenhof, über den man in zwei symmetrisch angelegte Ausstellungsräume gelangt. Eine Bedachung aus Wellblech bildet die Decke im Inneren der Lagerhalle, während ein einfacher Betonboden das intelligent konzipierte, minimalistische Innenraum-Design akzentuiert.

L'USINE DE LENSVELT réalisé pour un fabricant de mobilier dans un parc industriel se compose d'un entrepôt, de bureaux, d'une salle d'exposition et d'une aire de montage. La nuit, la structure à double-vitrage de 6 200 m² de surface et 8 m de haut semble embrasée de l'intérieur. Les panneaux de verre verticaux fixés à l'ossature d'acier à mi hauteur seulement donnent au bâtiment un caractère de simplicité et de transparence. Sur la façade est, une boîte métallique, formant un porte-à-faux de 2 m au-dessus du sol, abrite une salle de conférence. Une boîte similaire à l'ouest, mais beaucoup plus proche du sol, marque l'entrée principale et la salle de relaxation des employés. Un matériau de couverture en métal ondulé recouvre le plafond, tandis qu'un simple sol de béton accentue l'intelligent style minimaliste de l'ensemble.

The Lensvelt facility brings together at least two forms of twentieth century architectural tradition – Bauhaus/De Stijl geometric simplicity and industrial/factory design.

Der Gebäudekomplex der Firma Lensvelt kombiniert die geometrische Schlichtheit von Bauhaus und De Stijl, zwei Architekturtraditionen des 20. Jahrhunderts, mit Formen des Industrie- und Fabrikbaus.

L'usine de Lensvelt réunit au moins deux des traditions de l'architecture du XXe siècle : la simplicité géométrique et l'approche industrielle du Bauhaus et du groupe De Stijl.

Wiel Arets' minimalist sensibility is
apparent in these large, open spaces,
where light is an integral element
of the composition.

Wiel Arets' sensibler Minimalismus
zeigt sich in diesen großen, offenen
Räumen, in denen das Licht zu einem
integralen Gestaltungselement wird.

La sensibilité minimaliste de Wiel
Arets se manifeste dans ces vastes
espaces ouverts. La lumière est un
élément important de la composition.

At night the Lensvelt facility becomes a source of light, reversing the function of the large openings that bring in natural light during the day. From certain angles the structure is not readily apparent, giving the impression that the building has no visible means of support.

Nachts wird die Lensvelt Factory zur Lichtquelle, wobei sich die Funktion der großflächigen Verglasungen, die tagsüber natürliches Licht einlassen, in ihr Gegenteil verkehrt. Von bestimmten Standpunkten aus gesehen scheint das Gebäude nahezu frei zu schweben.

La nuit, les bâtiments de Lensvelt se transforment en une source lumineuse, inversant ainsi de la fonction des grandes baies qui s'ouvrent à la lumière naturelle pendant le jour. Sous certains angles, la structure est presque invisible, donnant l'impression d'absence de structures portantes.

ASYMPTOTE

Asymptote Architecture
561 Broadway, 5A
New York, NY 10012
United States

Tel: +1 212 343 7333
Fax: +1 212 343 7099
e-mail: info@asymptote.net
Web: www.asymptote-architecture.com

LISE ANN COUTURE (right) was born in Montreal in 1959. She received her B.Arch. degree from Carleton University, Ottawa, Canada, and her M.Arch. degree from Yale. She has been a Design Critic in the Master of Architecture program at Parsons School of Design, New York. **HANI RASHID** (left) received his M.Arch. degree from the Cranbrook Academy of Art, Bloomfield Hills, Michigan. They created Asymptote in 1989. Projects include the 1988 prize-winning commission for the Los Angeles West Coast Gateway, a commissioned housing project for Brig, Switzerland (1991), and their participation in the 1993 competition for an Art Center in Tours, France. They have also built a theater festival structure in Århus, Denmark in 1997. Presently Asymptote is designing a Edutainment Center in Kyoto, Japan and the Guggenheim Virtual Museum, published here in an initial version.

LISE ANN COUTURE (rechts), 1959 in Montreal geboren, erwarb ihren Bachelor of Architecture an der Carleton University in Kanada und ihren Master of Architecture an der Yale University. Anschließend war sie im Rahmen des Master of Architecture-Programms als Designkritikerin an der Parsons School of Design in New York tätig. **HANI RASHID** (links) machte seinen Master of Architecture an der Cranbrook Academy of Art, Bloomfield Hills, Michigan. Gemeinsam riefen sie 1987 Asymptote ins Leben. Zu ihren Projekten gehören der preisgekrönte Entwurf für den Los Angeles West Coast Gateway (1988), die Ausarbeitung eines Wohnhausprojekts für Brig in der Schweiz (1991) und ihr Wettbewerbsbeitrag für ein Kunstzentrum im französischen Tours (1993). Außerdem haben sie 1997 einen Bau für das Theaterfestival in Århus, Dänemark ausgeführt. Derzeit arbeiten Couture und Rashid an der Planung eines Technikmuseums in Kioto und am Guggenheim Virtual Museum, das hier in einer ersten Version vorgestellt wird.

LISE ANN COUTURE (à droite), née à Montréal en 1959, est Bachelor of Architecture de la Carleton University, Canada, et Master of Architecture de Yale. Elle a été « Design Critic » du programme de maîtrise en architecture de la Parsons School of Design, New York. **HANI RASHID** (à gauche) est Master of Architecture de la Cranbrook Academy of Art, Bloomfield Hills, Michigan. Ils créent Asymptote en 1989. Parmi leurs travaux : le projet primé de la West Coast Gateway (Los Angeles, 1988), un projet de logements (Brig, Suisse, 1991), leur participation au concours de 1993 pour un Centre d'art à Tours, France (1993), une structure pour un festival de théâtre (Århus, Danemark, 1997). Actuellement, Asymptote travaille à un Musée des Technologies pour Kyoto et sur le projet du Guggenheim Virtual Museum, publié ici dans sa version initiale.

VIRTUAL TRADING FLOOR

New York Stock Exchange, New York, NY, USA, 1998-99

Asymptote created two related projects for the New York Stock Exchange (NYSE). The first, the **3DTF** (Three Dimensional Trading Floor), is a "data-scape" that brings together information flow, data and correlation models into a single seamless three-dimensional architectural model. The 3DTF is intended to provide real-time information on the movements of the stock markets, and is an experiment in the gradual transfer of trading to a completely virtual environment. Before moving to that phase, however, Asymptote has also created the Advanced Trading Floor Operations Center off the main floor of the NYSE, a similarly inspired design that includes 60 high-resolution flat screen LCD monitors and an LED message board.

Asymptote schuf zwei miteinander verbundene Entwürfe für die New Yorker Börse (NYSE). Bei dem **3DTF** (Three Dimensional Trading Floor) genannten Projekt handelt es sich um eine »Daten-Landschaft«, die Informationsflüsse, Daten und Korrelationsmodelle zu einer zusammenhängenden, dreidimensionalen architektonischen Raumgestaltung zusammenführt. 3DTF ist für die Erfassung von Echtzeit-Informationen über alle Vorgänge auf dem Aktienmarkt konzipiert und stellt einen weiteren, experimentellen Schritt in der allmählichen Verlagerung des Börsenhandels auf ein vollständig virtuelles Environment dar. Zuvor hat Asymptote in einem ähnlich inspirierten Entwurf auch das »Advanced Trading Floor Operations Center« neben dem Hauptbörsenparkett der NYSE gestaltet, das mit 60 hochauflösenden Flachbildschirmen und einer LED-Anzeigentafel ausgestattet ist.

Asymptote est à l'origine de deux projets conjoints pour le New York Stock Exchange (NYSE). Le premier, appelé **3DTF** (Three Dimensional Trading Floor), est un « datascape » qui réunit des flux d'information, des modèles de données et de corrélations en un modèle architectural unique et tridimensionnel. Le 3DTF fournit en temps réel des informations sur les mouvements des marchés boursiers. C'est une expérimentation de transfert graduel du trading vers un environnement totalement virtuel. Avant d'en arriver là, Asymptote a par ailleurs conçu le Advanced Trading Floor Operations Center un peu à l'écart du plateau principal du NYSE, projet d'inspiration similaire qui comprend 60 écrans plats haute-résolution et un panneau d'affichage LED.

A "virtual" trading area that gives real-time data on the ebb and flow of stock prices, is placed in juxtaposition with an actual space (left) designed by Asymptote at the edge of the NYSE trading floor.

Das virtuelle Börsenparkett übermittelt Echtzeit-Informationen über den aktuellen Stand der Aktienkurse und ist einem realen Raum (links) gegenübergestellt, den Asymptote für die New Yorker Börse (NYSE) gestaltet hat.

L'aire de marchés virtuelle qui fournit des informations en temps réel sur les variations et les flux des actions, est juxtaposée à une salle réelle (à gauche) conçue par Asymptote à côté de la salle des marchés du New York Stock Exchange.

GUGGENHEIM
VIRTUAL MUSEUM

New York, NY, USA, 1999-2002

As part of a larger project intended to commission Internet-based works of art, the Guggenheim Museum in New York has asked Asymptote to create the "first important virtual building of the 21st Century," a fusion of "information space, art, commerce and architecture." This ambitious plan, calling for "navigable three-dimensional spatial entities accessible on the Internet as well as a real-time interactive component installed at the various Guggenheim locations," imagines a virtual architecture that would change according to visitor preferences or uses. In this sense, the **GUGGENHEIM VIRTUAL MUSEUM** will be in constant flux, corresponding, according to the architects, to the real requirements of truly contemporary art and art appreciation.

Als Teil eines größeren Projekts zur Vermittlung von Kunstwerken im Internet hat das Guggenheim Museum Asymptote mit der Gestaltung des »ersten bedeutenden virtuellen Gebäudes des 21. Jahrhunderts« beauftragt. Dieser ehrgeizige Plan hat die Verbindung von »Information, Kunst, Handel und Architektur« zum Ziel und erfordert »ein dreidimensionales, interaktives Environment für das Internet sowie eine interaktive Echtzeit-Komponente, die in den verschiedenen Guggenheim Einrichtungen installiert werden soll.« Die zugrunde liegende Idee ist eine virtuelle Architektur, die sich mit den Vorlieben oder Bedürfnissen der Benutzer verändert. In diesem Sinne wird sich das **GUGGENHEIM VIRTUAL MUSEUM** ständig im Fluß befinden und damit, nach Aussage der Architekten, den realen Anforderungen einer wirklich aktuellen Kunst und Kunstbetrachtung entsprechen.

Elément d'un important projet de commandes d'œuvres d'art par Internet, le Guggenheim Museum de New York a demandé à Asymptote de créer le premier grand « batiment virtuel » du XXIᵉ siècle, fusion « d'espaces d'information, de l'art, du commerce et de l'architecture. » Ce plan ambitieux, qui fait appel à des « entités spatiales accessibles par Internet ainsi qu'à des échanges interactifs en temps réel entre les diverses implantations du Guggenheim, » imagine une architecture virtuelle modifiable selon les préférences ou les besoins du visiteur. En ce sens, le **GUGGENHEIM VIRTUAL MUSEUM** apparaîtra comme un flux constant de données, ce qui correspond, pour les architectes, aux attentes concrètes de l'art réellement contemporain et à son appréciation.

Asymptote displayed their designs for the Guggenheim Virtual Museum at TZ Art and Henry Urbach Galleries.

Asymptotes Entwürfe für das Guggenheim Museum wurden in der TZ Art und Henry Urbach Galerie ausgestellt.

Asymptote a exposé ses projets pour le Guggenheim Virtual Museum dans la TZ Art et Henry Urbach galerie.

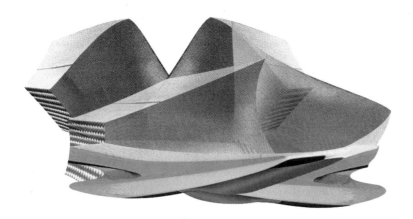

Unlike any existing traditional building, the Guggenheim Virtual Museum
could change its form to correspond
to visitor patterns, for example.

Im Gegensatz zu gebauten Museen
kann das Guggenheim Virtual Museum
jederzeit seine Form verändern, um
sich den Bedürfnissen der Besucher
anzupassen.

A la différence des constructions
traditionnelles, le Guggenheim virtuel
peut changer de forme en fonction
du profil des visiteurs.

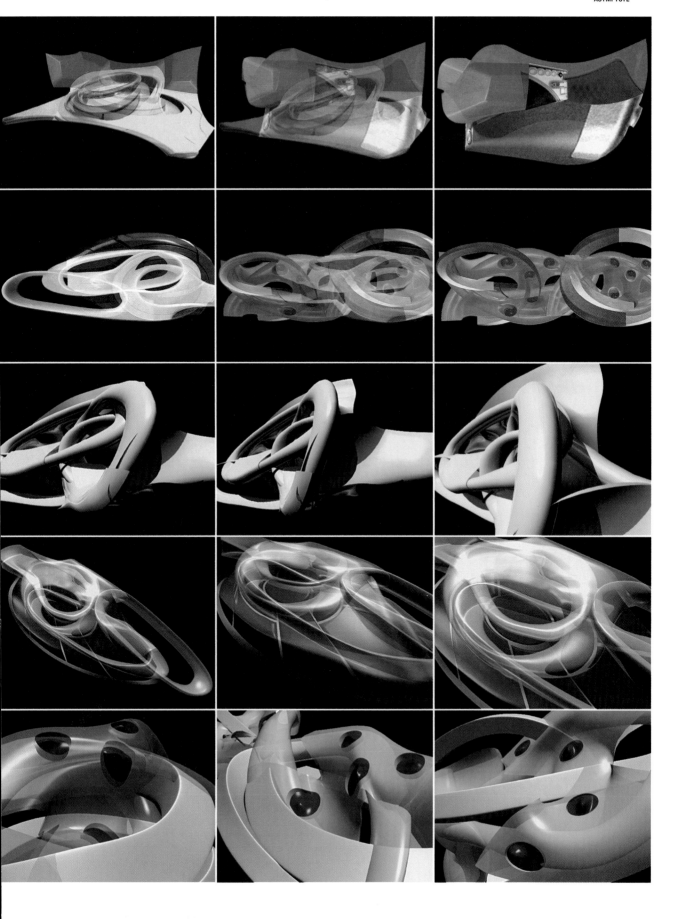

SHIGERU BAN

Shigeru Ban Architects
5-2-4 Matubara Ban Bldg.
Setagaya, Tokyo 156-0043
Japan

Tel: +81 3 3324 6760
Fax: +81 3 3324 6789
Web: www.dnp.co.jp/millennium/SB/VAN.html

Born in 1957 in Tokyo, **SHIGERU BAN** studied at the Southern California Institute of Architecture from 1977 to 1980. He also attended the Cooper Union School of Architecture, New York, where he studied under John Hejduk (1980-82, 83-84). He worked in the office of Arata Isozaki (1982-83) before founding his own firm in Tokyo in 1985. His work includes numerous exhibition designs (Alvar Aalto exhibition at the Axis Gallery, Tokyo, 1986). His buildings include the Curtain Wall House (Tokyo, 1995), the Wall-less House (Nagano, 1997), the Paper House (Lake Yamanaka, 1995), and the Paper Church (Takatori, Hyogo, 1995), all in Japan. He has also designed ephemeral structures such as his Paper Refugee Shelter made with plastic sheets and paper tubes for the United Nations High Commissioner for Refugees (UNHCR). He also to designed the Japan Pavilion for Expo 2000, Hanover, Germany, published here.

SHIGERU BAN, geboren 1957 in Tokio, studierte von 1977 bis 1980 am Southern California Institute of Architecture und von 1980 bis 1982, 1983 bis 1984 bei John Hejduk an der Cooper Union School of Architecture in New York. 1982-83 arbeitete er im Büro von Arata Isozaki, bevor er 1985 sein eigenes Büro in Tokio gründete. Er gestaltete zahlreiche Ausstellungen, so 1986 die Alvar-Aalto-Ausstellung in der Axis Gallery in Tokio. Zu seinen Bauten gehören das Curtain Wall House in Tokio (1995) und das Wall-less House (Nagano, 1997), das Paper House am Yamanaka-See (1994-95) und die Paper Church in Takatori, Hyogo (1995), alle in Japan. Shigeru Ban hat auch Behelfsbauten aus Plastikfolie und Pappröhren für den Hohen Flüchtlingskommissar der Vereinten Nationen (UNHCR) entworfen und baute den hier vorgestellten Japanischen Pavillon für die Expo 2000 in Hannover.

Né en 1957 à Tokyo, **SHIGERU BAN** étudie au Southern California Institute of Architecture de 1977 à 1980 puis à la Cooper Union School of Architecture où il suit l'enseignement de John Hejduk (1980-82, 83-84). Il travaille pour Arata Isozaki (1982-83) avant de fonder son agence à Tokyo en 1985. Il a conçu de nombreuses expositions (dont celle d'Alvar Aalto, Axis Gallery, Tokyo, 1986). Parmi ses réalisations architecturales : la Maison mur-rideau (Tokyo, 1995), la Maison sans murs (Nagano, 1997), la Maison de papier (Lac Yamanaka, 1995) et l'Église de papier (Takatori, Hyogo, 1995). Il conçoit également des structures éphémères comme un abri en papier, feuilles de plastique et tubes de papier pour le Haut Commissariat aux Réfugiés (HCRNU). Il a construit le Pavillon Japonais à Expo 2000, Hanovre, publié ici.

JAPAN PAVILION

Expo 2000, Hanover, Germany, 2000

Construction: 9/99-5/2000. Client: Japan External Trade Organization.
Floor area: 4 252 m².

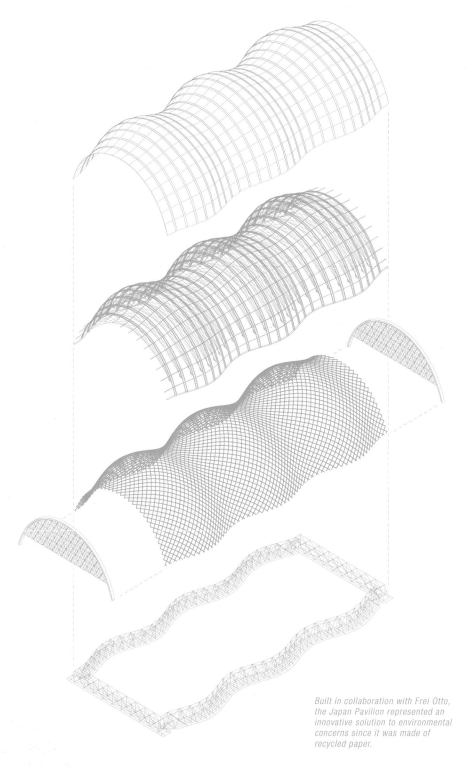

Der von Shigeru Ban in Zusammenarbeit mit Frei Otto gestaltete Japanische Pavillon stellte eine innovative Lösung für ökologische Probleme dar, da er größtenteils aus recyceltem Papier bestand.

Built in collaboration with Frei Otto, the Japan Pavilion represented an innovative solution to environmental concerns since it was made of recycled paper.

Construit en collaboration avec Frei Otto, le pavillon japonais a été en grande partie réalisé en papier. C'est une solution novatrice aux préoccupations environnementales.

Aware of the environmental agenda of Expo 2000, Shigeru Ban designed a **"PAPER PAVILION"** using recycled paper tubes as the primary structural material, and sand and stones for the foundations, which are to be resold within Germany for re-use after the exhibition closes. He also used rented scaffolding to minimize construction costs further. Although Ban has used the paper tube technique in Japan with approval of Japanese authorities, he has never before attempted such a large-scale structure, and therefore called on the expertise and assistance of the noted light-architecture specialist Frei Otto.

Unter Bezugnahme auf die umweltpolitische Agenda der Expo 2000 entwarf Shigeru Ban als Ausstellungsgebäude für sein Heimatland Japan einen **»PAPIER PAVILLON«**. Als Baumaterial dienten recycelte Pappröhren sowie Sand und Natursteine für das Fundament, die nach Ausstellungsende innerhalb Deutschlands weiterverkauft und wiederverwendet werden sollten. Um die Baukosten noch weiter zu senken, benutzte Ban ein gemietetes Gerüst. Obgleich der Architekt diese Pappröhren-Bauweise in Japan mit Bewilligung der Behörden bereits erfolgreich eingesetzt hatte, war es das erste Mal, dass er sie bei einem so großen Bauwerk anwendete, weshalb er mit Frei Otto, dem Spezialisten für leichte Schalentragwerke, zusammengearbeitet hatte.

Conscient des préoccupations environnementales d'Expo 2000, Shigeru Ban a proposé un **« PAVILLON DE PAPIER »** présentant une structure en tubes et papier recyclé, et des fondations en sable et en pierre, matériaux qui seront revendus en Allemagne pour être réutilisés une fois l'exposition achevée. Il s'est également servi d'échafaudages loués pour minimiser les coûts de construction. Bien qu'il ait déjà utilisé des tubes de papier pour d'autres projets, avec l'approbation des autorités japonaises, il ne s'était jusqu'alors jamais attaqué à une construction de telles dimensions, et a dû faire appel aux conseils de Frei Otto, du célèbre spécialiste de l'architecture légère.

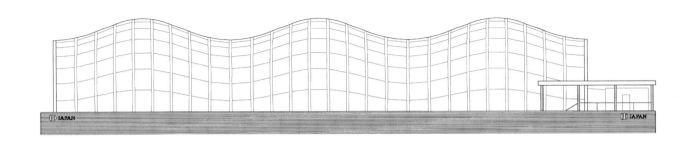

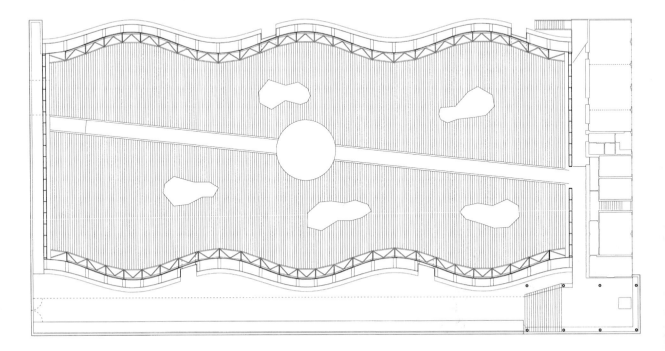

The design of the Pavilion undulates in both plan and elevation, giving a dynamic impetus to a structure that otherwise might have been unduly heavy.

Sowohl der Grundriss als auch die äußere Gestalt des Pavillons wurden wellenförmig angelegt, was dem Bauwerk trotz seiner Größe einen dynamischen Schwung verlieh.

Les ondulations de la structure, en plan comme en élévation, confèrent un mouvement dynamique à un volume qui aurait pu sembler pesant.

BERGER + PARKKINEN

Berger + Parkkinen Architekten
Fillgradergasse 16
1060 Vienna
Austria

Tel: + 43 1 581 4935
Fax: + 43 1 581 4937
e-mail: info@berger-parkkinen.com
www.berger-parkkinen.com

Alfred Berger is Austrian and **TIINA PARKKINEN** is Finnish; she was, however, born in Vienna in 1965, where she attended the Akademie der Bildenden Künste, graduating in 1994. **ALFRED BERGER** was born in Salzburg in 1961, and attended the Technical University in Vienna before going on to the Akademie der Bildenden Künste, which he left in 1989. He established his first architectural office, Berger & Krismer in 1990, followed by Penttilä – Berger – Krismer in 1992. They founded Berger + Parkkinen in 1995. Berger + Parkkinen's work includes the Ice Stadium (Vienna, 1994), a renovation for the Akademie der Bildenden Künste (1998), and the master plan of the Nordic Embassies in Berlin, Germany, published here. Current projects comprise a Biomedical Research Center in Vienna and a Court House in Leoben, Austria (2000).

Die Finnin **TIINA PARKKINEN** wurde 1965 in Wien geboren, wo sie 1994 ihren Abschluß an der Akademie der bildenden Künste machte. Der Österreicher **ALFRED BERGER**, geboren 1961 in Salzburg, besuchte die Technische Universität in Wien bevor er zur Akademie der bildenden Künste wechselte, die er 1989 verließ. 1990 gründete er sein erstes Architekturbüro, Berger & Krismer, dem 1992 Penttilä – Berger – Krismer folgte. 1995 schlossen sich Alfred Berger und Tiina Parkkinen zum Büro Berger + Parkkinen zusammen. Zu ihren Arbeiten gehören das Eisstadion in Wien (1994), eine Renovierungsarbeit für die Akademie der bildenden Künste (1998) und der hier vorgestellte Masterplan für die Botschaften der Nordischen Länder in Berlin. Aktuelle Projekte sind ein biomedizinisches Forschungszentrum in Wien und ein Gerichtsgebäude in Leoben, Österreich (2000).

Alfred Berger est autrichien et son associée **TIINA PARKKINEN** finlandaise, bien que née à Vienne en 1965 où elle a suivi les cours de l'Akademie der Bildenden Künste dont elle est sortie diplômée en 1994. **ALFRED BERGER**, né à Salzbourg en 1961, a étudié à l'Université Technique de Vienne avant d'entrer à l'Akademie der Bildenden Künste qu'il quitte en 1989. Il fonde sa première agence d'architecture, Berger & Krismer en 1990, puis Penttilä – Berger – Krismer en 1992. L'agence Berger + Parkkinen a été fondée en 1995. Parmi les réalisations de Berger + Parkkinen figurent la patinoire de Vienne (1994) ; un chantier de rénovation pour l'Akademie der Bildenden Künste (1998) et le plan directeur des ambassades des Pays Nordiques à Berlin, publié ici. Ils travaillent actuellement sur un centre de recherche biomédicale à Vienne et sur un palais de justice pour Leoben, Autriche (2000).

NORDIC EMBASSIES
Berlin, Germany, 1995-99

Planning: 12/95-12/98. Construction: 5/97-9/99.
Client: The countries Denmark, Finnland, Iceland, Norway and Sweden. Floor area: 15 550 m². Costs: Euro 49 500 000 .

The Austrian-Finnish partnership Berger + Parkkinen won the 1995 competition to design the master plan for the **NORDIC EMBASSIES** in Berlin. Their design, marked by their four-story undulating exterior wall of green patinated copper, and the common building called the Felleshus, encloses the buildings designed by Viiva Arkkitehtuuri for Finland, Gert Wingardh for Sweden, Nohetta for Norway, Palmar Kristmundsson for Iceland, and Nielsen & Nielsen for Denmark. Allocated in roughly similar geographic conditions, the embassies share a certain minimalist vocabulary. Within the inner courtyard, the Norwegian Embassy establishes its presence with a spectacular monolithic granite slab almost 14 m high and 71 cm thick. Playing on the effect of transparency versus opacity created by the louvers, screens, perforated metal panels, and the stone walls of the embassies, a common thread can be seen to emerge in the apparently monolithic appearance of the embassies of Finland, Denmark and Iceland.

Die österreichisch-finnische Architekturbüro Berger + Parkkinen gewann 1995 den Wettbewerb für den Masterplan der **NORDISCHEN BOTSCHAFTEN** in Berlin. Charakteristisches Merkmal ihres Entwurfes ist eine 15 m hohe, wellenförmige Umfassungsmauer, die das von Berger + Parkkinen entworfene und von allen fünf Botschaften gemeinschaftlich genutzte »Felleshus« umschließt, sowie die von Viiva Arkkitehtuuri für Finnland, von Gert Wingardh für Schweden, von Nohetta für Norwegen, von Palmar Kistmundsson für Island und von Nielsen & Nielsen für Dänemark entworfenen Gebäude. Die fünf Botschaftsgebäude haben einen gewissen Minimalismus in der Formensprache gemeinsam, der den sehr ähnlichen geographischen Bedingungen der Länder entspricht. Die im Bereich des Innenhofs gelegene Norwegische Botschaft macht mit einer spektakulären, fast 14 m hohen und 71 cm dicken Granitplatte auf sich aufmerksam. Dagegen lässt sich ein gemeinsamer Geist in der fast monolithischen Erscheinung der Botschaften von Finnland, Dänemark und Island erkennen. Auffällig ist hier ein spielerischer Umgang mit dem Kontrast von Transparenz und Undurchlässigkeit, der von den Lüftungsschlitzen, Sichtblenden, perforierten Stahlplatten und den Steinwänden der Gebäude erzeugt wird.

L'agence auto-finlandaise Berger + Parkkinen a remporté le concours (1995) pour le plan directeur des **AMBASSADES DES PAYS NORDIQUES** à Berlin. Compris entre quatre murs d'enceinte revêtus de cuivre ondulé à patine verte, le projet regroupe le Felleshus (bâtiment commun) ainsi que les ambassades de Finlande (Viiva Arkkitehtuuri), de Suède (Gert Wingardh), de Norvège (Nohetta), d'Islande (Palmar Kristmundsson), et du Danemark (Nielsen & Nielsen). La disposition des ces bâtiments au langage formel minimaliste reprend la géographie de la région. Située dans la cour intérieure, l'ambassade de Norvège affirme sa présence par une énorme dalle monolithique de 14 m de hauteur et de 71 cm d'épaisseur. Des effets de transparence et d'opacité engendrés par des persiennes, écrans, panneaux de métal perforé et murs de pierre soulignent la communauté d'esprit et les volumes des bâtiments finlandais, danois et islandais.

Seen from the air, the complex can be likened to a fortress. However, the whole seems to have an organic relationship to its surroundings.

Aus der Luft betrachtet ähnelt der Gebäudekomplex einer Festung. Dennoch scheint das Ganze in einer organischen Verbindung mit der Umgebung zu stehen.

En vue aérienne, ce complexe diplomatique fait penser à une forteresse. L'ensemble paraît entretenir une relation organique avec son environnement.

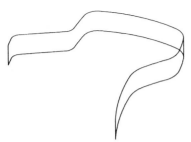 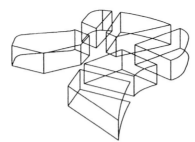 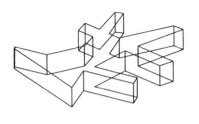

The compositional lines apparent in the aerial view are translated at ground level by bands in the walkways. The whole composition gives an impression not unlike that of a painting with multiple vanishing points. Opacity and transparency are strongly contrasted in each individual building design.

Die im Luftbild erkennbaren Umrisslinien der Gebäude wiederholen sich in einem Streifenmuster auf den Gehwegen. So wirkt die gesamte Komposition wie ein Gemälde mit mehreren Fluchtpunkten. In der Gestaltung der einzelnen Gebäude bilden lichtundurchlässige und transparente Elemente einen starken Kontrast.

Les lignes de la compositions, visibles sur la vue aérienne, sont matérialisées au niveau du sol par des bandes claires dans les allées. L'ensemble donne l'impression d'un tableau à plusieurs points de fuite. Chaque immeuble joue avec les contratses d'opacité et de transparence.

The entrance to the Embassy complex or Felleshus, designed by Berger + Parkkinen.

Das von Berger + Parkkinen entworfene Felleshus bildet den Eingang zum Botschaftskomplex.

L'entrée du complexe diplomatique ou Felleshus, conçue par Berger + Parkkinen.

The formal glass stairway provides
public access to the complex in
the Felleshus building designed
by Berger + Parkkinen.

Die formal strenge Glastreppe
in dem von Berger + Parkkinen
entworfenen Felleshus bildet
den öffentlichen Zugang zu dem
Komplex.

Le grand escalier en verre permet l'accès du public au bâtiment du Felleshus conçu par
Berger + Parkkinen.

The reception and waiting areas of the Felleshus.

Der Empfangs- und Wartebereich im Felleshus.

Aires de repos et de réception du Felleshus.

BOORA ARCHITECTS

BOORA Architects, Inc.
720 SW Washington St
Suite 800
Portland, Oregon 97205-3510
United States

Tel: +1 503 226 1575
Fax: +1 503 241 7429
Web: www.boora.com

Autobistro ▶

Created in 1958, **BOORA ARCHITECTS** is managed by 11 principals and has a staff of 106 employees. The firm does architectural planning and interior design work both in the United States and in other countries. They have completed master plans and buildings for 37 college and university campuses and 65 performing arts spaces. Current work includes the new performing arts center for the University of California, Davis, the National Underground Railroad Freedom Center, Cincinnati, Ohio, the Arts and Entertainment Center, Mesa, Arizona, and the Mark O. Hatfield Courthouse, Portland, Oregon.

Die 1958 gegründete Firma **BOORA ARCHITECTS** hat elf Leiter und 106 Mitarbeiter. BOORA ist international tätig in den Bereichen Architektur, Planung und Innenausstattung und hat bislang Masterpläne und Gebäude für 37 Colleges und Universitäten sowie 65 Einrichtungen für die darstellenden Künste ausgeführt. Zu den jüngsten Projekten gehören das neue Zentrum für Schauspiel und Tanz der University of California in Davis, das National Underground Railroad Freedom Center in Cincinnati, Ohio, das Arts and Entertainment Center in Mesa, Arizona und das Mark O. Hatfield Gerichtsgebäude in Portland, Oregon.

Fondé en 1958, **BOORA ARCHITECTS** regroupe onze associés et 106 collaborateurs. L'agence se consacre à l'architecture et à l'urbanisme et à l'architecture intérieure. Elle intervient aux Etats-Unis et dans d'autres pays. Elle a été chargée des plans directeurs et de la construction de 37 campus de collèges et d'universités et 65 salles de spectacles. Parmi ses travaux actuels : la nouvelle salle de spectacles de l'University of California, Davis, le National Underground Railroad Freedom Center, (Cincinnati, Ohio), l'Arts and Entertainment Center (Mesa, Arizona) et le Palais de justice Mark O. Hatfield (Portland, Oregon), toutes aux Etats-Unis.

AUTOBISTRO
Newport Beach, California, USA, 1997-98

*Planning: 8/97-1/98. Construction: 2/98-7/98. Client: Autobistro, Inc.
Floor area: 120 m². Costs: $1 100 000.*

California is well known for its roadside architecture. This prototype of a "quick service restaurant featuring healthy haute cuisine and specialty drinks to go" designed for a site on the Pacific Coast Highway breaks new ground. The 120-m² building has an elevated kitchen that accommodates vehicles driving below it, but its ambition is clearly to be more than an eye-catching diner. According to the architects **AUTOBISTRO** is intended to be a "commercial building that serves as public art, local landmark and commercial icon." A considerable effort has been made through landscaping and other means such as the blue color of the structure to make clear that it is no ordinary drive-in.

Kalifornien ist berühmt für seine Autobahn-Architektur. Dieser für einen Standort am Pacific Highway entworfene Prototyp eines »Schnellimbiss, in dem gesunde Kost und Spezialgetränke zum Mitnehmen« angeboten werden, ist wegweisend. Das 120 m² umfassende Gebäude verfügt über eine höher gelegene Küche, unter der die Fahrzeuge parken können. Sein Anspruch geht jedoch eindeutig darüber hinaus, lediglich ein Blickfang zu sein. Nach Aussage der Architekten soll das **AUTOBISTRO** ein »kommerzielles Gebäude sein, das als öffentliches Kunstwerk, lokales Baudenkmal und gewerbliches Symbol fungiert«. Sowohl die aufwendige Gestaltung der umliegenden Landschaft als auch die auffällige Farbgebung demonstrieren, dass es sich hier nicht um eine gewöhnliche Autobahnraststätte handelt.

La Californie est connue pour son architecture routière. Ce prototype d'établissement de restauration rapide conçu pour un emplacement au bord de la Pacific Coast Highway lui ouvre de nouvelles perspectives. Le bâtiment de 120 m² possède une cuisine surélevée où se préparent les repas pour les conducteurs des véhicules qui passent en dessous. Selon les architectes, cet **AUTOBISTRO** est un « immeuble commercial qui veut être à la fois un monument local, une œuvre d'art publique et une icône commerciale. » Les aménagements paysagers ainsi que d'autres détails comme la couleur bleue qui distingue ce restaurant des drive-in ordinaires témoignent des recherches formelles entreprises.

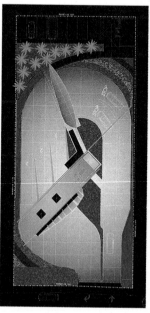

BOORA Architects took on the problem of California roadside architecture in a flamboyant and yet efficient way, making use of road space by setting the bulk of the structure above the carports.

BOORA Architects schuf einen auffallenden und funktionalen Beitrag zur kalifornischen Autobahn-Architektur. Der Raum wurde optimal genutzt, indem man den Hauptteil des Gebäudes über die Parkplätze verlegte.

BOORA Architects a traité le problème de l'architecture du bord des routes de façon étonnante mais efficace, en montant ce restaurant sur pilotis.

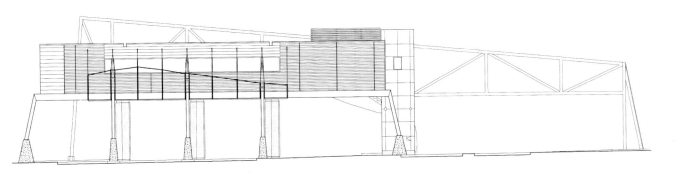

MARIO BOTTA

Mario Botta
Via Ciani 16
6904 Lugano
Switzerland

Tel: +41 91 972 8625
Fax: +41 91 970 1454
e-mail: mario.botta@botta.ch

Born in Mendrisio, Switzerland (1943), **MARIO BOTTA** left school at 15 to become an apprentice in an architectural office in Lugano. A year later, he designed his first house. During the studies at the University Institute of Architecture (IUAV) in Venice, where he graduated with Carlo Scarpa and Giuseppe Mazzariol, he worked briefly in the offices of Le Corbusier and Louis I. Kahn. He built private houses in the Ticino (Cadenazzo, 1970-71, Riva San Vitale, 1971-73, Ligornetto, 1975-76, and Stabio, 1980-82). Major buildings include Mediathèque (Villeurbanne, 1984-88), Malraux Cultural Center (Chambéry, 1982-87), Evry Cathedral (1988-95), all in France, San Francisco Museum of Modern Art (1992-95), and Chapel (Monte Tamaro, 1992-96), Museum Jean Tinguely (Basel, 1993-96), Church of St. John the Baptist (Mogno, 1986-98), all in Switzerland, the Municipal Library (Dortmund, Germany, 1995-99), and the recently completed Friedrich Dürrenmatt Center (Neuchâtel, Switzerland, 1992/97-2000). Current projects are the design for a church at Malpensa Airport (2000), and the Museum of Modern and Contemporary Art and Cultural Center (Rovereto, Italy, 1993-). In 1996 he founded the new Academy of Architecture in Mendrisio.

MARIO BOTTA, geboren 1943 im schweizerischen Mendrisio, verließ mit 15 Jahren die Schule und begann eine Lehre in einem Architekturbüro in Lugano. Dort entwarf er 1959 sein erstes Wohnhaus. Während seiner Studien am Istituto Universitario di Architettura (IUAV) in Venedig, die er bei Carlo Scarpa und Giuseppe Mazzariol abschloss, arbeitete er zeitweilig bei Le Corbusier und Louis I. Kahn. Danach baute er Einfamilienhäuser im Tessin (Cadenazzo, 1970-71, Riva San Vitale, 1971-73, Ligornetto, 1975-76 und Stabio, 1980-82). Zu Bottas Großprojekten gehören die Mediathèque in Villeurbanne (1984-88), das Malraux Kulturzentrum in Chambéry (1982-87) und die Kathedrale in Evry (1988-95), alle in Frankreich; das San Francisco Museum of Modern Art (1992-95), eine Kapelle auf dem Monte Tamaro (1992-96), das Museum Jean Tinguely in Basel (1993-96) und die Kirche Johannes der Täufer in Mogno (1986-98), alle in der Schweiz; die Stadtbibliothek in Dortmund (1995-99) sowie das erst kürzlich vollendete Friedrich Dürrenmatt Zentrum in Neuchâtel (Schweiz, 1992/97-2000). Seine jüngsten Projekte sind der Entwurf für eine Kirche für den Flughafen Malpensa (2000) sowie das Museum für Moderne und Zeitgenössische Kunst und Kulturzentrum in Rovereto, Italien (seit 1993). 1996 gründete er die neue Architektur-Akademie in Mendrisio.

Né à Mendrisio, Suisse, en 1943, **MARIO BOTTA** quitte l'école à 15 ans pour faire son apprentissage dans une agence d'architecture de Lugano. Il dessine sa première maison l'année suivante. Pendant ses études à l'University Institute of Architecture (IUAV) à Venise, qu'il a terminé chez et Carlo Scarpa et Giuseppe Mazzariol, il a brièvement travaillé dans l'entourage de Le Corbusier et Louis I. Kahn. Il a construit des villas en Suisse à Cadenazzo (1970-71), à Riva San Vitale (1971-73), à Ligornetto (1975-76) et à Stabio (1980-82). Parmi ses principales réalisations : la mediathèque de Villeurbanne (1984-88), le Centre culturel André Malraux (Chambéry, 1982-87), la cathédrale d'Evry (1988-95), le San Francisco Museum of Modern Art (1992-95), la chapelle de Tamaro (Monte Tamaro, Suisse, 1992-96), le musée Tinguely (Bâle, 1993-96), la chapelle de Saint Jean-Baptiste (Mogno, Suisse, 1986-98), la bibliothèque municipale (Dortmund, Germany, 1995-99) et le centre Friedrich Dürrenmatt (Neuchâtel, Suisse, 1992/97-2000). Parmi ses projets récents : la chapelle pur l'aéroport de Malpensa (2000) et le Musée d'art moderne et contemporain – Centre culturel de Rovereto (Italie, 1993-).

MODEL OF SAN CARLO ALLE QUATTRO FONTANE

Lugano, Switzerland, 1999

Promotors: Università della Svizzera italiana, Accademia di architettura. Planning: 2/99.
Construction: 3/99-8/99. Timber cut: 400 m³. Mounted panels: 491.

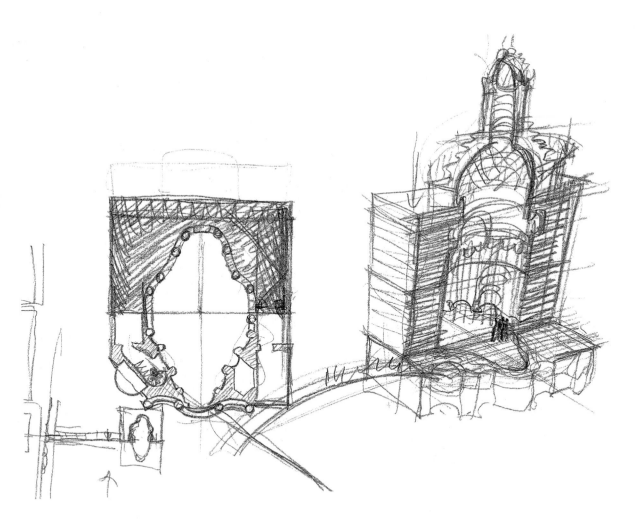

Mario Botta's drawings show the model's open, hollowed-out form. Baroque architects often created elaborate wooden models, but never at full scale. Botta's model is a masterpiece of craftsmanship.

Oben: Bottas Zeichnungen zeigen die offene Hohlform des Modells. Rechts: Die Architekten des Barock fertigten zwar häufig kunstvolle Holzmodelle ihrer Bauwerke an, aber nie im Maßstab 1:1. Bottas Arbeit ist ein Meisterwerk der Handwerkskunst.

Ci-dessus : Les dessins de Mario Botta montrent la maquette ouverte, en creux. A droite : Les architectes baroques créaient souvent des maquettes élaborées, mais jamais à échelle réelle. Celle de San Carlo est un chef d'œuvre de réalisation.

Mario Botta designed a 33 m-high full-scale wooden model of **SAN CARLO ALLE QUATTRO FONTANE** and the exhibition at the Museo Cantonale d'arte di Lugano to mark the 400th anniversary of the birth of architect Francesco Borromini. Set on a 22 m²-platform anchored a few meters off the shore-line in the lake near the entrance to the Parco Ciani, the model is made up of 35 000 planks, each 4.5 cm thick. Held together by steel cables, the whole structure is attached to a 100-ton steel frame. Based on a survey of Borromini's church by Professor Sartor in Rome, the model was built thanks to the efforts of the Swiss Italian University, Accademia di architettura, Mendrisio, and realized on a work-creation scheme involving unemployed people, architects, designers, carpenters and craftsmen working under Mario Botta's supervision.

Mario Botta entwarf ein 33 m hohes, originalgroßes Modell der Kirche **SAN CARLO ALLE QUATTRO FONTANE** in Rom für die im Museo Cantonale d'arte di Lugano veranstaltete Ausstellung zum 400. Geburtstag des italienischen Baumeisters Francesco Borromini. Das Modell steht auf einer 22 m² großen Plattform, die einige Meter vor dem Ufer und in der Nähe des Eingangs zum Parco Ciani im See verankert wurde. Es besteht aus 35 000, jeweils 4,5 cm dicken Holzplanken. Durch Stahlseile zusammengehalten, hängt die gesamte Konstruktion an einem 100 t schweren Stahlrahmen. Der Entwurf des Modells beruht auf dem Aufmaß von Borrominis Kirche durch Professor Sartor in Rom und wurde dank der Bemühungen der italienisch-schweizerischen Universität Accademia di architettura in Mendrisio unter Mario Bottas Leitung von arbeitslosen Architekten, Designern, Zimmerleuten und Handwerkern realisiert.

Mario Botta a conçu cette reproduction grandeur nature de 33 m de haut de l'église de **SAN CARLO ALLE QUATTRO FONTANE** et l'exposition du Musée cantonal d'art de Lugano pour le 400ème anniversaire de la naissance de l'architecte Francesco Borromini. Posée sur une plate-forme de 22 m² ancrée à quelques mètres de la rive du lac près de l'entrée du Parc Ciani, elle a nécessité 35 000 planches de 4,5 cm d'épaisseur. Maintenue par des câbles d'acier, elle repose sur une ossature d'acier de 100 t. Réalisée grâce aux efforts de l'université italo-helvétique Accademia di architettura de Mendrisio, d'après une étude de l'église de Borromini par le Professeur Sartor à Rome, elle a été construite par des chômeurs, des architecte, des designers, des charpentiers et des artisans travaillant sous le contrôle de Mario Botta.

BRANSON COATES

Branson Coates Architecture Ltd.
1-5 Honduras Street
London EC1Y OTH
England

Tel: +44 20 7336 1400
Fax: +44 20 7336 1401
e-mail: info@bransoncoates.com
Web: www.bransoncoates.com

The Body Zone, Millennium Dome ▶

DOUG BRANSON, born in 1951, and **NIGEL COATES**, born in 1949, formed Branson Coates in 1983. Both were educated at the Architectural Association (AA) in London. Coates taught at the AA for many years, first as an assistant to Bernard Tschumi and then as Unit Master of Unit 10 (1977-89). The work of Branson Coates includes the Bohemia Jazz Club (1986), Caffé Bongo (1986), the Nishi Azubu Wall (1990), all in Tokyo, and the Nautilus Bar and Seafood Restaurant at Schiphol Airport, Netherlands (1993). One of their most recent buildings is the National Centre for Popular Music in Sheffield (1996-98), whose quatrefoil form inspired that of Powerhouse::UK, an inflatable, temporary structure built for the Department of Trade and Industry on Horse Guards Parade in 1998. Current work includes the refurbishment of the King Street offices of the auctioneers Christie's in London.

DOUG BRANSON, geboren 1951, und **NIGEL COATES**, geboren 1949, gründeten 1983 das Büro Branson Coates. Beide studierten an der Architectural Association (AA) in London. Nigel Coates lehrte viele Jahre an der AA, zunächst als Assistent von Bernard Tschumi und danach als Unit Master der Unit 10 (1977-89). Zu ihren ausgeführten Bauten gehören der Bohemia Jazz Club (1986), das Caffé Bongo (1986) und die Nishi Azubu Wall (1990), alle in Tokio; außerdem die Nautilus Bar und das Fischrestaurant auf dem Flughafen Schiphol bei Amsterdam (1993). Eines ihrer jüngsten Projekte ist das National Centre for Popular Music in Sheffield (1996-98). Dessen Kleeblattform hat auch die Gestaltung des Powerhouse::UK inspiriert, einer aufblasbaren Konstruktion, die 1998 vorübergehend auf Horse Guards Parade in London errichtet wurde. Derzeit arbeiten sie unter anderem am Umbau der King Street-Filiale des Londoner Auktionshauses Christie's.

DOUG BRANSON, né en 1951 et **NIGEL COATES**, né en 1949, fondent l'agence Branson Coates en 1983, après avoir tous deux étudié à l'Architectural Association (AA) de Londres. Coates enseigne à l'AA pendant de nombreuses années, d'abord comme assistant de Bernard Tschumi, puis comme Unit Master de l'Unit 10 (1977-89). Parmi leurs travaux : le Bohemia Jazz Club (Tokyo, 1996), le Caffé Bongo (Tokyo, 1986), le Nishi Azubu Wall (Tokyo, 1990) et le Nautilus Bar et Seafood Restaurant de l'aéroport de Schiphol près d'Amsterdam (Pays-Bas, 1993). L'une de leurs plus récentes réalisations en Grande-Bretagne est le National Centre for Popular Music de Sheffield, (1996-98), dont la forme en trèfle a inspiré celle de Powerhouse::UK, une structure temporaire gonflable édifiée pour le Ministère du commerce et de l'industrie sur Horse Guards Parade, à Londres, en 1998. Parmi leurs chantiers récents : la rénovation des bureaux de Christie's, King Street, à Londres.

THE BODY ZONE

Millennium Dome, London, England, 2000

Planning: 4/98-8/98. Construction: 4/99-11/99. Client: New Millennium Experience Company.
Floor area: 458 m². Costs: £ 653 000

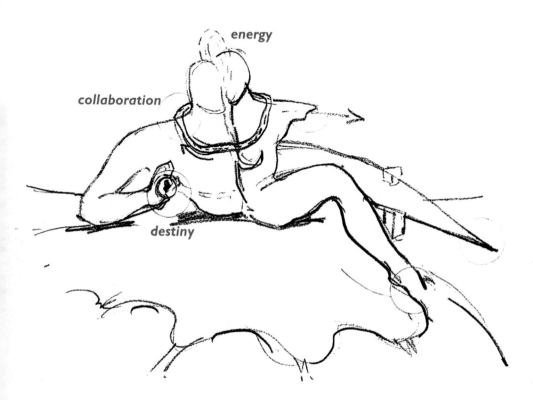

The pavilions in the interior of Richard Rogers' Millennium Dome relate to themes symbolic of daily life in the 21st Century. Branson Coates began working on the **BODY ZONE** in January 1999. They intended to create "a figure with a legendary status," neither man nor woman but rather two interlocking half-figures that represent both the sexes. The completed structure is 28 m high and 70 m long, providing about 400 m² of exhibition space. Clay and plaster models were made from drawings and digitally scanned for use with Microstation CAD software. An internal steel structure is covered with an external "skin" made of GRC (glass reinforced concrete). Although Branson Coates has built striking structures in the past, this figurative pavilion is undoubtedly one of the most unexpected sights under the Millennium Dome.

Die Ausstellungspavillons im Inneren von Richard Rogers' Millennium Dome beziehen sich auf Themen, die das Alltagsleben im 21. Jahrhundert versinnbildlichen. Branson Coates begannen im Januar 1999 mit ihrer Arbeit an der **BODY ZONE** (Körperzone). Ziel war die Darstellung einer »mythischen Figur«, die weder Mann noch Frau ist, sondern aus zwei sich gegenseitig durchdringenden, beide Geschlechter symbolisierenden Hälften besteht. Die fertige Konstruktion ist 28 m hoch, 70 m lang und bietet etwa 400 m² Ausstellungsfläche. Nach gezeichneten Vorlagen wurden Modelle aus Ton und Gips angefertigt und eingescannt, um sie mit Microstation CAD Software zu bearbeiten. Eine Stahlkonstruktion wurde mit einer Außenhaut aus GRC (glass reinforced concrete – glasfaserverstärkter Beton) versehen. Auch wenn Branson Coates bereits in der Vergangenheit außergewöhnliche Konstruktionen erbaut hat, bietet dieses figurative Ausstellungsgebäude zweifellos einen der überraschendsten Anblicke im Millennium Dome.

Les pavillons édifiés sous le Millennium Dome de Richard Rogers illustrent des thèmes symboliques de la vie quotidienne au XXIe siècle. Branson Coates a commencé à travailler sur cette **ZONE DU CORPS** en janvier 1999. Il voulait créer « une figure légendaire », ni homme ni femme, mais plutôt deux demi-personnages imbriqués qui représentent les deux sexes. La structure achevée mesure 28 m de haut et 70 m de long, pour un espace d'exposition de 400 m². Les maquettes en argile et plâtre ont été réalisées à partir de dessins et scannées pour être traitées par un logiciel de CAD. L'ossature interne en acier est recouverte d'une « peau » externe en GRC (béton renforcé de verre). Si Branson Coates est déjà connu pour certaines étonnantes réalisations, ce pavillon figuratif est certainement l'une des images les plus inattendues que l'on peut découvrir sous le Millennium Dome.

The unusual, figurative design of
The Body Zone corresponded to its
design function but caused considerable criticism, as did the rest of
the Dome's attractions.

Bienque les contours figuratifs de la
Body Zone répondent à la fonction
demandée, ce pavillon a soulevé de
nombreuses critiques, comme le reste
des attractions du Dome d'ailleurs.

Die außergewöhnliche figurative Form
der »Body Zone« nimmt Bezug auf
ihre Funktion als Ausstellungsraum.
Dennoch löste sie – ebenso wie die
anderen Attraktionen des Millennium
Dome – beträchtliche Kritik aus.

WILL BRUDER

william p. bruder-architect, ltd
1314 West Circle Mountain Road
New River, Arizona 85087
United States

Tel: +1 623 465 7399
Fax: +1 623 465 0109
e-mail: bruder@netwest.com

Byrne Residence ▶

Born in Milwaukee, Wisconsin in 1946, **WILL BRUDER** has a B.F.A. degree in sculpture from the University of Wisconsin-Milwaukee, and is self-trained as an architect. He apprenticed under Paolo Soleri and Gunnar Birkerts. He obtained his architecture license in 1974 and created his own studio the same year. In 1987, he was a fellow at the American Academy in Rome for six months. He has taught and lectured at Massachusetts Institute of Technology (MIT), ASU and the "cable works" in Helsinki. His most important built work is the Phoenix Central Library in Phoenix, Arizona (1989-95). Recent projects include the Teton County Library and Riddell Advertising, Jackson, Wyoming, Temple Kol Ami, Scottsdale, Arizona, the Deer Valley Rock Art Center, Phoenix, Arizona, and residences in Boston, Colorado, Arizona, Canada and Australia, as well as a restaurant in Manhattan.

WILL BRUDER, geboren 1946 in Milwaukee, Wisconsin, erwarb den Bachelor of Fine Arts (B.F.A.) in Bildhauerei, als Architekt ist er Autodidakt. Er ging bei Paolo Soleri und Gunnar Birkerts in die Lehre, bevor er 1974 die Zulassung als Architekt erhielt und sein eigenes Büro gründete. 1987 war er ein halbes Jahr an der American Academy in Rom tätig. Gelehrt hat Will Bruder am Massachusetts Institute of Technology (MIT), der ASU und bei »cable works« in Helsinki. Sein bedeutendster Bau ist die Phoenix Central Library in Phoenix, Arizona (1989-95). Zu seinen neueren Projekten gehören die Teton County Library und Riddell Advertising in Jackson, Wyoming, die Kol Ami-Synagoge in Scottsdale, Arizona, das Deer Valley Rock Art Center in Phoenix, Arizona, ein Restaurant in Manhattan sowie Wohnhäuser in Boston, Colorado, Arizona, Kanada und Australien.

Né à Milwaukee, Wisconsin en 1946, **WILL BRUDER** est diplômé de sculpture de l'Université de Wisconsin-Milwaukee et architecte autodidacte. Il fait son apprentissage auprès de Paolo Soleri et de Gunnar Birkerts. Licencié en architecture en 1974, il crée son propre atelier la même année, puis étudie à l'American Academy de Rome pendant six mois en 1987. Il enseigne et donne des conférences au MIT à l'ASU et à « cable works » (Helsinki). Son œuvre la plus importante aux Etats-Unis est la Phoenix Central Library (Phoenix, Arizona, 1988-95). Parmi ses projets récents : la Teton County Library, l'agence Riddell Advertising (Jackson, Wyoming), le Temple Kol Ami (Scottsdale, Arizona), le Valley Rock Art Center (Phoenix, Arizona) et des résidences à Boston, dans le Colorado, l'Arizona, au Canada et en Australie, ainsi qu'un restaurant à Manhattan.

BYRNE RESIDENCE

North Scottsdale, Arizona, USA, 1994-98

Design: 1994-95. Construction: 1996-98. Client: Bill and Carol Byrne. Floor area: 250m².

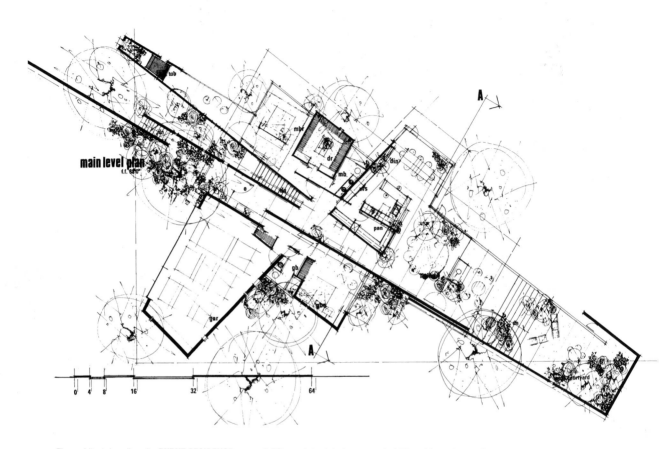

main level plan

The architect describes the **BYRNE RESIDENCE** very well, "The sculptural design concept of this residence is one of creating a metaphorical series of abstract canyon walls of concrete masonry, emerging like geological gestures from the home's natural desert site." This 250-m² house is located on a 2-hectare lot roughly 80 km north of Phoenix. Its angled surfaces evoke the sandstone surfaces of the area, and the architect has respected the clients' request for an energy-efficient and "organic" type of architecture. Will Bruder refers to Frank Lloyd Wright's Price House (1954, Phoenix) as an indirect source of inspiration for his design, and the two residences do in fact share, among other features, the idea of concrete-block walls.

Der Architekt selbst beschreibt die **BYRNE RESIDENCE** so: »Das bildhauerische Gestaltungskonzept dieses Wohnhauses bestand darin, eine metaphorische Serie stilisierter Felswände aus Betonmauerwerk zu schaffen, die wie geologische Formationen aus der natürlichen Wüstenumgebung des Hauses erwachsen.« Das Gebäude mit einer Nutzfläche von 250 m² liegt auf einem 2 ha großen Grundstück ca. 80 km nördlich von Phoenix. Seine schrägen Außenwände, die dem Wunsch der Bauherren nach einem energiesparenden und »organischen« Bautypus nachkommen, erinnern an die für diese Gegend typischen Sandsteinformationen. Will Bruder nennt Frank Lloyd Wrights Price House in Phoenix (1954) als indirekte Inspirationsquelle für seine Gestaltung, und tatsächlich haben die beiden Wohnhäuser, neben anderen Merkmalen, die Idee der Wände aus Betonformstein gemeinsam.

Le descriptif de la **BYRNE RESIDENCE** de Will Bruder est précis : « Le concept sculptural de cette résidence repose sur la création d'une succession de parois métaphoriques formant une sorte de ‹ canyon › abstrait en maçonnerie de béton qui émerge du site désertique environnant à la manière de plissements géologiques. » La maison de 250 m² s'élève sur un terrain de 2 ha à 80 km environ au nord de Phoenix. Les surfaces anguleuses évoquent le paysage minéral de la région. L'architecte a respecté les souhaits du client qui voulait un projet « organique » et économe en énergie. Will Bruder cite la Price House de Frank Lloyd Wright (Phoenix, Arizona, 1954) parmi ses sources d'inspiration indirectes. D'ailleurs, les murs en parpaings de béton sont une caractéristique commune à les deux résidences.

Despite its apparent sophistication, this design calls on the idea of the ephemeral shelter, thus differentiating itself from the more deeply anchored architecture of Frank Lloyd Wright for example.

Trotz seines raffinierten Entwurfs erinnert das Gebäude in der Ausführung eher an Behelfsbauten. Dadurch unterscheidet es sich beispielsweise von der massiveren Architektur eines Frank Lloyd Wright.

La sophistication apparente de ce projet repose en fait sur l'idée d'abri temporaire, ce qui le différencie, entre autres, des architectures solidement ancrées dans le sol de Frank Lloyd Wright.

As the topographical plan to the left
indicates, the house draws part of its
inspiration from the very lay of the
land (below left). It is intended to
be in harmony with its spectacular
natural setting.

Inspirationsquellen für die Gestaltung
waren sowohl die geographischen
Gegebenheiten (unten links) als auch
die spektakuläre Landschaft, in die
die Byrne Residence harmonisch
eingefügt ist.

Comme le montre le plan du site
(en bas à gauche), la maison tire en
partie son inspiration de la forme
même du terrain et s'harmonise avec
son spectaculaire environnement
naturel.

Will Bruder is one of the recognized masters of contemporary architecture in the Southwestern United States. Open to its environment, this house shows a mastery of form that is more than regional.

Will Bruder ist einer der anerkanntesten Vertreter zeitgenössischer Architektur im Südwesten der USA. Die Offenheit gegenüber der Umgebung und die ungewöhnliche Formensprache machen seine Byrne Residence zu einem Meisterwerk von überregionaler Bedeutung.

Will Bruder est l'un des maîtres reconnus de l'architecture contemporaine dans le Sud-Ouest américain. Ouverte à son environnement, cette maison témoigne d'un traitement des formes qui n'est pas seulement d'inspiration régionale.

SANTIAGO CALATRAVA

Santiago Calatrava, S. A.
Höschgasse 5
8008 Zurich
Switzerland

Tel: +41 1422 7500
Fax: +41 1422 5600
www.calatrava.com

City of Arts and Sciences ▶

Born in Valencia in 1951, **SANTIAGO CALATRAVA** studied art and architecture at the Escuela Técnica Superior de Arquitectura in Valencia (1969-74) and engineering at the Eidgenössische Technische Hochschule in Zurich (doctorate in technical science, 1981). He opened his own architecture and civil engineering office the same year. His built work includes Gallery & Heritage Square, BCE Place (Toronto, 1987), the Bach de Roda Bridge (1985-87) and the Torre de Montjuic (1989-92) in Barcelona, the Kuwait Pavilion and the Alamillo Bridge at Expo '92, Seville, and the Lyon-Satolas TGV Station (1989-94). He recently completed the Oriente Station in Lisbon. He was a finalist in the competition for the Reichstag in Berlin. His most recently completed project is the City of Arts and Sciences in Valencia, published here.

SANTIAGO CALATRAVA, geboren 1951 in Valencia, studierte an der dortigen Escuela Técnica Superior de Arquitectura Kunst und Architektur (1969-74) sowie Ingenieurbau an der Eidgenössischen Technischen Hochschule (ETH) in Zürich, wo er 1981 promovierte. Im selben Jahr gründete er sein eigenes Büro für Architektur und Bauingenieurwesen. Zu Calatravas Bauten gehören Gallery & Heritage Square, BCE Place in Toronto (1987), die Bach de Roda-Brücke (1985-87) und die Torre de Montjuic (1989-92) in Barcelona, der Kuwait-Pavillon und die Alamillo-Brücke für die Expo '92 in Sevilla sowie der TGV-Bahnhof Lyon-Satolas (1989-94). Kürzlich vollendete er den Oriente-Bahnhof in Lissabon. Calatravas Entwurf für den Reichstag in Berlin kam in die Endauswahl. Sein jüngstes Projekt ist das hier vorgestellte Wissenschaftsmuseum in Valencia.

Né à Valence, Espagne, en 1951, **SANTIAGO CALATRAVA** étudie l'art et l'architecture à la Escuela Técnica Superior de Arquitectura de Valencia (1969-74) et l'ingénierie à l'ETH (Zurich) dont il est docteur en sciences techniques, en 1981, date à laquelle il ouvre son agence d'architecture et d'ingénierie. Parmi ses réalisations : la Gallery & Heritage Square, BCE Place (Toronto, 1987), le pont Bach de Roda (Barcelone, 1985-87), la Torre de Montjuic (Barcelone, 1989-92), le pavillon du Koweit à Expo '92 (Séville), le pont Alamillo pour la même manifestation, ainsi que la gare TGV de Lyon-Satolas (1989-94). Il a récemment achevé la gare de l'Oriente à Lisbonne. Finaliste du concours pour le Reichstag, à Berlin, il vient d'achever le Musée des sciences de Valence.

CITY OF ARTS AND SCIENCES

Valencia, Spain, 1991-

Planetarium: Planning: 1991-95. Construction: 1996-98. Floor area: 2 561 m². Costs: Ptas 3 000 000 000.
Museum: Planning: 1991-95. Construction: 1996-2000. Floor area: 41 530 m². Cost estimate: Pts 10 400 000 000.
Opera: Planning: 1995-97. Construction: 1997-. Floor area: 44 150 m². Cost estimate: Pts 11 380 000 000.
Client: Generalitat Valenciana.

Part of a long-standing effort of the government of Valencia to rehabilitate an area at the eastern periphery of the city, lodged between a large highway and the dried-up bed of the Turia River, Calatrava's **CITY OF ARTS AND SCIENCES** took almost ten years to be completed. A native of Valencia, he won the 1991 competition for the project that, at the time, included a telecommunications tower resting on three elongated feet. Rising to a height of 327 m, the tower would have been the most visible element of the whole complex. Changes in the city's government led to a replacement of the tower in 1996 by a music center and an Opera, the Palacio de las Artes. The Planetarium, with its eye-shaped plan and hemispheric dome with movable ribbed covering, was built on an area of almost 2 561 m² between 1996 and 1998. The 241 m-long, 41 530-m² Museum of Science is based on an asymmetrical repetition of tree- and rib-like forms filled with glass to admit ample daylight. The Palacio de las Artes (under construction since 1997) will eventually complete the composition.

Calatravas **STADT DER KÜNSTE UND WISSENSCHAFTEN**, deren Fertigstellung beinahe zehn Jahre erforderte, ist das Ergebnis der langjährigen Bemühungen der Provinzregierung von Valencia, das am östlichen Stadtrand zwischen einer großen Autobahn und dem ausgetrockneten Flussbett des Turia liegende Gebiet zu sanieren. Calatrava, selbst aus Valencia gebürtig, gewann 1991 den Wettbewerb für das Projekt, das zum damaligen Zeitpunkt noch einen Telekommunikationsturm auf drei spitz zulaufenden Pfeilern einschloss. Mit einer Höhe von 327 m wäre dieser Turm das beherrschende Element des gesamten Komplexes geworden. Veränderungen innerhalb der Stadtverwaltung führten dazu, dass der Turm 1996 durch den Palacio de las Artes, der eine Oper, ein Theater und ein Musik- und Tanzzentrum umfaßt, ersetzt wurde. Das Planetarium mit seinem, an ein Auge erinnernden Grundriss und seiner Kuppel in Form einer Halbkugel unter einer Verkleidung aus beweglichen Rippen wurde zwischen 1996 und 1998 auf einer Fläche von 2 561 m² errichtet. Die Anlage des 241 m langen und 41 530 m² umfassenden Wissenschaftsmuseums basiert formal auf einer asymmetrischen Wiederholung verästelter- oder rippenartiger Formen, die mit Glas ausgefüllt wurden, durch das reichlich Tageslicht einfällt. Der seit 1997 im Bau befindliche Palacio de las Artes wird schließlich die Komposition vervollständigen.

Dans le cadre d'un vaste effort du gouvernement de la région de Valence pour réhabiliter une zone de la périphérie est de la ville, entre une importante autoroute et le lit asséché du fleuve Turia, il a fallu presque dix ans pour mener à bien le projet de cette **CITÉ DES ARTS ET DES SCIENCES.** Né à Valence, Calatrava avait remporté le concours lancé pour ce projet en 1991. Le concours comprenait alors une tour de télécommunications de 327 m de haut, appuyée sur trois pieds allongés. Elle fut remplacée en 1996 par un centre de musique et un opéra, le Palacio de las Artes. Le Planétarium et son dôme hémisphérique en forme d'œil à couverture mobile et nervuré a été édifié sur un terrain de 2 561 m² de 1996 à 1998. Le Musée des Sciences de 41 530 m² et 241 m de long est une répétition asymétrique de formes végétales et de nervures réunies par une verrière qui favorise un généreux éclairage naturel. Dans l'avenir, le Palacio de las Artes (en construction depuis 1997) complétera la composition.

Set at the eastern fringe of Valencia, near the end of the long green belt formed by the Turia River gardens (designed by Ricardo Bofill), the City of Arts and Sciences presents a ribbed design not unlike a gigantic thoracic cage.

Die Gestaltung der am Ostrand von Valencia und am Ausläufer des von Ricardo Bofill entworfenen Turia Park- und Grüngeländes gelegenen Stadt der Künste und Wissenschaften ähnelt mit ihrer Reihung breiter Rippen einem riesigen Brustkorb.

A la limite est de la commune de Valence et vers l'extrémité de la longue ceinture verte des jardins de la Turia (dessinés par Ricardo Bofill), la Cité des Arts et des Sciences et son squelette nervuré font penser à une gigantesque cage thoracique.

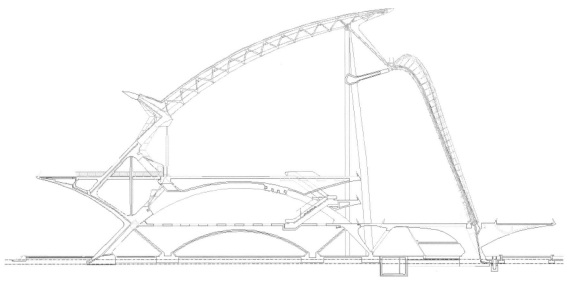

The 240 m-long atrium space of
the City of Sciences brings to mind
Calatrava's BCE Place, Galleria &
Heritage Square (Toronto, Canada,
1987-92), with its six story-high
115 m-long gallery.

Die 240 m lange Vorhalle des Wissenschaftsmuseums erinnert an Calatravas BCE Place, Galleria & Heritage
Square in Toronto (1987-92), mit seiner sechsgeschossigen, 115 m langen
Galerie.

L'atrium de 240 m de long rappelle
une autre réalisation de Calatrava :
la galerie de 115 m de long et six
étages de haut de BCE Place, Galleria
& Heritage Square (Toronto, Canada,
1987-92).

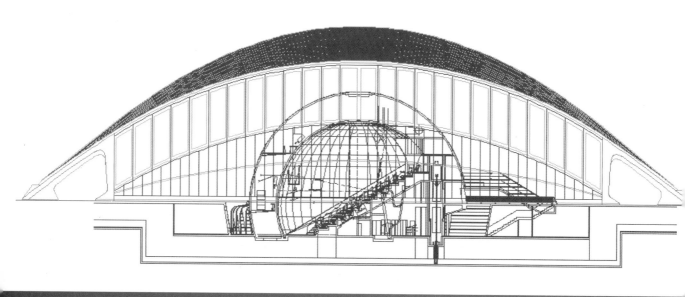

The Planetarium, which was the first part of the complex to reach completion, clearly resembles an eye – and even includes a moving "eyelid." The hemispheric form of the theater naturally lends itself to this interpretation, but Calatrava often uses the form of the eye in his work.

Das Planetarium, das als erstes Gebäude der Anlage fertiggestellt wurde, erinnert mit seinem halbkugelförmigen Kuppelsaal an ein Auge, und hat sogar ein bewegliches »Augenlid«. Calatrava hat die Form des Auges bereits in früheren Arbeiten verwendet.

Le Planétarium, première partie du complexe achevée, ressemble à un œil, « paupière » mobile comprise. La forme hémisphérique de la salle se prête à cette interprétation, d'ailleurs l'architecte a souvent utilisé la forme de l'œil dans ses créations.

SONDICA AIRPORT

Bilbao, Spain, 1990-2000

Planning: 1990-95. Construction: 1997-2000. Floor area: 74 430 m².
Client: AENA (Aeropuertos Españoles y Navigación Aéra).
Cost: Ptas 11 000 000 000.

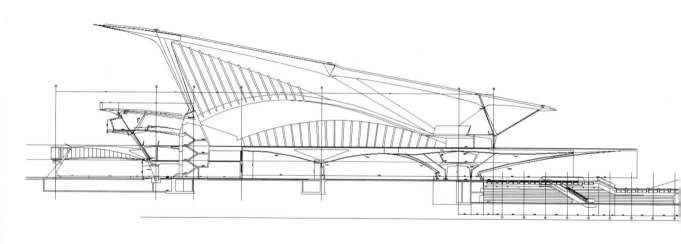

Part of an ongoing campaign by
municipal and regional authorities
to make Bilbao a tourist destination,
the Sondica Airport is a stylized
interpretation of aircraft movement,
somewhat akin to Calatrava's Lyon
Satolas TGV Station (now called Lyon-
Saint-Exupéry, Lyon, France, 1989-
94).

Der Bau des Flughafens Sondica
gehört zu den laufenden Bemühungen
von Stadt- und Bezirksverwaltung,
Bilbao zu einer Touristenattraktion zu
machen. Seine Formgebung beruht
auf der stilisierten Darstellung von
Flugbewegungen und hat gewisse
Ähnlichkeit mit Calatravas 1994 fer-
tiggestelltem Lyon Satolas TGV-Bahnhof (jetzt Lyon-Saint-Exupéry genannt)
im französischen Lyon.

Dans le cadre d'un programme municipal et régional qui veut faire de
Bilbao une destination touristique
plus séduisante, l'aéroport de Sondica est une interprétation stylisée des
mouvements d'un avion. Ce bâtiment
n'est pas sans rapport avec la gare
T. G. V. de Lyon-Satolas, également de
Calatrava (aujourd'hui Lyon-Saint-
Exupéry, France, 1989-94).

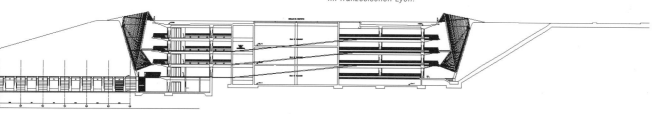

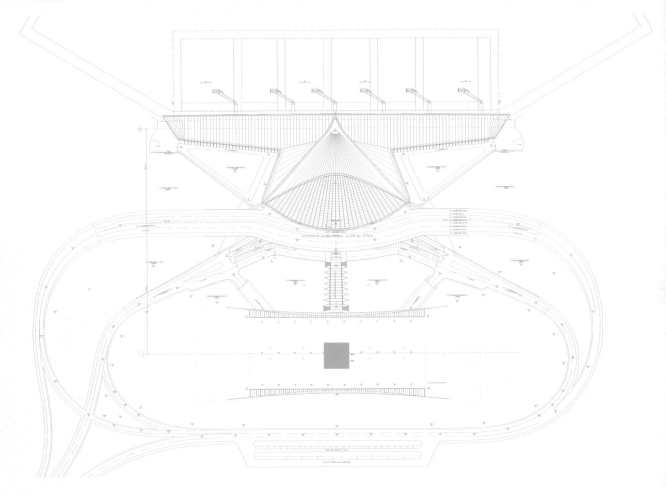

Located on the Bay of Biscay to the north of Bilbao, this new terminal of **SONDICA AIRPORT** includes a total of eight gates, intended to process 2 million passengers per year with possible future expansion to accomodate 10 million travellers. Options for later construction include hotels and a recreational complex. Spanish Airport authorities first asked Calatrava to design a smaller four-gate version of this terminal, but the growing number of flights required an increase in the size of the design in 1994. The most spectacular feature of the complex is its large, triangular glazed hall. As the architect puts it, "The steel structure of its aerodynamic roof rises up towards the airfield to span the administrative areas and restaurants, as well as the waiting areas behind the canted glazed facades that overlook the apron and runways." The old terminal of the Bilbao Airport, intended for domestic flights only, is situated on the opposite side of the runways.

Der nördlich von Bilbao am Golf von Biscaya gelegene neue Terminal des **SONDICA AIRPORT** verfügt über insgesamt acht Gates und soll zunächst jährlich zwei Millionen Passagiere abfertigen, eine Ausweitung auf 10 Millionen Reisende ist möglich. Die Option auf zukünftige Erweiterungen beinhaltet den Bau eines Hotels und eines Erholungszentrums. Die spanische Flughafenbehörde hatte Calatrava ursprünglich mit dem Entwurf einer kleineren Version mit vier Gates beauftragt. Aber die wachsende Zahl von Flügen machte 1994 eine Planung in größerem Maßstab erforderlich. Das hervorstechendste Element der Anlage ist die große, dreieckig geschnittene und verglaste Halle. Dazu erklärt der Architekt: »Die Stahlkonstruktion des aerodynamischen Hallendachs schwingt sich in Richtung Flugplatz empor und umspannt die Bereiche Verwaltung und Gastronomie sowie die Wartezonen hinter den abgeschrägten Glasfassaden mit Aussicht auf Vorfeld und Rollbahnen.« Das alte Abfertigungsgebäude des Flughafens Bilbao, das nur für Inlandsflüge konzipiert ist, befindet sich auf der gegenüberliegenden Seite der Start- und Landebahnen.

En bordure de l'océan, au nord de Bilbao, ce nouveau terminal d'**AÉROPORT DE SONDICA** comprend sept portes qui devraient accueillir deux millions de passagers par an, avec une possibilité d'extension à 10 millions. Le projet s'accompagnera de la création d'hôtels et d'un ensemble de loisirs. A l'origine, les autorités aéroportuaires espagnoles avaient commandé à Calatrava un projet à quatre portes, mais qui fut revu et développé en 1994. L'élément le plus spectaculaire est un vaste hall d'accueil triangulaire en verre. Comme l'explique l'architecte : « La structure en acier du grand toit aérodynamique s'élève vers l'aérodrome pour abriter les installations administratives, les restaurants, les zones et salles d'attente placées derrière les façade de verre inclinées qui dominent l'aire de stationnement et les pistes. L'ancien terminal, réservé aux vols nationaux, se trouve à l'autre extrémité des pistes.

The impression of movement is heightened when the airport structure is viewed from certain angles, but the idea of a forward-leaning design is apparent everywhere. A plan alludes to anthropomorphic intent in the design.

Die Idee vorwärts strebender Formen ist überall präsent, und der dynamische Eindruck wird noch verstärkt, wenn man das Flughafengebäude aus bestimmten Blickwinkeln betrachtet. Die Planskizze lässt auf anthropomorphe Bezüge in der Gestaltung schließen.

L'impression d'un mouvement vers l'avant est omniprésente, elle devient encore plus forte quand on regarde l'aéroport sous un certain angle. Le plan révèle quelques allusions anthropomorphiques.

ALBERTO CAMPO BAEZA

Alberto Campo Baeza
Arquitecto
Almirante, 9
28004 Madrid
Spain

Tel/Fax: +34 91 521 7061
e-mail: campo-baeza@redestb.es

Center for Innovative Technologies BIT

Born in Cadiz, Spain, in 1946, **ALBERTO CAMPO BAEZA** studied in Madrid, where he graduated in 1971 and obtained his Ph.D. in 1982. He has taught in Madrid, at the ETH Zurich (1989-90), at Cornell University, Ithaca, New York and at the University of Pennsylvania, Philadelphia (1999). His work includes the Fene Town Hall (1980), S. Fermin Public School (Madrid, 1985), Public Library (Orihuela, 1992) and a Public School (Cadiz, 1992), all in Spain, as well as a number of private houses. Current work includes a bank in Granada, and a house for Tom Ford of Gucci in Santa Fe, New Mexico.

Der 1946 im spanischen Cádiz geborene **ALBERTO CAMPO BAEZA** schloß 1971 sein Universitätsstudium in Madrid ab und erwarb dort 1982 den Doktorgrad. Seither lehrte er an der Universität Madrid, der Eidgenössischen Technischen Hochschule (ETH) in Zürich (1989-90), der Cornell University, Ithaca, New York und der University of Pennsylvania, Philadelphia (1999). Zu seinen Bauten gehören das Rathaus in Fene (1980), die Schule S. Fermin in Madrid (1985), die Stadtbücherei in Orihuela (1992) und eine weitere Schule in Cádiz (1992), alle in Spanien, sowie eine Reihe von Privathäusern. Gegenwärtig arbeitet er an einer Bank in Granada und einem Haus für Tom Ford von Gucci in Santa Fe, New Mexico.

Né en 1946 à Cadix (Espagne), **ALBERTO CAMPO BAEZA** étudie l'architecture à Madrid (diplôme en 1971 et doctorat en 1982). Il a enseigné à Madrid, à l'ETH (Zurich, 1989-90), à la Cornell University, Ithaca, New York, et à l'University of Pennsylvania, Philadelphie (1999). Parmi ses interventions en Espagne : l'hôtel de ville de Fene (1980), l'école publique S. Firmin (Madrid, 1985), une bibliothèque publique (Orihuela, 1992), un collège (Cadix, 1992) ainsi qu'un certain nombre de villas. Ses projets actuels concernent une banque à Grenade, et une maison pour Tom Ford (Gucci) à Santa Fe (Nouveau Mexique, Etats-Unis).

CENTER FOR INNOVATIVE TECHNOLOGIES BIT

Inca, Majorca, Spain, 1995-98

Competition: 4/95. Construction: 3/97-3/98. Floor area: 4 900 m²
Client: Govern Balear. Costs: $4 000 000.

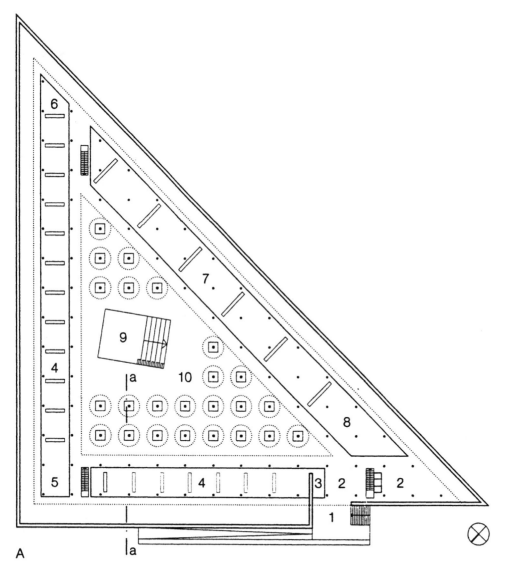

A

Alberto Campo Baeza's taste for a geometric simplicity is carried through from the basic triangular plan of the Center (left) to its extremely minimalist design (right).

Campo Baezas Vorliebe für geometrisch schlichte Formen zieht sich durch das gesamte Zentrum: von seinem dreieckigen Grundriss (links) bis zu seiner äußerst minimalistischen Gestaltung (rechts).

Le goût d'Alberto Campo Baeza pour la pureté géométrique est porté ici à son paroxysme : un plan triangulaire (à gauche) et sa réalisation minimaliste (à droite).

The spare, triangular design of the **CENTER FOR INNOVATIVE TECHNOLOGIES BIT** is very minimal. Alberto Campo Baeza, winner of a 1995 competition, chose to isolate the building, a 4900-m² structure (3200 m² in the basement), from its industrial environment with limestone walls. The interior walls are clad in Roman Travertine marble. Unframed glass and white steel columns complete the concrete slab design, with orange trees in the patio and wisteria, jasmine and grapes growing on the walls. The 2-m overhang of the slab roof shades the windows from the strong sun. The whole building presents a very distinct impression of a minimal style that the architect call its "CB flavor" (after his own initials).

Alberto Campo Baeza gewann 1995 den Wettbewerb für das **CENTER FOR INNOVATIVE TECHNOLOGIES BIT** auf Mallorca. Er grenzte das 4900 m² große (davon befinden sich 3200 m² im Untergeschoss) Zentrumsgebäude, das auf dreieckigem Grundriß errichtet wurde, durch Kalksteinwände von seiner industriellen Umgebung ab. Die Innenwände sind mit römischem Travertin und Betonplatten verkleidet. Diese sparsame Gestaltung wird durch rahmenloses Glas und weiße Stahlstützen vervollständigt. Im Patio wachsen Orangenbäume, und auf den Wänden ranken sich Glyzinien, Jasmin und Wein in die Höhe. Der um 2 m überhängende Teil des Plattendachs schirmt die Fenster vor dem starken Sonnenlicht ab. Das gesamte Bauwerk vermittelt den für Campo Baeza charakteristischen, minimalistischen Stil, von ihm selbst nach seinen eigenen Initialen der »CB-Touch« genannt.

Ce centre, de conception austère et très minimaliste, suit un plan triangulaire. Alberto Campo Baeza, qui en avait remporté le concours en 1995, a choisi d'isoler le **CENTER FOR INNOVATIVE TECHNOLOGIES BIT** de 4900 m² (dont 3200 m² en sous-sol) de son contexte industriel par des murs de grès. Les parois intérieures sont parées de travertin romain. Des panneaux de verre sans cadre apparent et des colonnes d'acier blanches complètent l'ensemble édifié en béton. Des orangers ont été plantés dans le patio tandis que des glycines, des jasmins et de la vigne poussent sur les murs. L'avancée de 2 m de profondeur de la dalle du toit protège les fenêtres des ardeurs du soleil local. L'ensemble reflète de façon exemplaire ce style minimaliste que l'architecte lui-même qualifie de « saveur CB » (d'après ses propres initiales).

Even the trees planted in the inner courtyard of the complex take on an almost geometric regularity in this powerful, modern design.

Selbst die im Innenhof des Komplexes gepflanzten Bäume sind in diesem kraftvollen, modernen Entwurf in beinahe geometrischer Regelmäßigkeit angeordnet.

Même les arbres plantés dans la cour intérieure se sont pliés au rythme géométrique régulier de ce projet plein de force.

DALY, GENIK

Daly, Genik
1558 10th Street
Santa Monica, California 90401
United States

Tel: +1 310 656 3180
Fax: +1 310 656 3183
email: kevin@dalygenik.com or
chris@dalygenik.com
Web: www.dalygenik.com

Valley Center House ▶

KEVIN DALY received his M.Arch. degree at Rice University and his B.Arch. at the University of California at Berkeley. He has participated in the studio faculty of the Southern California Institute of Architecture (1992-99). Before becoming a principal of Daly, Genik in 1989, he worked at the Design Build Studio in Berkeley (1980-85), with Hodgetts & Fung (1985-86), and as an associate in the office of Frank O. Gehry (1986-90). **CHRIS GENIK** received his B.Arch. degree from Carleton University, Ottawa (1983) and his M.Arch. from Rice University, Houston, Texas (1985). Following graduate school, he formed a partnership with Rice University professor Peter Waldman and undertook a series of institutional, residential, and theoretical projects. While practicing, he held a teaching position at the University of Houston, Texas. He moved to Los Angeles to create **DALY, GENIK** in 1989.

KEVIN DALY erwarb seinen Bachelor of Architecture an der Rice University, Houston, Texas und seinen Master of Architecture an der University of California in Berkeley. Von 1992 bis 1999 lehrte er am Southern California Institute of Architecture (SCI-Arc). Bevor er 1989 einer der Leiter von **DALY, GENIK** wurde, war Kevin Daly Mitarbeiter im Design Studio in Berkeley (1980-85), bei Hodgetts & Fung (1985-86) und im Büro von Frank O. Gehry (1986-90). **CHRIS GENIK** erwarb 1983 den Bachelor of Architecture an der Carleton University und 1985 den Master of Architecture an der Rice University. Nach seinem Graduiertenstudium bildete er eine Partnerschaft mit dem an der Rice University als Professor tätigen Peter Waldman und führte eine Reihe praktischer und theoretischer Projekte durch. Daneben unterrichtete er an der University of Houston. 1989 zog er nach Los Angeles und gründete zusammen mit Kevin Daly das Architekturbüro Daly, Genik.

KEVIN DALY est Bachelor of Architecture de l'University of California de Berkeley et Master of Architecture de la Rice University. Il a enseigné au Southern California Institute of Architecture (1992-99). Avant de s'associer à Chris Genik, il avait travaillé pour l'agence Design Build Studio de Berkeley (1980-85), chez Hodgetts & Fung (1985-86) et comme associé chez Frank O. Gehry (1986-90). **CHRIS GENIK** est diplômé en architecture de la Carleton University (1983) et Master of Architecture de la Rice University, Houston, Texas (1985). Associé à un professeur de Rice University, Peter Waldman, il réalise une série de projets institutionnels, résidentiels et théoriques. En même temps, il enseigne à l'Université de Houston, Texas. Il s'installe à Los Angeles où il crée **DALY, GENIK** en 1989.

VALLEY CENTER HOUSE

North San Diego County, California, USA, 1998

Construction: 1998. Client: withheld at owner's request. Floor area: 265 m².

Located at an altitude of 550 m above sea level near a citrus and avocado ranch 70 km northeast of San Diego, the **VALLEY CENTER HOUSE** was intended to replace a residence destroyed by a wildfire in November 1996. Laid out in a skewed "U" form, the house offers 265 m² of space, and features large perforated aluminum screens attached to aluminum tube frames that can swing down to shield the house from the sun or offer privacy at night. The screens also protect the residence in case of another wildfire. The bare concrete floors and reinforced concrete fireplace inside the structure are designed to survive earthquakes. The combination of aluminum and concrete gives the house an almost industrial look that seems inspired by temporary housing or shipping containers.

Das **VALLEY CENTER HOUSE** liegt 550 m über dem Meeresspiegel, in der Nähe einer Zitronen- und Avocado-Farm, 70 km nordöstlich von San Diego. Es ersetzt ein Wohnhaus, das im November 1996 bei einem Waldbrand zerstört wurde. Das Gebäude ist in Form eines angeschrägten »U« geschnitten und hat eine Wohnfläche von 265 m². Es ist mit großen Blendschirmen aus perforiertem Aluminium ausgestattet, die ausschwenkbar sind, um die Bewohner tagsüber vor der Sonne zu schützen und nachts die notwendige Privatsphäre zu bieten. Darüber hinaus dienen die Blenden als Feuerschutz. Die nackten Betonböden und der Kamin aus Stahlbeton im Hausinneren sind erdbebensicher konstruiert. Während die Kombination von Aluminium und Beton an Industriebauten erinnert, scheint die Form des Gebäudes von Behelfsbauten oder Schiffscontainern inspiriert zu sein.

Située à 70 km au nord-est de San Diego et 550 m d'altitude, en bordure d'une plantation de citronniers et d'avocatiers, le **VALLEY CENTER HOUSE** remplace une précédente résidence détruite par un incendie de forêt en novembre 1996. Ses 265 m² se répartissent selon un plan en U en biais. Elle présente d'importants écrans d'aluminium perforé fixés sur une structure en tube d'aluminium, qui se rabattent pour protéger la maison du soleil ou des regards pendant la nuit. Ils jouent également un rôle de protection en cas d'incendie. Les sols en béton nu sont antisismiques. La combinaison d'aluminium et de béton donne à la maison une allure presque industrielle qui semble inspirée des abris temporaires ou des conteneurs de transport.

The swinging perforated aluminum screens allow the house to be almost completely open to its environment or, on the contrary, completely closed.

Durch die ausschwenkbaren Blendschirme aus perforiertem Aluminium lässt sich das Gebäude entweder zu seiner Umgebung hin öffnen oder von ihr abschirmen.

Des écrans d'aluminium perforé pivotants permettent à la maison de s'ouvrir sur son environnement ou de se refermer totalement sur elle-même.

DILLER + SCOFIDIO

Diller + Scofidio
36 Cooper Square
New York, NY 10003
United States

Tel: +1 212 260 7971
Fax: +1 212 260 7924
e-mail: disco2@flashcom.net

ELIZABETH DILLER is an Associate Professor at Princeton University, and **RICARDO SCOFIDIO** is a Professor of Architecture at The Cooper Union in New York. According to their own description, "**DILLER + SCOFIDIO** is a collaborative, interdisciplinary studio involved in architecture, the visual arts and the performing arts. The team is primarily involved in thematically-driven experimental work that takes the form of architectural commissions, temporary installations and permanent site-specific installations, multimedia theater, electronic media, and print." Their recent work includes Slither, 100 units of social housing in Gifu, Japan (under construction), and Moving Target, a collaborative dance work with Charleroi/Danses, Belgium, as well as The Brasserie in the Seagram Building, New York, published here. Installations by Diller + Scofidio have been seen at the Fondation Cartier in Paris (Master/Slave, 1999), the Museum of Modern Art in New York and the Musée de la Mode in Paris.

ELIZABETH DILLER ist außerordentliche Professorin in Princeton, **RICARDO SCOFIDIO** Professor an der Cooper Union School of Architecture in New York. Ihrer eigenen Beschreibung zufolge ist »**DILLER + SCOFIDIO** ein interdisziplinäres Gemeinschaftsprojekt, das sich mit Architektur, den bildenden und den darstellenden Künsten beschäftigt. Das Team führt hauptsächlich experimentelle Arbeiten durch, die sich auf der Grundlage von Architektur, Installation, Multimediaveranstaltung, elektronischen Medien und Druckgrafik mit bestimmten Themen auseinandersetzen.« Zu ihren jüngsten Projekten gehören Slither, 100 Einheiten des sozialen Wohnungsbaus in Gifu, Japan (im Bau), Moving Target, eine Tanztheaterproduktion in Zusammenarbeit mit der belgischen Tanzgruppe Charleroi/Danses sowie das hier vorgestellte Restaurant The Brasserie im Seagram-Building, New York. Installationen von Diller + Scofidio wurden in der Fondation Cartier in Paris (Master/Slave, 1999), im Museum of Modern Art in New York und im Musée de la Mode in Paris gezeigt.

ELIZABETH DILLER est professeur associé à Princeton, **RICARDO SCOFIDIO** Professeur d'architecture à la Cooper Union, New York. Selon leur présentation: « **DILLER + SCOFIDIO** est une agence interdisciplinaire coopérative qui se consacre à l'architecture, aux arts plastiques et aux arts du spectacle. L'équipe travaille essentiellement sur des recherches thématiques expérimentales qui se concrétisent sous forme de commandes architecturales, d'installations temporaires, d'installations permanentes adaptées au site, théâtre multimédia, médias électroniques et imprimés. » Parmi leurs projets récents : Slither, 100 logements sociaux à Gifu, Japon (en construction) et Moving Target, une œuvre chorégraphique en collaboration avec Charleroi/Danses, Belgique, ainsi que The Brasserie dans le Seagram Building, New York, publiée ici. Les installations de Diller + Scofidio ont été présentées à la Fondation Cartier à Paris (Master/Slave, 1999) au Museum of Modern Art de New York et au Musée de la mode à Paris.

THE BRASSERIE

Seagram Building, New York, NY, USA, 1998-2000

Planning: 1998-2/99. Construction: 3/99-1/2000. Client: Restaurant Associates
Floor area: 650 m². Costs: withheld at owner's request.

THE BRASSERIE is one of the best-known restaurants in New York. Originally designed by Philip Johnson at the same time as the Four Seasons Restaurant, it is located in Mies van der Rohe's Seagram Building. Set in a 650-m² underground space, the Diller + Scofidio project (completed with Charles Renfro and Deane Simpson) started out by "removing all traces of Philip Johnson's interior," that had been severely damaged by fire some time ago. Seating 230 guests, the restaurant is built with sensitivity to the apparent transparency of the Seagram Building, contrasting here with the windowless underground space. Each guest who comes in is videotaped, and his or her image is projected on 15 monitors above the bar. A long glass stairway descends into the middle of the main room, allowing arriving guests to be viewed by the seated patrons. Other features include a 15 m-long lenticular glass wall that partially blurs the vision from most angles. Pear wood is used for some of the ceiling surfaces and the madrone on the floor. Dining room tables are made of poured resin formed around stainless steel structural supports.

THE BRASSERIE in Mies van der Rohes Seagram Building ist eines der bekanntesten Restaurants in New York. Sie wurde wie auch das Four Seasons Restaurant ursprünglich von Philip Johnson gestaltet. Diller + Scofidio begannen ihr Projekt (zusammen mit Charles Renfro und Deane Simpson) für den 650 m² umfassenden Bereich im Untergeschoss damit, »alle Spuren von Philip Johnsons Innenausstattung zu entfernen«, wobei hinzugefügt werden muß, dass das Restaurant vor einiger Zeit durch ein Feuer stark beschädigt worden war. Das für 230 Gäste ausgelegte Restaurant wurde mit viel Gespür für die Transparenz des Seagram Building gestaltet, der die Architekten einen fensterlosen unterirdischen Raum entgegensetzten. Jeder der eintretenden Gäste wird mit einer Videokamera aufgenommen, woraufhin ihr oder sein Bild auf 15 über der Bar hängenden Monitoren erscheint. Eine lange Glastreppe führt in die Mitte des Hauptraums, so werden neuankommende Gäste für die an den Tischen Sitzenden bereits beim Hinabsteigen sichtbar. Zu den weiteren Gestaltungsmitteln gehört eine 15 m lange linsenförmige Glaswand, die für eine teilweise verschwommene Sicht sorgt. Teile der Deckentäfelung sind aus Birnbaum, die Böden aus Madrone. Die Esstische bestehen aus gegossenen Kunstharzplatten, die plastisch um Stützkonstruktionen aus Edelstahl geformt wurden.

THE BRASSERIE est l'un des plus célèbres restaurants new yorkais. Conçu à l'origine par Philip Johnson au même moment que celui des Four Seasons, il est installé dans le Seagram Building de Mies van der Rohe. Le projet de 650 m² en sous-sol de Diller + Scofidio (avec la collaboration de Charles Renfro et de Deane Simpson) a consisté dans un premier temps à « supprimer toute trace des aménagements de Philip Johnson, » d'autant plus qu'un incendie avait ravagé les lieux quelque temps plus tôt. Conçue pour 230 couverts, la salle n'est pas sans rendre hommage à la transparence du Seagram Building, même dans cet espace souterrain sans fenêtre. Chaque client est enregistré en vidéo à son arrivée et son image se retrouve projetée sur 15 moniteurs disposés au-dessus du bar. Un long escalier de verre descend jusqu'au milieu de la salle principale, ce qui permet à chacun de voir les nouveaux arrivants. Le restaurant comporte également un mur de verre lenticulaire de 15 m de long qui brouille partiellement la vision sous la plupart des angles. Certains plafonds sont revêtus de poirier et le sol de madrone. Les tables sont en résine coulée sur une structure en acier inoxydable.

Diller + Scofidio radically transformed one of New York's most famous restaurant interiors, the original Brasserie, designed by Philip Johnson, although the basic below-grade volume was necessarily maintained.

Diller + Scofidio gestalteten den Innenraum des berühmten, von Philip Johnson entworfenen New Yorker Restaurants radikal um. Die Grundform des Untergeschosses blieb jedoch erhalten.

Diller + Scofidio ont radicalement transformé l'un des plus célèbres décors de restaurant de New York, créé à l'origine par Philip Johnson. Ils ont dû néanmoins respecter les proportions de ce grand volume en sous-sol.

BLUR BUILDING

International Expo 2002, Yverdon, Switzerland, 1998-2002

Planning: 1998-2000. Construction: 2000-5/2002. Client: EXPO 02 by Extasia.
Dimensions: 100 x 60 x 12 m (fog structure). Budget: $7 500 000.

The **BLUR BUILDING**, realized in collaboration with the Extasia-Team, is designed to appear like a cloud hovering above Lake Neuchâtel. 100 m wide, 60 m deep, and 12 m thick, it rises up to a height of 25 m above the water. The "cloud" effect will be achieved through the use of filtered lake water "shot as a fine mist through a dense array of high-pressure water nozzles integrated into a large cantilevered tensegrity structure." A ramp will lead into the cloud where visitors will experience a kind of sensory deprivation due to the "white-out" accompanied by "white noise" produced by mist projectors. A "black-out shell" in the center of the structure will be used to project a panoramic image in the round for 250 visitors at a time. Omnimax movies would be used to "twist spatial conventions to challenge geographical continuity and linear time."

Das **BLUR BUILDING**, in Zusammenarbeit mit dem Extasia-Team realisiert, ist so gestaltet, dass es wie eine über dem Neuburger See schwebende Wolke aussieht. Bei einer Länge von 100 m, einer Breite von 60 m und einer Tiefe von 12 m erhebt es sich 25 m über dem Wasserspiegel. Der »Wolken-Effekt« wird durch den Einsatz gefilterten Seewassers erzielt, das »als feiner Nebel aus einer dichten Anordnung von Hochdruck-Wasserdüsen versprüht wird, die in eine große, freitragende Seilnetz-Konstruktion eingebaut sind.« Die Besucher gelangen über eine Rampe in das Innere der Wolke, wo sie aufgrund eines optischen »weißen Nichts«, begleitet vom »weißen Rauschen« der Nebelapparate eine Art sensorischen Entzug erleben. Im Zentrum der Konstruktion befindet sich eine muschelförmige »black-out« Plattform für bis zu 250 Besucher, auf der ein Panoramabild auf eine kreisförmige Leinwand projiziert wird. Dazu werden Omnimax-Filme eingesetzt, die »die räumlichen Sehgewohnheiten verzerren und so die geographische Kontinuität und zeitliche Linearität infragestellen«.

Le **BLUR BUILDING**, un collaboration avec le Extasia-Team, est conçu pour donner l'impression d'un nuage suspendu au-dessus du lac de Neuchâtel. De 100 m de large, 60 de profondeur et 12 d'épaisseur, il s'élèvera jusqu'à 25 m au-dessus du niveau de l'eau. L'effet de nuage sera obtenu « au moyen d'eau du lac filtrée et projetée en brume par un réseau serré de jets haute pression intégrés à une vaste structure suspendue ». Une rampe conduira les visiteurs à l'intérieur du nuage où ils éprouveront une sensation de privation due à un « blanc optique » renforcé par le « bruit blanc » produit par les projecteurs de brume. Une « coquille d'isolement » au centre de la structure servira de salle de projection panoramique circulaire pour 250 visiteurs. Des films Omnimax seront projetés « qui perturberont les conventions spatiales et remettront en jeu la continuité géographique et la linéarité du temps. »

The almost surreal idea of a stationary cloud that is in fact a building challenges all existing notions of facade, volume and relation to the earth in architecture.
Because it is actually intended to be built, this is a fundamentally radical design.

Die fast surreal anmutende Idee eines Gebäudes in Form einer Wolke, die beständig an einem Ort schwebt, stellt sämtliche in der Architektur bestehenden Vorstellungen von Fassade, Rauminhalt und Bezug zum Boden in Frage und ist damit ein von Grund auf radikaler Entwurf.

L'idée presque surréaliste d'un bâtiment en forme de nuage remet en question toutes les notions architecturales de façade, de volume et de relations au sol. Ce projet radical a néanmoins été étudié pour être réalisé.

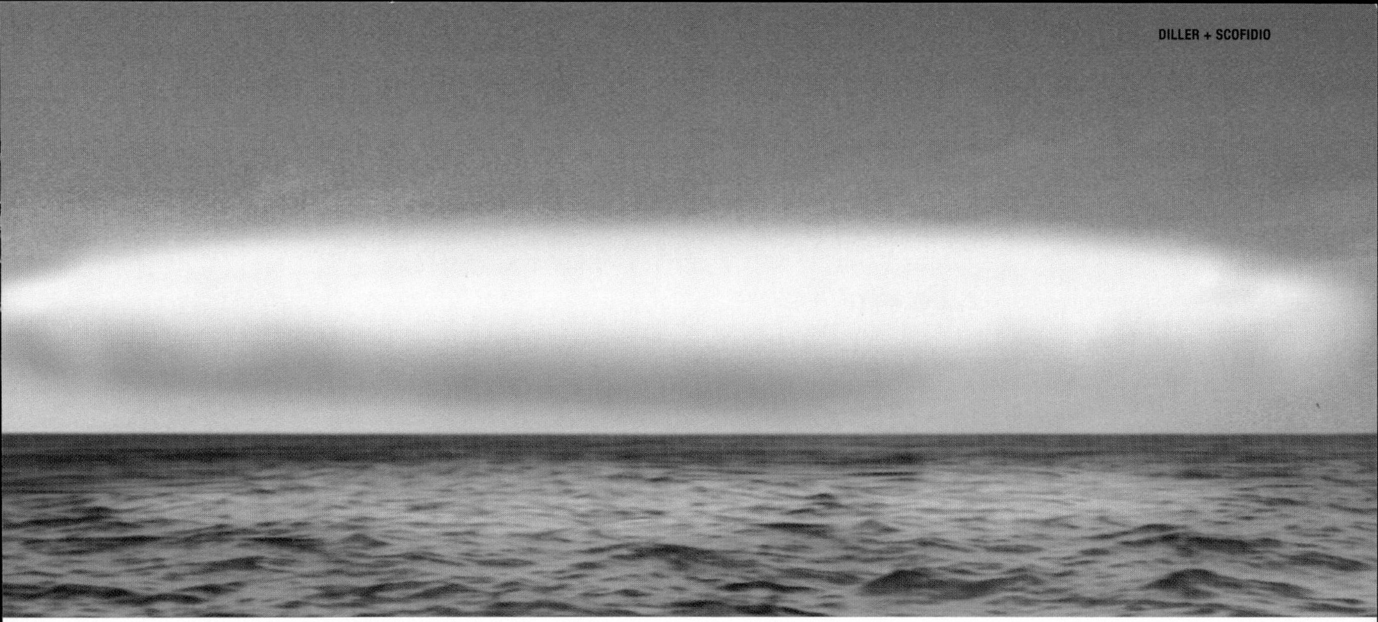

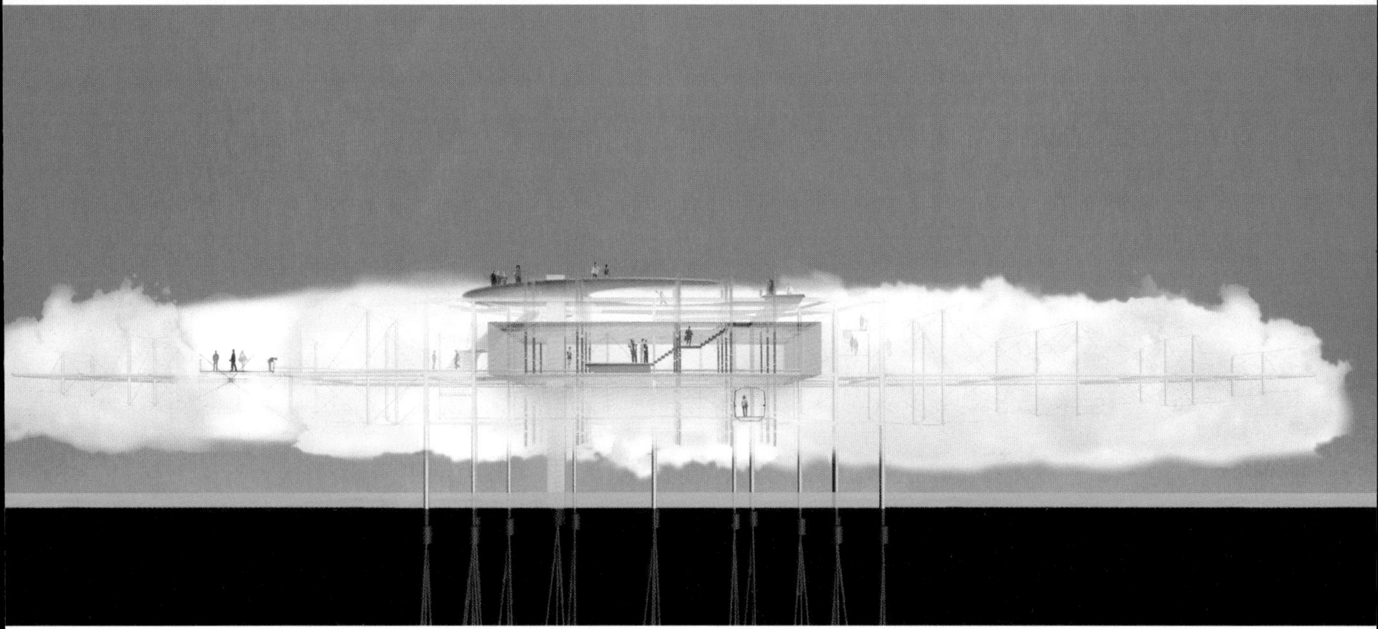

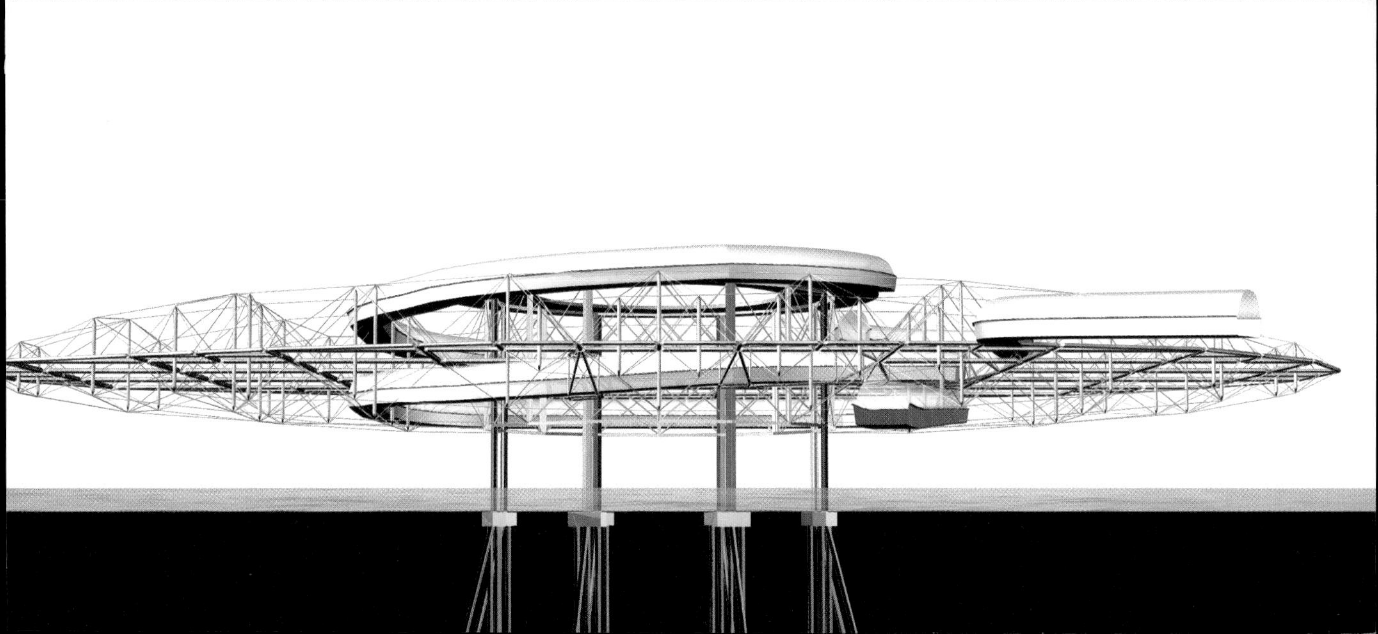

The so-called "Glass Box" within the structure is a space where visitors, surrounded by glass on six sides, will experience a "sense of physical suspension only heightened by an occasional opening in the fog."

Die sogenannte »Glass Box« ist ein sechsseitig verglaster Raum im Gebäudeinneren, in dem die Besucher ein Gefühl des Schwebens verspüren, das sich noch verstärkt, wenn sich der Nebel gelegentlich lichtet.

La « Boîte de verre » à l'intérieur de la structure est un espace dans lesquels les visiteurs, entourés de verre sur six côtés, expérimenteront « le sentiment physique d'être en suspension, renforcé à l'occasion par une percée dans le brouillard. »

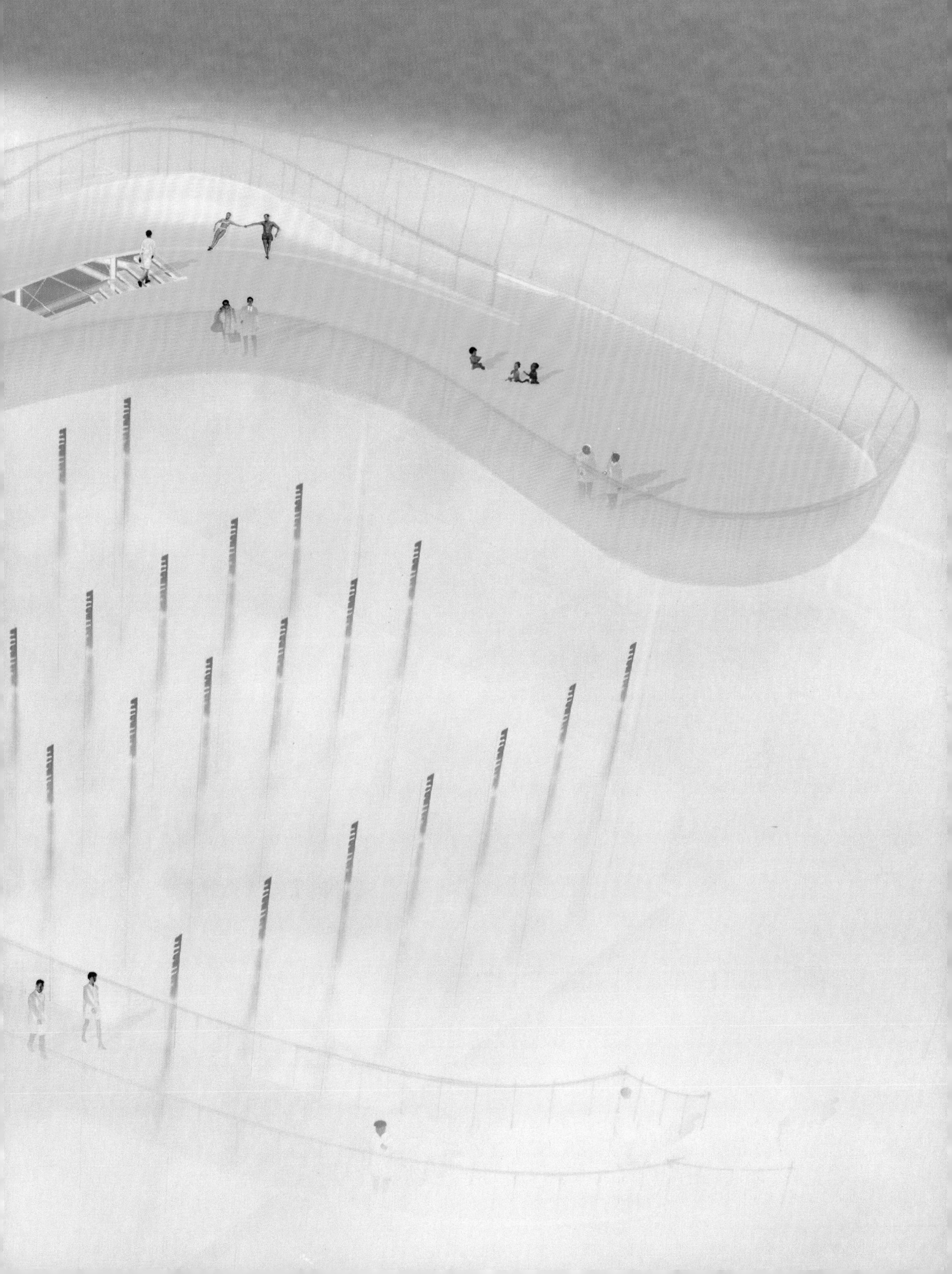

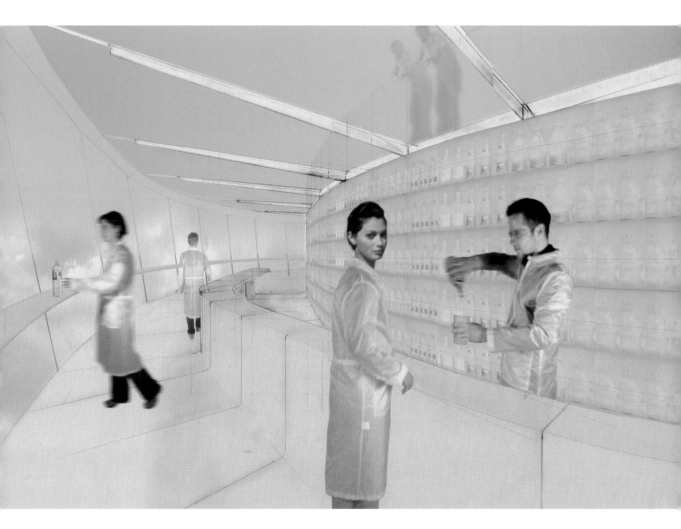

The Angel Bar deck is set above the fog, offering a panoramic view of the landscape and the lake. It serves only mineral water from a variety of international sources.

Die »Angel Bar« liegt auf einer Plattform über dem Nebel und bietet einen Rundblick über die Landschaft und den See. Es wird dort nur Mineralwasser aus vielen verschiedenen Ländern serviert.

La terrasse du Bar des Anges, qui ne propose que des eaux minérales venues du monde entier, se trouve au dessus du brouillard. Elle offre une vue panoramique sur le paysage et le lac.

STEVEN EHRLICH

Steven Ehrlich Architects
10865 Washington Blvd.
Culver City, California 90232
United States

Tel: +1 310 838 9700
Fax: +1 310 838 9737
e-mail: inquire@s-ehrlich.com
web: www.s-ehrlich.com

Canyon Residence ▶

Born in New York in 1946, **STEVEN EHRLICH** received his B.Arch. degree from the Rensselaer Polytechnic Institute in Troy, New York (1969). He studied indigenous vernacular architecture in North and West Africa from 1969 to 1977. He has completed numerous private residences, including the Friedman Residence (1986), the Ehrman-Coombs Residence (1989-1991, Santa Monica), and the Shulman Residence (Brentwood, 1989-1992) all in the Los Angeles area. Other built work includes the Shatto Recreation Center (Los Angeles, 1991); Sony Music Entertainment Campus (Santa Monica, 1993); Child Care Center for Sony, Culver City (1993-95); Game Show Network, Culver City (1995) as well as the Robertson Branch Library (Los Angeles, 1996). More recently, he has worked on the DreamWorks SKG Animation Studios, Glendale, California, 1998; the Orange Coast Collage Art Center, Costa Mesa, 2000; and the Biblioteca Latinoamericana & Washington Youth Center, San Jose, 1999. A recent widely published project was his House Extension (Santa Monica, California, 1996-98) for Richard Neutra's 1938 Lewin House.

STEVEN EHRLICH, 1946 in New York geboren, erwarb 1969 den Bachelor of Architecture am Rensselaer Polytechnic Institute in Troy, New York. Von 1969 bis 1977 studierte er die Architektur der Eingeborenen Nord- und Westafrikas. Ausgeführt hat er zahlreiche Privathäuser, darunter das Haus Friedman (1986), das Haus Ehrmann-Coombs in Santa Monica (1989-91) und das Haus Shulman in Brentwood (1989-92), die alle in der Region Los Angeles liegen. Zu seinen weiteren realisierten Bauten gehören das Shatto Recreation Center in Los Angeles (1991), der Sony Music Entertainment Campus in Santa Monica (1993), das Child Care Center für Sony (1993-95) und das Game Show Network (1995), beide in Culver City, sowie die Robertson Branch Library in Los Angeles (1996). Seine jüngsten Arbeiten sind die Dream-Works SKG Animation Studios in Glendale, Kalifornien (1998), das Orange Coast College Art Center in Costa Mesa (2000) sowie die Biblioteca Latinoamericana und das Washington Youth Center in San Jose (1999). Große Beachtung fand seine Erweiterung von Richard Neutras 1938 erbauten Haus Lewin in Santa Monica, Kalifornien (1996-98).

Né à New York en 1946, **STEVEN EHRLICH** est Bachelor of Architecture du Rensselaer Polytechnic Institute de Troy, New York (1969). Il étudie ensuite l'architecture vernaculaire indigène d'Afrique du Nord et de l'Ouest de 1969 à 1977. Il a construit de nombreuses résidences privées dont la Friedman Residence (1986), la Ehrman-Combs Residence (Santa Monica, 1989-1991) et la Shulman Residence (Brentwood, 1989-1992), toutes trois dans la région de Los Angeles en Californie. Parmi ses autres réalisations : le Shatto Recreation Center (Los Angeles, 1991), le Sony Music Entertainment Campus (Santa Monica, 1993), le Child Care Center Sony (1993-95) et le Game Show Network (1995) à Culver City ainsi que la Robertson Branch Library (Los Angeles, 1996). Plus récemment, il a réalisé les Dreamworks SKG Animation Studios (Glendale, Californie, 1998), le Orange Coast Collage Art Center (Costa Mesa, 2000), ainsi que la Biblioteca Latinoamericana et le Washington Youth Center (San Jose, 1999). Une des ses interventions souvent publiée est l'extension de la Lewin House de Richard Neutra (1938) à Santa Monica, Californie (1996-98).

CANYON RESIDENCE

Los Angeles, California, USA, 1996-98

Planning and construction: 1996-98. Floor area: 687 m².
Client: withheld at owner's request.

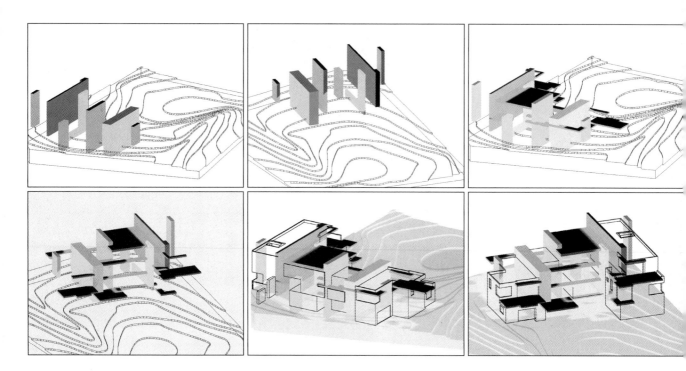

In this 687-m² house, the architect uses a series of vertical masses in stucco to house fireplaces, stairway, service cores and storage. Their counterpoint is a set of horizontal canopies clad in copper. Set on a sloping site, the **CANYON RESIDENCE** steps down the hillside, never exceeding a height of two stories, but permitting a living room height that approaches 6 m. The living room divides the two-story bedroom area from the "family-kitchen zone." Designed around large trees, the house is meant to be closely connected to its natural environment. Architecture critic Joseph Giovannini has likened the composition of this house to that of the De Stijl artists, and more specifically to the lines of Mondrian's "Boogie Woogie" paintings.

Das 687 m² umfassende Wohnhaus ist stufenförmig auf einem Hanggrundstück errichtete. Es geht nicht über eine Höhe von zwei Geschossen hinaus, wobei das Wohnzimmer eine Deckenhöhe von annähernd 6 m hat. Dieser Wohnraum trennt den zweistöckigen Schlafzimmertrakt vom Essbereich und der Küche. Bei der **CANYON RESIDENCE** kontrastiert eine Serie von vertikalen, mit Gips verputzten Baukörpern, die der Unterbringung von Kaminen, Treppenaufgang, Versorgungsschächten und Speicher dienen, mit einer Reihe horizontaler, kupferbeschichteter Schutzdächer. Das Haus wurde bewusst um große Bäume herum angelegt, um eine enge Verbindung mit seiner natürlichen Umgebung herzustellen. Der Architekturkritiker Joseph Giovannini hat die Gestaltung dieses Bauwerks mit der Formensprache der De Stijl-Künstler, insbesondere mit den Linien von Mondrians »Boogie Woogie«-Gemälden verglichen.

Pour cette maison de 687 m², l'architecte a imaginé une succession de masses verticales en stuc qui abritent les cheminées, l'escalier, les locaux techniques et de rangement. Des dais horizontaux revêtus de cuivre viennent en contrepoint. La **CANYON RESIDENCE** descend en escalier la pente de la colline sans jamais dépasser deux niveaux, la hauteur du séjour approchant cependant 6 m. Ce séjour sépare les deux chambres de la zone « famille-cuisine ». Dessinée autour de grands arbres existants, le projet cherche à créer un lien étroit avec son cadre naturel. Le critique d'architecture Joseph Giovannini a comparé sa composition à celles d'artistes du groupe De Stijl et en particulier aux peintures de la série « Boogie-Woogie » de Mondrian.

Right: Calling both on local architectural tradition, such as the houses of Richard Neutra, and on modern painting as inspiration, Steven Ehrlich integrates this design into the lush Southern California vegetation.

Rechts: Steven Ehrlich integriert seinen sowohl von lokaler Architekturtradition – wie den Häusern von Richard Neutra – als auch von modernen Gemälden inspirierten Entwurf in die üppige Vegetation Südkaliforniens.

A droite : S'appuyant à la fois sur les traditions architecturales locales, comme les maisons de Richard Neutra, et sur la peinture moderne, Steven Ehrlich a cherché à intégrer son projet dans la luxuriante végétation de Californie du Sud.

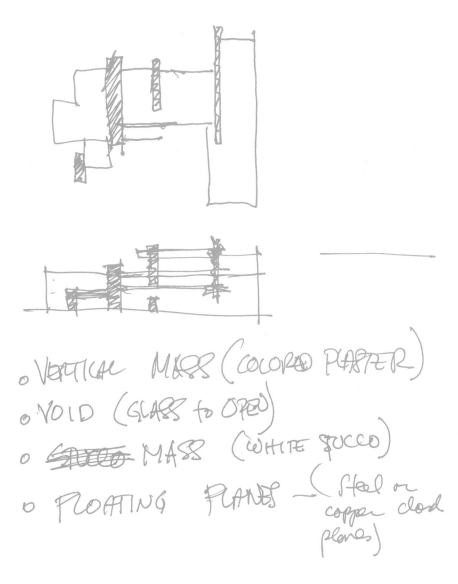

Benerron   1/26/97

o VERTICAL MASS (COLORED PLASTER)
o VOID (GLASS to OPEN)
o ~~STUCCO~~ MASS (WHITE STUCCO)
o FLOATING PLANES — (steel or copper clad planes)

The architect's own reference to voids and floating planes (above) in the drawing above becomes apparent in the interior views of the house, where openings and perspectives penetrate the volumes, particularly in the generous space of the living room (above left).

Die vom Architekten skizzierten Hohlräume und freischwebenden Flächen (oben) sind im Inneren des Hauses, besonders im großzügig bemessenen Wohnraum, in Form von Öffnungen und Ausblicken, die den Baukörper durchdringen, umgesetzt (oben links).

Les vides et les plans flottants esquissés par l'architecte (dessins ci-dessus) se retrouvent dans les vues intérieures de la maison, où des ouvertures et des perspectives pénètrent les volumes, en particulier dans le généreux espace du séjour (en haut à gauche).

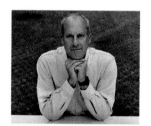

NORMAN FOSTER

Foster and Partners
Riverside Three
22 Hester Road
London SW11 4AN
England

Tel: +44 20 7738 0455
Fax: +44 20 7738 1107/08
e-mail: enquiries@fosterandpartners.com
Web: www.fosterandpartners.com

Born in Manchester in 1935, **NORMAN FOSTER** studied architecture and city planning at Manchester University (1961). Awarded the Henry Fellowship to Yale University, he received the M.Arch. degree, and met Richard Rogers, with whom he created Team 4. He received the Royal Gold Medal for Architecture (1983) and the American Institute of Architects Gold Medal for Architecture (1994). He was knighted in 1990 and made a life peer in 1999. Norman Foster has built the IBM Pilot Head Office (Cosham, 1970-71), Sainsbury Centre for Visual Arts and Crescent Wing, University of East Anglia (Norwich, 1976-77; 1989-91), Hong Kong and Shanghai Banking Corporation Headquarters (Hong Kong, 1981-86), London's third airport, Stansted (1987-91), the Faculty of Law of Cambridge University (1993-95), and the Commerzbank Headquarters (Frankfurt, Germany, 1994-97). Recent projects include the Hong Kong International Airport (1995-98), the new Reichstag (Berlin, 1993-99), and the British Museum Redevelopment (London, 1997-2000).

NORMAN FOSTER, geboren 1935 in Manchester, studierte bis 1961 Architektur und Stadtplanung an der Manchester University. Er wurde mit dem Henry Fellowship der Yale University ausgezeichnet und schloss dort seine Studien mit dem Master of Architecture ab. In Yale lernte er Richard Rogers kennen, mit dem er Team 4 gründete. 1983 wurde Foster mit der Royal Gold Medal for Architecture ausgezeichnet und 1990 geadelt. 1994 wurde ihm die Gold Medal for Architecture des American Institute of Architects verliehen, 1999 wurde er zum Lord ernannt. Zu seinen Bauten gehören das IBM Pilot Head Office in Cosham (1970-71), das Sainsbury Centre for Visual Arts und der Crescent Wing der University of East Anglia in Norwich (1976-77; 1989-91), der Sitz der Hong Kong and Shanghai Bank in Hongkong (1981-86), Londons dritter Flughafen, Stansted (1987-91), die Juristische Fakultät der University of Cambridge (1993-95) und die Commerzbank-Zentrale in Frankfurt am Main (1994-97). Zu seinen jüngsten Projekten gehören der Internationale Flughafen Hongkong (1995-98), der Umbau des Reichstags in Berlin zum neuen Sitz des Deutschen Bundestags (1993-99) und die Modernisierung des British Museum in London (1997-2000).

Né à Manchester en 1935, **NORMAN FOSTER** étudie l'architecture et l'urbanisme à la Manchester University (1961). Titulaire d'un Henry Fellowship de la Yale University, il passe son Master of Architecture à Yale (1963), où il rencontre Richard Rogers avec lequel il crée Team 4. Il est titulaire de la Royal Gold Medal for Architecture (1983) et de l'American Institute of Architects Gold Medal for Architecture (1994). Fait chevalier en 1990, Norman Foster est nommé pair à vie en 1999. Parmi ses réalisations : le siège pilote d'IBM (Cosham, Grande-Bretagne, 1970-71), le Sainsbury Centre for Visual Arts et la Crescent Wing de l'Université d'East Anglia (Norwich, Grande-Bretagne, 1976-77, 1989-91), la tour de la Hong Kong and Shanghai Bank (Hongkong, 1981-86), le terminal de l'aéroport de Stansted, Grande-Bretagne (1987-91), la faculté de droit de Cambridge (1993-95), le siège de la Commerzbank (Francfort, Allemagne, 1994-97), l'aéroport international de Hongkong (1995-98), le Reichstag (Berlin, 1993-99) et la rénovation du British Museum (Londres 1997-2000).

GREATER LONDON AUTHORITY

London, England, 1999-2002

Planning: 2/99-2/2000. Construction: 3/1999-2002 (scheduled).
Client: CIT Group. Floor area: ca. 17 187 m². Budget: £65 000 000.

Located on the Thames near the Tower Bridge, directly opposite the Tower of London, these new 10-story headquarters for the **GREATER LONDON AUTHORITY** will provide about 17 000 m² of available floor space and be built at a cost of approximately £65 million. An office for the Mayor of London and the Cabinet will be located on the eighth floor of the "flask-like form." An exhibition or function room on the ninth floor has been dubbed "London's Living Room" and can accommodate about 200 people. The unusual spherical shape of the building "has been generated as a result of thorough scientific analysis, aiming to reduce both solar gain and heat loss via the building's skin, thus reducing the building's energy needs." More specifically, energy consumption is to be reduced to 25% of a typical air-conditioned office building.

Der Entwurf dieses am Themse-Ufer, nahe der Tower Bridge und direkt gegenüber dem Tower of London gelegenen neuen Sitzes der **GREATER LONDON AUTHO-RITY** sieht eine Gesamtnutzfläche von ca. 17 000 m² auf zehn Geschossen vor und ist mit ca. 65 Millionen Pfund veranschlagt. In der achten Etage des »glaskolbenförmigen« Gebäudes wird ein Büro für den Bürgermeister von London und sein Kabinett eingerichtet. Ein Ausstellungs- oder Empfangssaal im neunten Stock, der den Namen »Londons Wohnzimmer« erhalten hat, kann etwa 200 Personen fassen. Die ungewöhnliche, kugelförmige Gestalt des Gebäudes »beruht auf gründlichen wissenschaftlichen Untersuchungen, die zum Ziel hatten, den Verlust an Sonnenenergie und Wärme durch die Außenhaut des Gebäudes und damit den Energiebedarf zu minimieren«. Dadurch wird der Energieverbrauch auf 25% eines typischen Bürogebäudes mit Klimaanlage gesenkt.

Situé au bord de la Tamise, près de Tower Bridge, juste en face de la Tour de Londres sur l'autre rive, le nouveau siège de la **GREATER LONDON AUTHORITY** offrira environ 17 000 m² de surface brute sur 10 niveaux pour un coût estimé à £65 millions. Le bureau du Maire de Londres et son cabinet seront installés au huitième niveau de cet immeuble « en forme de bocal ». Une salle d'exposition ou de réception au neuvième niveau a déjà été surnommée le « London Living Room », et pourra recevoir 200 personnes. La forme sphérique inhabituelle de l'immeuble vient d'une analyse scientifique visant à réduire l'effet du soleil et la déperdition de chaleur et donc de diminuer les besoins énergétiques du bâtiment au moyen de son enveloppe. La consommation d'énergie devrait être de 25% inférieure à celle d'un immeuble climatisé classique.

As in many of his recent designs, Norman Foster is most attentive to problems of solar gain and heat flow, doing the utmost to give the building a large degree of energy self-sufficiency.

Wie in vielen seiner neueren Entwürfe hat sich Norman Foster auch hier besonders mit der Nutzung von Sonnenenergie und Wärmestrom auseinandergesetzt, um den Energieverbrauch des Gebäudes möglichst gering zu halten.

Comme dans beaucoup de ses projets récents, Foster, particulièrement attentif aux problèmes de l'exposition solaire et des flux de chaleur, s'est efforcé d'assurer au projet un degré élevé d'autonomie énergétique.

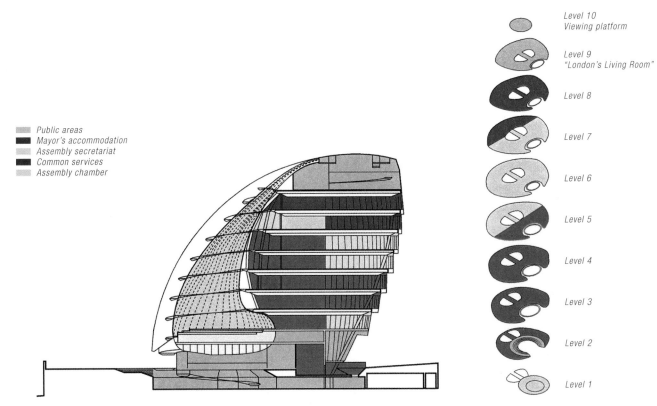

Level 10
Viewing platform

Level 9
"London's Living Room"

Level 8

Level 7

Level 6

Level 5

Level 4

Level 3

Level 2

Level 1

Public areas
Mayor's accommodation
Assembly secretariat
Common services
Assembly chamber

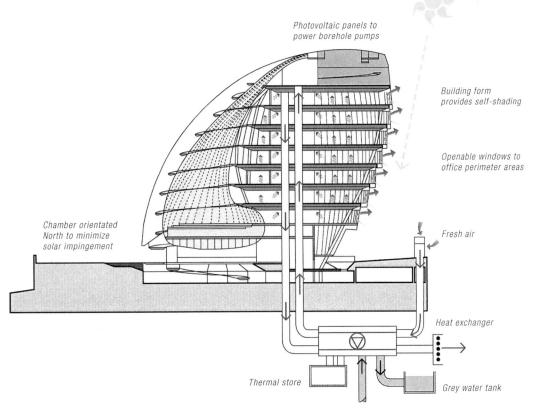

Photovoltaic panels to
power borehole pumps

Building form
provides self-shading

Openable windows to
office perimeter areas

Chamber orientated
North to minimize
solar impingement

Fresh air

Heat exchanger

Thermal store

Grey water tank

Borehole cooling

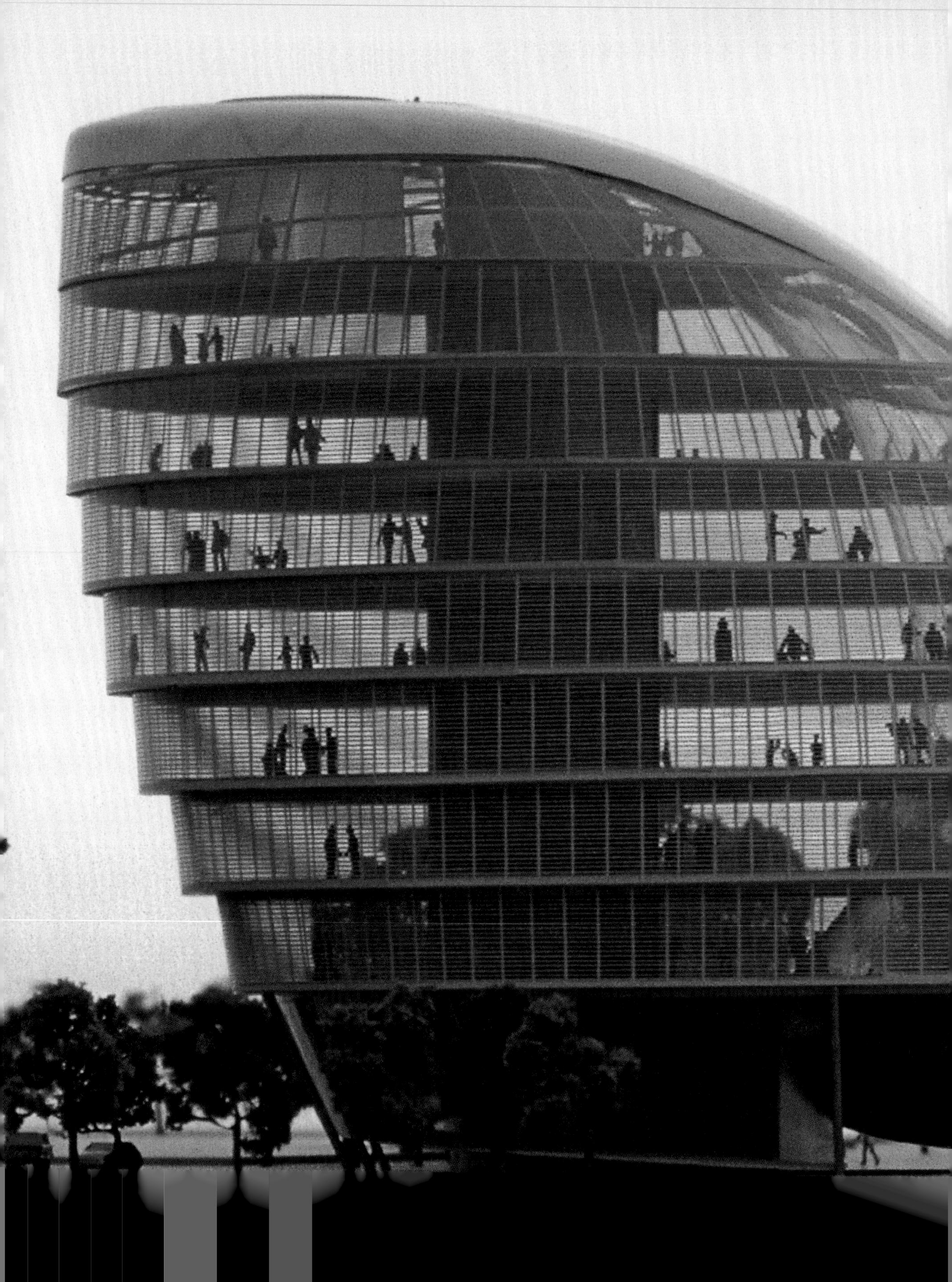

Calling on CAD-design to work out the complex curves in this structure, the architect has placed an emphasis on the building's transparency.

Die komplexen Windungen des Gebäudes sind mit CAD-Programmen ausgearbeitet. Foster hat viel Betonung auf die Transparenz des Gebäudes gelegt.

Utilisant la CAO pour mettre au point les courbes complexes de la structure, l'architecte a mis l'accent sur la transparence.

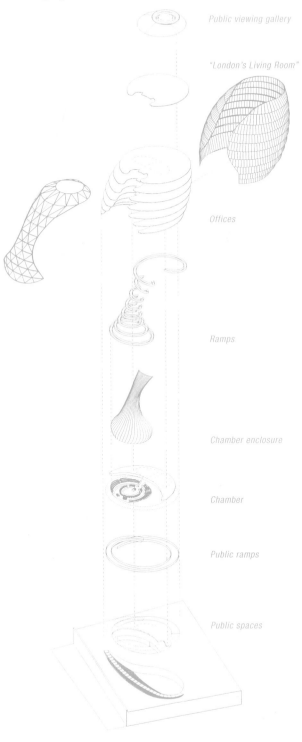

Public viewing gallery

"London's Living Room"

Offices

Ramps

Chamber enclosure

Chamber

Public ramps

Public spaces

MASSIMILIANO FUKSAS

Massimiliano Fuksas Architetto
Piazza del Monte di Pietà, 30
0186 Rome
Italy

Tel: +39 06 6880 7871
Fax: +39 06 6880 7872
e-mail: fuksas@interbusiness.it
Web: www.art.dada.it/fuksas/home.htm

Born in Rome in 1944, **MASSIMILIANO FUKSAS** received his degree from the Faculty of Architecture, La Sapienza University, Rome in 1969. He established the architectural office "Granma" with Anna Maria Sacconi (1969-88). Having completed a large number of projects in Italy, Fuksas became known in both Italy and France in the late 1980s with projects such as his Cemetery extension in Orvieto (1984-91), Town Hall (1985-90) and Library (1990) of Cassino, both in Italy, and the Médiathèque (Rézé, 1991) and the École nationale d'Ingénieurs ENIB (Brest, 1990-92), both in France. More recently, he completed the restruction of a city block on the Rue Candie in Paris (1987-96) with Enzo Cucchi. Recent work includes the Lycée Maximilien Perret (Alfortville, France, 1994-97), the Place des Nations in Geneva, a tower in Vienna, 150 m high, and the Europark Spar in Salzburg, published here. Massimiliano Fuksas was the Director of the 2000 Architecture Biennial in Venice.

MASSIMILIANO FUKSAS, 1944 in Rom geboren, schloss 1969 sein Architekturstudium an der Universität La Sapienza in seiner Heimatstadt ab und gründete im selben Jahr zusammen mit Anna Maria Sacconi das Architekturbüro »Granma«, in dem er bis 1988 tätig war. Nachdem er zahlreiche Bauwerke in Italien ausgeführt hatte, wurde er in den späten 80er-Jahren über die Landesgrenzen hinaus bekannt mit Projekten wie der Friedhofserweiterung in Orvieto (1984-91), dem Rathaus (1985-90) und der Bibliothek (1990) von Cassino, alle in Italien, sowie der in Frankreich gebauten Médiathèque in Rézé (1991) und der École nationale d'Ingenieurs (ENIB) in Brest (1990-92). Zu Fuksas' jüngeren Arbeiten gehören der Umbau eines Häuserblocks in der Rue Candie in Paris (1987-96), das Lycée Maximilien Perret im französischen Alfortville (1994-97), die Place des Nations in Genf, ein 150 m hoher Turm in Wien und der hier vorgestellte Europark Spar in Salzburg. 2000 war Massimiliano Fuksas Direktor der Biennale in Venedig.

Né dans la capitale italienne en 1944, **MASSIMILIANO FUKSAS** est diplômé de la Faculté d'architecture de Rome, La Sapienza (1669). Il fonde aussitôt l'agence d'architecture Granma avec Anna Maria Sacconi (1969-88). Après avoir réalisé un grand nombre de projets en Italie, il se fait aussi connaître hors des frontières et surtout en France à la fin des années 80 par des projets comme l'extension du cimetière d'Orvieto (1994-91), l'hôtel de ville (1985-90) et la bibliothèque de Cassino (1990), la médiathèque de Rézé (France,1991), et l'Ecole nationale d'Ingénieurs de Brest (ENIB, 1990-92). Plus récemment, il a achevé la restructuration d'un ensemble urbain, rue Candie, à Paris (1987-96), le Lycée Maximilien Perret (Alfortville, France, 1994-97), la Place des Nations à Genève, une tour de 150 m de haute à Vienne et le grand centre commercial Europark Spar à Salzbourg. En 2000, il a été le directeur de la Biennale de Venise.

EUROPARK SPAR

Salzburg, Austria, 1994-97

*Planning: 3/94-2/95. Construction: 3/95-9/97. Client: Spar Warenhandels AG, Salzburg.
Site area: 65 000m²; retail area: 28 000m². Costs: DM 120 000 000.*

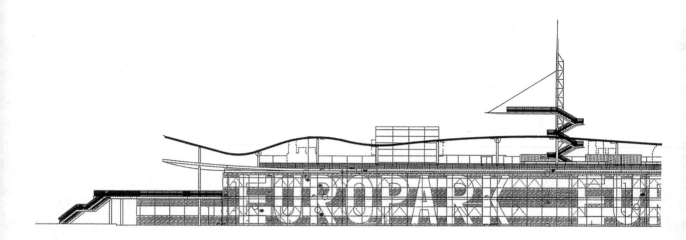

Intended as a commercial center, **EUROPARK SPAR** covers an area 320 m long and 140 m wide. It comprises three food halls and about 30 additional shops. Parking facilities for 600 cars on the roof and 1 200 cars under ground cover about 60 000 m² of space defined by two metal grid waves. Full-length external glass walls with large-scale serigraphy reflected in a "moat" define the most visible facade areas. As the architect puts it, "In this project I worked in sections proceeding from the inside to the outside. The use of voids placed lengthwise or crosswise provides a variety of spatial sequences," and brings daylight into the complex.

Der als Einkaufszentrum konzipierte **EUROPARK SPAR** hat eine Fläche von 320 x 140 m und verfügt über drei Markthallen und ca. 30 Geschäfte. Parkdecks für 600 Fahrzeuge auf dem Dach und 1 200 Fahrzeuge im Untergeschoss (insgesamt ca. 60 000 m²) sind durch zwei wellenförmige Metallgitter markiert. Die sichtbaren Teile der Außenfassade sind in voller Länge mit Glaswänden verkleidet. Diese sind mit großformatigen Siebdrucken dekoriert, welche sich in einem das Gebäude umgebenden »Wassergraben« spiegeln. Der Architekt erläutert: »Bei diesem Projekt habe ich etappenweise von Innen nach Außen gearbeitet. Die längs oder quer angeordneten Aussparungen schaffen eine abwechslungsreiche räumliche Strukturierung und lassen Tageslicht in den Komplex einfallen.«

Ce centre commercial **EUROPARK SPAR** couvre une surface de 320 m de long par 140 de large. Il comprend trois halls pour les produits alimentaires et environ 30 boutiques. Les parkings – 600 voitures sur le toit et 1 200 en sous-sol – occupent une surface d'envisou 60 000 m², définie par deux vagues en grillage métallique. Les murs extérieurs en verre qui courent sur toute la longueur sont ornés de grands motifs sérigraphiés qui se reflètent dans une « douve ». Comme le précise l'architecte : « J'ai travaillé à ce projet par étapes en procédant de l'intérieur vers l'extérieur. L'utilisation des vides disposés longitudinalement ou en transversales offre toute une variété de séquences spatiales » et permet de laisser entrer la lumière du jour.

In designing the Europark Spar, Fuksas has accepted the challenge of achieving interesting architectural results with the forcibly limited budget of a mass-market commercial space, making use, as these images testify, of lighting and large-scale graphics to draw attention to the complex (right).

Mit dem Europark Spar ist es Fuksas gelungen, trotz des begrenzten Budgets für dieses Einkaufszentrums architektonisch interessante Resultate zu erzielen. Die Verwendung von Licht und großformatigen grafischen Elementen als Gestaltungsmittel lenken die Aufmerksamkeit auf das Gebäude (rechts).

En concevant l'Europark Spar, Fuksas a accepté le défi de faire tenir une proposition architecturale originale dans le budget limité alloue à un espace commercial grand public. Il crée des effets d'éclairage et de grandes compositions graphiques pour attirer l'attention (à droite).

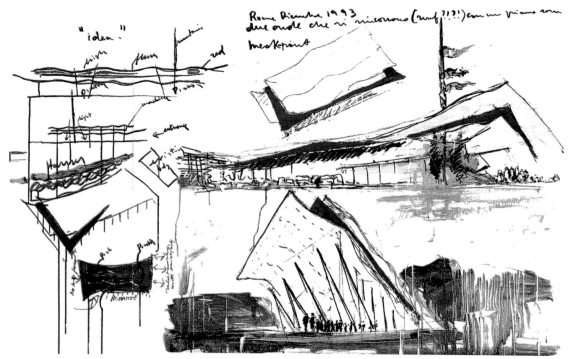

Below left: Massimiliano Fuksas makes frequent use of small models and drawings to work out his architectural ideas before actually putting them into the form of concrete designs.

Unten links: Massimiliano Fuksas arbeitet seine Ideen häufig in kleinen Modellen und Zeichnungen aus, bevor er sie in konkrete Entwürfe umsetzt.

En bas à gauche : Massimiliano Fuksas se sert souvent de petites maquettes et dessins pour mettre au point ses idées architecturales avant de passer à des dessins précis.

GAROFALO, LYNN, MCINTURF

Garofalo Architects
3752 North Ashland Avenue, Chicago, Illinois 60613, United States
Tel: +1 773 975 2069, Fax: +1 773 975 3005, e-mail: garofalo@a-node.net

Greg Lynn FORM
1813-1817 Lincoln Boulevard, Venice, California 90291, United States
Tel: +1 310 821 2629, Fax: +1 310 821 9729, e-mail: node@glform.com, web: www.glform.com

Michael McInturf Architects
1136 St. Gregory Street, Suite #110, Cincinnati, Ohio 45202, United States
Tel: +1 513 639 2351, Fax: +1 513 639 2353, e-mail: go@mcinturf.com, web: www.mcinturf.com

The New York Presbyterian Church was a collaboration between **GAROFALO ARCHITECTS** in Chicago, **GREG LYNN FORM** in Los Angeles and **MICHAEL MCINTURF ARCHITECTS** in Cincinnati. Douglas Garofalo received his B.Arch. from the University of Notre Dame School of Architecture (1981) and his M.Arch. degree from Yale University, Graduate School of Architecture (1987). He is president of Garofalo Architects, created in 1992, and Associate Professor of Architecture of the University of Illinois at Chicago. Greg Lynn was born in 1964. He received his Bachelor of Philosophy and Bachelor of Environmental Design from Miami University of Ohio, Oxford, Ohio (1986), and his M.Arch. from Princeton University (1988). He created his present firm Greg Lynn FORM in 1994. Michael McInturf received his Bachelor of Environmental Design from Miami University of Ohio, Oxford (1985), and his M. Arch. from the University of Illinois, Chicago (1988). He presently is an Assistant Professor of Architecture at the College of Design, Architecture, Art, and Planning of the University of Cincinnati. He created his own firm, Michael McInturf Architects in 1995.

Die hier vorgestellte Koreanische Presbyterial-Kirche in New York entstand in Zusammenarbeit von **GAROFALO ARCHITECTS** in Chicago, **GREG LYNN FORM** in Los Angeles und **MICHAEL MCINTURF ARCHITECTS** in Cincinnati. Douglas Garofalo schloss 1981 sein Architekturstudium an der Universität von Notre Dame mit dem Bachelor of Architecture ab und erwarb 1987 seinen Master of Architecture an der Graduate School of Architecture der Yale University. Er ist Präsident von Garofalo Architects in Chicago, 1992 gegründet, und Professor an der Architekturfakultät der University of Illinois, Chicago. Greg Lynn wurde 1964 geboren. Er erwarb 1986 seinen Bachelor of Philosophy und seinen Bachelor of Environmental Design an der Miami University of Ohio in Oxford und 1988 seinen Master of Architecture an der Princeton University. Derzeit ist er in seinem 1994 gegründeten Büro Greg Lynn FORM tätig. Michael McInturf erwarb 1985 seinen Bachelor of Environmental Design an der Miami University of Ohio, Oxford und 1988 seinen Master of Architecture an der University of Illinois, Chicago. Gegenwärtig ist er als außerordentlicher Professor für Architektur am College of Design, Architecture, Art and Planning der University of Cincinnati tätig. 1995 gründete er seine eigene Firma, Michael McInturf Architects.

La New York Presbyterian Church est le fruit d'une collaboration entre **GAROFALO ARCHITECTS**, Chicago, **GREG LYNN FORM**, Los Angeles et **MICHAEL MCINTURF ARCHITECTS**, Cincinnati. Douglas Garofalo obtient son Bachelor of Architecture de l'Ecole d'architecture de l'Université de Notre Dame (1981) et son Master of Architecture de la Graduate School of Architectur de la Yale University (1987). Il est président de Garofalo Architects à Chicago, crée en 1992. Greg Lynn est né en 1964. Il est Bachelor of Philosophy et Bachelor of Environmental Design de la Miami University of Ohio, Oxford (1986) et Master of Architecture de Princeton University (1988). Il a ouvert son agence, Greg LynnFORM, en 1994. Michael McInturf obtient son Bachelor of Environmental Design de Miami University of Ohio, Oxford (1985) et son Master of Architecture de l'University of Illinois, Chicago (1988). Il est actuellement Professeur assistant d'architecture au College of Design, Architecture, Art and Planning, University of Cincinnati. Il a ouvert sa propre agence en 1995.

THE KOREAN PRESBYTERIAN CHURCH OF NEW YORK

Long Island City, NY, USA, 1995-99

Planning: 6/95-9/97. Construction: 9/97-9/99. Client: The Korean Presbyterian Church of New York.
Floor area: 11 198 m². Costs: $11 000 000

Designed for the **KOREAN PRESBYTERIAN CHURCH OF NEW YORK** in Sunnyside, Queens, the building is the result of a collaboration between three firms: Garofalo Architects in Chicago, Greg Lynn FORM in Los Angeles and Michael McInturf Architects in Cincinnati. Shared digital technologies and web connections allowed these three small firms to exchange CAD files, images of models and other project information. The church is in fact a re-purposed Laundromat with an addition, integrating the existing building and a new space. The church's functions are housed within the original factory building while a series of new elements "both engage and absorb the host structure." In the newly added sanctuary, the church provides services for 2 500 people. Within the same structure, multiple programs can take place simultaneously in 80 classrooms used by schools and social groups. The complex also includes a 600-seat wedding chapel, assembly spaces, a choir rehearsal area, a cafeteria, a library and a daycare center.

Die Kirche für die **KOREANISCHE PRESBYTERIAL-GEMEINDE VON NEW YORK** in Sunnyside, Queens, ist das Ergebnis einer Zusammenarbeit von drei Architektenbüros: Garofalo Architects in Chicago, Greg Lynn FORM in Los Angeles und Michael McInturf Architects in Cincinnati. Mittels digitaler Technologien und Netzverbindungen konnten die drei kleineren Firmen CAD-Files, Bilder von Baumodellen und andere Projektinformationen austauschen. Das Gebäude war ehemals eine Großwäscherei mit einem Anbau, der heute den alten mit dem neuen Teil verbindet. Die Kirchenräume sind im ursprünglichen Bau untergebracht, während eine Reihe neuer Bauteile die Grundstruktur sowohl mit einbezieht als auch in sich aufnimmt. Die Kirche bietet Platz für 2 500 Menschen. Im selben Gebäude wurden 80 Unterrichtsräume geschaffen, die von Schulen und Vereinen genutzt werden. Der Komplex enthält außerdem eine Hochzeitskapelle mit 600 Sitzen, Versammlungsräume, einen Proberaum für den Chor, ein Café, eine Bücherei und ein Tagesheim.

Conçue pour **L'ÉGLISE PRESBYTÉRIENNE CORÉENNE DE NEW YORK** à Sunnyside, Queens, cette construction est issue de la collaboration de trois agences : Garofalo Architects de Chicago, Greg Lynn FORM de Los Angeles et Michael McInturf Architectes de Cincinnati. Ces trois petites agences communiquent par Internet et se transmettent des fichiers CAO, images de maquettes et toutes sortes d'informations nécessaires. L'église, qui intègre un bâtiment ancien et une extension nouvelle, est en fait la reconversion d'une laverie. Les fonctions spécifiquement religieuses trouvent place dans le bâtiment industriel d'origine tandis qu'une série de composants nouveaux « dialogent avec la structure tout en l'absorbant. » L'extension consacrée aux divers services paroissiaux accueille jusqu'à 2 500 personnes. De multiplies activités peuvent se tenir simultanément dans 80 salles de classe utilisées par des écoles et des associations. Le complexe comprend également une chapelle de mariages de 600 places, des salles de réunion, un salle de répétition de chorale, une cafétéria, une bibliothèque et un dispensaire.

The building's most spectacular exterior feature is its accordion-like succession of apertures that give, together with the undulating roof, an impression of movement.

Das auffallendste äußere Merkmal des Gebäudes ist ein Reihe akkordeonartig ineinander greifender Blenden, die im Zusammenspiel mit dem wellenförmigen Dach den Eindruck von Bewegung vermitteln.

La caractéristique extérieure la plus spectaculaire de ce projet est une succession d'ouvertures en accordéon qui, combinées avec l'ondulation du toit, génèrent une impression de mouvement.

Above: A view from the parking lot emphasizes the presence of a large-scale cross on the exterior of the church. Right: Within the church itself, the ribbed roof and pew patterns echo the successive external apertures.

Oben: Auf der zum Parkplatz gelegenen Seite betont ein großformatiges Kreuz die Außenwand der Kirche. Rechts: Im Kirchenraum finden die gestaffelten Blenden der Außenfassade ihr Echo in der gerippten Decke und der Anordnung der Bankreihen.

Ci-dessus : A l'extérieur, une énorme croix domine le parking. A droite : A l'intérieur, le toit nervuré et le dessin des bancs font écho aux ouvertures sur l'extérieur.

FRANK O.GEHRY

Frank O. Gehry & Associates, Inc.
1520-B Cloverfield Boulevard
Santa Monica, California 90404
United States

Tel.: +1 310 828 6088
Fax: +1 310 828 2098

Experience Music Project

Born in Toronto, Canada in 1929, **FRANK O. GEHRY** studied at the University of Southern California, Los Angeles (1949-51), and at Harvard (1956-57). Principal of Frank O. Gehry and Associates, Los Angeles, since 1962, he received the 1989 Pritzker Prize. Among his notable projects are the Loyola Law School, Los Angeles, California (1981-84); the Norton Residence, Venice, California (1983); the California Aerospace Museum, Los Angeles, California (1982-84); the Schnabel Residence, Los Angeles, California (1989); the Festival Disney, Marne-la-Vallée, France (1989-92); the University of Toledo Art Building, Toledo, Ohio (1990-92); the American Center, Paris, France (1993); the Disney Concert Hall, Los Angeles, California (construction temporarily halted); the Nationale-Nederlanden Building, Prague, Czech Republic (1994-96); the Guggenheim Bilbao, Spain (1993-97); Pariser Platz 3, Berlin, Germany (1994-2001) and the Experience Music Project, Seattle, Washington (1996-2000). Gehry is recognized as one of the most creative and influential architects of the latter part of the 20th century.

FRANK O. GEHRY, geboren 1929 in Toronto, studierte von 1949 bis 1951 an der University of Southern California (USC) in Los Angeles und von 1956 bis 1957 in Harvard. Seit 1962 ist er Leiter von Frank O. Gehry and Associates in Los Angeles und erhielt 1989 den Pritzker Prize. Zu seinen bekanntesten Bauten gehören die Loyola Law School in Los Angeles (1981-84), das Haus Norton in Venice (1983), das California Aerospace Museum (1982-84) und das Haus Schnabel in Los Angeles (1989), das Festival Disney im französischen Marne-la-Vallée (1989-92), das University of Toledo Art Building in Toledo, Ohio (1990-92), das Amerikahaus in Paris (1993), die Disney Concert Hall, Los Angeles (die Bauarbeiten wurden vorübergehend eingestellt), das Nationale Nederlanden-Gebäude in Prag (1994-96), das Guggenheim Bilbao, Spanien (1993-97), das Gebäude Pariser Platz 3 in Berlin (1994-2001) und das hier vorgestellte Experience Music Project in Seattle, Washington (1996-2000). Gehry ist anerkanntermaßen einer der kreativsten und einflussreichsten Architekten des ausgehenden 20. Jahrhunderts.

Né à Toronto (Canada) en 1929, **FRANK O. GEHRY** étudie à l'University of Southern California, Los Angeles (1949-51) et à Harvard (1956-57). A la tête de Frank O. Gehry and Associates, Los Angeles, depuis 1962, il se voit attribuer le Prix Pritzker en 1989. Parmi ses projets les plus remarqués : la Loyola Law School, Los Angeles, Californie (1981-84) ; la Norton Residence, Venice, Californie (1983) ; le California Aerospace Museum, Los Angeles, Californie (1982-84) ; la Schnabel Residence, Los Angeles (1989) ; Festival Disney, Marne-la-Vallée, France (1989-92) ; l'Art Building, University of Toledo, Ohio (1990-92) ; l'American Center, Paris, France (1993) ; le Disney Concert Hall, Los Angeles (construction provisoirement interrompue) ; l'immeuble Nationale Nederlanden, Prague, République Tchèque (1994-96) ; le Guggenheim Bilbao, Espagne (1993-97) ; Pariser Platz 3, Berlin, Allemagne (1994-2000) et l'Experience Music Project, Seattle, Washington (1996-2000). Il est considéré comme l'un des architectes les plus créatifs et les plus influents de la dernière partie du XXe siècle.

EXPERIENCE MUSIC PROJECT

Seattle, Washington, USA, 1995-2000

Planning: 1995-97. Construction: 1997-2000. Client: Experience Music Project.
Floor area: 13 006 m². Costs: $240 000 000.

One of the most surprising and ambitious of Frank O. Gehry's recent buildings, the 13 000 m² **EXPERIENCE MUSIC PROJECT** was financed largely by Microsoft co-founder Paul Allen. Built at a cost of $240 million, it became a constructive response to I. M. Pei's Rock and Roll Hall of Fame in Cleveland, Ohio (1995), although it was originally intended to house only Allen's collection of Jimi Hendrix memorabilia. Clad in aluminum and stainless steel panels, an unusual feature of the building is the use of color not typical of Gehry's work. The choice of colors is inspired by rock and roll or guitar themes: blue for the Fender, gold for Les Paul and purple for Jimi Hendrix (inspired by his song Purple Haze). Gehry adds that the red passages are a tribute to the faded old trucks rock and roll stars used to drive. One source of inspiration for the forms was the idea of a shattered 1960s Fender Stratocaster guitar, but for the most part the project consists of abstract, sculptural volumes similar to those used in the Guggenheim Bilbao. In both projects, Gehry uses computer-assisted design on a large scale, feeding images of guitars into the imaging software and morphing them almost beyond recognition. Each of the building's 21 000 panels has a unique shape and size, and is cut and bent to fit its specific location. Gehry insists on the conviviality of the design, saying "With its folds, the building is intended to be huggable, like a mother cradling a baby in her arms against the folds of her garment."

Eines der erstaunlichsten und anspruchsvollsten unter Frank O. Gehrys jüngsten Bauwerken ist das 13 000 m² umfassende **EXPERIENCE MUSIC PROJECT,** das hauptsächlich von Microsoft-Mitbegründer Paul Allen finanziert wurde. Obwohl das Gebäude ursprüglich nur Allens Sammlung von Jimi Hendrix-Memorabilien beherbergen sollte, beliefen sich die Gesamtbaukosten schließlich auf 240 Millionen Dollar; es wurde zu einer architektonischen Replik der 1995 von I. M. Pei erbauten Rock and Roll Hall of Fame in Cleveland, Ohio. Ein besonderes Merkmal dieses mit Aluminium- und Edelstahltafeln verkleideten Gebäudes ist die Verwendung von Farben, die eher untypisch für Gehrys Arbeiten ist. Die Farbwahl wurde von Themen aus dem Bereich Rock and Roll und Gitarrenmusik inspiriert: Blau steht für die Fender-Gitarre, Gold für Les Paul und Purpur für Jimi Hendrix (angeregt durch sein Lied Purple Haze). Gehry fügt hinzu, dass die rotgestrichenen Gänge ein Tribut an die alten, abgewetzten Trucks sind, in denen die Rock and Roll Stars früher gerne herumfuhren. Die Form wurde von einer zertrümmerten Fender Stratocaster E-Gitarre aus den 60er-Jahren inspiriert. Zum größten Teil setzt sich das Gebäude jedoch aus abstrakten, plastisch geformten Baukörpern zusammen, ähnlich denen, die Gehry für das Guggenheim Bilbao verwendet hat. Wie dort hat Gehry auch bei diesem Projekt mit einer CAD-Software gearbeitet. Für den Entwurf des Experience Music Project hat er Bilder von E-Gitarren in das Programm eingespeist und diese anschließend fast bis zur Unkenntlichkeit umgestaltet. Jede der 21 000 Tafeln, mit denen das Gebäude verkleidet ist, wurde individuell gefertigt und hat eine ihrem jeweiligen Platz entsprechende Form und Größe. Gehry betont die heitere Ausstrahlung des Designs und sagt: »Mit seinen Falten soll der Bau zum Umarmen einladen und an eine Mutter denken lassen, die ihr Baby auf dem Arm hält und es schützend in den Falten ihrer Kleidung birgt.«

Ce **EXPERIENCE MUSIC PROJECT** de 13 000 m² est l'une des plus surprenantes et ambitieuses réalisations récentes de Frank O. Gehry. Il a été en grande partie financé par le cofondateur de Microsoft, Paul Allen. Pour un coût de $240 millions, il est une réponse au Rock and Roll Hall of Fame de I. M. Pei à Cleveland (Ohio, 1995). A l'origine il devait simplement abriter la collection de souvenirs de Jimi Hendrix réunis par Allen. Habillé de panneaux d'aluminium et d'acier inoxydable, il se distingue par une utilisation de la couleur peu fréquente dans l'œuvre de Gehry. Le choix chromatique a été inspiré par des thèmes de guitare ou de Rock'n roll : bleu pour Fender, or pour Les Paul et pourpre pour Jimi Hendrix (inspiré de sa chanson, Purple Haze). Gehry ajoute que les passages en rouge sont un hommage aux vieux camions rouge délevé que les stars du rock avaient l'habitude de conduire. Une des sources formelles est une vieille guitare Fender Stratocaster des années 1960, mais pour l'essentiel, le projet se compose de volumes abstraits et sculpturaux similaires à ceux du Guggenheim Bilbao. Ici, Gehry a en abondamment secours à la CAO, alimentant les logiciels d'images de guitares soumises à un traitement de morphing à la limite de la reconnaissance. Le bâtiment est recouvert de 21 000 panneaux de taille et de forme différentes, chacun ayant été découpé et façonné en fonction de sou emplacement. Gehry insiste sur la convivialité de ce projet : « Avec ses plis et ses replis, le bâtiments est plein de tendresse, comme une mère berçant un bébé dans ses bras contre les plis de son vêtement. »

Although its extravagant, sculptural forms are not unfamiliar to those who know his work, Gehry's Experience Music Project makes use on a large scale of strong colors.

Während die extravaganten skulpturalen Formen des Experience Music Project den Kennern von Gehrys Arbeiten durchaus vertraut sind, setzt er hier zusätzlich eine ungewöhnlich breite Palette kräftiger Farben ein.

Si les formes sculpturales et extravagantes de l'Experience Music Project n'étonnent plus chez Gehry, le recours aux couleurs fortes à grande échelle surprend.

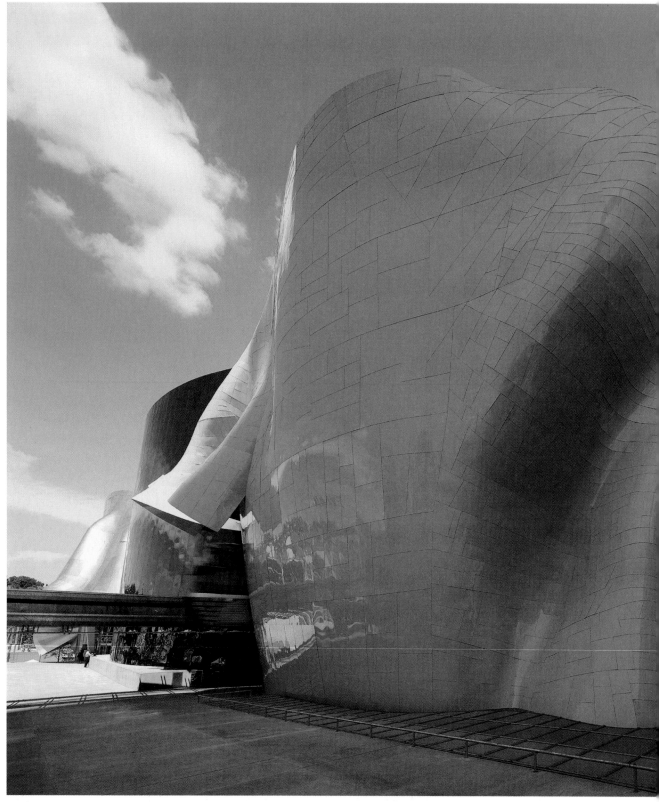

Though obviously not contradictory with the ebb and flow of rock and roll, Gehry's architecture again underlines his position as a sculptural master, redefining architecture at a level that brings it closer to art.

Gehry unterstreicht mit diesem Bauwerk, das den Rhythmus des Rock and Roll formal umsetzt, abermals seine Position als Meister der bildhauerischen Gestaltung. Damit rückt er die Architektur an die Grenze zur Kunst.

Dans l'esprit du rock and roll, l'intervention de Gehry met une fois encore en valeur sa maîtrise de la sculpture et des formes qui élève son architecture à un niveau proche de la création artistique.

Here, as in the Guggenheim Bilbao, the surprising architectural forms of the exterior of the building are an integral part of the conception of the interior.

Ebenso wie in Gehrys Guggenheim Bilbao sind auch hier die ungewöhnlichen äußeren Bauformen ein Teil der Innenraumgestaltung.

Ici, comme pour le Guggenheim Bilbao, les suprenantes formes architecturales extérieures se retrouvent dans les volumes intérieurs.

The powerful sculptural volumes of Frank Gehry take on a life of their own in the interior, just like the music they are intended to celebrate.

Die kraftvollen skulpturalen Baukörper, die das Innere des Gebäudes beherrschen, entwickeln ein Eigen- leben, so wie die Musik, die sie versinnbildlichen sollen.

Les puissants volumes plastiques de Frank Gehry possèdent une vie intérieure propre, de même que la musique qu'ils célèbrent.

CONDÉ NAST CAFETERIA

New York, NY, USA, 1998-2000

Planning: 1996-1998. Construction: 1998-2000. Client: Condé Nast Publications.
Floor area: 1003 m². Costs: withheld at owner's request.

Not open to the general public, the Condé Nast Cafeteria may recall the rough inventiveness of Frank Gehry's early work in some choices of materials, but on the whole, the design is closer to his more sophisticated recent work.

Einige Materialien des der Öffentlichkeit nicht zugänglichen Condé Nast Cafes erinnern an den Einfallsreichtum Gehrys früherer Arbeiten. Die Gestaltung jedoch steht seinen eleganten neueren Arbeiten näher.

Etablissement privé, la cafétéria Condé Nast peut rappeler l'inventivité débridée de Gehry par certains choix de matériaux, mais, dans l'ensemble, son projet est plus proche de la sophistication de ses œuvres récentes.

The 260-seat **CONDÉ NAST CAFETERIA** is located in the Condé Nast Building in Times Square. Gehry's style is apparent in the thick curving glass walls and other features, like the plywood tabletops that bring to mind his early work in and around Los Angeles. The ash-veneer floor and the blue titanium ceiling conspire, creating the atmosphere of a trendy nightclub, an allusion that the architect clearly rejects. "It's made to be cafeteria-like," he says, "it's warm and fuzzy." Frank Gehry has come a long way since he designed Rebecca's Restaurant in Venice, California (1982-85). There, spontaneity, exposed concrete, brick, ceramic tile, and a stuffed alligator on the ceiling were his trademarks. Here, a very high degree of sophistication was required and achieved. Though one might argue that a continent and more separates the beaches of Venice from Times Square, the spontaneity of Gehry's work is vibrantly alive and expresses itself in different forms today than it did 20 years ago. Artistic assemblages of ordinary materials have been replaced by computer-driven curves of the most worldly kind.

Das mit Sitzplätzen für 260 Gäste ausgestattete **CONDÉ NAST CAFÉ** befindet sich im Condé Nast Building am Times Square. Der für Gehry typische Stil zeigt sich hier in den geschwungenen Glaswänden und anderen Elementen wie den Tischplatten aus Furnierholz, die an seine frühen kalifornischen Arbeiten erinnern. Das Zusammenwirken von Fußböden aus Eschenfurnier und der Decke in blauem Titan erzeugt die Atmosphäre eines trendigen Nachtclubs, ein Eindruck, den der Architekt jedoch entschieden zurückweist: »Es soll wie eine Cafeteria wirken, warm und locker.« Frank Gehry hat einen weiten Weg zurückgelegt, seit er Anfang der 80er-Jahre Rebecca's Restaurant im kalifornischen Venice gestaltete. Dort waren Sichtbeton, Backstein, Keramikfliesen und ein von der Decke hängender ausgestopfter Alligator seine Markenzeichen. Hier dagegen wurde ein hohes Maß an Raffinesse verlangt und erzielt. Obwohl sich einwenden ließe, dass ein ganzer Kontinent und mehr zwischen dem Strand von Venice und dem Times Square liegt, ist die für Gehry so charakteristische Spontanität immer noch sprühend lebendig und spürbar, drückt sich hier nur in anderen Formen aus als vor 20 Jahren. So wurde die künstlerische Zusammenstellung alltäglicher Materialien durch computergenerierte Bogenlinien ersetzt.

La **CONDÉ NAST CAFÉTÉRIA** de 260 places est située dans l'immeuble de Condé Nast sur Times Square. Le style de Gehry transparaît dans les épais murs de verre incurvé et d'autres détails comme les tables en contre-plaqué qui rappellent ses premiers travaux à Los Angeles et dans les environs. Le sol en hêtre verni et le plafond de titane bleu conspirent pour créer une atmosphère de night-club à la mode, allusion que l'architecte rejette. « Tout ceci est pensé pour être une vraie cafétéria, c'est chaleureux et plein d'énergie. » Frank Gehry a beaucoup évolué depuis le projet du Rebecca's restaurant de Venice, Californie (1982-85) où il avait imposé son style au moyen de béton brut, de briques, de carrelage et d'un grand alligator empaillé suspendu au plafond. A New York, il atteint un degré élevé de sophistication. Bien qu'un continent, et même davantage, sépare les plages de Venice de Times Square, la vibrante spontanéité stylistique de Gehry s'exprime aujourd'hui dans des formes différentes d'il y a 20 ans. Les assemblages artistiques de matériaux ordinaires ont été remplacés par d'élégantes courbes générées par ordinateur.

A relatively calm furniture pattern contrasts with the undulating walls and ceiling. When the room is full however, the animation on the floor gives another, less static image.

Die eher strenge Möblierung steht in Kontrast zu den geschwungenen Formen von Wänden und Decke. Sobald der Raum belebt wird, verliert er seine Starrheit.

Le plan d'implantation du mobilier relativement sage contraste avec les ondulations des murs et des plafonds. La salle remplie donne une impression moins statique.

GIGON/GUYER

Annette Gigon/ Mike Guyer Architekten
Carmenstrasse 28
8032 Zurich
Switzerland

Tel: +41 1 257 1111
Fax: +41 1 257 1110
e-mail: info@gigon-guyer.ch
Web: www.gigon-guyer.ch

Born in 1959 in Herisau, Switzerland, **ANNETTE GIGON** received her diploma from the ETH in Zurich in 1984. She worked in the office of Herzog & de Meuron in Basle (1985-88) before setting up her own practice (1987) and creating her present firm with **MIKE GUYER** in 1989. Born in 1958 in Columbus, Ohio, Mike Guyer also graduated from the ETH in 1984. He worked with Rem Koolhaas (OMA, 1984-87) and taught with Hans Kollhoff at the ETH (1987-88). Gigon/Guyer's built work includes the Kirchner Museum (Davos, 1990-92); the Vinikus Restaurant (Davos, 1990-92); a renovation of the Oskar Reinhart Collection am Römerholz (Winterthur, 1997-98), all in Switzerland. They have participated in numerous international competitions: for the Nelson-Atkins Museum extension (Kansas City, Missouri, 1999), or the Santiago de Compostela "City of Culture" project (1999). Current work includes the extension of the Aviation/Space Museum (Lucerne, Switzerland, 2000-03). The office currently employs 18 architects.

ANNETTE GIGON, geboren 1959 im schweizerischen Herisau, erwarb 1984 ihr Diplom an der Eidgenössischen Technischen Hochschule (ETH) in Zürich. Von 1985 bis 1988 arbeitete sie im Büro von Herzog & de Meuron in Basel, bevor sie 1987 ein eigenes Büro und 1989 zusammen mit **MIKE GUYER** ihre jetzige Firma gründete. Auch der 1958 in Columbus, Ohio, geborene Mike Guyer schloss 1984 sein Studium an der ETH ab. Von 1984 bis 1987 arbeitete er im Office for Metropolitan Architecture (OMA) von Rem Koolhaas und lehrte von 1987 bis 1988 zusammen mit Hans Kollhoff an der ETH Zürich. Zu den Schweizer Bauprojekten von Gigon/Guyer gehören das Kirchner-Museum in Davos (1990-92), das Restaurant Vinikus in Davos (1990-92) und die Renovierung der Sammlung Oskar Reinhart am Römerholz in Winterthur (1997-98). Darüber hinaus nahmen sie an zahlreichen internationalen Wettbewerben teil, wie dem für die Erweiterung des Nelson-Atkins Museum in Kansas City, Missouri (1999) oder dem für das »City of Culture«-Projekt in Santiago de Compostela (1999). Derzeit arbeiten sie und ihre 18 Angestellten unter anderem an einem Erweiterungsbau des Museums für Flugwesen und Raumfahrt in Luzern, der 2003 fertiggestellt werden soll.

Né en 1959 à Herisau, Suisse, **ANNETTE GIGON** est diplômée de l'ETH de Zurich (1984). Elle a travaillé dans l'agence d'Herzog & de Meuron à Bâle (1985-88) avant de créer sa propre structure (1987) et de s'associer à **MIKE GUYER** en 1989. Né en 1958 à Columbus, Ohio, celui-ci est également diplômé de l'ETH (1984). Il a travaillé auprès de Rem Koolhaas (OMA) (1984-87), et enseigné avec Hans Kollhoff à l'ETH (1987-88). Parmi leurs réalisations, toutes en Suisse : le Kirchner Museum (Davos, 1990-92) ; le restaurant Vinikus (Davos, 1990-92) ; la rénovation de la Collection Oskar Reinhart am Römerholz (Winterthur, 1997-98). Ils ont participé à de nombreux concours internationaux comme celui de l'extension du Nelson-Atkins Museum (Kansas City, Missouri, 1999), et du projet de « Cité de la culture » de Saint-Jacques de Compostelle (1999). Ils travaillent actuellement sur un projet de musée de l'aviation et de l'espace pour Lucerne (2000-03). Leur agence emploie aujourd'hui 18 architectes.

MUSEUM LINER

Appenzell, Switzerland, 1996-98

Planning: 6/96-6/97. Construction: 7/97-8/98. Client: Stiftung Carl Liner Vater und Sohn, Appenzell
Floor area: 1 600 m². Exhibition area: 650 m². Costs: SF 6 200 000.

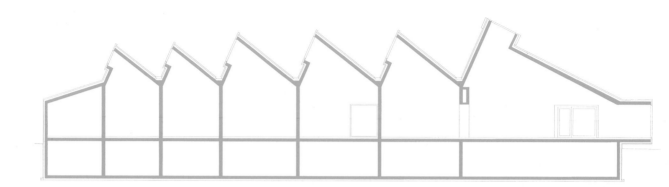

The **MUSEUM LINER** is intended to display the work of two local artists, Carl August Liner and his son Carl Walter Liner. The display areas create a rather sober impression with poured concrete floors and natural overhead lighting, supplemented when necessary by fluorescent tube lighting. There are ten rooms varying in size, forming a total exhibition area of 650 m². The structure also includes a lobby, cloakroom, lounge, screening room, two offices and storage space. Exterior cladding of the roof and walls is in sandblasted chrome steel. The sawtooth roof facilitates natural lighting, but it also echoes local industrial architecture and the surrounding mountainous countryside. Construction cost was 6.2 million Swiss francs excluding the land.

Das **MUSEUM LINER** wurde neben Wechselausstellungen für die Präsentation der Werke der beiden einheimischen Künstler Carl August Liner und seines Sohns Carl Walter Liner konzipiert. Die Ausstellungsräume mit ihren Böden aus Gussbeton und den Oberlichtern, deren natürliche Belichtung bei Bedarf durch fluoreszierende Leuchtstoffröhren ergänzt werden kann, erzeugen eine eher sachliche Atmosphäre. Zehn Räume von unterschiedlicher Größe ergeben zusammen eine Ausstellungsfläche von 650 m². Das Haus enthält außerdem ein Foyer, eine Garderobe, einen Raum für Filmvorführungen, zwei Büros und einen Lagerraum. Dach und Außenwände sind mit sandgestrahltem Chromstahl verkleidet. Das Sheddach sorgt nicht nur für eine natürliche Belichtung, sondern greift darüber hinaus die Formensprache der lokalen Industriearchitektur sowie der umliegenden Berglandschaft auf. Die Baukosten ohne Grundstück beliefen sich auf 6,2 Millionen Schweizer Franken.

Le **MUSEUM LINER** est consacré à l'œuvre de deux artistes locaux, Carl August Liner et son fils, Carl Walter Liner. Les espaces d'exposition aux sols de béton coulé éclairés par des verrières zénithales complétées en cas de necessité par un éclairage fluorescent, donnent une impression de grande sobriété. Les dix salles offrent une surface totale de 650 m². Le bâtiment comprend par ailleurs un hall d'accueil, un vestiaire, un salon, une salle de projection, deux bureaux et un espace de stockage. Le revêtement extérieur du toit et des murs est en acier chromé sablé. Le toit en dents de scie facilite l'éclairage naturel et rappelle certaines architectures industrielles locales ainsi que l'environnement montagneux. L'ensemble a coûté 6,2 millions de SF, terrain non compris.

In line with a good deal of recent Swiss architecture, Gigon/Guyer adopt the simplest possible approach to the design of the museum, eliminating all superfluous elements.

In Anlehnung an zahlreiche Beispiele der neueren schweizerischen Architektur entschieden sich Gigon/Guyer für eine möglichst schlichte und formal reduzierte Gestaltung des Museums.

Dans l'esprit d'une tendance de l'architecture suisse récente, Gigon/Guyer ont adopté l'approche la plus simple possible et éliminé tous les éléments superflus.

The sandblasted chrome steel panels on the exterior facades are set in an irregular, overlapping pattern, giving a more organic "scaly" impression than might be expected at first. Window openings at ground level are few, but powerful in their brutal simplicity.

Die sandgestrahlten Chromstahl-platten der Außenfassaden sind über-lappend in einem unregelmäßigen Muster angeordnet, wodurch der Bau eine unerwartet organische, schup-penartige Gestalt erhält. Die wenigen, durch ihre breiten Rahmungen beton-ten Fensteröffnungen im Erdgeschoss durchbrechen die Fassaden auf fast brutale Art.

Les panneaux en acier chromé et sablé des façades extérieures se chevauchent pour créer un effet « d'écaille » organique et inattendu. Les ouvertures au niveau du sol sont rares, mais très présentes par leur simplicité brutaliste.

ZAHA HADID

Zaha M Hadid Ltd.
Studio 9
10 Bowling Green Lane
London EC1R 0BQ
England

Tel: +44 20 7253 5147
Fax: +44 20 7251 8322
e-mail: zaha@hadid.u-net.com

Landscape Formation One

ZAHA HADID, born in Baghdad in 1950, studied architecture at the Architectural Association (AA) in London, beginning in 1972, and was awarded the Diploma Prize in 1977. She then became a partner of Rem Koolhaas in the Office for Metropolitan Architecture, and taught at the AA, at Harvard, the University of Chicago, in Hamburg and at Columbia University in New York. Well-known for her paintings and drawings she has had a substantial influence, despite having built relatively few buildings. She has completed the Vitra Fire Station (Weil am Rhein, Germany, 1990-94) and exhibition designs such as that for "The Great Utopia," Solomon R. Guggenheim Museum, New York (1992). Significant competition entries include her design for the Cardiff Bay Opera House (Wales, 1994-96), the Habitable Bridge (London, 1996), and the Luxembourg Philharmonic Hall (1997).

ZAHA HADID, 1950 in Bagdad geboren, studierte ab 1972 an der Architectural Association (AA) in London und erhielt 1977 den Diploma Prize. Danach wurde sie Partnerin von Rem Koolhaas im Office for Metropolitan Architecture (OMA) und lehrte an der AA und in Harvard, der University of Chicago, in Hamburg und an der Columbia University in New York. Hadid ist durch ihre Gemälde und Zeichnungen bekannt geworden. Obwohl nur wenige ihrer Entwürfe realisiert wurden, so das Vitra-Feuerwehrhaus in Weil am Rhein (1990-94), hat sie großen Einfluß ausgeübt. 1992 entwarf sie das Ausstellungsdesign für »The Great Utopia« im New Yorker Guggenheim Museum. Zu ihren bedeutendsten Wettbewerbsbeiträgen gehören Entwürfe für das Cardiff Bay Opera House in Wales (1994-96), für die Habitable Bridge in London (1996) und die Luxemburger Philharmonie (1997).

Née en 1950 à Bagdad, **ZAHA HADID** a étudié l'architecture à l'Architectural Association (AA) de Londres de 1972 à 1977, date à laquelle elle obtient le Prix du diplôme. Elle est ensuite associée dans l'agence de Rem Koolhaas, Office for Metropolitan Architecture, et enseigne à l'AA, Harvard, University of Chicago, Columbia University, New York, et à l'Université de Hambourg. Elle est connue pour ses peintures et ses dessins. Bien que n'ayant pas beaucoup construit, elle exerce une réelle influence. Parmi ses réalisations : le poste d'incendie de Vitra (Weil-am-Rhein, Allemagne, 1990-94) et des projets d'expositions comme « La Grande utopie », Solomon R. Guggenheim Museum, New York, 1992. Elle a participé à des concours dont les plus importants sont le projet de la Cardiff Bay Opera House (Pays-de-Galles, 1994-96), le Pont habitable (Londres, 1996) et la Salle de concerts philharmoniques de Luxembourg (1997).

LANDSCAPE FORMATION ONE

Weil am Rhein, Germany, 1996-99

Planning: 12/96-12/97. Construction: 1/98-1/99. Floor area: 845 m². Costs: DM 3 200 000
Client: Landesgartenschau Weil am Rhein 1999 GmbH by order of the city Weil am Rhein.

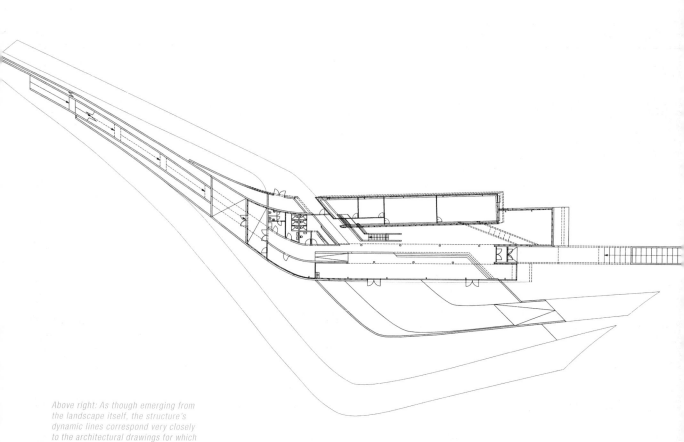

Above right: As though emerging from the landscape itself, the structure's dynamic lines correspond very closely to the architectural drawings for which Zaha Hadid has become famous.

Oben rechts: Mit seinen dynamischen Umrisslinien wirkt der Bau, als sei er aus der Landschaft selbst hervorgegangen und erinnert damit stark an die Architekturzeichnungen, für die Zaha Hadid berühmt wurde.

En haut à droite : Semblant émerger du sol, les lignes dynamiques de la construction sont très proches des dessins architecturaux qui ont fait la célébrité de Zaha Hadid.

Built for the 1999 horticulture show hosted by Weil am Rhein, **LANDSCAPE FORMATION ONE** (in colaboration with Schumacher, mayer bährle) was conceived as a series of paths that integrate themselves directly into the surrounding gardens. Located in close proximity to the Vitra factories, which were built by such renowned architects as Frank O. Gehry, Tadao Ando, Álvaro Siza and Zaha Hadid, the 845-m² building includes a restaurant, offices and an exhibition space. Constructed of three distinct concrete strands, the building is inserted with remarkable sensitivity into its site so as to maximize its temperature stability both in winter and in summer. With its terraces and walkways, the building is not such an alien presence as its complex design might have implied, and as Zaha Hadid's reputation might have led some to expect. Rather it blends gently into the landscape and fulfills its assigned role admirably well.

LANDSCAPE FORMATION ONE wurde (in Zusammenarbeit mit Schumacher, mayer bährle) für die 1999 in Weil am Rhein eröffnete Landesgartenschau als eine Serie von Wegen und Räumen entworfen, die sich unmittelbar in die umgebende Gartenanlage eingliedern. In der Nähe der Vitra Fabrikgebäude gelegen, die von Architekten wie Frank O. Gehry, Tadao Ando, Álvaro Siza und Zaha Hadid gestaltet wurden, beherbergt der 845 m² große Komplex ein Restaurant, Büroräume und einen Ausstellungsraum. Er wurde aus drei scharf konturierten Betonelementen konstruiert und so sensibel in seine Umgebung eingepasst, dass sowohl im Winter wie auch im Sommer eine optimale Temperaturstabilität gewahrt bleibt. Mit seinen Terrassen und Gehwegen wirkt der Bau keineswegs so fremdartig, wie man es aufgrund des komplexen Entwurfs und bei Zaha Hadids Ruf für extreme Architektur vielleicht hätte erwarten können. Vielmehr fügt es sich sanft in die umgebende Landschaft ein und erfüllt damit seine Funktion auf bewundernswert gelungene Weise.

Édifiée pour une exposition sur le jardin qui s'est tenue à Weil-am-Rhein en 1999, **LANDSCAPE FORMATION ONE** (en collaboration avec Schumacher, mayer bährle) consiste en une série de cheminements qui viennent s'intégrer aux jardins voisins. Situé non loin du complexe Vitra, édifié par des architectes comme Frank O. Gehry, Tadao Ando, Álvaro Siza et Zaha Hadid, le bâtiment de 845 m² comprend un restaurant, des bureaux et un espace d'exposition. Construit en trois parties distinctes, il s'inscrit de manière remarquablement sensible dans son site au point de réguler la stabilité de sa température en été comme en hiver. Avec ses terrasses et ses allées, il ne semble pas aussi étrange que sa conception complexe pourrait le laisser supposer compté tenu de la réputation de Zaha Hadid. Il se fond délicatement dans le paysage et rempli admirablement le rôle qui lui a été assigné.

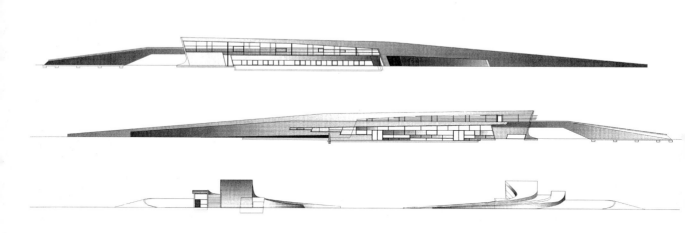

Characterized by an extended horizontality, the structure gives an even stronger impression of movement at night than during the day.

Der durch seine strenge Horizontalität gekennzeichnete Komplex wirkt bei Nacht noch dynamischer als bei Tag.

Caractérisé par son horizontalité dilatée, le bâtiment donne une impression de mouvement encore plus forte la nuit que le jour.

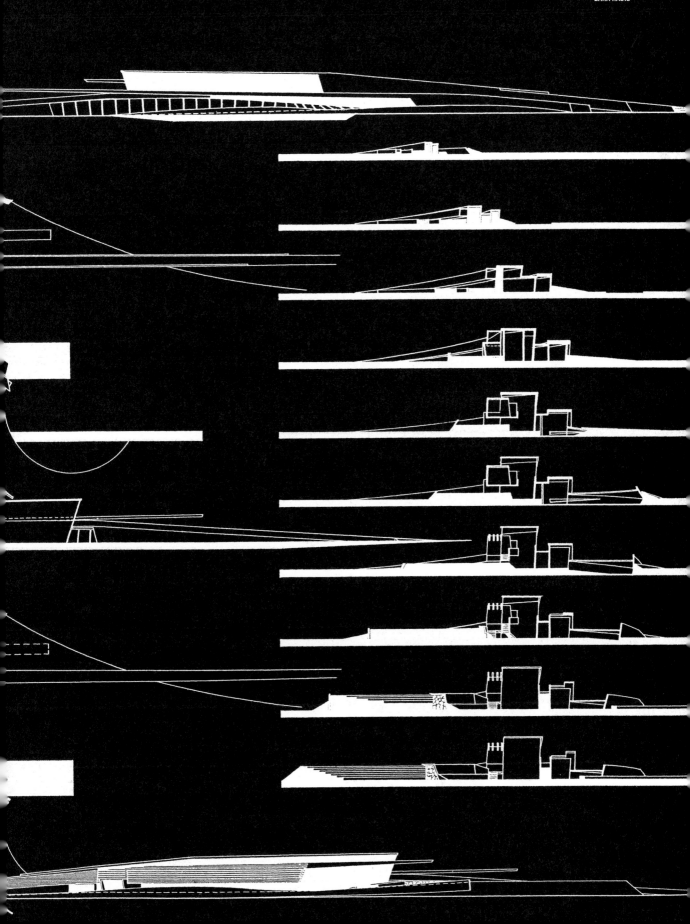

MIND ZONE

Millennium Dome, London, England, 1999

Construction: 2/99-12/99. Client: New Millennium Experience Company.
Floor area: 1 500 m². Costs: £12 000 000.

Situated in the midst of the world's-fair type atmosphere of the Millennium Dome in Greenwich, London, Zaha Hadid's **MIND ZONE** stands out with its spectacular cantilevered steel structure. As the architect says, "Our minds are amazingly complex machines and our aim is to unravel some of their mysteries in a truly memorable fashion." Working with a number of talented artists such as Ron Mueck, Gavin Turk and Richard Deacon, Hadid indeed succeeds in creating spaces that appear to defy gravity and to prepare the visitor for the technologically oriented exhibits within the pavilion. Although risky for a serious architect as Hadid to participate in this circus-like venture she has once again proved by her forceful design that good architecture can impose itself even in the most difficult conditions.

Zaha Hadids **MIND ZONE** (Bewußtseinszone), die das Zentrum des im Londoner Stadtteil Greenwich erbauten Millennium Dome bildet, fällt mit ihrer spektakulären freitragenden Stahlkonstruktion aus ihrer Umgebung heraus. Die Architektin erklärt ihr Projekt so: »Das menschliche Bewußtsein ist eine erstaunlich komplexe Maschine, und unser Ziel ist es, einige seiner Rätsel auf eine wirklich einprägsame Weise aufzudecken.« In Zusammenarbeit mit einer Reihe talentierter Künstler wie Ron Mueck, Gavin Turk und Richard Deacon ist es Hadid tatsächlich gelungen, Räume zu schaffen, die der Schwerkraft zu trotzen scheinen und die Besucher auf die technologisch orientierten Ausstellungsstücke im Inneren des Pavillons einstimmen. Es war für Hadid als eine ernst zu nehmende Architektin sicher riskant, an dieser zirkushaften Veranstaltung teilzunehmen. Aber durch ihre eindrucksvolle Gestaltung hat sie ein weiteres Mal bewiesen, dass sich gute Architektur selbst unter sehr schwierigen Bedingungen durchsetzen kann.

Dans l'ambiance de foire internationale du Millennium Dome de Greenwich, la **MIND ZONE** (Zone de l'esprit) se fait remarquer par ses spectaculaires structure d'acier en porte-à-faux. Pour Zaha Hadid : « L'esprit est une machine étonnement complexe, et notre but est de dévoiler certains de ses mystères pour qu'ils puissent être mémorisés. » En collaboration avec quelques artistes de talent comme Ron Mueck, Gavin Turk et Richard Deacon, elle a réussi à créer des espaces qui semblent défier la gravité et préparer le visiteur à la découverte de l'exposition d'orientation technologique présentée à l'intérieur du pavillon. Participer à cette manifestation hautement populaire était un pari risqué pour cette architecte éminemment sérieuse, mais une fois de plus elle fait preuve de la puissance de sa réflexion et démontre que la bonne architecture peut s'imposer, même dans des conditions difficiles.

Mixed together with other pavilions of dubious architectural distinction, within Richard Rogers' Millennium Dome, the Mind Zone retained a powerful presence with its impressive cantilevered volume.

Im Vergleich mit benachbarten Pavillons von eher zweifelhafter architektonischer Qualität besitzt Zaha Hadids freitragende Konstruktion für die Mind Zone in Richard Rogers' Millennium Dome eine eindrucksvolle Präsenz.

Sous le Dome du Millennium de Richard Rogers, au voisinage de pavillons d'intérêt architectural variable, la Mind Zone (Zone de l'esprit) manifeste sa forte présence par son impressionnant volume en porte-à-faux.

Hadid's strong volumes undoubtedly
expressed her own style, yet their
intimate relation to the concept of
the Mind Zone might be harder to
discern.

*Während in Hadids imponierenden
Baukörpern zweifellos ihr persönlicher
Stil zum Ausdruck kommt, ist deren
Übereinstimmung mit dem Ausstel-
lungskonzept der Mind Zone weniger
eindeutig auszumachen.*

*Les puissants volumes expriment sans
aucun doute le style de l'architecte,
bien que leur relation réelle avec le
concept de la Mind Zone soit assez
difficile à discerner.*

HIROSHI HARA Φ

Hiroshi Hara + Atelier
10-3 Hachiyama-cho
Shibuya-ku, Tokyo 150-0035
Japan

Tel: +81 3 3464 8670
Fax: +81 3 3464 8612
e-mail: atelier-phi@mvg.biglobe.ne.jp

Ito House

Born in Kawasaki, Japan, in 1936, **HIROSHI HARA** received his B.A. from the University of Tokyo (1959), his M.A. in 1961 and his Ph.D. from the same institution in 1964, before becoming an associate professor in the university's Faculty of Architecture. Though his first work dates from the early 1960s, he began his collaboration with Atelier Φ in 1970. Notable structures include numerous private houses, such as his own residence, Hara House (Machida, Tokyo, 1973-74). He participated in the 1982 International Competition for the Parc de la Villette, Paris, and built the Yamato International Building (Ota-ku, Tokyo, 1985-86), the Ida City Museum (Nagano, 1986-88), and the Sotetsu Culture Center (Yokohama, Kanagawa, 1988-90). His recent work includes the Umeda Sky Building (Kita-ku, Osaka, 1988-93), and the JR Kyoto Railway Station (Sakyo-ku, Kyoto, 1991-97).

HIROSHI HARA, geboren 1936 in Kawasaki, erwarb 1959 den Bachelor of Arts, 1961 den Master of Arts und 1964 den Doktorgrad an der Universität Tokio, wo er zum außerordentlichen Professor an der dortigen Architekturfakultät berufen wurde. Obwohl sein erster Bau aus den frühen 60er-Jahren datiert, begann seine Zusammenarbeit mit Atelier Φ erst 1970. Zu Haras Bauten zählen zahlreiche Wohnhäuser, so sein eigenes Haus, Haus Hara in Machida, Tokio (1973-74). 1982 nahm Hara am internationalen Wettbewerb für den Parc de la Villette in Paris teil. Weitere von Hara ausgeführte Bauten sind das Yamato International Building in Ota-ku, Tokio (1985-86), das Ida City Museum in Nagano (1986-88) und das Sotetsu-Kulturzentrum in Yokohama, Kanagawa (1988-90). Zu seinen jüngeren Arbeiten gehören das Umeda Sky Building in Kitaku, Osaka (1988-93) und der Bahnhof der Japan Railway (JR) in Sakyo-ku, Kioto (1991-97).

Né à Kawasaki, Japon, en 1936, **HIROSHI HARA** est Bachelor of Arts de l'Université de Tokyo (1959), Master of Arts (1961) et docteur de cette même université (1964) avant de devenir professeur associé de la faculté d'architecture. Ses premières œuvres datent du début des années 1960, mais il n'entame sa collaboration avec l'atelier Φ qu'en 1970. Parmi ses réalisations notoires : de nombreuses résidences privées, dont la sienne, Hara House (Machida, Tokyo, 1973-74). Il participe en 1982 au concours international pour le Parc de la Villette, construit le Yamamoto International Building (Ota-ku, Tokyo, 1985-86), le musée municipal d'Ida (Nagasaki, 1986-88) et le centre culturel Sotetsu (Yokohama, Kanagawa, 1988-90). Œuvres récentes au Japon : l'Umeda Sky Building (Kita-ku, Osaka, 1988-93) et la gare JR de Kyoto (Sakyo-ku, Kyoto, 1991-97).

ITO HOUSE

Chijiwa, Nagasaki, Japan, 1997-98

*Design: 5/97-10/97. Construction: 12/97-8/98.
Floor area: 176 m² (all three buildings).*

ITO HOUSE is divided into three sections, and covers a total floor area of 176 m². The "parent's" section measuring 100 m² in floor area, consists of a basement and two stories built of reinforced concrete and steel; the "children's" section, covering a floor area of 41 m², consists of two stories constructed of wood and steel. Both sections have a gray wood cladding on their upper sections. The third section, a one-story "study" covering a floor area of 35 m², is built of wood. Placed in a spectacular wooded setting, these three units stand out from the surrounding pine trees like geometric objects – upright rectangular forms for the two-story houses for parents and children, and a lower triangular shape for the study. The gray wood of the residence spaces rests upon the fully glazed ground floors set on concrete podiums, creating an unexpected visual imbalance.

Das **ITO HOUSE** ist in drei Teile gegliedert, die insgesamt eine Nutzfläche von 176 m² bieten. Der 100 m² umfassende Wohnbereich für die Eltern, der aus einem Souterrain und zwei aus Stahlbeton und Stahl erbauten Etagen besteht, sowie ein 41 m² großer Wohnbereich für die Kinder, dessen zwei Stockwerke aus Holz und Stahl konstruiert sind, haben im oberen Teil eine graue Holzverkleidung. Der dritte Teil, ein eingeschossiges Atelier, nimmt eine Fläche von 35 m² ein und besteht aus Holz. Auf einem besonders schön bewaldeten Grundstück gelegen, heben sich diese drei Gebäudeteile – hochaufgerichtete, rechteckige Formen für die zweistöckigen Gebäude der Eltern und der Kinder und der niedrigere, dreieckige Baukörper des Ateliers – wie geometrische Objekte von den Kiefern der Umgebung ab. Die graue Holzverkleidung der Wohnbereiche ruht auf vollständig verglasten Untergeschossen, die wiederum auf Betonsockeln aufliegen, wodurch ein ungewöhnliches optisches Ungleichgewicht entsteht.

La **MAISON ITO** est divisée en trois zones et totalise une surface de planchers de 176 m². La partie «parents», de 100 m², consiste en un sous-sol et deux niveaux en béton armé. La partie «enfants», de 41 m² se répartit sur deux étages en bois et acier. Leur partie haute est habillée de bois gris. La troisième zone, le «bureau», de 35 m² sur un seul niveau, est en bois. Ces trois volumes se détachent de leur environnement de pins à la manière d'objets géométriques : volumes rectangulaires des parties des parents et des enfants, volume triangulaire, moins haut, pour le bureau. Les volumes d'habitation, en bois gris, reposent sur un rez-de-chaussée entièrement vitré appuyé sur un soubassement en béton, créant ainsi un déséquilibre visuel inattendu.

Despite an extremely simple plan, the scaling and volumetric distribution of the Ito House give it an unusual appearance. The essentially vertical form echoes the pine trees, and the mostly horizontal cladding gives the upper cube a more stable aspect.

Die besondere Formgebung und Raumaufteilung verleihen dem Ito House trotz seines äußerst einfachen Grundrisses ein ungewöhnliches Aussehen. Seine im Wesentlichen vertikale Form harmoniert mit den umstehenden Kiefern, während die weitgehend horizontal angelegte Holzverkleidung den oberen Baukörpern Gewicht verleiht.

L'extrême simplicité du plan n'empêche pas une forme originale obtenue par un travail sur la distribution des volumes et les échelles. Essentiellement verticale, la forme de la maison rappelle celle d'un pin, tandis que le bardage horizontal confère poids et stabilité au cube de la partie supérieure.

A Parents
B Children
C Study
D Planned

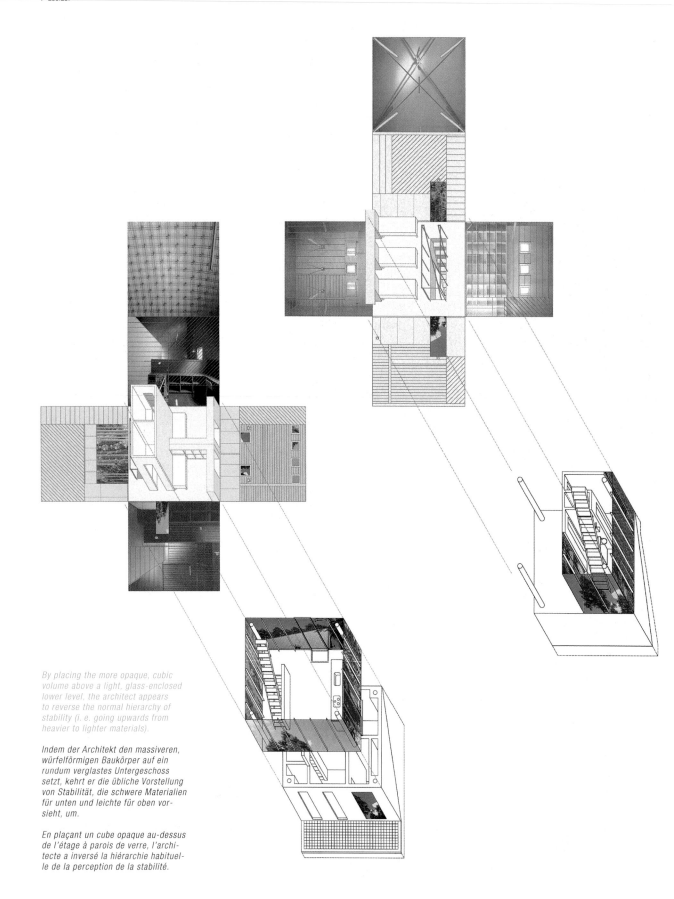

By placing the more opaque, cubic
volume above a light, glass-enclosed
lower level, the architect appears
to reverse the normal hierarchy of
stability (i. e. going upwards from
heavier to lighter materials).

Indem der Architekt den massiveren,
würfelförmigen Baukörper auf ein
rundum verglastes Untergeschoss
setzt, kehrt er die übliche Vorstellung
von Stabilität, die schwere Materialien
für unten und leichte für oben vor-
sieht, um.

En plaçant un cube opaque au-dessus
de l'étage à parois de verre, l'architecte a inversé la hiérarchie habituel-
le de la perception de la stabilité.

ZVI HECKER

Zvi Hecker Architekt
Oranienburger Strasse 41
10117 Berlin
Germany

Tel: +49 30 282 6914
Fax: +49 30 282 7322
e-mail: z.hecker@berlin.snafu.de

Palmach Museum of History

Born in 1931 in Krakow, Poland, **ZVI HECKER** grew up in Samarkand and Krakow before moving to Israel in 1950. He studied architecture at Krakow Polytechnic (1949-50), the Israeli Institute of Technology (Technion), Haifa (1950-54) receiving a degree in engineering and architecture (1955). He studied painting at Avni Academy of Art, Tel Aviv (1955-57). After two years of military service in the Corps of Engineers of Israeli Army, Hecker set up private practice in 1959, working with Eldar Sharon until 1964 and Alfred Neumann until 1966. His buildings include the City Hall, (Bat-Yam, 1960-63), Club Méditerranée (Ahziv, 1961-62), Aeronautic Laboratory, Technion Campus (Haifa, 1963-66), Ramot Housing (Jerusalem, 1973, 1979-82, and 1984-86), and Spiral Apartment House (Ramat Gan, 1981-89), all in Israel. Recent projects include the Heinz Galinski School (1991-95) and the "Berliner Berge" residential neighborhood (1994) in Berlin, and the Palmach Museum of History, Tel Aviv (1992-98), published here.

ZVI HECKER, geboren 1931 im polnischen Krakau, wuchs in Samarkand und Krakau auf, bevor er 1950 nach Israel auswanderte. Von 1949 bis 1950 studierte er Architektur am Krakauer Polytechnikum und von 1950 bis 1954 am Israeli Institute of Technology (Technion) in Haifa, wo er 1955 seinen Abschluß in Ingenieurbau und Architektur machte. Anschließend studierte er bis 1957 Malerei an der Avni Academy of Art in Tel Aviv. Nach seinem zweijährigen Militärdienst im Ingenieurskorps der israelischen Armee eröffnete Hecker 1959 sein eigenes Büro, wo er bis 1964 mit Eldar Sharon und bis 1966 mit Alfred Neumann zusammenarbeitete. Zu seinen Bauten gehören das Rathaus von Bat-Yam (1960-63), der Club Méditerranée in Ahziv (1961-62), die Luftfahrtforschungsanstalt auf dem Technion-Campus in Haifa (1963-66), die Ramot-Wohnanlage in Jerusalem (1973, 1979-82 und 1984-86) sowie das Spiral-Etagenhaus in Ramat Gan (1981-89), alle in Israel. Neuere Projekten sind die Heinz Galinski-Schule (1991-95) und die Wohnhausanlage »Berliner Berge« (1994) in Berlin sowie das hier vorgestellte Palmach Museum of History in Tel Aviv.

Né en 1931 à Cracovie, Pologne, **ZVI HECKER** grandit à Samarkhande et à Cracovie avant d'émigrer en Israël en 1950. Il étudie l'architecture à l'Ecole polytechnique de Cracovie (1949-50), à l'Institut israélien de Technologie (Technion) de Haïfa (1950-54) dont il est diplômé en ingénierie et architecture. Il étudie également la peinture à l'Académie d'art Avni (Tel-Aviv, 1955-57). Après deux ans de service militaire dans le Corps des ingénieurs de l'armée israélienne, il crée son agence en 1959 et collabore avec Eldar Sharon jusqu'en 1964 ainsi qu'avec Alfred Neumann jusqu'en 1966. Parmi ses réalisations : un hôtel de ville (Bat-Yam, 1960-63), le Club Méditerranée (Ahziv, 1961-62), le laboratoire d'aéronautique (campus de Technion, Haïfa, 1963-66), les logements Ramot (Jérusalem 1973, 1979-82 et 1984-86), l'immeuble d'appartements Spiral (Ramat Gan, 1981-89). Il a récemment réalisé l'école Heinz Galinski (1991-95) et les immeubles d'habitation Berliner Berge (1994), ainsi que le Musée d'histoire Palmach (Tel Aviv) publié ici.

PALMACH MUSEUM OF HISTORY

Tel Aviv, Israel, 1992-98

*Construction: 1992-98. Client: Palmach Veterans Association.
Floor area: ca. 5 100 m². Costs: ca. DM 13 500 000.*

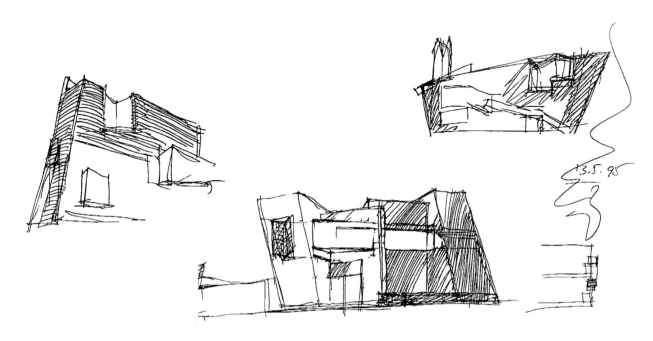

Palmach was a Jewish underground organization fighting British rule in Palestine, before being incorporated into the Israeli Defense Forces. The 5 100-m² **PALMACH MUSEUM OF HISTORY** made of bare concrete, local sandstone, and plaster houses a permanent exhibition as well as a 400-seat auditorium, a youth center, a cafeteria and offices. As the architect says, "The Museum is not a building, but rather a sequence of retaining walls, wrapped around a central courtyard and its existing trees. To preserve the natural character of the site, much of the Museum space has been designed underground. The plan of the building reflects the form of the site, as the elevation mirrors the terraced character of the landscape." Indeed, the high cost of preserving the landscape dictated that many architectural details in this complex were left intentionally rough. Hecker collaborated with the architect Rafi Segal on this project.

Palmach war eine jüdische Untergrundorganisation, die vor ihrer Eingliederung in die israelische Armee gegen die britische Mandatsherrschaft in Palästina kämpfte. Das 5 100 m² große **PALMACH MUSEUM OF HISTORY** aus nacktem Beton, örtlichem Sandstein und Gipsputz beherbergt eine ständige Ausstellung zur Geschichte der Palmach, ein Auditorium mit 400 Sitzen, ein Jugendzentrum, ein Café sowie Büroräume. Der Architekt erklärt dazu: »Das Museum ist weniger ein Gebäude als eine Abfolge von Schutzmauern, die einen zentralen Innenhof und dessen Baumbestand umschließen. Um den natürlichen Charakter des Grundstücks zu erhalten, wurde ein großer Teil der Ausstellungsfläche ins Untergeschoss verlegt. Der Grundriss des Gebäudes nimmt Bezug auf die Form des Geländes, so wie die Schrägen und die unterschiedlichen Ebenen die terrassenförmig angelegte Landschaft spiegeln.« Tatsächlich geboten die hohen Kosten der Landschaftserhaltung, viele architektonische Details dieses Gebäudes bewußt im Rohzustand zu belassen. Bei diesem Projekt arbeitete Hecker mit dem Architekten Rafi Segal zusammen.

Palmach était une organisation clandestine juive qui avait combattu les Britanniques en Palestine avant d'être incorporée aux forces de défense israéliennes. La **PALMACH MUSEUM OF HISTORY** de 5 100 m² en béton brut, grès local et plâtre enduit abrite une exposition permanente ainsi qu'un auditorium de 400 places, un centre de jeunesse, une cafétéria et des bureaux. Pour Hecker, « Le Musée n'est pas un bâtiment, mais plutôt une séquence de murs de soutènement autour d'une cour centrale plantées d'arbres existants. Pour préserver le caractère naturel du site, une grande partie des espaces muséaux est aménagée en sous-sol. Le plan reflète la forme du terrain, en particulier en section, où il suit les contours en terrasses du paysage. » Le coût élevé qu'a entraîné le respect du site explique que de nombreux détails d'exécution aient été volontairement laissés bruts. Hecker a collaboré sur ce projet avec l'architecte Rafi Segal.

Zvi Hecker has shown a capacity to create powerful, unexpected buildings, whose style has an organic relationship to both their sites and to programmatic requirements.

In diesem Entwurf zeigt sich Zvi Heckers Fähigkeit, kraftvolle, ungewöhnliche Bauten zu schaffen, die in Stil und Aufbau genau ihrem Standort und ihren inhaltlichen Anforderungen entsprechen.

Zvi Hecker a souvent montré sa capacité à créer de surprenantes architectures, dont le style plein de force reste en relation organique avec le site et fidèle au programme.

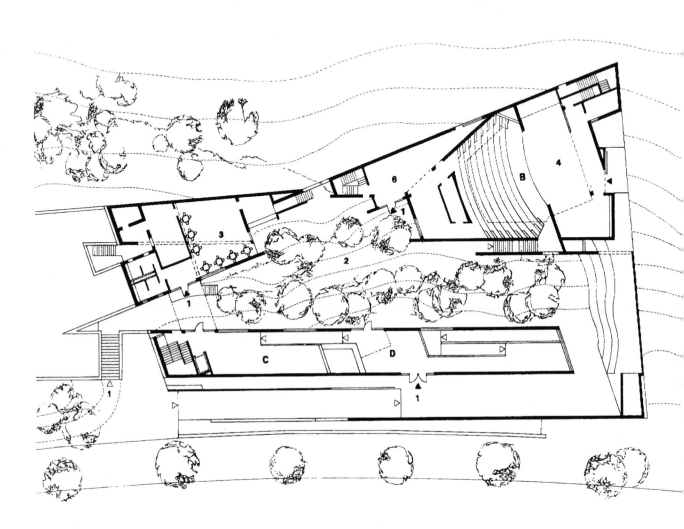

<table>
<tr><td>A - Exibition space</td><td>A - Ausstellungsbereich</td><td>A - Espace d'exposition</td></tr>
<tr><td>B - Auditorium</td><td>B - Auditorium</td><td>B - Auditorium</td></tr>
<tr><td>C - Administration</td><td>C - Verwaltung</td><td>C - Administration</td></tr>
<tr><td>D - Reception</td><td>D - Empfang</td><td>D - Réception</td></tr>
</table>

A - Exibition space	A - Ausstellungsbereich	A - Espace d'exposition
B - Auditorium	B - Auditorium	B - Auditorium
C - Administration	C - Verwaltung	C - Administration
D - Reception	D - Empfang	D - Réception
1 - Entrance	1 - Eingang	1 - Entrée
2 - Courtyard	2 - Hof	2 - Cour intérieure
3 - Canten	3 - Cafeteria	3 - Rampe
4 - Memorial space	4 - Gedenkstätte	4 - Mémorial
5 - Stage	5 - Bühne	5 - Scène
6 - Lobby	6 - Lobby	6 - Vestibule
7 - Gallery	7 - Galerie	7 - Galerie

Blending a closed, fortress-like exterior (above) with the obvious need for a museum to be open to the public, Hecker laid out a plan in the form of overlapping triangles (left).

Links: Grundlage des Entwurfs sind einander überschneidende Dreiecke. Oben: Dadurch wird eine harmonische Verbindung zwischen der geschlossenen, festungsartigen Außenfassade und der für ein Museum notwendigen Offenheit geschaffen.

Combinant une forme fermée de forteresse aux besoins d'ouverture d'un musée (ci-dessus), Hecker a imaginé un plan composé de triangles imbriqués (à gauche).

HERZOG & DE MEURON

Herzog & de Meuron
Rheinschanze 6
4056 Basel
Switzerland

Tel: +41 61 385 5757
Fax: +41 61 385 5758
e-mail: info@herzogdemeuron.ch

JACQUES HERZOG and **PIERRE DE MEURON** were both born in Basel in 1950. They received degrees in architecture from the ETH Zurich in 1975 and founded their firm Herzog & de Meuron in Basel in 1978. **HARRY GUGGER** was born in Grezenbach, Switzerland in 1956, he studied at ETH Zurich and Columbia University, New York (1984-89) and received his degree in architecture from the ETH Zurich in 1989. He is a partner since 1991. **CHRISTINE BINSWANGER** was born in Kreuzlingen, Switzerland in 1964. She studied at the ETH Zurich (1984-90) and received her degree in 1990. She is a partner since 1994. Their built work includes the Antipoles I Student Housing at the Université de Bourgogne (Dijon, 1991-92) and the Ricola Europe Factory and Storage Building (Mulhouse, 1993), both in France, the Sammlung Goetz building (Munich, 1989-92), the Museum Küppersmühle/Sammlung Grothe (Duisburg, Germany, 1997-99), and the Kramlich Residence and Media Collection (Oakville, Napa Valley, California, 1999-2002). Most notably they were chosen early in 1995 to design the new Tate Modern gallery in London, situated in the Bankside Power Station on the Thames, opposite St. Paul's Cathedral, which opened in May 2000. They were also shortlisted in the competition for the new design of the Museum of Modern Art in New York (1997).

JACQUES HERZOG und **PIERRE DE MEURON** wurden beide 1950 in Basel geboren. Sie studierten an der ETH in Zürich, wo sie 1975 ihr Diplom machten. 1978 gründeten sie ihre Firma Herzog & de Meuron in Basel. **HARRY GUGGER** wurde 1956 in Grezenbach, Schweiz geboren. Er studierte an der ETH, Zürich und an der Columbia University, New York (1984-89) und erhielt sein Diplom von der ETH 1989. Seit 1991 ist er Partner. **CHRISTINE BINSWANGER** wurde 1964 in Kreuzlingen, Schweiz geboren. Sie studierte ebenfalls an der ETH (1984-90), wo sie 1990 ihr Diplom ablegte. Sie ist seit 1994 Partner. Zu ihren Bauten gehören das Studentenwohnheim Antipodes I der Université de Bourgogne in Dijon (1991-92), das Fabrik- und Lagergebäude der Firma Ricola Europe in Mühlhausen (1993), die Galerie der Sammlung Goetz in München (1989-92), das Museum Küppersmühle/Sammlung Grothe in Duisburg (1997-99) und die Kramlich Residenz und Media Sammlung in Oakville, Napa Valley, Kalifornien (1999-2002). 1995 erhielten sie ihren bedeutendsten Auftrag: die Tate Modern Gallery, die im Mai 2000 in der umgebauten Bankside Power Station an der Themse, gegenüber St. Paul's Cathedral, eröffnet wurde. Beim Wettbewerb für die Umgestaltung des Museums of Modern Art in New York (1997) kamen Herzog & de Meuron in die engere Wahl.

JACQUES HERZOG et **PIERRE DE MEURON**, sont tous deux nés à Bâle en 1950. Ils sont diplômés en architecture de l'ETH de Zurich (1975) et fondent leur agence, Herzog & de Meuron, à Bâle en 1978. **HARRY GUGGER**, naît à Grezenbach, Suisse en 1956, étudie à l'ETH Zurich et à la Columbia University, New York (1984-90) et est diplômé de l'ETH (1989). Depuis 1991, il est accocié. **CHRISTINE BINSWANGER** est née en 1964 à Kreuzlingen en Suisse. Elle a aussi étudié à l'ETH (1984-90) dont elle a été diplômée en 1990. Elle est associée depuis 1994. Parmi leurs réalisations: le foyer d'étudiants Antipodes I pour l'Université de Bourgogne à Dijon (1991-92), l'usine-entrepôt Ricola Europe, à Mulhouse (1993), une galerie pour une collection privée d'art contemporain, la Sammlung Goetz, à Munich (1989-92), le Musée Küppersmühle/Sammlung Grothe de Duisburg (1997-99) et la Kramlich Residence and Media Collection en Oakville, Napa Valley, Californie (1999-2002). Ils sont été sélectionnés en 1995 pour l'extension de la Tate Modern gallery de Londres, installée dans l'ancienne centrale électrique de Bankside Power Station, au bord de la Tamise, face à la cathédrale St. Paul. La Tate Modern a été inaugurée en Mai 2000. Ils comptaient parmi les architectes retenus pour le concours de la transformation du Museum of Modern Art de New York (1997).

HOUSE
Leymen, France, 1996-97

Planning: 1996. Construction: 1997. Client: Hanspeter Rudin.
Floor area: 260 m². Costs: FF 3 300 000.

This 260-m² **HOUSE**, made of pale gray exposed concrete, is placed unexpectedly on a platform resting on pilotis that makes it appear to float, despite the weight of its concrete walls. The entrance stairway made of cast concrete is set beneath the house, as if to heighten the distance between the residence and the land on which it is placed, almost precariously. In the interior, a relatively simple plan allows for unexpected spaces like the large, high bathroom. The stairway bisects the house, which consists of a kitchen and bedroom on the first level, bathroom and another bedroom on the second level, and a laundry under the eaves. Far from wanting to protect the rough concrete finish of the house, the architects have arranged for water runoffs to mark the west façade over time.

Weil dieses **HAUS** mit 260 m² Bruttogeschossfläche aus hellgrauem Sichtbeton auf eine Plattform gesetzt wurde, die auf Stützen ruht, wirkt es, als würde es trotz der Schwere seiner Betonmauern schweben. Die aus Gußbeton bestehende Eingangstreppe wurde unter das Haus verlegt, so als sollte die Distanz zwischen Wohnhaus und dem Gelände, auf dem es – beinahe unsicher – steht, noch zusätzlich betont werden. Im Inneren erlaubt ein relativ schlichter Grundriß die Gestaltung ungewöhnlicher Räume, wie etwa eines großen, hohen Badezimmers. Die Treppe teilt das Haus in zwei Hälften, die aus Küche und Schlafzimmer im ersten Obergeschoß, Badezimmer und einem weiteren Schlafzimmer im zweiten Stock und einer Waschküche unterhalb der Plattform bestehen. Die rauhen Betonoberflächen wurden bewußt ungeschützt gelassen, so dass die Westfront mit der Zeit durch die Spuren des Regenwassers markiert wird.

Cette **MAISON** de 260 m² en béton gris pâle est curieusement juchée sur une plate-forme qui repose elle-même sur des pilotis. Elle donne ainsi l'impression de flotter, malgré le poids de ses murs en béton. L'escalier d'entrée en béton brut est placé à l'arrière, comme pour accroître l'espace entre la partie résidentielle et le terrain sur lequel elle s'appuie de manière presque précaire. A l'intérieur, le plan relativement simple ne renonce pas pour autant à des volumes surprenants entre centres, une vaste salle-de-bains toute en hauteur. L'escalier sépare en deux la maison qui se compose d'une cuisine et d'une chambre au premier niveau, d'une salle-de-bains et d'une autre chambre au second et d'une buanderie sous le toit. Au lieu de vouloir protéger la surface de béton brut de la façade, les architectes ont fait en sorte que l'eau de ruissellement du toit ou des murs marque la façade ouest.

Against all expectations, the House sits above the ground, as though it had been dropped in this location by a mysterious force. Aside from this particularity, it retains relatively conventional lines, with large openings on its lower level.

Das Haus erhebt sich auf einer Plattform über dem Erdboden, wodurch es zu schweben scheint. Abgesehen von dieser Besonderheit hat es eine relativ konventionelle Form, mit großen Fensteröffnungen im unteren Stockwerk.

La maison se dresse sur son terrain, comme si elle venait d'y être déposée par quelque mystérieuse force. Elle conserve cependant une apparence conventionnelle. De grandes ouvertures ont été pratiquées au niveau du rez-de-chaussée.

Within, the house is faithful to the architectural austerity that Herzog & de Meuron are well known for.

Die Innenraumgestaltung zeigt die architektonische Strenge, für die Herzog & de Meuron bekannt sind.

L'intérieur de la maison est caractéristique de l'austérité architecturale qui a fait la notoriété d'Herzog & de Meuron.

LIBRARY OF THE EBERSWALDE TECHNICAL SCHOOL

Eberswalde, Germany, 1994-99

Planning: 1994-96. Construction: 1997-99. Client: Land Brandenburg.
Floor area: 1 504 m². Costs: DM 3 515 000.

Connected to an older building by a low passageway, the Library might seem at first glimpse to have more relation to the history of art, than to forestry and applied sciences for which it is intended.

Die durch einen niedrigen Korridor mit einem älteren Gebäude verbundene Bibliothek nimmt auf den ersten Blick eher Bezug auf die Kunstgeschichte als auf das Forstwesen und die Naturwissenschaften, für die sie konzipiert wurde.

Reliée à un autre bâtiment par un passage couvert, la bibliothèque semble, à première vue, au premier vue, entretenir plus de rapports avec l'histoire de l'art qu'avec celle de la forêt et des sciences appliquées pour lesquelles elle a été construite.

The most immediately visible feature of the 1 504-m² **LIBRARY OF THE EBERSWALDE TECHNICAL SCHOOL** devoted to forestry and the applied sciences is the facade created by the architects, together with Thomas Ruff, using a curious mixture of historic images from his private picture collection, including a Canadian warplane, Walter Gropius' 1923 Weimar House, and works of art such as Lorenzo Lotto's Venus and Cupid and a still-life by Pieter Potter applied on the windows and on the exterior concrete panels. Although this is not an art library, the facade with images systematically repeating themselves in bands around the rectangular box-like structure brings to mind "multiples" by artist Andy Warhol. Serigraphy on such a scale would seem to be an innovation in architecture. The images are, in fact, marked on the concrete panels using a cure retardant.

Das auffallendste Merkmal dieser **BIBLIOTHEK DER FACHHOCHSCHULE EBERSWALDE** für Forstwesen und angewandte Naturwissenschaften mit 1 504 m² Bruttogeschossfläche ist die von den Architekten in Zusammenarbeit mit dem Künstler Thomas Ruff gestaltete Fassade: Auf den Wandflächen und den dazwischenliegenden verglasten Fassadenschlitzen weist sie eine seltsame Zusammenstellung historischer Bilder aus Ruffs privater Sammlung auf, einschließlich eines kanadischen Kriegsflugzeugs, Walter Gropius' Weimarer Haus von 1923 und anderer Kunstwerke wie Lorenzo Lottos Venus und Amor und einem Stillleben von Pieter Potter. Obwohl es sich nicht um eine kunstgeschichtliche Bibliothek handelt, weckt die Fassade mit ihren Bildern, die sich regelmäßig auf den Glasbändern und Betonplatten, welche das kistenartige Gebäude umlaufen, wiederholen, Erinnerungen an Andy Warhols »Multiples«. Siebdrucke in diesem Maßstab dürften eine Neuerung in der Architektur darstellen. So wurden die Bilder auch unter Verwendung eines Konservierungsmittels auf die Betonplatten aufgetragen.

La caractéristique la plus frappante de cette **BIBLIOTHÈQUE DE L'ÉCOLE TECHNIQUE SUPÉRIEURE D'EBERSWALDE** de 1 504 m² consacrée aux sciences et techniques forestières est sa façade, conçue par les architectes en collaboration avec Thomas Ruff. Un étonnant mélange d'images historiques appartenant à la collection de Ruff s'affiche sur les fenêtres et sur le revêtement extérieur en béton. On y décourse dont un avion de guerre canadien, la maison de Weimar de Walter Gropius (1923) et des reproductions d'œuvres d'art comme la Vénus et Cupidon de Lorenzo Lotto ou une nature-morte de Pieter Potter. Ces images systématiquement répétées en bandeaux tout autour du bâtiment rectangulaire rappellent les « multiples » d'Andy Warhol. A une telle échelle, l'iconographie est presque une innovation en architecture. Elle fait appel à la sérigraphie sur les fenêtres et à une technique de retardement du séchage du béton sur les murs.

Despite its unusual facade treatment, the Library has an extremely simple rectangular plan, with regular, horizontal notch windows.

Die ungewöhnliche Fassadengestaltung kontrastiert mit der äußerst einfachen, rechteckigen Grundform mit horizontalen Fensteröffnungen.

Malgré le traitement original de la façade et le rythme des fenêtres horizontales, la bibliothèque présente un plan rectangulaire extremement simple.

TATE MODERN

London, England, 1998-2000

Competition: 1994-95. Planning: 1995-97. Construction: 1998-5/2000. Client: Tate Gallery, London.
Total floor area: 34 000 m². Total project costs: £134 000 000. Total construction costs: £81 000 000.

Located opposite St. Paul's Cathedral on the Thames, the Bankside Power Station was built in two phases in 1947 and 1963 by Sir Giles Gilbert Scott, who was also the inventor of the famous red English telephone box, and finally shut down in 1981 because it was polluting London too much. The Bankside Power Plant is dominated by a 99-m-high chimney, visible from much of inner London. The Tate Gallery took an option to purchase the building in 1994, and organized a competition the following year that selected Herzog & de Meuron as architects, over competitors like Tadao Ando, Rem Koolhaas, and Renzo Piano. Preserving the spectacular space of the former Turbine Hall as the entrance area, Jacques Herzog, Pierre de Meuron, Harry Gugger and Christine Binswanger have opted for an approach that conserves the rough, industrial qualities of the building, while providing 10 000 m² of state-of-the-art exhibition space, the **TATE MODERN**, on the Thames side of the building. Polished concrete and rough-cut wood alternate on the floor surfaces, and numerous viewpoints permit visitors to orient themselves vis-à-vis the Thames and the Turbine Hall. A rather harsh fluorescent lighting scheme might appear to be the only fault of this ambitious project.

Das gegenüber von St. Paul's Cathedral am Themse-Ufer gelegene Bankside-Kraftwerk wurde in zwei Phasen, 1947 und 1963, von dem Architekten Sir Giles Gilbert Scott erbaut, der auch als Schöpfer der berühmten roten englischenTelefonzellen bekannt geworden ist. 1981 wurde die Anlage, die von einem weithin sichtbaren, 99 m hohen Schornstein überragt wird, wegen zu hoher Emissionswerte stillgelegt. Die Tate Gallery erwarb 1994 eine Kaufoption auf das Gebäude und beauftragte ein Jahr später, nach einem internationalen Wettbewerb mit Teilnehmern wie Tadao Ando, Rem Koolhaas und Renzo Piano, Herzog & de Meuron mit der Umgestaltung des Kraftwerks zu einem Museum für moderne Kunst, der **TATE MODERN**. Jacques Herzog, Pierre de Meuron, Harry Gugger und Christine Binswanger entschieden sich für die Erhaltung des rauhen, industriellen Charakters des Bauwerks: Der spektakuläre Raum der früheren Turbinenhalle wurde als Eingangsbereich genutzt, während man den 10 000 m² umfassenden Ausstellungsbereich auf die Uferseite des Gebäudes verlegte. Für die Böden wurde abwechselnd geschliffener Beton und grob bearbeitetes Holz verwendet; zahlreiche Aussichtspunkte ermöglichen den Besuchern die Orientierung. Das eher kalt wirkende, fluoreszierende Lichtdesign könnte sich als einziger Makel dieses ehrgeizigen Projekts herausstellen.

Face à la cathédrale St. Paul de l'autre côté de la Tamise, la centrale électrique de Bankside fut édifiée en deux phases, 1947 et 1963, par Sir Giles Gilbert Scott – par ailleurs designer de la célèbre cabine téléphonique rouge britannique – puis fermée en 1981 pour pollution excessive. Elle est dominée par une cheminée de 99 m de haut, visible d'une grande partie de la capitale. La Tate Gallery prit une option d'achat en 1994, organisa un concours l'année suivante et choisit l'agence Herzog & de Meuron parmi des concurrents comme Tadao Ando, Rem Koolhaas ou Renzo Piano. En décidant de conserver le magnifique espace de l'ancien hall des turbines pour en faire le hall d'entrée, Jacques Herzog, Pierre de Meuron, Harry Gugger et Christine Binswanger ont opté pour une approche qui préserve les qualités industrielles et « brutes » du bâtiment tout en dégageant 10 000 m² d'espaces d'exposition de la **TATE MODERN** derrière la façade donnant sur la Tamise. Le béton poli et le bois brut alternent au sol et de nombreux points de vue permettent aux visiteurs de s'orienter. Un éclairage fluorescent assez brutal semble être le seul défaut de cet ambitieux projet.

Rather than the monumental Thames-side entrance that one might expect for such an institution, the architects have opted for a low, recessed entrance on the western side of the building.

Statt eines monumentalen Haupteingangs auf der Uferseite haben die Architekten einen niedrigen, in die Westwand des Gebäudes eingelassenen Zugang gewählt.

Les architectes ont préféré une entrée basse et en retrait sur la façade ouest à une entrée monumentale donnant sur la Tamise.

Altering the austere facade of the
original structure only at some points,
such as for the glazed ground level
cafeteria (above), Herzog & de Meuron
have carried the austerity of the
exterior over into the galleries, with
their untreated wood floors (right).

Oben: Herzog & de Meuron haben die
nüchterne Fassadengestaltung des
ehemaligen Kraftwerks nur an wenigen Stellen verändert – so für die
verglaste Cafeteria im Erdgeschoss.
Rechts: In den Ausstellungsräumen
wird der schlichte und nüchterne
Eindruck in den Böden aus unbehandeltem Holz fortgeführt.

Ne modifiant l'austère façade originale qu'à certains endroits, comme pour
la cafétéria vitrée du rez-de-chaussée
(ci-dessus), Herzog & de Meuron ont
maintenu cette austérité dans les
salles d'exposition aux sols en bois
brut (à droite).

The most spectacular internal feature of the Tate Modern is indisputably the Turbine Hall, whose volume has been left essentially intact. The large neon-filled light boxes on the sides of the space correspond to openings where visitors can look down on the Turbine Hall from the galleries.

Das spektakulärste Element der Innenraumgestaltung der Tate Modern ist zweifellos die ehemalige Turbinenhalle, deren Ausmaße im Wesentlichen unverändert blieben. Von den großen Neon-Leuchtkästen an den Seitenwänden können die Besucher in die Halle blicken.

L'élément intérieur le plus impressionnant est le hall des turbines, dont le volume a été pratiquement laissé intact. Les vastes boîtes latérales éclairées au néon sont des balcons d'ou les visiteurs peuvent regarder le hall à partir des galeries.

STEVEN HOLL

Steven Holl Architects
435 Hudson Street, Suite 402
New York, NY 10014
United States

Tel: +1 212 989 0918
Fax: +1 212 463 9718
e-mail: mail@stevenholl.com
Web: www.stevenholl.com

STEVEN HOLL, born in 1947 in Bremerton, Washington, gained his B.Arch. at the University of Washington, Seattle (1970), and then studied in Rome and at the Architectural Association (AA) in London (1976). He began his career in California and opened his own office in New York in 1976. He taught at the University of Washington, Syracuse University, and, since 1981, at Columbia University in New York. Notable buildings: Hybrid Building (Seaside, Florida, 1984-88); Berlin AGB Library (Berlin, competition entry, 1988); Void Space/Hinged Space, Housing, Nexus World (Fukuoka, Japan, 1989-91); Stretto House (Dallas, Texas, 1989-92); Makuhari Housing (Chiba, Japan, 1992-97); Chapel of St. Ignatius, Seattle University (Seattle, Washington, 1994-97); and the Kiasma Museum of Contemporary Art (Helsinki, Finland, 1993-98). Recent work also includes the renovation and extension of the Cranbrook Institute of Science (Bloomfield Hills, Michigan) published here. Winner of the 1998 Alvar Aalto Medal, Holl is presently working on the Bellevue Art Museum, Bellevue, Washington, and the Knut Hamsun Museum, Hamarøy, Norway.

STEVEN HOLL, geboren 1947 in Bremerton, Washington, erwarb 1970 den Bachelor of Architecture der University of Washington in Seattle und studierte anschließend in Rom sowie bis 1976 an der Londoner Architectural Association. Er begann seine Karriere als Architekt in Kalifornien und eröffnete 1976 ein eigenes Büro in New York. Holl lehrte zunächst an der University of Washington und der Syracuse University und seit 1981 an der Columbia University in New York. Zu seinen Projekten gehören: das Hybrid Building in Seaside, Florida (1984-88), der Wettbewerbsbeitrag für die Amerika-Gedenkbibliothek in Berlin (1988), das Wohnungsprojekt Void Space/Hinged Space Nexus World in Fukuoka, Japan (1989-91), das Haus Stretto in Dallas, Texas (1989-92), die Wohnsiedlung Makuhari in Chiba, Japan (1992-97), die St. Ignatius-Kapelle der Seattle University in Seattle, Washington (1994-97) und das Kiasma Museum für Zeitgenössische Kunst in Helsinki, Finnland (1993-98). Zu seinen jüngsten Arbeiten gehören der hier vorgestellte Umbau und die Erweiterung des Cranbrook Institute of Science in Bloomfield Hills, Michigan. Gegenwärtig arbeitet Steven Holl, der 1998 mit der Alvar-Aalto-Medaille ausgezeichnet wurde, am Art Museum in Bellevue, Washington und am Knut-Hamsun-Museum in Hamarøy, Norwegen.

STEVEN HOLL, né en 1947 à Bremerton (Washington), Bachelor of Architecture de l'University of Washington (1970), études à Rome et à l'Architectural Association, Londres (1976). Il débute sa carrière en Californie et ouvre sa propre agence à New York, en 1976. Enseignant à l'University of Washington, à la Syracuse University, et, depuis 1981, à la Columbia University, New York. Principales réalisations : Hybrid Building (Seaside, Floride, 1984-88) ; participation au concours de la Bibliothèque AGB, Berlin (1988) ; immeuble d'habitatious Void Space/Hinged Space, Nexus World (Fukuoka, Japon,1989-91), Stretto House (Dallas, Texas, 1989-92) ; immeuble d'habitatious Makuhari (Chiba, Japon, 1992-97) ; Kiasma Musée d'art contemporain (Helsinki, Finlande, 1993-98). Parmi ses travaux récents : rénovation et extension du Cranbrook Institute of Science (Bloomfield Hills, Michigan), publié ici. Médaille Alvar Aalto en 1998, Holl travaille actuellement sur le Bellevue Art Museum (Bellevue, Washington) et sur le Knut Hamsun Museum (Hamarøy, Norvège).

CRANBROOK INSTITUTE OF SCIENCE

Bloomfield Hills, Michigan, USA, 1996-99

Construction: 9/96-6/98 (addition), 1/98-8/99 (renovation). Client: Cranbrook Educational Community.
Floor area: 2 778 m² (addition), 5 946 m² (renovation).

Winner of the 1995 New York AIA Design Award, the **CRANBROOK INSTITUTE OF SCIENCE** includes approximately 2 800 m² of new addition and 6 000 m² renovation of the existing science museum, originally built by Eliel Saarinen. "Our aim," says the architect, "is to make the least intrusion on the architecture of the original Saarinen building while maximizing the potential for circulation and visiting experiences with the addition." The addition is intended to be free and open-ended – easily adaptable to change. Shaped roughly like a "U", the structure is composed of a steel truss frame spanned in precast concrete planks, clad in yellow Kasota stone near the entrance and concrete block to the north. The inner part of the "U" faces the similarly shaped existing museum, forming a new plaza space between the two buildings.

Mit dem **CRANBOOK INSTITUTE OF SCIENCE** gewann Steven Holl 1995 den Design Award des American Institute of Architects in New York. Das Projekt umfasst die Renovierung einer 6 000 m² großen Fläche des ursprünglich von Eliel Saarinen erbauten Wissenschaftsmuseums sowie einen neuen Anbau von ca. 2 800 m². »Unser Ziel war es«, sagt der Architekt, »so wenig wie möglich in die Architektur des Originalgebäudes von Saarinen einzugreifen und zugleich den Besucherverkehr und das Besuchserlebnis zu maximieren.« Der Anbau soll offen, erweiterbar und leicht zu verändern sein. Der fast U-förmig gestaltete Bau besteht aus einem Stahlhängewerk, das in großflächige Betonfertigteile eingespannt wurde, welche in der Nähe des Eingangs mit gelbem Kasota-Stein und auf der Nordseite mit Betonformstein verkleidet sind. Die offene Seite des »U« liegt der des ähnlich geformten Museums gegenüber, wodurch zwischen den beiden Gebäuden ein neuer Platz entsteht.

Le **CRANBROOK INSTITUTE OF SCIENCE** qui a remporté le Design Award 1995 de l'American Institute of Architecture de New York comprend la rénovation des 6 000 m² du musée des sciences existant, édifié par Eliel Saarinen, et une extension de 2 800 m². «Notre but», précise Steven Holl, «est d'intervenir le moins possible sur l'architecture originale de Saarinen tout en maximisant le potentiel de circulation et d'intérêt de la visite au moyen de l'extension.» Celle-ci, de plan libre, ne se «termine» pas, ce qui la rend facilement adaptable à une future évolution. Sa structure, qui reprend en gros le contour d'un U, se compose d'une ossature de portiques d'acier recouverte de plaques de béton préfabriquées, habillées de pierre de Kasota jaune près de l'entrée et de parpaings en béton au Nord. La partie interne de l'U fait face au musée existant, de forme similaire, ce qui crée une sorte de place publique entre les deux bâtiments.

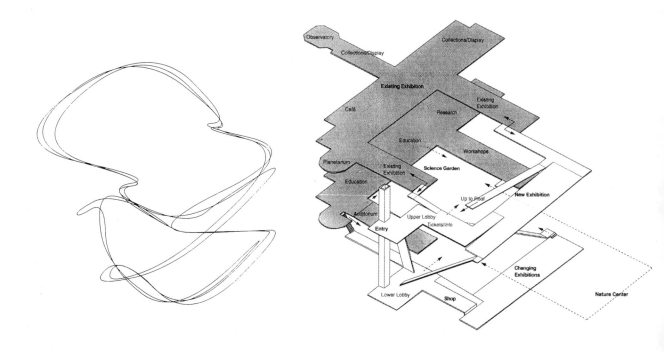

The complex articulated volumes of the Cranbrook Institute are typical of the architectural designs of Steven Holl.

Komplex gegliederte Baukörper, wie die des Cranbrook Institute of Science, sind charakteristisch für die Architekturentwürfe von Steven Holl.

La complexité de l'articulation des volumes du Cranbrook Institute est typique du style de Steven Holl.

These two views of the same stairway give an idea of Holl's handling of volumes, but also of light. Despite being relatively simple in appearance, the stairway design is quite distant from Modernist purity.

Die beiden Ansichten des Treppenaufgangs vermitteln einen Eindruck von Holls Umgang mit räumlichen Formen und Licht. Obwohl die Gestaltung relativ schlicht wirkt, ist sie weit entfernt von modernistischem Purismus.

Ces deux vues du même escalier illustrent le traitement des volumes cher Holl et son approche de la lumière. Bien que d'apparence relativement simple, son dessin est assez éloigné de la pureté moderniste.

Y-HOUSE

Catskills, NY, USA, 1997-99

Planning and construction: 1997-99. Floor area: 330 m². Client: withheld. Costs: withheld.

This 330-m² house is located in Schoharie County in the Catskill Mountains. The two rectangular volumes of the **Y-HOUSE** split apart to create spaces for two generations of the Austrian family that commissioned the residence. Clad in red painted cedar, the house responds to the topology of the site and not specifically to the red painted wood barns that are typical of the region, so the architect. Divided into "day" and "night" zones, the interior spaces flow into each other in an effect that Steven Holl likens to flying. He also notes that this client was the first to accept his initial drawing for a project, allowing him an unprecedented degree of "artistic" freedom in the design. Large, open balconies face from the front of the house toward slightly different views of the countryside.

Das 330 m² große **Y-HOUSE** liegt im Schoharie County in den Catskill Mountains. In den beiden lang gestreckten, im spitzen Winkel zueinander angeordneten Bauteilen befinden sich getrennte Wohnbereiche für zwei Generationen einer österreichischen Familie, die dieses Haus für sich entwerfen ließ. Die Verkleidung aus rot gestrichenem Zedernholz wurde laut Architekt eher von der Topologie des Grundstücks inspiriert als von den für diese Region typischen roten Holzscheunen. Die in »Tag- und Nacht-Zonen« unterteilten Innenräume gehen fließend ineinander über. Steven Holl weist darauf hin, dass seine Auftraggeber bei diesem Projekt erstmalig bereits die erste Entwurfsskizze akzeptierten, was ihm ein bis dahin nicht gekanntes Maß an künstlerischer Freiheit erlaubte. Große, offene Balkone auf der Vorderseite des Hauses bieten leicht variierende Aussichten auf die umgebende Landschaft.

Cette maison de 330 m² est située dans le comté de Schoharie dans les Catskill Mountains. La **MAISON EN Y** se divise en deux volumes rectangulaires que se partagent les propriétaires, deux générations d'Autrichiens. Son bardage de cèdre peint en rouge est une réponse à la topographie locale et non un écho aux granges de cèdre rouge courantes dans la région, a expliqué l'architecte. Divisés en zones de jour et de nuit, les espaces intérieurs s'imbriquent les uns dans les autres créant un effet que Steven Holl aime comparer à un « envol. » Il fait également remarquer que le client fut le premier a accepter d'emblée son premier projet, lui laissant une liberté artis-tique sans précédent. De vastes balcons-loggias ouverts sur la façade offrent des vues légèrement différents sur le paysage agreste environnant.

The architect deals here with the need for distinct housing arrange-ments within the same residence. His Y-shaped collision of two essentially rectangular forms solves the design problem and adds a spatial richness to the house.

Der Forderung nach getrennten Wohn-bereichen innerhalb eines Hauses kam der Architekt durch die Y-förmige Anordnung zweier fast rechteckiger Baukörper nach, die dem Gebäude zudem räumliche Fülle verleiht.

L'architecte était confronté au besoin de distinguer deux zones résiden-tielles à l'intérieur d'une même maison. La solution retenue – la collision en Y de deux formes à peu près rectangulaires – accroît la spatialité du bâtiment.

BASEMENT

WINE CELLAR

Careful, painterly compositions give the interior a wealth of varying effects, with an emphasis on openness and free movement, even in the bedroom seen above.

Sorgfältige, malerische Kompositionen sorgen für eine effektvolle Innenraumgestaltung, bei der Offenheit und die Möglichkeiten der freien Bewegung im Raum im Vordergrund stehen.

Des compositions soignées, presque picturales, créent de multiples effets à l'intérieur. L'accent est mis sur l'ouverture et la liberté de mouvement, même dans la chambre.

DAVID HOVEY

Optima, Inc.
630 Vernon Avenue
Glencoe, Illinois 60022
United States

Tel: +1 847 835 8400
Fax: +1 847 835 3073

Modular Steel House

Born in Wellington, New Zealand, in 1944, **DAVID HOVEY** attended the Illinois Institute of Technology (1967-70) and worked as an assistant architect in the 20th Century Art Department at The Art Institute of Chicago (1967-70), before working in the offices of A. S. Takeuchi (1971-74) and C. F. Murphy (1974-78). He created his present firm, Optima, Inc., in 1978. His work includes a number of multi-family residential developments in Evanston, Wilmette, Deerfield, and Chicago, Illinois, mixed-use developments in Glenview, Wilmette, and Highland Park, as well as single family prototype residences like the one published here. David Hovey has been Associate Professor of Architectural Design at the Illinois Institute of Technology since 1978.

DAVID HOVEY, 1944 in Wellington, Neuseeland geboren, studierte von 1967 bis 1970 am Illinois Institute of Technology und hatte während dieser Zeit eine Assistentenstelle als Architekt in der Abteilung Kunst des 20. Jahrhunderts am Art Institute of Chicago inne. Von 1971 bis 1974 war er Mitarbeiter im Büro von A. S. Takeuchi und von 1974 bis 1978 bei C. F. Murphy. 1978 gründete er sein eigenes Büro, Optima Inc. Zu seinen Bauten gehören mehrere Wohnhausanlagen in Evanston, Wilmette, Deerfield und Chicago, Illinois, Mehrzweckgebäude in Glenview, Wilmette und Highland Park sowie verschiedene Prototypen für Einfamilienhäuser wie das hier vorgestellte Modular Steel House. David Hovey ist seit 1978 als außerordentlicher Professor für Architekturdesign am Illinois Institute of Technology tätig.

Né à Wellington, Nouvelle-Zélande, en 1944, **DAVID HOVEY** suit l'enseignement de l'Illinois Institute of Technology (1967-70) et fait ses débuts comme architecte assistant au département d'art du XXe siècle de l'Art Institute de Chicago (1967-70) avant d'entrer dans l'agence de A. Soane. Takeuchi (1971-74), puis dans celle de C. F. Murphy (1974-78). Il crée son agence actuelle, Optima Inc. en 1978. Parmi ses réalisations : plusieurs programmes immobiliers à Evanston, Wilmette, Deerfield et Chicago, immeubles mixtes à Glenview, Wilmette et Highland Park ainsi que des prototypes de maisons individuelles comme celle publiée dans ces pages. David Hovey est Professeur associé de conception architecturale à l'Illinois Institute of Technology depuis 1978.

MODULAR STEEL HOUSE

Glencoe, Illinois, USA, 1998

Design and construction period: 6 months. Floor area: 790 m².

Set on a lot above Lake Michigan, the 830-m² **MODULAR STEEL HOUSE** was designed and built in a remarkably short six-month period. The architect explains that "The design integrates existing materials and systems from every industry rather than developing customized components to perform the same function. Off-site pre-fabrication of all components ensured an efficient, fast-track construction schedule and simplified the assembly of the building on this steeply sloped site." Hovey used press-formed aluminum panels made for buses as the exterior cladding, for example. Intended to evolve over time, with different elements being added or removed, this residence, the architect's own, is conceived as a laboratory for the design of modernist industrially inspired houses.

Das auf einem Grundstück oberhalb des Michigans-Sees gelegene 820 m² große **MODULAR STEEL HOUSE** wurde in der erstaunlich kurzen Zeit von sechs Monaten geplant und ausgeführt. Der Architekt erklärt, dass »die Gestaltung auf bereits bestehende Baumaterialien und -systeme aus verschiedenen Industriezweigen zurückgreift, statt für die gleiche Funktion maßgeschneiderte Teile anzufertigen. Durch die Vorfabrikation sämtlicher Bauteile wurde ein zügiger Bauzeitplan gewährleistet und die Errichtung auf diesem steil abfallenden Hanggrundstück erleichtert.« So setzte Hovey z. B. als Außenverkleidung pressgeformte Aluminiumtafeln ein, wie sie für die Karosserie von Bussen verwendet werden. Dieses für den Architekten selbst erbaute Wohnhaus soll sich durch Hinzufügen oder Entfernen verschiedener Bauteile mit der Zeit entwickeln und damit als Prototyp für die Gestaltung neuartiger, von der modernen Industriebauweise inspirierter Häuser dienen.

Sur un terrain qui domine le Lac Michigan, la **MODULAR STEEL HOUSE** de 830 m² conçue et construite dans le délai remarquablement court de six mois est la résidence personnelle de D. Hovey. Il explique que dès le départ « Le projet a pris en compte des matériaux et des procédés existants plutôt que d'avoir à imaginer des éléments spéciaux pour remplir la même fonction. La préfabrication en atelier de tous les composants a permis de respecter un calendrier de construction ultra rapide tout en simplifiant l'assemblage sur un terrain en pente raide. » Pour l'extérieur, Hovey s'est servi de panneaux d'aluminium emboutis d'habitude utilisés pour les carrosseries de bus. Prévue pour évoluer dans le temps, par l'adjonction ou la suppression d'éléments, cette résidence est en fait un laboratoire de recherche pour des maisons modernistes d'inspiration industrielle.

Although it does share a rectangular purity of outline with early Modernist houses, the Modular Steel House also has a close connection to efficient industrial architecture.

Mit seinen klaren rechteckigen Konturen erinnert das Gebäude sowohl an Häuser der frühen Moderne als auch an funktionale Industrie-architektur.

Proche de certaines compositions modernistes par la pureté des lignes, la Modular Steel House cultive un rapport étroit avec l'architecture industrielle.

0   25'

The use of pilotis combined with its
industrial vocabulary gives the house
an ephemeral or movable feeling,
and certainly does not emphasize
its residential character.

Le recours aux pilotis et à un vocabulaire industriel crée une impression
d'éphémère et de mobilité qui atténue
le caractère résidentiel.

*Die Verwendung von Stahlstützen und
einer industriellen Formensprache
erweckt den Eindruck von Veränderbarkeit und Mobilität, der eher
untypisch für ein Wohnhaus ist.*

ARATA ISOZAKI

Arata Isozaki & Associates
9-6-17 Akasaka, Minato-ku
Tokyo 107-0052
Japan

Tel: +81 3 3405 1526
Fax: +81 3 3475 5265

COSI ●

Born in Oita City on the Island of Kyushu in 1931, **ARATA ISOZAKI** graduated from the Architectural Faculty of the University of Tokyo in 1954 and established Arata Isozaki & Associates in 1963, having worked in the office of Kenzo Tange before. Winner of the 1986 Royal Institute of British Architects Gold Medal, he has been a juror of major competitions such as the 1988 competition for the new Kansai International Airport. Notable buildings include: The Museum of Modern Art, Gunma (Takasaki, Japan, 1971-74), the Tsukuba Center Building (Japan, 1978-83), the Museum of Contemporary Art (Los Angeles, 1981-86), Art Tower Mito (Japan, 1986-90), Team Disney Building (near Orlando, Florida, 1990), Center of Japanese Art and Technology (Krakow, Poland, 1991-94), and B-con Plaza (Oita, Japan, 1991-95). Recent projects include the Higashi Shizuoka Plaza Cultural Complex and the Convention and Arts Center "Granship" (1993-98), both in Shizuoka, Japan, the Nara Centennial Hall (Nara, Japan, 1992-98), and the Center of Science and Industry (COSI), Columbus, Ohio, published here.

ARATA ISOZAKI, geboren 1931 in Oita auf der Insel Kyushu, beendete 1954 sein Architekturstudium an der Universität Tokio. Danach arbeitete er im Büro von Kenzo Tange und gründete 1963 Arata Isozaki & Associates. 1986 wurde er mit der Gold Medal des Royal Institute of British Architects ausgezeichnet. Er war Preisrichter in bedeutenden Wettbewerben, so 1988 bei der Ausschreibung für den Internationalen Flughafen Kansai. Zu Isozakis Bauten zählen das Gunma Prefectural Museum of Fine Arts in Takasaki (1971-74) und das Tsukuba Center Building (1978-83), beide in Japan, das Museum of Contemporary Art in Los Angeles (1981-86), der Art Tower Mito, Japan (1986-90), das Team Disney Building bei Orlando, Florida (1990), das Zentrum für japanische Kunst und Technologie in Krakau, Polen (1991-94) und die B-con Plaza in Oita, Japan (1991-95). Seine neuesten Projekte sind der Kulturkomplex Higashi Shizuoka und das Konferenz- und Kunstzentrum »Granship« (1993-98), beide im japanischen Shizuoka, die Nara Centennial Hall in Nara, Japan (1992-98) sowie das hier vorgestellte Center of Science and Industry (COSI) in Columbus, Ohio.

Né à Oita, (île de Kyushu) en 1931, **ARATA ISOZAKI** est diplômé de la faculté d'architecture de l'Université de Tokyo en 1954. Il fonde Arata Isozaki & Associates en 1963 après avoir travaillé dans l'agence de Kenzo Tange. Titulaire de la médaille d'or du Royal Institute of British Architects en 1986, il est juré dans de nombreux concours internationaux dont celui de l'aéroport international de Kansai (1988). Parmi ses réalisations les plus connues : Le Musée d'art moderne, Gunma (Takasaki, Japon, 1971-74), le Centre Tsukuba (Tsukuba, Japon, 1978-83), le Museum of Contemporary Art (Los Angeles, 1981-86), la Tour d'art Mito (Japon, 1986-90), l'immeuble Team Disney (près d'Orlando, Floride, 1990-94), B-con Plaza (Oita, Japon, 1991-95). Projets récents : le complexe culturel Higashi Shizuoka Plaza, et le Centre des Arts « Granship » (1993-98) tous deux à Shizuoka, Japon, le Hall du Siècle de Nara (Nara, Japon, 1992-98) et le Center of Science and Industry (COSI) à Columbus, Ohio, publié ici.

COSI

Columbus, Ohio, USA, 1994-99

Planning: 4/94-1/97. Construction: 4/97-11/99. Client: State of Ohio and COSI Building Development & Financial Resource Corporation. Floor area: 29 796 m²

Located on a 6.87-hectares site on the west bank of the Scioto River across from the downtown area of Columbus, Ohio's 21st Century Center of Science & Industry is made up of a new westward-facing structure of 21 367 m² and a renovated eastward-facing former high school containing a further 8 361 m². The new building, very much in the spirit of Arata Isozaki's recent work, is a partial ellipse 20 m high and 293 m long. It is made of white-gray, precast concrete panels articulated by stainless steel joints. A sky-lit cubic atrium measuring 23 m on each side and a 230-seat dome theater for interactive digital presentations on astronomy, oceanography and life sciences are among the prominent features of the building, which also offers 10 219 m² of exhibition space. A "civic gathering place," the new **COSI** complex is part of a broader urban development plan for Columbus.

Ohio's 21st Century Center for Science & Industry befindet sich auf einem 6,87 ha großen Gelände am Westufer des Scioto Flusses gegenüber dem Stadtzentrum von Columbus. Es besteht aus einem neuen, nach Westen ausgerichteten Trakt mit 21 367 m² und einem renovierten, nach Osten ausgerichteten Teil mit 8 361m², der früher eine High School beherbergte. Der im Geist von Isozakis jüngsten Arbeiten gestaltete Neubau hat die Form einer Halb-Ellipse mit einer Länge von 293 m und einer Höhe von 20 m. Er besteht aus großflächigen weiß-grauen Betonfertigteilen, die durch Verfugungen aus Edelstahl gegliedert sind. Ein von oben natürlich belichtetes, auf jeder Seite 23 m messendes kubisches Atrium und ein Kuppelsaal mit 230 Sitzen für interaktive digitale Vorführungen über Astronomie, Ozeanographie und Life Sciences (Gen- und Arzneimitteltechnologie) gehören zu den hervorstechenden Merkmalen des Gebäudes, das außerdem über eine Ausstellungsfläche von 10 219 m² verfügt. Ein im neuen **COSI** eingerichteter »Versammlungsraum für die Bürger« ist Teil eines größeren Stadtentwicklungsplans für Columbus.

Situé sur la terrain de 6,87 ha sur la rive ouest de la Scioto River face au centre de Columbus, Ohio's 21st Century Center of Science & Industry se compose d'un bâtiment neuf de 21 367 m² orienté ouest, et d'un ancien collège de 8 361 m² orienté est. Le nouveau bâtiment, bien dans l'esprit des plus récentes réalisations d'Isozaki, est un segment d'ellipse de 20 m de haut et 293 de long. Il est construit en panneaux de béton moulé gris-blanc entre lesquels courent des joints d'acier inox. Un atrium cubique à éclairage zénithal de 23 m de côté et un théâtre sous coupole de 230 places, prévu pour des présentations numérisées interactives d'astronomie, d'océanographie et de sciences de la vie, font partie des points forts de ce bâtiment qui offre par ailleurs 10 219 m² d'espaces d'exposition. « Lieu de réunions publiques » le nouveau complexe **COSI** fait partie d'un vaste programme de développement urbanistique de la ville de Columbus.

Isozaki's first large-scale US commission since he designed the Los Angeles Museum of Contemporary Art (MoCA, 1981-86), COSI's shape shares the broad sweeping curves of works like the Shizuoka Convention and Arts Center "Granship" (Shizuoka, Japan, 1995-98).

COSI ist Isozakis erstes Großprojekt in den USA seit dem Los Angeles Museum of Contemporary Art (MoCA, 1981-86). Die weit geschwungenen Bogenlinien (oben rechts) lassen sich mit dem Konferenz- und Kunstzentrum »Granship« in Shizuoka Japan, 1995-98) vergleichen.

Première commande américaine importante d'Isozaki depuis le Museum of Contemporary Art de Los Angeles (1981-86), COSI (en haut à droite) rappelle les amples courbes de réalisations comme le Centre d'arts et de congrès de Shizuoka « Granship » (Japon, 1995-98).

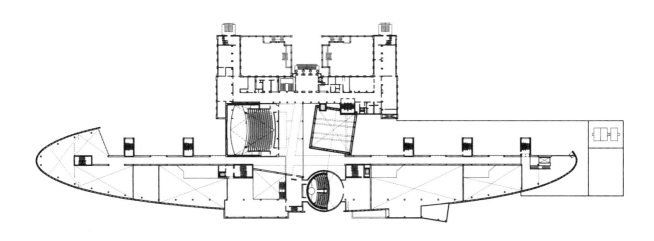

Far from his Post-Modern days, Isozaki has evolved towards the type of mega-form that is popular in many contemporary architectural circles, using computer-aided design to solve construction problems.

Im Gegensatz zu seiner postmodernen Phase neigt Isozaki inzwischen zu Mega-Formen, die heute bei vielen Architekten beliebt sind; dabei verwendet er CAD-Programme zur Lösung von Konstruktionsproblemen.

En s'éloignant de sa phase postmoderne, Isozaki a évolué vers un type de « méga-formes » apprécié de nombreux cercles architecturaux contemporains et pour lesquelles la CAO joue un rôle important.

JAKOB + MACFARLANE

Jakob + MacFarlane SARL d'Architecture
13-15, rue des Petites Écuries
75010 Paris
France

Tel: +33 1 4479 0572
Fax: +33 1 4800 9793
e-mail: jakmak@club-internet.fr

DOMINIQUE JAKOB, born in Paris in 1966, received her degree in art history at the Université de Paris 1 (1990) before obtaining her degree in architecture at the École d'Architecture Paris-Villemin (1991). She has taught at the École Spéciale d'Architecture (1998-99) and the École d'Architecture Paris-Villemin (1994-2000). Born in Christ Church, New Zealand in 1961, **BRENDAN MACFARLANE** received his B.Arch. degree at the Southern California Institute of Architecture (1984), and his M.Arch. degree at the Harvard Graduate School of Design (1990). He has taught at the Berlage Institute, Amsterdam (1996), the Bartlett School of Architecture in London (1996-98), and the École Spéciale d'Architecture in Paris (1998-99). Both Jakob and MacFarlane have worked in the office of Morphosis in Santa Monica. Their main projects include the T House, La-Garenne-Colombes, France (1994,1998), the restaurant of the Centre Georges Pompidou, Paris, published here, and the reconstruction of the Maxime Gorki Theater, Le-Petit-Quévilly, France (1999-2000).

DOMINIQUE JAKOB, 1966 in Paris geboren, schloss 1990 ihr Studium der Kunstgeschichte an der Université de Paris 1 ab und machte 1991 ihren Abschluss in Architektur an der École d'Architecture Paris-Villemin. Von 1998 bis 1999 lehrte sie an der École Spéciale d'Architecture und von 1994 bis 2000 an der École d'Architecture Paris Villemin. Der 1961 in Christ Church, Neuseeland geborene **BRENDAN MACFARLANE** erwarb 1984 seinen Bachelor of Architecture am Southern California Institute of Architecture (SCI-Arc) und 1990 seinen Master of Architecture an der Harvard Graduate School of Design (GSD). Er lehrte am Berlage-Institut in Amsterdam (1976), der Bartlett School of Architecture in London (1996-98) und an der École Spéciale d'Architecture in Paris (1998-99). Sowohl Jakob als auch MacFarlane haben im Architekturbüro Morphosis in Santa Monica gearbeitet. Zu ihren wichtigsten Projekten gehören das T-Haus im französischen La-Garenne-Colombes (1994, 1998), das hier vorgestellte Restaurant im Pariser Centre Georges Pompidou und die Neugestaltung des Maxime Gorki-Theaters in Le-Petit-Quévilly in Frankreich (1999-2000).

DOMINIQUE JAKOB, née à Paris en 1966, est diplômée d'histoire de l'art de l'Université de Paris 1 (1990) puis diplômée d'architecture de l'Ecole d'architecture de Paris-Villemin (1991). Elle a enseigné à l'Ecole Spéciale d'Architecture (1988-99) puis à l'Ecole d'architecture de Paris-Villemin (1994-2000). Né en Christ Church, Nouvelle-Zélande en 1961, **BRENDAN MACFARLANE** est Bachelor of Architecture du Southern California Institute of Architecture (1994) et Master of Architecture de l'Harvard Graduate School of Design (1990). Il a enseigné à l'Institut Berlage, Amsterdam (1996), à la Bartlett School of Architecture, Londres (1996-98) et à l'Ecole Spéciale d'Architecture de Paris (1998-99). Tous deux ont travaillé dans l'agence de Morphosis à Santa Monica. Parmi leurs principaux projets : la Maison T (La Garenne-Colombes, France, 1994-98), le restaurant du Centre Georges Pompidou (1999-2000), publiée ici, et la restructuration du Théâtre Maxime Gorki (Le Petit Quevilly, France, 1999-2000).

CENTRE GEORGES POMPIDOU RESTAURANT

Paris, France, 1998-2000

Competition: 1998. Construction: 3/99-1/2000. Client: Costes.
Floor area: 900 m² (restaurant), 450 m² (terrace). Costs: 16 000 000 FF.

Designed in conjunction with the overall renovation of the Centre by Renzo Piano and Jean-François Baudin, the **CENTRE GEORGES POMPIDOU RESTAURANT** occupies a corner with a spectacular view of Paris. The aluminum floor rises up to form four "sky grottoes" that house the kitchen, toilets, a bar and a VIP guestroom. The overall silver color scheme is broken in the interior rooms with bright red, yellow, green and orange rubber coating applied to the aluminum walls. Steel-frame tables, with battery-operated lights that make them appear to glow from within, were designed by the architects to fit into the overall grid, as were the steel and polyurethane chairs. Although the design competition was organized by the Centre before the operators of the restaurant, the well-known Costes brothers, had been selected, they were able to participate in the decision regarding the final details of the concept.

Das **CENTRE GEORGES POMPIDOU RESTAURANT**, das einen phantastischen Ausblick auf Paris bietet, wurde im Rahmen der von Renzo Piano und Jean-François Baudin durchgeführten umfassenden Renovierung des Gebäudes entworfen. Der Aluminiumboden erhebt sich zu vier Volumen, den »Himmelshöhlen«, in denen die Küche, Toiletten, eine Bar und ein VIP-Raum untergebracht sind. Die insgesamt vorherrschende silberne Farbgebung wird in den Innenräumen von hellroten, gelben, grünen und orangen Gummibelägen auf den Aluminiumwänden durchbrochen. Stahlrahmentische, die mit batteriebetriebenen Lampen von innen beleuchtet werden, und die Stühle aus Stahl und Polyurethan wurden von den Architekten entworfen. Obwohl der Designwettbewerb vom Centre Pompidou durchgeführt wurde, bevor die bekannten Costes-Brüder als Restaurantbetreiber ausgewählt waren, konnten sie sich an der Entscheidung über das endgültige Baukonzept beteiligen.

Créé dans le cadre de la rénovation d'ensemble du Centre par Renzo Piano et Jean-François Bodin, le **CENTRE GEORGES POMPIDOU RESTAURANT** occupe un angle du bâtiment, au 6ème étage, et bénéficie donc d'une vue spectaculaire sur Paris. Le sol d'aluminium semble se soulever pour former quatre « grottes » qui abritent la cuisine, les toilettes, un bar et un salon VIP. Leur intérieur revêtu de caoutchouc rouge vif, jaune, vert et orange, rompt avec la coloration générale argentée. Des tables à piétement d'acier, dotées d'un éclairage sur batterie qui leur donne l'impression de luire de l'intérieur, ont été dessinées par les architectes pour s'intégrer dans la trame générale, de même que les sièges en acier et polyuréthane. Si le concours a été organisé avant que le concessionnaire – les Frères Costes – n'ait été choisi, celui-ci a pu participer à la mise au point des détails.

The aluminum volumes added to the Pompidou Center's top floor house bathrooms, kitchens and a bar.

Im Restaurant im obersten Stock des Centre Pompidou sind in von Aluminium-Wänden begrenzten Volumen, die Küche, Toiletten, eine Bar und ein VIP-Raum untergebracht.

Les volumes d'aluminium du dernier étage abritent la cuisine, un bar et les toilettes.

FRANÇOISE-HÉLÈNE JOURDA

JOURDA Architectes
9-11 Passage Bullourde
75011 Paris
France

Tel: +33 1 5528 8220
Fax: +33 1 5528 8518

Mont-Cenis Academy and Municipal District Centre

Born in 1955, **FRANÇOISE-HÉLÈNE JOURDA** received her diploma as an architect in 1979. She has taught at the École d'architecture in Lyons, at University of Architecture in Oslo, at the University of Minnesota, and at the Technical University of Kassel, Germany. She has worked most notably on the Law Courts of Melun, France (1994), Futuroscope and Entertainment Center (Krefeld, Germany, 1996), a park and housing area with a 13 000-m² greenhouse (Potsdam, Germany, 1997), the Clinique de l'Europe (Lyons, France, 1998), and the Decathlon Store in Hanover, Germany (1999), which is serving as the French Pavilion for Expo 2000. Current work includes glass houses for the Botanical Garden Bordeaux, and the National Technical Rugby Center in Le Creusot, both in France.

FRANÇOISE-HÉLÈNE JOURDA, 1955 geboren, machte 1979 ihr Diplom in Architektur. Sie lehrte an der École d'architecture in Lyon, in Oslo, an der University of Minnesota und an der Technischen Hochschule in Kassel. Zu ihren wichtigsten Projekten gehören der Gerichtshof von Melun, Frankreich (1994), das Futuroscope and Entertainment Center in Krefeld (1996), eine Park- und Wohnhausanlage mit einem 13 000 m² großen Gewächshaus in Potsdam (1997), das Hôpital de l'Europe in Lyon (1998) und die Decathlon-Niederlassung in Hannover, die auch als Französischer Pavillon für die Expo 2000 dient. Gegenwärtig arbeitet sie am Centre Hospitalier Jean Mermoz in Lyon, am botanischen Garten in Bordeaux und am National Technical Rugby Center in Le Creusot, alle in Frankreich.

Née en 1955, **FRANÇOISE-HÉLÈNE JOURDA** est diplômée d'architecture en 1979. Elle a enseigné à l'Ecole d'architecture de Lyon, à Oslo, à l'Université du Minnesota et à l'Université Technique de Kassel, Allemagne. Elle a principalement travaillé sur les projets du Palais de Justice de Melun (1995), du Futuroscope (Poitiers), d'un Centre de loisirs (Krefeld, Allemagne, 1997), d'un parc et ensemble de logements avec une serre de 13 000 m² (Potsdam, Allemagne, 1998), sur l'Hôpital de l'Europe (Lyon, France, 1998) et le Magasin Decathlon (Hanovre, Allemagne) qui a servi de Pavillon français pour Expo 2000. Parmi ses chantiers actuels : le Centre hospitalier Jean Mermoz à Lyon, un jardin botanique à Bordeaux, et le Centre Technique National du Rugby au Creusot.

MONT-CENIS ACADEMY
AND MUNICIPAL DISTRICT CENTER

Herne, Germany, 1992-99

Competition: 1992. Planning: 1996. Completion: 8/99. Landscape: Latz, Riehl und Schulz, Kassel.
Client: EMC Mont-Cenis. Floor area: 7 100 m² (total interior: 11 700 m²).
Costs: DM 100 000 000

The IBA Emscher Park International Building Exhibition in Herne-Sodingen consists of roughly 100 renovation, architectural, and landscaping projects spread over an area of approximately 800 km² in the Ruhr Valley. Set in a former coal-mining area, the **MONT-CENIS ACADEMY**, originally intended as a training center for government employees, consists of a library, a social welfare center and a community center. The 168-m long building, essentially a timber "shed" with a glass skin, was designed with ecological concerns in mind by Jourda & Perraudin Architectes, Jourda Architectes, HHS Planer + Architekten BDA. The roof of the structure includes a 10 000-m² array of photovoltaic cells intended to amply cover the building's electrical needs. Methane gas released from the former mining zones is recycled to generate electricity, which can be stored in an on-site battery plant. The architect designed the wooden furniture.

Die Internationale Bauausstellung (IBA) Emscher Park in Herne-Sodingen besteht aus fast 100 über eine Fläche von ca. 800 km² im Ruhrtal verteilten Projekten der Renovierung, Architektur und Landschaftsgestaltung. Im ehemaligen Zentrum des Kohlebergbaus gelegen, umfasst der Bau die **AKADEMIE MONT-CENIS** (eine Fortbildungsakademie des Landes Nordrhein-Westfalen) und außerdem eine Bibliothek, einen Bürgersaal und ein Stadtteilbüro. Das 168 m lange Gebäude, das aussieht wie ein »Holzschuppen« mit einer Glashaut, wurde nach ökologischen Gesichtspunkten von der Architektengemeinschaft Jourda & Perraudin Architectes, Jourda Architectes, HHS Planer + Architekten BDA geplant. Das Dach des Gebäudes enthält auf einer Fläche von insgesamt 10 000 m² Photovoltaik-Zellen, die den Energiebedarf des Komplexes decken sollen. Aus den ehemaligen Bergwerksbetrieben gewonnenes Grubengas wird für die Elektrizitätsgewinnung recycelt und in einer vor Ort installierten Batteriespeicheranlage gespeichert. Die Inneneinrichtung aus Holz wurde von der Architektin entworfen.

L'Exposition internationale de la construction (IBA) de Emscher Park à Herne-Sodingen, regroupe environ 100 projets de rénovation, d'architecture et d'aménagements paysagers répartis sur un secteur de 800 km² dans la vallée de la Ruhr. Implantée dans une ancienne région minière, l'**ACADÉMIE MONT-CENIS** qui était au départ un centre de formation pour les fonctionnaires fédéraux, comprend une bibliothèque, un centre social et un centre communautaire. Le bâtiment de 168 m de long – un shed en bois à peau de verre – a été conçu par Jourda & Perraudin Architectes, Jourda Architectes, HHS Planer + Architekten BDA dans un esprit écologique. Le toit est équipé d'un réseau de 10 000 m² de cellules photovoltaïques qui devraient amplement couvrir les besoins énergétiques. Le gaz de méthane récupéré dans les anciennes mines est recyclé pour produire de l'électricité qui peut être accumulée dans une installation in situ. L'architecte a conçu le mobilier en bois.

Various architectural metaphors are used here including references to the industrial shed, or to large greenhouses. Rough wood columns, green plants and water within the confines of the building symbolize the ecological concerns of the architects.

Form und Konstruktion der Akademie erinnern an einen Industriebau oder ein Gewächshaus. Unten rechts: Im Innern symbolisieren Säulen aus roh bearbeitetem Holz, Grünpflanzen und Wasserbecken das ökologische Anliegen der Architekten.

Diverses métaphores architecturales rappelent des entrepôts industriels et des serres. En bas à droite : colonnes de bois brut, plantes vertes et présence de l'eau à l'intérieur du bâtiment reflètent les préoccupations écologiques des architectes.

*Within the shelter of the simple
outside shed, pavilions house a
hotel, the activities of the Academy,
a casino, and a municipal center.*

*Die schlichte Außenhülle umgibt
eine Reihe von Pavillons, in denen ein
Hotel, die Arbeitsräume der Akademie,
ein Casino, ein Bürgersaal und ein
Stadtteilzentrum untergebracht sind.*

*A l'abri de cette vaste serre, des
pavillons abritent un hôtel, les activités de l'académie et un centre
municipal.*

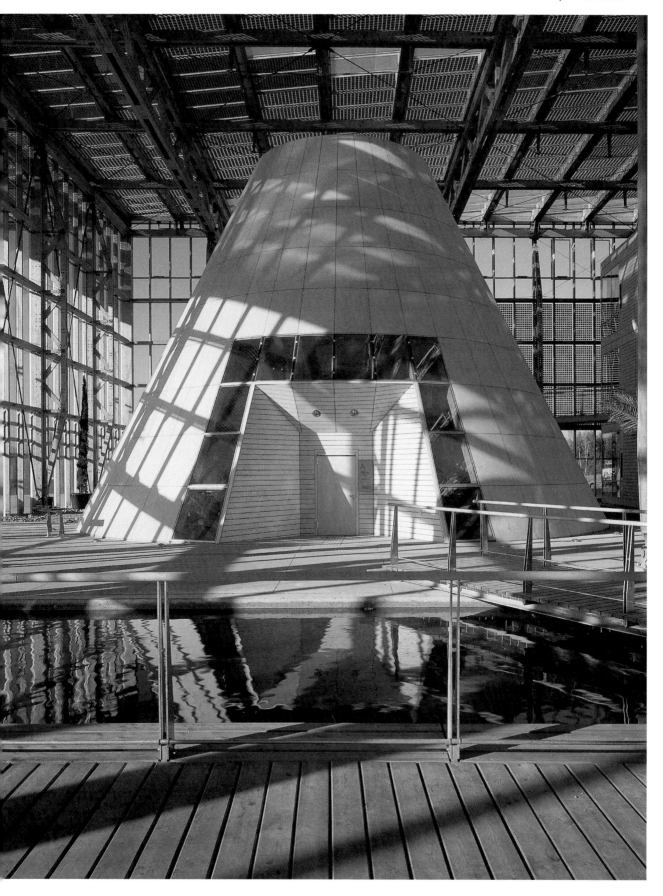

REI KAWAKUBO

Comme des Garçons Co., Ltd.
5-11-5 Minamiaoyama
Minato-ku
Tokyo
Japan

Tel.: +81 3 3407 2480
Fax.: +81 3 5485 2439

REI KAWAKUBO created the Comme des Garçons label in 1969 and established Comme des Garçons Co. Ltd. in Tokyo in 1973. She opened her Paris boutique in 1982, and one in New York one year later. Although she is best known as a fashion designer, she has long had an interest in furniture and architecture. Rei Kawakubo introduced the Comme des Garçons furniture line in 1983. The Flagship Store in Aoyama, Tokyo, which she recently redesigned with the assistance of Takao Kawasaki (interior design), Future Systems (architect/facade), Christian Astuguevieille (art director/interior) and Sophie Smallhorn (artist/interior), was first opened in 1989. Rei Kawakubo received an Honorary Doctorate from the Royal College of Art, London, in 1997. The New York boutique, published here, was designed by Rei Kawakubo with Takao Kawasaki and Future Systems.

REI KAWAKUBO schuf 1969 das Modelabel Comme des Garçons und gründete 1973 die Firma Comme des Garçons Co. Ltd. in Tokio. 1982 eröffnete sie ihre Boutique in Paris und zwei Jahre später eine in New York. Obwohl sie vor allem als Modedesignerin bekannt ist, hat sie seit langem ein großes Interesse an Inneneinrichtung und Architektur. 1983 brachte sie ihre erste Kollektion von Comme des Garçons-Möbeln heraus, 1997 wurde ihr vom Royal College of Art in London der Titel eines Ehrendoktors verliehen. Rei Kawakubo hat ihr 1989 eröffnetes Hauptgeschäft in Aoyama, Tokio, vor einem Jahr in Zusammenarbeit mit Takao Kawasaki (Inneneinrichtung), Future Systems (Fassade), Christian Astuguevieille (Artdirector/Interieur) und Sophie Smallhorn (Künstlerin/Interieur) neu gestaltet. Die ebenfalls hier vorgestellte New Yorker Boutique wurde von Rei Kawakubo zusammen mit Takao Kawasaki und Future Systems entworfen.

REI KAWAKUBO a créé la marque Comme des Garçons en 1969 et fondé Comme des Garçons Co. Ltd à Tokyo en 1973. Elle a ouvert sa boutique parisienne en 1982, puis celle de New York en 1984. Bien qu'elle soit surtout connue comme styliste de mode, elle s'intéresse depuis longtemps au design de mobilier et à l'architecture. Elle a lancé une ligne de meubles Comme des Garçons en 1983. Son magasin principal à Aoyama, Tokyo, qu'elle a récemment rénové en collaboration avec Takao Kawasaki (architecte d'intérieur), Future Systems (architecture, façade), Christian Astuguevieille (directeur artistique, aménagements intérieurs) et Sophie Smallhorn (artiste, aménagements intérieurs) avait été ouverte en 1989. Elle est docteur honoraire du Royal College of Arts de Londres (1997). La boutique new-yorkaise, également publiée ici, a été conçue par Rei Kawabuko avec Takao Kawasaki et Future Systems.

COMME DES GARÇONS
FLAGSHIP STORE

Tokyo, Japan, 1999

Planning: 1998. Construction: 1999 (one month)
Client: Comme des Garçons. Floor area: 698 m².

Set on Aoyama Street as are several other exclusive fashion boutiques, the **COMME DES GARÇONS FLAGSHIP STORE** was built under the direction of Rei Kawakubo by Takao Kawasaki (interior design), Future Systems (architect/facade), Christian Astuguevieille (art director/interior), and Sophie Smallhorn (artist/interior). The undulating glass facade, overlaid with blue circular dots, allows passersby to look in, but not enough to really capture the interior of the space. The large enameled forms of the interior partitions, designed by Kawakubo, divide the space, at the same time making it appear rather complex. Visitors discover clothes or shoes, displayed in small quantities, as they stroll through and around Kawakubo's units. Here architecture and fashion converge, and the design further contributes to setting out the intention Comme des Garçons wishes to project – an image that goes beyond clothing.

Der in der Aoyama-Straße neben mehreren anderen exklusiven Modeboutiquen gelegene Tokioter **COMME DES GARÇONS FLAGSHIP STORE** wurde unter der Leitung von Rei Kawakubo von Takao Kawasaki (Innenarchitekt), Future Systems (Architekt/Fassade), Christian Astuguevieille (Artdirector/Interieur) und Sophie Smallhorn (Künstlerin/Interieur) ausgeführt. Die wellenförmige, mit blauen, kreisrunden Tupfen bedeckte Glasfront erlaubt den Vorübergehenden, hineinzusehen, ohne dass sie jedoch das Innere konkret erkennen könnten. Die vuluminösen Formen der von Kawakubo entworfenen emaillierten Trennwände gliedern den Raum einerseits und lassen ihn gleichzeitig sehr komplex erscheinen. Während man in und zwischen diesen Einheiten umhergeht, entdeckt man die sparsam dekorierten Kleidungsstücke und Schuhe. Hier ergänzen sich Architektur und Mode, und das Design trägt zusätzlich zu dem Image bei, das Comme des Garçons vermitteln möchte: ein Image, das über den Verkauf von Bekleidung hinausgeht.

Situé rue Aoyama, comme de nombreuses boutiques de mode de luxe, le **COMME DES GARÇONS FLAGSHIP STORE** a été aménagé sous la direction de Rei Kawakubo par Takao Kawasaki (architecture intérieure), Future Systems (Architecte/façade), Christian Astuguevieille (directeur artistique/aménagements intérieurs) et Sophie Smallhorn (artiste/aménagements intérieurs). La façade en verre ondulé, plaquée de disques bleus, permet aux passants de voir l'intérieur, sans qu'il puisse en capter le volume. Les grands cocons émaillés, dessinés par Kawabuko, divisent l'espace tout en lui conférant une plus grande complexité. Les visiteurs découvrent les vêtements ou les chaussures présentés en très petit nombre, en se promenant autour d'eux. Cette convergence de la mode et de l'architecture contribue à l'image de Comme des Garçons qui va bien au delà de l'univers vestimentaire.

The undulating glass facade of Comme des Garçons' Aoyama Flagship Store was designed by the architects Future Systems, transforming a relatively innocuous modern space into a remarkable boutique.

Die wellenförmige Glasfront des Tokioter Hauptgeschäfts von Comme des Garçons wurde vom Architekturbüro Future Systems entworfen, das damit ein konventionelles Ladenlokal in eine auffallende Boutique verwandelte.

La façade ondulée en verre du magasin mère de Comme des garçons d'Aoyama a été conçue par Future Systems. Elle fait d'un volume moderne relativement anodin un lieu remarquable.

Rei Kawakubo designed the interior volumes of the shop with the assistance of architect Takao Kawasaki. Their unusual shapes give an almost labyrinthine aspect to the space.

Die Innenräume wurden von Rei Kawakubo in Zusammenarbeit mit dem Architekten Takao Kawasaki ausgeführt. Die ungewöhnlichen Formen geben dem Raum fast labyrinthischen Charakter.

Rei Kawabuko a conçu les volumes intérieurs de son magasin avec l'assistance de l'architecte Takao Kawasaki. Leur forme inhabituelle donne l'impression d'être dans un labyrinthe.

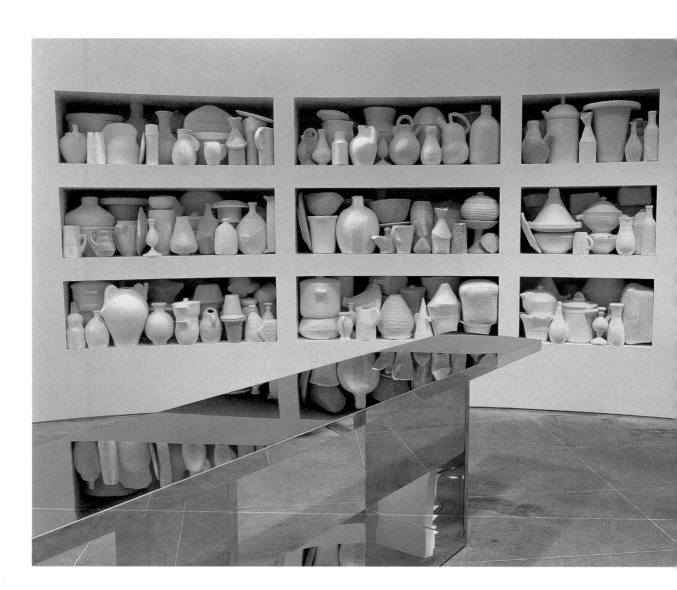

Art director Christian Astuguevieille
and artist Sophie Smallhorn collaborated with Rei Kawakubo on the artistic elements of the interior.

Artdirector Christian Astuguevieille
und die Künstlerin Sophie Smallhorn
schufen gemeinsam mit Rei Kawakubo
die Kunstwerke im Verkaufsraum.

Le directeur artistique Christian
Astuguevieille et l'artiste Sophie
Smallhorn ont collaboré avec
Rei Kawabuko pour créer le décor
intérieur du magasin.

COMME DES GARÇONS STORE

New York, NY, USA, 1999

Planning: 1998. Construction: 1999 (3 months)
Client: Comme des Garçons. Floor area: 465 m².

The striking aluminum monocoque structure, designed by Future Systems, sits just inside the unmarked entrance to the New York store in the Chelsea gallery district of Manhattan.

Die auffallende, von Future Systems entworfene Tunnelkonstruktion aus Aluminium wurde in einen Eingang integriert, der keinerlei Hinweis auf die Boutique im Gebäude gibt.

L'étonnante structure monocoque en aluminium conçue par Future Systems annonce l'entrée sans enseigne du magasin new-yorkais de Rei Kawabuko à Chelsea, le quartier des galeries de Manhattan.

EXIT

Set in the midst of the new gallery district in Chelsea in Manhattan, the **COMME DE GARÇONS STORE** is located in the former car repair shop Heavenly Body Works, whose sign has been retained over the door. The original brick facade was also kept intact. The only clear signal that there is an unusual space is the entrance to a seamless aluminum monocoque tunnel leading into the store, designed by Future Systems and built in a Cornwall shipyard, with a large, free-form glass door. Inside, the large space is divided using the same system of enameled partitions (or "pods" as she calls them) used by Rei Kawakubo in her Tokyo Flagship Store. Both store interiors have a maze-like quality, allowing visitors to discover the clothing or objects for sale in an unexpected or surprising way. Just as she broke traditional merchandizing rules by deciding, from the very outset, that this boutique should have no windows, Kawakubo breaks new ground as to how her clothes should be presented within the space.

Der inmitten des neuen Manhattaner Kunstviertels Chelsea gelegene New Yorker **COMME DE GARÇONS STORE** ist in den Räumen der ehemaligen Autowerkstatt Heavenly Body Works untergebracht, deren Schild über der Eingangstür belassen wurde. Ebenfalls beibehalten wurde die ursprüngliche Backsteinfassade. Einzige Anzeichen für die Existenz eines architektonisch ungewöhnlichen Raums hinter dieser Fassade sind der Eingang zu einem Tunnel in selbsttragender Schalenbauweise, der von Future Systems entworfen und in einer Schiffswerft im englischen Cornwall gefertigt wurde, sowie eine große, frei geformte Glastür, die in das Ladeninnere führt. Der großzügig angelegte Verkaufsraum ist durch die gleichen emaillierten Trennwände (oder »Kokons«, wie die Designerin sie nennt) unterteilt, die Rei Kawakubo für die Gestaltung ihres Flagship Store in Tokio eingesetzt hat. Die Ladeninterieurs ermöglichen den Kunden durch ihre labyrinthartige Anlage, die Verkaufsobjekte auf neue und ungewöhnliche Weise zu entdecken. Ebenso wie sie herkömmliche Vermarktungsregeln brach, als sie von Anfang an beschloss, dass diese Boutique keine Fenster haben sollte, ist Kawakubo wegweisend in der Art, wie sie ihre Modeartikel innerhalb des Verkaufsraums präsentiert.

Situé au milieu du nouveau quartier de galeries de Chelsea, à Manhattan, le **MAGASIN COMME DES GARÇONS** abritait naguère un atelier de carrosserie, Heavenly Body Works, dont l'enseigne a été conservée tout comme la façade d'origine en brique. Le seul signal évident annonçant l'originalité du lieu est l'entrée, un tunnel monocoque en aluminium, dessiné par Future Systems et fabriqué par un chantier naval de Cornouailles. Il est fermé par une grande porte vitrée de forme libre. A l'intérieur, le vaste espace est divisé par le même système de cloisonnements émaillées ou «cocons» que Rei Kawabuko a utilisé dans son magasin de Tokyo. Les deux boutiques donnent l'impression d'un parcours labyrinthique, qui permet aux visiteurs de découvrir les vêtements ou les objets en vente comme par surprise. De même qu'elle rompt avec les règles traditionnelles de la commercialisation en éliminant toute vitrine, Kawabuko expérimente ainsi de nouvelles façons de présenter ses vêtements dans l'espace.

The same dark curving volumes used in Tokyo grace the interior of the New York Comme des Garçons store, giving a continuity of spirit to two very different spaces.

Das Interieur des New Yorker Comme des Garcons Stores ist mit den gleichen dunkelfarbigen, geschwungenen Trennwänden ausgestattet, wie sie für das Tokioter Hauptgeschäft verwendet wurden. Dies verleiht den beiden sonst sehr unterschiedlichen Räumen einen einheitlichen Stil.

Les mêmes volumes sombres et incurvés utilisés à Tokyo décorent la boutique de New York, en signe de continuité d'esprit entre des espaces très différents.

Alternating light and dark volumes, Rei Kawakubo sets out a relatively limited number of her designs for shoppers to see. Although her approach may not follow strict commercial logic, it does set her apart from other fashion designers.

Im Wechsel zwischen hellen und dunklen Elementen präsentiert Rei Kawakubo eine begrenzte Auswahl an Kleidungsstücken. Indem sie sich einer streng kommerziellen Logik verweigert, hebt sie sich von anderen Modedesignern ab.

En alternant des volumes sombres et clairs, Rei Kawabuko ne met en valeur qu'un nombre limité de ses créations de vêtements. Sa démarche éloignée des règles commerciales strictes la distingue de celle des autres stylistes de mode.

KHRAS

KHRAS arkitekter
Teknikerbyen 7
2830 Virum
Denmark

Tel: +45 4585 4444
Fax: +45 4585 3615

e-mail: khr@khras.dk
Web: www.khras.dk

Bang & Olufsen Headquarters

JAN SØNDERGAARD was born in 1947. He attended the Copenhagen Advanced College of Building Technology (1972), and the School of Architecture, Royal Academy of Fine Arts, Copenhagen (1979), and is a certified carpenter. He has been a partner of KHRAS architects since 1988. Nominated for the European Mies van der Rohe Award in both 1992 and 1994, he has designed the Danish Pavilion for Expo '92, Seville, Spain, the headquarters of Pihl & Son, Lyngby, near Copenhagen (1993-94), Denmark, an extension of the Royal Danish Embassy in Moscow (1995-97) and the headquarters for Bayer Denmark (1995-97) and Unicon Beton (1986-88), both in Copenhagen.

JAN SØNDERGAARD wurde 1947 geboren. Er ist ausgebildeter Zimmermann, studierte in Kopenhagen bis 1972 an der höheren Lehranstalt für angewandte Bautechnik und bis 1979 an der Architekturschule der Königlichen Akademie der Künste. Seit 1988 ist er Partner von KHRAS arkitekter. Zu seinen Projekten gehören der Dänische Pavillon für die Expo '92 in Sevilla, die Zentrale von Pihl & Son in Lyngby bei Kopenhagen, Dänemark (1993-94), die Erweiterung der Königlich Dänischen Botschaft in Moskau (1995-97) und die Hauptsitze von Bayer Dänemark (1995-97) und Unicon Beton (1986-88), beide in Kopenhagen. 1992 und 1994 wurde er für den Mies-van-der-Rohe-Preis der Europäischen Gemeinschaft nominiert.

Né en 1947, JAN SØNDERGAARD est diplômé de l'Ecole d'architecture de l'Académie Royale des Beaux-Arts de Copenhague (1979), du Collège Supérieur de Technologie de la Construction de Copenhague (1972). Il est par ailleurs charpentier diplômé. Associé de KHRAS architects depuis 1988. Cité pour le Prix européen Mies van der Rohe en 1992 et 1994, il a conçu le Pavillon danois pour Expo '92 à Séville, le siège de Pihl & Son, Lyngby, près de Copenhague Danemark (1993-94), une extension de l'Ambassade royale du Danemark à Moscou (1995-97), et le siège de Bayer Danemark (1995-97) et d'Unicon Beton (1986-88) à Copenhague.

BANG & OLUFSEN HEADQUARTERS

Struer, West Jutland, Denmark, 1996-99

Planning and construction: 7/96-8/99. Client: Bang & Olufsen A/S.
Floor area: 5 150 m². Costs: ca. 70 000 000 DKR.

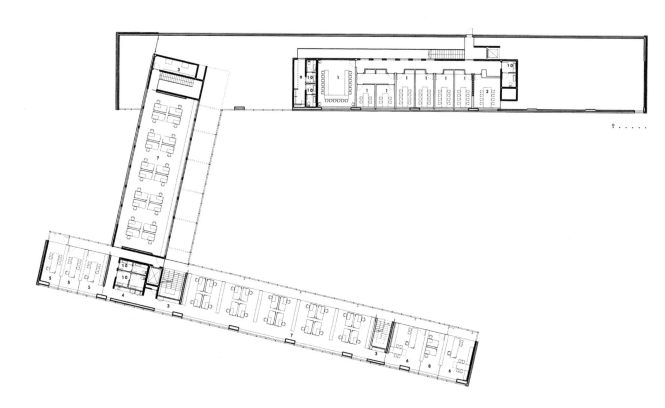

As the architect of the **BANG & OLUFSEN HEADQUARTERS** Jan Søndergaard says, "The design of the building borrows its inspiration from the typical solitary farmhouses of the area. The farm building with its courtyard forms an introverted space with the possibility of visual contact between all functions of the production." Using a simple geometric vocabulary, he nonetheless succeeds in creating a complex spatial experience. Icelandic basalt, brick, sandblasted glass, and poured-in-place concrete contrast with the light wood floors. The clients, well known for their high-quality audio equipment, wanted "a building which in its essence expressed the identity of B&O." They also demanded that the building be "unpretentious" and held within "average or normal" Danish construction cost schedules. The architects were also responsible for the furniture, lamp and sanitation designs. Natural ventilation systems improve the energy consumption of the building.

Der Architekt Jan Søndergaard beschreibt seine **BANG & OLUFSEN HEADQUARTERS** so: »Der Entwurf des Gebäudes geht auf die für diese Gegend charakteristischen Bauernhöfe zurück. Zusammen mit seinem Hof bildet ein solches Gebäude einen nach außen abgeschlossenen Raum, der den Blickkontakt zwischen allen Produktionsbereichen ermöglicht.« Trotz seiner schlichten Formensprache ist es dem Architekten gelungen, ein komplexes Raumerlebnis zu erzeugen. Isländischer Basalt, Backstein, sandgestrahltes Glas und vor Ort gegossener Beton kontrastieren mit den hellen Holzböden. Die für ihre hochwertigen Audiogeräte bekannten Auftraggeber wollten »ein Gebäude, das die Identität von B&O zum Ausdruck bringt«. Sie verlangten außerdem, das Gebäude solle »unprätentiös« sein und seine Baukosten sollten sich innerhalb eines für Dänemark »durchschnittlichen oder normalen« Rahmens bewegen. Die Architekten waren auch verantwortlich für die Entwürfe von Möbeln, Lampen und sanitären Einrichtungen. Ein natürliches Belüftungssystem sorgt für einen reduzierten Energieverbrauch des Gebäudes.

Comme l'explique l'architecte Jan Søndergaard : « Les **BANG & OLUFSEN HEADQUARTERS** s'inspire des fermes isolées typiques de la région. Le corps de bâtiment de la ferme et sa cour forment un espace introverti qui permet un contact visuel entre toutes les fonctions de production. » S'appuyant sur un vocabulaire géométrique simple, il réussit néanmoins à créer un jeu spatial complexe. Le basalte d'Islande, la brique, le verre sablé et le béton coulé sur place contrastent avec les sols en bois clair. Le client, connu pour la qualité exceptionnelle de sa production audio et vidéo, souhaitait « un bâtiment dont essence exprime l'identité de B&O, » tout en restant « sans prétention », dans le cadre des budgets « moyens ou normaux », que l'on consacre à l'architecture au Danemark. Les architectes ont également dessiné le mobilier, les luminaires et les sanitaires. Des systèmes de ventilation naturelle réduisent la consommation d'énergie.

Depending on the angles from which
they are seen, the rectangular volumes of the Bang & Olufsen building
take on a more or less solid (right),
or weighty (left) appearance.

Je nach Blickwinkel wirken die rechteckigen Bauteile des Bang & Olufsen-
Gebäudes massiv und gewichtig
(rechts) oder transparent und leicht
(unten).

Selon l'angle de vision, les volumes
du siège de Bang & Olufsen semblent
massifs (à droite) ou transparents
(ci-dessous).

The placement of an office block on thin pilotis permits it to hover above the landscape, at once both solid and immaterial.

Der auf dünne Pilotis gesetzte Gebäudetrakt scheint über der Landschaft zu schweben – gleichzeitig schwerelos und erdverbunden.

L'implantation d'une aile de bureaux sur pilotis la fait flotter au-dessus du terrain, objet à la fois massif et immatériel.

Left: The spectacular overhang of the suspended office block emphasizes its incongruity in the relatively untouched landscape. Above: Within, light and views to the exterior soften the corporate atmosphere.

Links: Fast fremd wirkt dieser weit vorkragende Bauteil in der nahezu unberührten Landschaft. Oben: Einfallendes Tageslicht und Ausblicke in die Umgebung sollen die korporative Atmosphäre im Inneren mildern.

A gauche : Le spectaculaire porte-à-faux de l'aile des bureaux souligne son incongruité dans un paysage resté relativement intact. Ci-dessus : A l'intérieur, la lumière et les cadrages des vues sur l'extérieur atténuent l'atmosphère austère de ce siège social.

WARO KISHI

Waro Kishi + K. Associates
3F Yamashita Bldg.
10 Nishimotomachi
Koyama, Kita-ku
Kyoto 603 8113
Japan

Tel.: +81 75 492 5175
Fax: +81 75 492 5185
e-mail: warox@ja2.so-net.ne.jp

Born in Yokohama in 1950, **WARO KISHI** graduated from the Department of Electronics of Kyoto University in 1973, and from the Department of Architecture of the same institution two years later. He completed his postgraduate studies in Kyoto in 1978, and worked in the office of Masayuki Kurokawa in Tokyo from 1978 to 1981. He established Waro Kishi + K. Associates in Kyoto in 1993. In Japan he completed the Autolab Automobile Showroom (Kyoto, 1989), Kyoto-Kagaku Research Institute (Kizu-cho, Kyoto, 1990), Yunokabashi Bridge (Ashikita-cho, Kumamoto, 1991), Sonobe SD Office (Sonobe-cho, Funai-gun, Kyoto, 1993), and numerous private houses. Recent work includes his Memorial Hall (Ube, Yamaguchi, 1997), and houses in Higashi-nada (Kobe, 1997) in Suzuka (Nara, 1998) and in Bunkyo (Bunkyo-ku, Tokyo, 2000).

WARO KISHI, geboren 1950 in Yokohama, studierte an der Universität Tokio bis 1973 Elektrotechnik und bis 1975 Architektur. 1978 schloss er sein Graduierten-studium an der Universität Kioto ab und arbeitete danach bis 1981 im Büro von Masayuki Kurokawa in Tokio. 1993 gründete Kishi dort seine eigene Firma, Waro Kishi + K. Associates. In Japan hat er den Automobilsalon Autolab in Kioto (1989), das Forschungsinstitut Kioto-Kagaku in Kizu-cho (1990), die Yunokabashi-Brücke in Ashikita-cho, Kumamoto (1991), das Bürogebäude Sonobe SD in Sonobe-cho, Funai-gun, Kioto (1993) sowie zahlreiche Wohnhäuser gebaut. Zu seinen jüngsten Werken gehören die Memorial Hall in Ube, Yamaguchi (1997) und Häuser in Higashi-nada (Kobe, 1997) in Suzuka (Nara, 1998) und in Bunkyo (Bunkyo-ku, Tokio, 2000).

Né à Yokohama en 1950, **WARO KISHI** est diplômé du département d'électronique de l'Université de Kyoto en 1973, et du département d'architecture de la même institution en 1975. Il poursuit des études de spécialisation à Kyoto de 1978 à 1981. Il fonde Waro Kishi + K. Associates à Kyoto en 1993. Au Japon, il a réalisé, entre autres, le hall d'exposition automobile Autolab (Kyoto, 1989), l'Institut de Recherches Kyoto-Kagaku (Kizu-cho, Kyoto, 1990), le pont Yunokabashi (Ashikita-cho, Kumamo-to, 1991), les bureaux de Sonobe SD (Sonobe-cho, Funai-gun, Kyoto, 1993) ainsi que de nombreuses résidences privées. Parmi ses récents chantiers : le mémorial de Ube (Yamaguchi, 1997) et des maisons à Higashi-nada (Kobe, 1997) à Suzuka (Nara, 1998) et à Bunkyo (Bunkyo-ku, Tokyo, 2000).

HOUSE IN SUZAKU

Nara, Japan, 1997-98

*Completion: April 1998. Client: withheld. Floor area: 178 m². Construction: 10/97-10/98
Costs: withheld.*

Situated in a new residential area on the outskirts of Nara, the **HOUSE IN SUZAKU** is made up of two separate 9 x 5.4-m units, the one on the east containing the living room, dining room and roof garden, the one on the west housing the bedrooms and a tea ceremony room. A courtyard connects the two areas, and the whole building has a floor space of 178 m², set on a 304-m² lot. Built of reinforced concrete, the House in Suzaku displays the minimalist purity for which Waro Kishi is known, combining a modernist vocabulary with a respect for a Japanese sensibility of space and light.

Das **HAUS IN SUZAKU** Haus liegt in einem Neubaugebiet an der Peripherie von Nara und besteht aus zwei getrennten, jeweils 9 x 5,4 m großen Einheiten. Der östliche Teil enthält das Wohnzimmer, das Esszimmer und einen Dachgarten, während im westlichen die Schlafzimmer und ein Raum für die Teezeremonie untergebracht sind. Ein Hof verbindet die beiden auf einem 304 m² großen Grundstück errichteten Bereiche, die insgesamt eine Nutzfläche von 178 m² haben. In seiner Gestaltung aus Stahlbeton und der Kombination einer modernen Formensprache mit der japanischen Sensibilität im Umgang mit Raum und Licht verkörpert das Haus in Suzaku einen minimalistischen Purismus, der für Waro Kishi charakteristisch ist.

Située dans une banlieue résidentielle de Nara, la **MAISON DE SUZAKU** se compose de deux éléments de 9 x 5,4 m, celui de l'est abrite la salle-de-séjour, la salle-à-manger et le toit-terrasse aménagé en jardin, l'autre à l'ouest est consacré aux chambres et à un salon pour la cérémonie du thé. Une cour les relie. L'ensemble représente une surface de 178 m² sur une parcelle de 304 m². Construite en béton armé, cette maison illustre la pureté minimaliste à laquelle Kishi doit sa réputation : vocabulaire moderniste et respect de la sensibilité japonaise pour l'espace et la lumière.

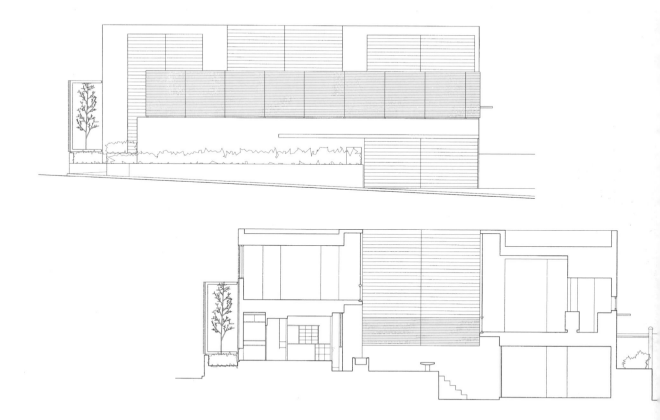

The internal courtyard is a typical feature of traditional Japanese houses, emphasizing the connection to nature that is recalled in Japanese architecture, even in dense urban areas.

Der Innenhof ist ein charakteristisches Merkmal der traditionellen japanischen Wohnhausarchitektur und schafft selbst in dicht besiedelten Stadtgebieten eine Verbindung zur Natur.

La cour intérieure est caractéristique des maisons japonaises traditionnelles. Elle illustre un lien avec la nature qu'aime maintenir l'architecture japonaise, même en zone urbaine dense.

Right: Space for the tea ceremony is laid out along essentially traditional lines, but this is in no way contradictory with the very modern design of the house itself.

Rechts: Die Gestaltung des Raums für die Teezeremonie folgt im Wesentlichen traditionellen Prinzipien, steht jedoch nicht in Widerspruch zu dem äußerst modernen Entwurf des Hauses selbst.

A droite : L'espace prévu pour la cérémonie du thé est conçu de façon traditionnelle, sans contredire pour autant la conception très actuelle de la maison.

KOHN PEDERSEN FOX

Kohn Pedersen Fox Associates
Architects & Planning Consultants
111 West 57th Street
New York, NY 10019
United States

Tel: +1 212 977 6500
Fax: +1 212 956 2526
e-mail: info@kpf.com
Web: www.kpf.com

13 Langley Street
Covent Garden
London WC 2 H9JG
England

Tel: +44 20 7836 6668
Fax: +44 20 7497 1175

KOHN PEDERSEN FOX (KPF) was founded in 1976. With offices in New York, London and Tokyo, KPF currently works in 30 countries. The 300-person firm is led by the 12 principals: A. Eugene Kohn, William Pedersen, Robert L. Cioppa, William Louie, Lee Polisano, David Leventhal, Gregory Clement, Paul Katz, James von Klemperer, Kevin Kennon, Michael Greene, and Peter Schubert. KPF's notable projects include the DG Bank Headquarters (Frankfurt, Germany, 1993), the World Bank (Washington D. C., 1996), IBM Corporate Headquarters (Armonk, New York, 1997), and the Shanghai World Financial Center (Shanghai, 2001-04), published here. William Pedersen, born in St. Paul, Minnesota, in 1938, obtained his M Arch. degree from MIT in 1963. He was an associate with I. M. Pei and Partners (1967-71) and Vice President of John Carl Warnecke and Associates (1971-76) before founding KPF.

Das 1976 gegründete Büro KOHN PEDERSEN FOX (KPF) mit Niederlassungen in New York, London und Tokio arbeitet gegenwärtig in 30 Ländern. Es hat insgesamt 300 Mitarbeiter und wird von zwölf Architekten geleitet: A. Eugene Kohn, William Pedersen, Robert L. Cioppa, William Louie, Lee Polisano, David Leventhal, Gregory Clement, Paul Katz, James von Klemperer, Kevin Kennon, Michael Greene und Peter Schubert. Zu den wichtigsten Bauten von KPF gehören die Hauptverwaltung der DG-Bank in Frankfurt am Main (1993), der Sitz der Weltbank in Washington, D. C. (1996), die IBM-Hauptverwaltung in Armonk, New York (1997) und das hier vorgestellte Shanghai World Financial Center (2001-04). William Pedersen, der Planungschef des Shanghai World Financial Center, erwarb 1963 seinen Master of Architecture am Massachusetts Institute of Technology (MIT). Bevor er KPF gründete, war Pedersen von 1967 bis 1971 Mitarbeiter bei I. M. Pei and Partners und von 1971 bis 1976 Vizepräsident von John Carl Warneck and Associates.

L'agence KOHN PEDERSEN FOX (KPF) a été fondée en 1976. Possédant des bureaux à New York, Londres et Tokyo, elle intervient actuellement dans 30 pays. 300 collaborateurs et 12 architectes associés y travaillent : A. Eugene Kohn, William Pedersen, Robert L. Cioppa, William Louie, Lee Polisano, David Leventhal, Gregory Clement, Paul Katz, James von Klemperer, Kevin Kennon, Michael Greene et Peter Schubert. Parmi ses principales réalisations : le siège de la DG Bank (Francfort, Allemagne, 1993), la banque Mondiale (Washington, 1996), le siège d'IBM à Armonk, New York, 1997) et le Shanghai World Financial Center (Shanghai, 2001-04), publié ici. William Pedersen est M. Arch. du MIT (1963). Il a été associé à I. M. Pei and Partners (1967-71) et vice-président de John Carl Warneck and Associates (1971-76) avant de fonder KPF.

SHANGHAI WORLD FINANCIAL CENTER

Shanghai, China, 2001

Developer: Mori Building Co., Ltd., Tokyo, Japan. Design architect: KPF Associates PC, New York, USA.
Planning: 1995-. Completion: 2005 (scheduled). Client: Forest Overseas Co., Ltd. Floor area: 312 152 m².

To be completed in 2005, the **SHANGHAI WORLD FINANCIAL CENTER** is slated to be the tallest building in the world (460 m). Located in the Lujiazui Financial and Trade District in Pudong, the building's most spectacular feature, apart from its height, is the 50 m cylindrical void at the top, dubbed the "moon gate." This opening, which gives the tower the appearance of an archaic Chinese artifact, serves to relieve wind pressure on the structure. The tower's form is based on the intersection of a square prism and a cylinder; it will contain office and retail space as well as a hotel. Retail space will be housed in the lower, podium area, and the building will rise to a total of 95 stories, clearly marking the emergence of China in general and Shanghai in particular as economic forces to be reckoned with.

Das **SHANGHAI WORLD FINANCIAL CENTER**, dessen Fertigstellung für 2005 geplant ist, soll bei seiner Fertigstellung mit 460 m das höchste Gebäude der Welt sein. Auffälligstes Kennzeichen dieses im Finanz- und Handelsdistrikt Lujiazui gelegenen Baus, ist neben seiner Höhe eine 50 m große zylindrische Öffnung an der Turmspitze, die den Namen »moon gate« (Mondtor) erhielt. Diese Öffnung, die ihm die Gestalt eines frühzeitlichen chinesischen Artefakts verleiht, dient der Verminderung des Winddrucks auf das Gebäude. Die äußere Gestalt des Wolkenkratzers entsteht aus der Durchdringung eines quadratischen Prismas und eines Zylinders. Im Inneren wird er Büros, Verkaufsräume und ein Hotel enthalten, die Geschäfte werden im unteren Sockelbereich liegen. Das Gebäude mit insgesamt 95 Stockwerken soll China im Allgemeinen und Shanghai im Besonderen als Ernst zu nehmende und kommende Wirtschaftsmächte symbolisieren.

Prévu pour être achevé en 2005, le **SHANGHAI WORLD FINANCIAL CENTER** édifié dans le quartier d'affaires de Lujiazui à Pudong, devrait être la plus haute tour du monde (460 m et 95 étages). Ce qui le caractérise, hormis ses dimensions, est une ouverture cylindrique de 50 m de haut à son sommet, appelé «porte de la lune.» Cette ouverture, qui évoque certains objets archaïques chinois, sert en fait à alléger la pression du vent sur la structure. La forme de la tour est générée par l'intersection d'un prisme carré et d'un cylindre. Elle contient des bureaux, des installations commerciales et un hôtel. Les commerces seront implantés dans la partie inférieure, dans le socle. Cette nouvelle tour marque l'émergence de la Chine en général et de Shanghai en particulier parmi les puissances avec lesquelles il faut compter.

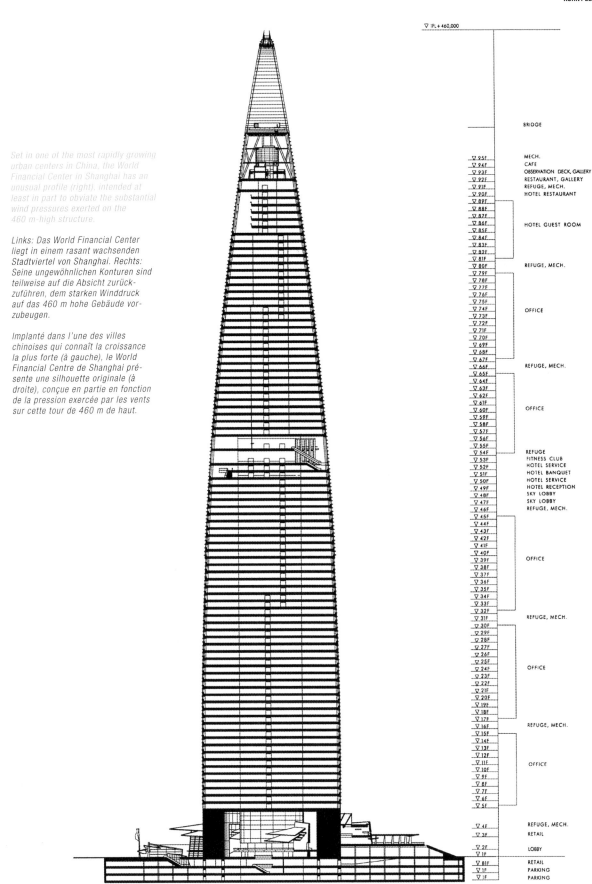

Set in one of the most rapidly growing
urban centers in China, the World
Financial Center in Shanghai has an
unusual profile (right), intended at
least in part to obviate the substantial
wind pressures exerted on the
460 m-high structure.

Links: Das World Financial Center
liegt in einem rasant wachsenden
Stadtviertel von Shanghai. Rechts:
Seine ungewöhnlichen Konturen sind
teilweise auf die Absicht zurückzuführen, dem starken Winddruck
auf das 460 m hohe Gebäude vor-
zubeugen.

Implanté dans l'une des villes
chinoises qui connaît la croissance
la plus forte (à gauche), le World
Financial Centre de Shanghai présente une silhouette originale (à
droite), conçue en partie en fonction
de la pression exercée par les vents
sur cette tour de 460 m de haut.

▽ IFL + 460,000

BRIDGE

▽ 95F MECH.
▽ 94F CAFE
▽ 93F OBSERVATION DECK, GALLERY
▽ 92F RESTAURANT, GALLERY
▽ 91F REFUGE, MECH.
▽ 90F HOTEL RESTAURANT
▽ 89F
▽ 88F
▽ 87F
▽ 86F HOTEL GUEST ROOM
▽ 85F
▽ 84F
▽ 83F
▽ 82F
▽ 81F
▽ 80F REFUGE, MECH.
▽ 79F
▽ 78F
▽ 77F
▽ 76F
▽ 75F
▽ 74F OFFICE
▽ 73F
▽ 72F
▽ 71F
▽ 70F
▽ 69F
▽ 68F
▽ 67F REFUGE, MECH.
▽ 66F
▽ 65F
▽ 64F
▽ 63F
▽ 62F
▽ 61F OFFICE
▽ 60F
▽ 59F
▽ 58F
▽ 57F
▽ 56F
▽ 55F
▽ 54F REFUGE
▽ 53F FITNESS CLUB
▽ 52F HOTEL SERVICE
▽ 51F HOTEL BANQUET
▽ 50F HOTEL SERVICE
▽ 49F HOTEL RECEPTION
▽ 48F SKY LOBBY
▽ 47F SKY LOBBY
▽ 46F REFUGE, MECH.
▽ 45F
▽ 44F
▽ 43F
▽ 42F
▽ 41F
▽ 40F
▽ 39F OFFICE
▽ 38F
▽ 37F
▽ 36F
▽ 35F
▽ 34F
▽ 33F
▽ 32F
▽ 31F REFUGE, MECH.
▽ 30F
▽ 29F
▽ 28F
▽ 27F
▽ 26F
▽ 25F
▽ 24F OFFICE
▽ 23F
▽ 22F
▽ 21F
▽ 20F
▽ 19F
▽ 18F
▽ 17F
▽ 16F REFUGE, MECH.
▽ 15F
▽ 14F
▽ 13F
▽ 12F
▽ 11F OFFICE
▽ 10F
▽ 9F
▽ 8F
▽ 7F
▽ 6F
▽ 5F

▽ 4F REFUGE, MECH.
▽ 3F RETAIL
▽ 2F
▽ 1F LOBBY

▽ B1F RETAIL
▽ 1F PARKING
▽ 1F PARKING

LAMOTT ARCHITEKTEN

Lamott Architekten BDA
Silberburgstraße 129 a
70176 Stuttgart
Germany

Tel.: +49 711 481 061
Fax: +49 711 4870 291
e-mail: mail@lamott.de
web: www.lamott.de

Public Library

ANSGAR LAMOTT was born in 1958 in Landau/Pfalz. He studied architecture at the University of Stuttgart (1978-85) and began to practice as an architect in 1985. A member of the architecture group Ostend 106 until 1996, he has taught at the Univeristy of Stuttgart (1994-96) and at the University College Biberach. He established his office with Caterina Lamott in 1996. **CATERINA LAMOTT** (née Karakitsou) was born in 1956 in Athens, Greece. She studied at the University of Stuttgart, obtaining her diploma as an architect in 1981. She was also a member of the Ostend 106 group until 1996. The firm's projects include an elementary school in Hardthausen-Gochsen (1997); a public library in Landau (1996-98); a sports hall in Herxheim (1999); a Catholic Church center in Völklingen/Saarland (2000); and a music school in Fellbach (2000), all in Germany.

ANSGAR LAMOTT, 1958 in Landau/Pfalz geboren, studierte von 1978 bis 1985 Architektur an der Universität Stuttgart. Bis 1996 war er Mitglied der Architekten-gruppe Ostend 106 und lehrte von 1989 bis 1992 und 1994 bis 1996 an der Universität Stuttgart und von 1994 bis 1996 am Universitätskolleg Biberach. 1996 gründete er zusammen mit seiner Frau Caterina Lamott das Architekturbüro Lamott Architekten. **CATERINA LAMOTT** (geborene Karakitsou) wurde 1956 in Athen geboren und stu-dierte wie ihr Mann an der Universität Stuttgart, wo sie 1981 ihr Architekturdiplom erwarb. Auch sie war bis 1996 Mitglied der Gruppe Ostend 106. Zu ihren gemeinsam ausgeführten Projekten gehören eine Grundschule in Hardthausen-Gochsen (1997), die Stadtbibliothek von Landau (1998), eine Sporthalle in Herxheim (1999), ein katho-lisches Gemeindezentrum in Völklingen/Saarland (2000) und eine Musikschule in Fellbach (2000).

ANSGAR LAMOTT est né en 1958 à Landau, Palatinat. Il étudie l'architecture à l'Université de Stuttgart (1978-85) et pratique dès 1985. Membre du groupe Ostend 106 jusqu'en 1996, il enseigne à l'Université de Stuttgart (1994-96) et au collège universitaire de Biberach. Il crée son agence en association avec Caterina Lamott en 1996. **CATERINA LAMOTT** (née Karakitsou) a vu le jour en 1956 à Athènes. Elle étudie à l'Université de Stuttgart dont elles est architecte diplômée en 1981. Elle est également membre du groupe Ostend 106 jusqu'en 1996. L'agence a réalisé une école primaire à Hardthausen-Gochsen (1997) ; une bibliothèque publique à Landau (1996-98) ; une salle de sport à Herxheim (1999) ; un centre paroissial catholique à Völklingen/Sarre, 2000, et une école de musique à Fellbach (2000), toutes en Allemagne.

PUBLIC LIBRARY

Landau, Germany, 1996-98

*Competition: 7/92. Planning: 11/94-7/96. Construction: 8/96-2/98. Client: Karl + Edith Fix-Stiftung, Landau.
Total floor area: 1 780 m². Costs: ca. 8 000 000 DM*

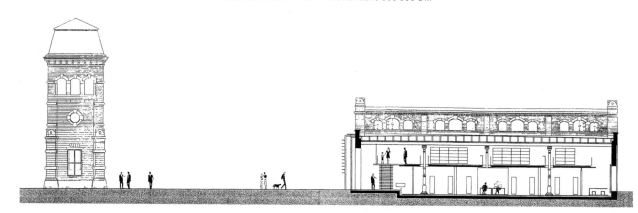

Built at a cost of 8 million DM, this 1 780-m² **PUBLIC LIBRARY** is housed in the former Landau slaughterhouse, originally built in 1895. Planned to accommodate a collection of some 75 000 books, CDs and periodicals, the original building was enlarged with a glass-enclosed annex, creating an obvious transition between the old and the new building. As the architects say, "The points at which the former outer wall has been perforated are rendered as wounds." The ground floor contains the entry, foyer, exhibition area and a café, the children's library and the main reading room with open stacks, connecting bridges that link the old and new spaces, the offices and meeting rooms are located above. Concerned that they were dealing with a heavy, antiquated structure originally used for a very different purpose the architects have created a thoroughly modern and convivial library.

Die 1 780 m² große, für 8 Millionen DM errichtete **STADTBIBLIOTHEK** befindet sich im ehemaligen Landauer Schlachthaus von 1895. Konzipiert für die Unterbringung eines Bestands von fast 75 000 Büchern, CD's und Zeitschriften, wurde das ursprüngliche Gebäude mit einem verglasten Anbau versehen, der alte und neue Gebäudeteile verbindet. Die Architekten erklären dazu: »Die Stellen, an denen die früheren Außenwände durchbrochen wurden, sind als Wunden kenntlich gemacht.« Im Erdgeschoss befinden sich der Eingang, ein Foyer, ein Ausstellungsbereich mit Café, die Kinderbücherei und der Hauptlesesaal mit dem Freihandmagazin sowie Laufstege, welche die alten und neuen Bereiche, die Büros und die darüberliegenden Konferenzräume miteinander verbinden. Angesichts der Tatsache, dass sie es mit einem massiven alten Baukörper zu tun hatten, der ursprünglich für einen völlig anderen Zweck konzipiert wurde, haben die Architekten eine durch und durch moderne und einladende Bibliothek geschaffen.

Construite pour un budget de DM 8 millions, cette **BIBLIOTHÈQUE PUBLIQUE** de 1 780 m² est installée dans les anciens abattoirs de Landau datant de 1895. Programmé pour 75 000 livres, CD et périodiques, le bâtiment original a été agrandi par une annexe de verre, qui différencie ainsi nettement les parties anciennes et nouvelles de l'ensemble. «Les endroits où l'ancien mur périphérique a été percé sont traités comme des blessures», explique l'architecte. Le rez-de-chaussée contient l'entrée, un hall d'accueil, une zone d'exposition et un café, l'étage abrite la bibliothèque des enfants, la salle de lecture principale à rayonnages ouverts, des passerelles qui relient les deux espaces, des bureaux et des salles de réunion. Conscient d'intervenir dans un édifice à la fois massif et ancien, conçu pour des fonctions très différents, les architectes ont réussi à créer une bibliothèque à la fois moderne et réellement conviviale.

The juxtaposition and interpenetration of old and new architectural forms is a theme in this design where industrial architecture intended for another purpose is augmented and transformed to meet new needs.

Das Nebeneinander und gegenseitige Durchdringen von alten und neuen Architekturformen bestimmt diesen Entwurf, auf dessen Grundlage ein ursprünglich als Schlachthaus genutzter Baukörper erweitert und den neuen Bedürfnissen angepasst wurde.

La juxtaposition et l'interpénétration de formes architecturales anciennes et nouvelles est un des thèmes de ce projet dans lequel l'architecture industrielle est détournée, enrichie et transformée pour répondre à de nouveaux besoins.

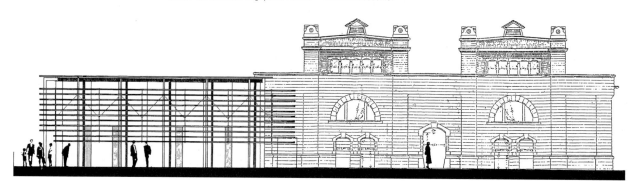

MAYA LIN

Maya Lin Studio
112 Prince Street
New York, NY 10012
United States

Tel: +1 212 941 6463
Fax: +1 212 941 6464
e-mail: MLinStudio@aol.com

Norton Apartment

MAYA LIN was born in Athens, Ohio, in 1959. She attended Yale College and the Yale School of Architecture, receiving her M.Arch. degree in 1986. She established her office, Maya Lin Studio, in New York the same year. By that time, she had already created what remains up to now her most famous work, the Vietnam Veterans' Memorial on the Mall in Washington D.C. (1981). Other sculptural work includes her Civil Rights Memorial (Montgomery, Alabama, 1989), and Groundswell, a landscape sculpture at the Wexner Center for the Arts (Columbus, Ohio, 1993). Before the Langston Hughes Library and the Norton Residence published here, she completed the designs for the Museum of African Art in New York (with David Hotson, 1993), the Weber Residence (Williamstown, Massachusetts, 1994), and the Asia/Pacific/American Studies Department, New York University (1997). New work includes a Chapel for the Children's Defense Fund in Clinton, Tennessee.

MAYA LIN wurde 1959 in Athens, Ohio geboren. Sie studierte am Yale College und an der Yale School of Architecture, wo sie 1986 ihren Master of Architecture erwarb. Im selben Jahr eröffnete sie in New York ihr eigenes Büro, Maya Lin Studio. Bereits 1981 hat sie ihr wohl berühmtestes Werk geschaffen, das Vietnam Veterans' Memorial auf der Mall in Washington, D. C. Zu Lins weiteren plastischen Arbeiten gehören das Civil Rights Memorial in Montgomery, Alabama (1989) und Groundswell, eine Landschaftsskulptur am Wexner Center for the Arts in Columbus, Ohio (1993). Außerdem entwarf sie das Museum of African Art in New York (in Zusammenarbeit mit David Hotson, 1993), die Villa Weber in Williamstown, Massachusetts (1994) und das Fakultätsgebäude für Asien/Pazifik/Amerika-Studien der New York University (1997). Zu ihren jüngsten Projekten gehört eine Kapelle für den Children's Defense Fund in Clinton, Tennessee.

Née à Athens, Ohio, en 1959, **MAYA LIN** suit les cours du Yale College et de la Yale School of Architecture dont elle est Master of Architecture en 1986. Elle crée son agence – Maya Lin Studio – à New York la même année. Elle a alors déjà signé ce qui reste son œuvre la plus connue, le Vietnam Veteran's Memorial sur le Mall de Washington (1981). Parmi ses autres œuvres relevant de la sculpture : le Civil Rights Memorial (Montgomery, Alabama, 1989) et la sculpture de plein air Groundswell au Wexner Center for the Arts (Columbus, Ohio, 1993). Avant de réaliser la Langston Hughes Library et la Norton Residence publiées ici, elle a achevé les plans du Museum of African Art (New York, avec David Hotson, 1993), de la Weber Residence (Williamstown, Massachusetts, 1994) et du Department of Asia/Pacific/American Studies (New York University, 1997). Elle travaille actuellement sur le projet d'une chapelle pour le Children's Defense Fund à Clinton, Tennessee.

NORTON APARTMENT

New York, NY, USA, 1996-98

Planning: 1996-1997. Construction: 1997-1998. Client: Peter and Eileen Norton. Floor area: 195 m².

The 195-m² **NORTON APARTMENT** was commissioned as "a surprise gift for the client's wife." Intended to be extremely flexible, it features two bedrooms that can be made into one, a single bathroom that can be divided, and a "dining table that reduces to a simple bar element." The apartment is set on two levels, the upper level housing the bedrooms and baths, the lower level comprising the public areas. The apartment benefited from an indulgent client who imposed "no fixed budget, no fixed schedule, no overriding design parameters, and no heavy-fisted client intervention." Frosted glass and sycamore paneling create a slightly austere but sophisticated atmosphere, which is heightened by the furniture, specially designed for the apartment by Maya Lin and her collaborator, the architect David Hotson.

Das 195 m² große **NORTON APARTMENT** wurde als »ein Überraschungsgeschenk für die Frau des Bauherrn« in Auftrag gegeben. Da es möglichst flexibel nutzbar sein sollte, wurde es mit zwei Schlafräumen ausgestattet, die zu einem einzigen zusammengelegt werden können, einem Badezimmer, das sich teilen lässt und einem Esstisch, der in eine kleine Bar verwandelt werden kann. Die Wohnung ist auf zwei Ebenen angelegt, in der oberen befinden sich Schlafzimmer und Bad, die untere enthält die Wohnräume. Das Bauprojekt profitierte von der Großzügigkeit des Auftraggebers, der »kein festes Budget und keinen Zeitplan vorgab« und der Architektin bei der Gestaltung völlig freie Hand ließ. Mattglas und Holztäfelungen aus Platane evozieren eine Atmospäre kühler Eleganz, die noch gesteigert wird durch die Möbel, die Maya Lin in Zusammenarbeit mit dem Architekten David Hotson eigens für dieses Apartment entworfen hat.

L'**APPARTEMENT NORTON** de 195 m² était «une surprise pour l'épouse du client». L'objectif était d'arriver à une souplesse extrême d'aménagement. Deux chambres peuvent ainsi se transformer en une seule, la salle-de-bains peut se diviser, ou «une table de salle-à-manger «se transformer en un simple bar». L'appartement s'étend sur deux niveaux. L'étage est occupé par les chambres et les salles-de-bains, le niveau inférieur par les pièces de réception. Le chantier a bénéficié de la collaboration d'un client à l'esprit ouvert qui n'a imposé «ni budget, ni calendrier, ni contraintes gênantes, et qui s'est abstenu de tout interventionnisme pesant». Le verre givré et des lambris de sycomore créent une atmosphère légèrement austère, mais sophistiquée, qui met en valeur le mobilier spécialement dessiné par Maya Lin et son collaborateur, l'architecte David Hotson.

As both an artist and an architect, Maya Lin was able to lay out the space of this apartment as a display area for some of her own work (the glass piece in the corner above) and the furniture she designed (right) in the dining area.

Maya Lin, Künstlerin und Architektin, gestaltete die Räume so, dass sie einige eigene Arbeiten präsentieren konnte, wie das Glasobjekt in einer Ecke des Wohnraums (oben) und die von ihr entworfenen Möbel im Essbereich (rechts).

A la fois artiste et architecte Maya Lin a aménagé cet appartement pour présenter un certain nombre de ses propres travaux et des meubles qu'elle a dessinés, comme dans la salle-à-manger (à droite).

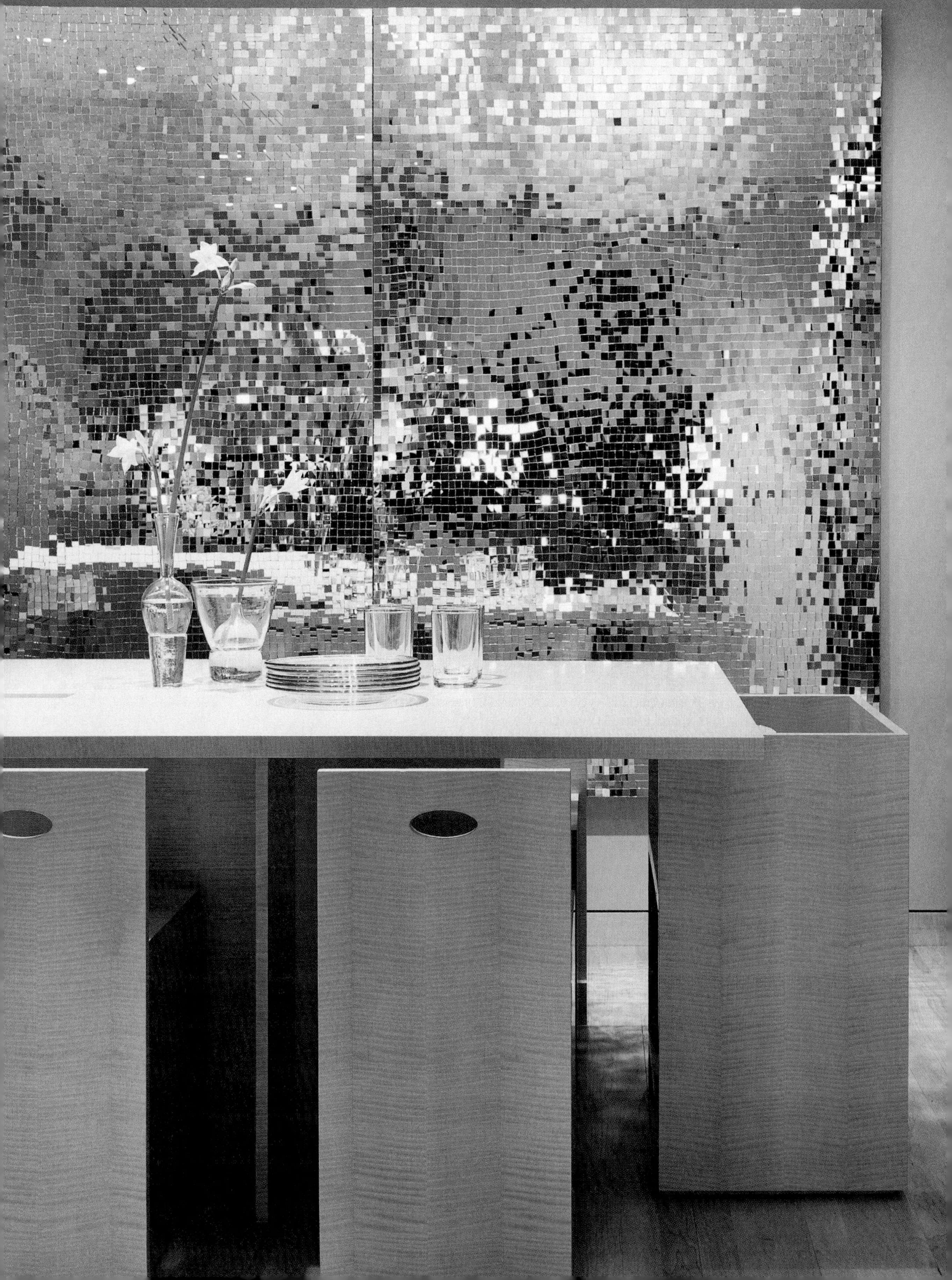

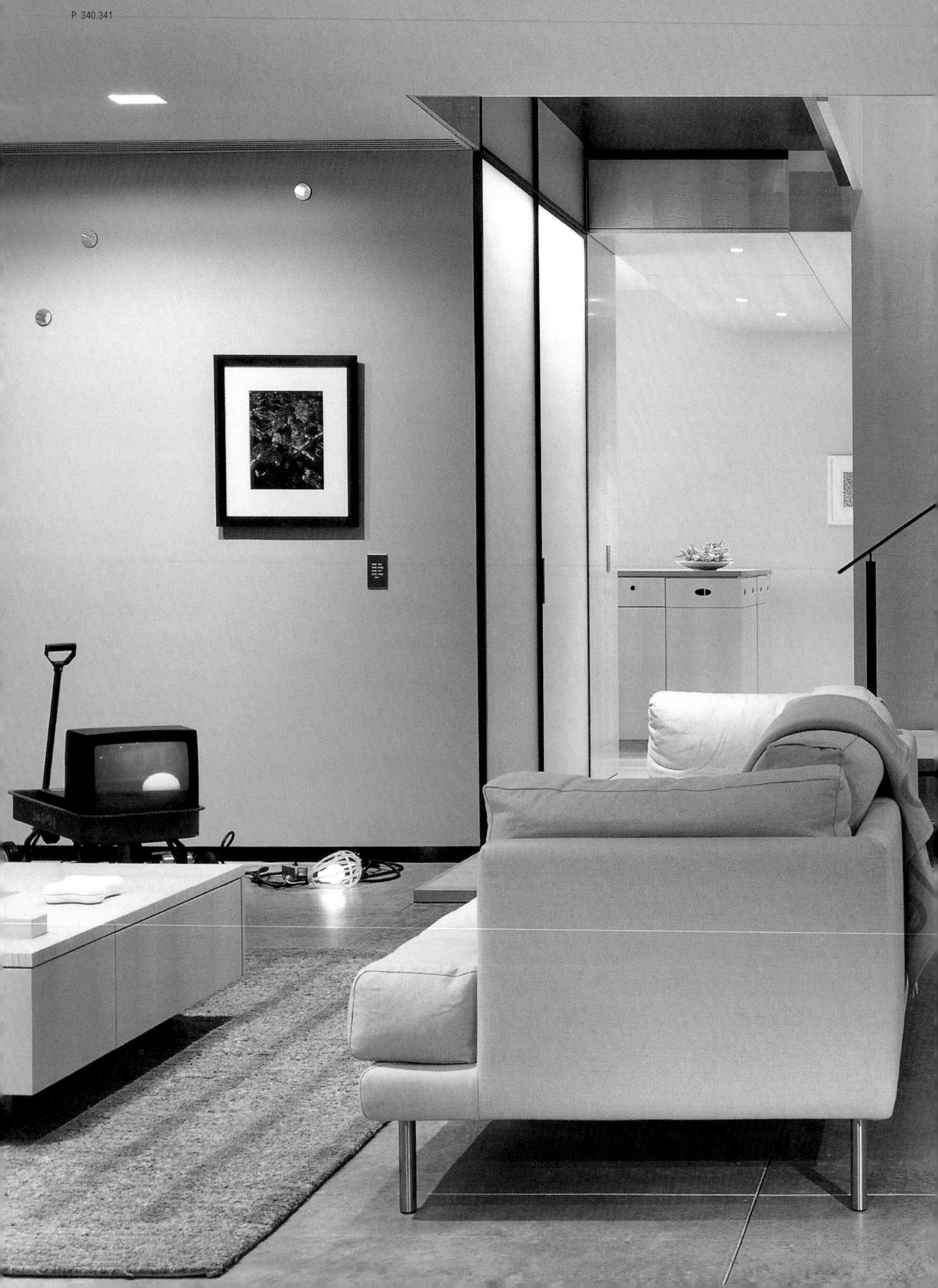

LANGSTON HUGHES LIBRARY

Knoxville, Tennessee, USA, 1997-99

Planning: 1997-98. Completion: 3/99. Clients: Len and Louise Reggio, donors; Children's Defense Fund, sponsors; Marian Wright Edelman, director of CDF. Total floor area: 186 m².

Designed as a library of African-American culture, the unusual **LANGSTON HUGHES LIBRARY** is based on a 100-year old cantilevered Tennessee barn that the architect literally took apart and set up on two supporting cribs. The library space, measuring about 153 m², is the single upper-level room, whose interior surfaces are clad in maple paneling, beige carpeting and brown recycled particleboard. Located on a farm owned by the Children's Defense Fund, the library's interior has little relation to the rough-hewn timber of the barn – a feature for which the architect has been criticized. Lin compares the design to a "diamond in the rough." "When you cut into it," she says, "it reveals a more-polished inner self." Despite its relatively closed appearance, the library receives good natural light through "cuts made throughout the stacks, reading areas and the entry stair hall."

Die ungewöhnliche, für die Bibliothek der afroamerikanischen Kultur konzipierte **LANGSTON HUGHES LIBRARY** entstand aus der Umnutzung einer 100 Jahre alten, freitragenden »Tennessee-Scheune«, die von der Architektin buchstäblich auseinander genommen und auf eine Balkenkonstruktion gesetzt wurde. Der gut 153 m² große Bibliothekssaal nimmt das gesamte Obergeschoss ein, dessen Inneres mit Ahorntäfelung, beigen Teppichböden und recycelten braunen Spanplatten ausgestattet ist. Obwohl der Bau auf einem im Besitz des Children's Defense Fund befindlichen Farmgelände steht, hat das Interieur der Bibliothek wenig mit der ursprünglichen, grob gearbeiteten Holzauskleidung der Scheune zu tun – ein Aspekt, für den die Architektin kritisiert wurde. Lin vergleicht ihren Entwurf mit einem »Rohdiamanten« und fügt hinzu: »Erst wenn man ihn aufschneidet, kommt sein glattes Inneres zum Vorschein.« Trotz ihrer relativ geschlossenen Form erhält die Bibliothek viel natürliches Licht durch Schlitze, die überall zwischen den Regalen, im Lesebereich und im Eingangstreppenhaus angebracht wurden.

Destinée à devenir la Bibliothèque de à la culture afro-américaine, la **LANGSTON HUGHES LIBRARY** est implantée dans une propriété agricole du Children's Defense Fund. Ce curieux projet résulte de la reconversion d'une grange à encorbellement séculaire du Tennessee, démontée et remontée sur deux systèmes de pilotis. La bibliothèque, d'environ 153 m², occupe la totalité de la pièce unique de l'étage, dont les murs sont habillés de lambris d'érable, de médium brun, et les sols recouverts de moquette beige. L'intérieur de la bibliothèque n'a que peu de rapport avec l'aspect extérieur de la grange, ce qui a valu certaines critiques à l'architecte. M. Lin compare le projet à « un diamant brut ». « Lorsque vous le taillez, il révèle un intérieur plus lisse. » En dépit de son aspect assez fermé, la bibliothèque reçoit un éclairage naturel de qualité par « des découpes pratiquées entre les rayonnages, dans les zones de lecture et l'escalier d'entrée. »

One very surprising aspect of this project is that the interior and the exterior of the original, elevated wood structure have very little to do with each other. Indeed the sophistication of the interior does contradict the rural surroundings.

Die wohl durchdachte und elegante Innenausstattung des auf eine Holzkonstruktion gesetzten Baus steht in deutlichem Widerspruch zu seinem Äußeren und der ländlichen Umgebung.

Un des aspects les plus surprenants de ce projet est l'absence presque totale de rapports entre le bâtiment d'origine, en bois, et son aménagement. Son intérieur raffiné est même en contradiction avec le cadre naturel.

The rough-hewn exterior of the
original barn building gives way to
a sophisticated interior that houses
the Langston Hughes Library.

Über die Unterbauten, die in ihrer
Gestaltung an die grob gearbeitete
Außenfassade der ehemaligen
Scheune angepasst sind, gelangt
man in den sachlich-kühlen Innen-
raum der Langston Hughes Library.

On accède à la belle salle de lecture
de la Langston Hughes Library par la
partie inférieure de cette ancienne
grange de construction rustique.

MAHLER GÜNSTER FUCHS

Mahler Günster Fuchs
Gutenbergstrasse 94 a
70197 Stuttgart
Germany

Tel.: +49 711 610 521
Fax: +49 711 615 9443

KLAUS MAHLER was born in 1940 in Stuttgart, Germany. He has taught at the University College in Cologne and at Kaiserslautern University. **ARMIN GÜNSTER** was born in 1959 in Weitersburg, Germany. He studied at Kaiserslautern and Darmstadt Universities (1979-86) and has been working as an architect since 1989. **HARTMUT FUCHS** was born in 1952 in Berlin, Germany, and studied at the University of Stuttgart (1971-78). He has been a practicing architect since 1981. The practice completed a Fashion House (Schwäbisch Hall, 1993), a Vocational School (Karlsruhe, 1994), a Nursing Home (Neuenbürg, 1996), and a Tax Office (Schwarzenberg, 1999), all in Germany. Current work includes the University College in Wiesbaden. They won second prize in the competition for the German Pavilion for Hanover Expo 2000. The firm was awarded the Mies van der Rohe Prize in 1999, the German Architecture Prize in 1989, 1995, 1997 and 1999, and the Balthasar Neumann Prize in 1996.

Der 1940 in Stuttgart geborene **KLAUS MAHLER** lehrte an der Kölner Fachhochschule und an der Universität Kaiserslautern. **ARMIN GÜNSTER,** geboren 1959 in Weitersburg, studierte von 1979 bis 1986 an den Universitäten Kaiserslautern und Darmstadt und ist seit 1989 als Architekt tätig. **HARTMUT FUCHS,** 1952 in Berlin geboren, studierte von 1971 bis 1978 an der Universität Stuttgart und arbeitet seit 1981 als Architekt. Zu ihren gemeinsam realisierten Bauten zählen ein Modehaus in Schwäbisch Hall (1993), eine Berufsschule in Karlsruhe (1994), ein Pflegeheim in Neuenbürg (1996) und das Finanzamt in Schwarzenberg (1999); die Fachhochschule (Fachbereich Gestaltung) in Wiesbaden ist eines ihrer aktuellen Projekte. Im Wettbewerb für den Deutschen Pavillon der Expo 2000 in Hannover erhielten sie den zweiten Preis. Das Architekturbüro wurde 1999 mit dem Mies-van-der-Rohe-Preis, 1989, 1995, 1997 und 1999 mit dem Deutschen Architekturpreis sowie 1996 mit dem Balthasar-Neumann-Preis ausgezeichnet.

KLAUS MAHLER naît en 1940 à Stuttgart, Allemagne. Il enseigne au collège universitaire de Cologne et à l'Université de Kaiserslautern. **ARMIN GÜNSTER** naît en 1959 à Weitersburg, Allemagne. Il étudie à l'Université de Kaiserslautern et à celle de Darmstadt (1978-86). Il exerce depuis 1989. **HARTMUT FUCHS** naît en 1952 à Berlin et étudie à l'Université de Stuttgart (1971-78). Il exerce depuis 1981. En Allemagne l'agence a réalisé un magasin de mode (Schwäbisch Hall, 1993), une école professionnelle (Karlsruhe, 1994), une maison de soins (Neuenbürg, 1996) et une agence des impôts (Schwartzenberg, 1999). Elle travaille actuellement à un collège universitaire pour Wiesbaden. Elle a remporté le deuxième prix du concours pour le pavillon allemand, de Hanovre Expo 2000. Elle a obtenu le Prix Mies van der Rohe 1999, le Prix allemand d'architecture en 1989, 1995, 1997 et 1999, ainsi que le Prix Balthasar Neumann en 1996.

SCHULZENTRUM MÜNCHEN-RIEM

Munich, Germany, 1996-98

Completion: 8/98. Client: Landeshauptstadt München, represented by MRG Maßnahmeträger München-Riem GmbH. Floor area: 10 290 m².

This 10 290-m² **SCHOOL** was built on the grounds of the former Riem airport. Consisting of a primary and main school, a daycare center and a gymnasium, the complex consists of a main structure to the south with smaller buildings attached to the north facade. Facing an open landscape, the design makes ample use of glazing, and a cantilevered brise-soleil provides protection from the summer sun. The use of untreated wood paneling for the exterior surfaces lends itself to a natural graying of the building, intended by the architects. Natural ventilation is used to the greatest possible extent. The architects also designed all the furniture for the complex.

Das 10 290 m² umfassende **SCHULZENTRUM** wurde auf dem Gelände des ehemaligen Flughafens München-Riem errichtet. Es besteht aus einem nach Süden ausgerichteten Hauptbau und mehreren kleineren, auf der nördlichen Seite befindlichen Nebengebäuden und umfasst eine Grund- und Hauptschule, einen Hort sowie ein Gymnasium. Große Glasflächen, die den Blick nach außen freigeben, beziehen die Landschaft der Umgebung in den Bau ein. Eine freitragende Brisesoleil-Konstruktion (Sonnenschutz an der Außenseite der Fenster) schützt im Sommer vor Sonnenlicht. Zudem wurde Wert auf eine weitestgehend natürliche Belüftung gelegt. Wie von den Architekten beabsichtigt, wird das Gebäude durch die Täfelung der Außenflächen mit unbehandeltem Holz allmählich auf natürliche Weise »ergrauen«. Die gesamte Inneneinrichtung des Komplexes wurde ebenfalls von den Architekten entworfen.

Cette **ÉCOLE** de 10 290 m² a été édifiée sur les terrains de l'ancien aéroport de Riem. Elle se compose d'un bâtiment principal au sud et de petites constructions rattachées au nord, l'ensemble étant destiné à une école primaire, une école secondaire, une crèche et un gymnase. Les architectes ont tenu compte du paysage ouvert et recouru à de grandes surfaces vitrées. Un système de pare-soleil se révèle très utile en été. Les architectes ont choisi un bardage en bois qui vieillira avec le temps et opté pour une ventilation naturelle. Tout le mobilier a été dessiné par Mahler Günster Fuchs.

The intentional contrast between the rough wood cladding of one wall and a perpendicular glass wall is typical of this austere school complex.

Der Kontrast der rauen Holzverkleidung einer Außenwand und der Glaswand ist charakteristisch für diesen nüchternen Schulkomplex.

Le contraste voulu entre le bardage de bois d'œuvre d'un mur et la paroi perpendiculaire en verre caractérise cette école à l'aspect austère.

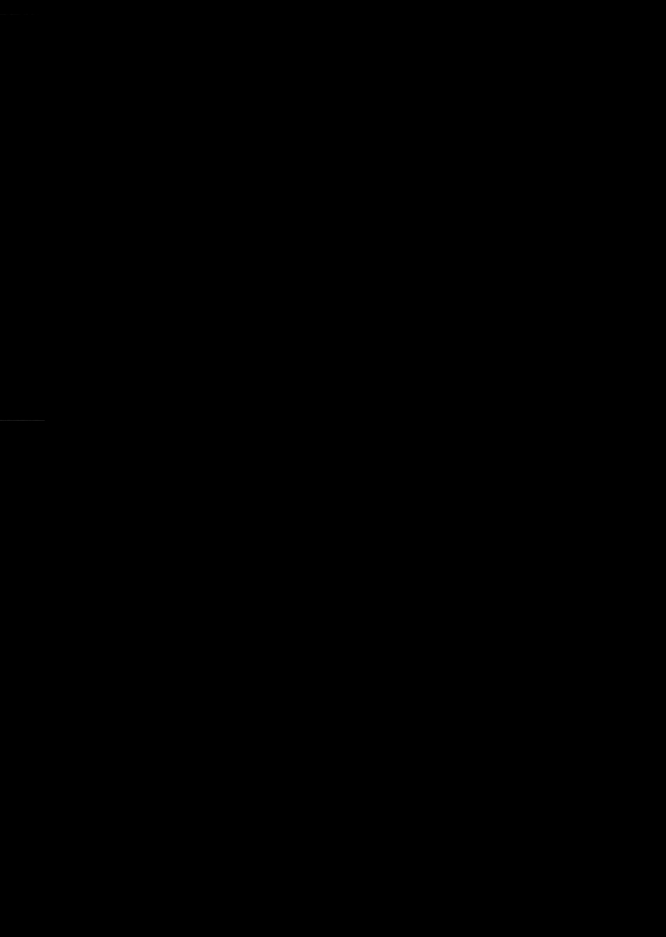

A dark, even difficult interior corresponds to the relative harshness of the exterior.

Das dunkle Innere des Gebäudes korrespondiert in seiner Gestaltung mit der relativ strengen Außenfassade.

L'aménagement intérieur sombre, presque difficile à vivre, répond à la rigueur de l'extérieur.

Glazed surfaces and the use of glass
blocks alleviate the rather heavy and
hard materials chosen for what should
perhaps be a more joyful space.

Große verglaste Flächen und Wände
aus Glasbausteinen erhellen die in
ihrer Materialwahl streng und sparsam, fast hart wirkenden Räumlichkeiten des Schulgebäudes.

Les surfaces vitrées et les pavés de
verre contrastent par leur légèreté
avec les matériaux durs et lourds
choisis pour des espaces qui
manquent peut-être de gaieté.

FUMIHIKO MAKI

Maki and Associates
Hillside West Building C
13-4 Hachiyama-cho
Shibuya-ku, Tokyo 150-0035
Japan

Tel: +81 3 3780 3880
Fax: +81 3 3780 3881

Born in Tokyo in 1928, **FUMIHIKO MAKI** received his B.Arch. degree from the University of Tokyo in 1952, and M.Arch. degrees from the Cranbrook Academy of Art (1953) and the Harvard Graduate School of Design (1954). He worked for Skidmore, Owings and Merrill in New York (1954-55) and Sert Jackson and Associates in Cambridge, Massachusetts (1955-58) before creating his own firm, Maki and Associates, in Tokyo in 1965. Notable buildings include Fujisawa Municipal Gymnasium (Fujisawa, Kanagawa, 1984), Spiral (Minato-ku, Tokyo, 1985), National Museum of Modern Art (Sakyo-ku, Kyoto, 1986), Tepia (Minato-ku, Tokyo, 1989), Nippon Convention Center Makuhari Messe (Chiba, 1989), Tokyo Metropolitan Gymnasium (Shibuya, Tokyo, 1990), and Center for the Arts Yerba Buena Gardens (San Francisco, California, 1993). Recent and current projects include Nippon Convention Center Makuhari Messe Phase II (Chiba, 1997) and the Hillside West buildings, part of his ongoing Hillside Terrace project, both completed in 1998, as well as the Asahi Television Headquarters & Studios (Tokyo, to be completed in 2003), and the MIT Media Laboratory (Cambridge, Massachusetts, to be completed in 2004).

FUMIHIKO MAKI, geboren 1928 in Tokio, erwarb 1952 den Bachelor of Architecture an der Universität Tokio, den Master of Architecture 1953 an der Cranbrook Academy of Art und 1954 an der Harvard Graduate School of Design (GSD). Er arbeitete in den Büros Skidmore, Owings and Merrill in New York (1954-55) und Sert Jackson and Associates in Cambridge, Massachusetts (1955-58), bevor er 1965 seine eigene Firma, Maki and Associates in Tokio gründete. Zu seinen herausragenden Bauten gehören die Städtische Sporthalle in Fujisawa, Kanagawa (1984), das Medienzentrum Spiral, Minato-ku, Tokio (1985), das Staatliche Museum für Moderne Kunst in Sakyo-ku, Kioto (1986), das Tepia-Gebäude in Minato-ku, Tokio (1989), das Nippon Convention Center Makuhari Messe in Chiba (1989), die Städtische Sporthalle in Shibuya, Tokio (1990) und das Center for the Arts Yerba Buena Gardens in San Francisco (1993). Zu seinen jüngsten Projekten gehören das Nippon Convention Center, Makuhari Messe Phase II in Chiba und die Hillside West-Gebäude als Teil seines laufenden Hillside Terrace-Projekts, beide 1998 fertiggestellt, außerdem die Asahi Television Headquarters & Studios (Tokio, geplante Fertigstellung 2003) und das Medienlabor des Massachusetts Institute of Technology (Cambridge, Massachusetts, geplante Fertigstellung 2004).

Né à Tokyo en 1928, **FUMIHIKO MAKI** est Bachelor of Architecture de l'Université de Tokyo en 1952, et Master of Architecture de la Cranbrook Academy of Art (1953) et de la Harvard Graduate School of Design (1954). Il travaille pour Skidmore, Owings and Merrill à New York (1954-55), et Sert Jackson and Associates à Cambridge, Massachusetts (1955-58), avant de créer sa propre agence, Maki and Associates, à Tokyo (1965). Parmi ses réalisations les plus connues : le gymnase municipal de Fujisawa (Fujisawa, Kanagawa, Japon,1984), Spiral (Minato-ku, Tokyo, 1985), Musée national d'art moderne (Sakyo-ku, Kyoto, 1986), Tepia (Minato-ku, Tokyo, 1989), le Centre de Congrès Nippon de Makuhari (Chiba, Japon, 1989), le gymnase métropolitain de Tokyo (Shibuya, Tokyo, 1990), le Center for the Arts Yerba Buena Gardens (San Francisco, Californie, 1993). En 1998, il achève la phase II (extension) du Centre de Congrès Nippon de Makuhari (Chiba) et les immeubles de Hillside West qui font partie de Hillside Terrace, son projet en cours ainsi que les quartiers généraux et les studios de Asahi (date prévue des travaux 2003) et le laboratoire de développement pour les médias du Massachusetts Institute of Technology (Cambridge, Massachusetts, date prévue des travaux 2004).

HILLSIDE WEST

Tokyo, Japan, 1996-98

Planning: 3/96-6/97. Completion: 11/98. Client: Asakura Real Estate.
Floor area: 2 958 m². Costs: withheld at owner's request.

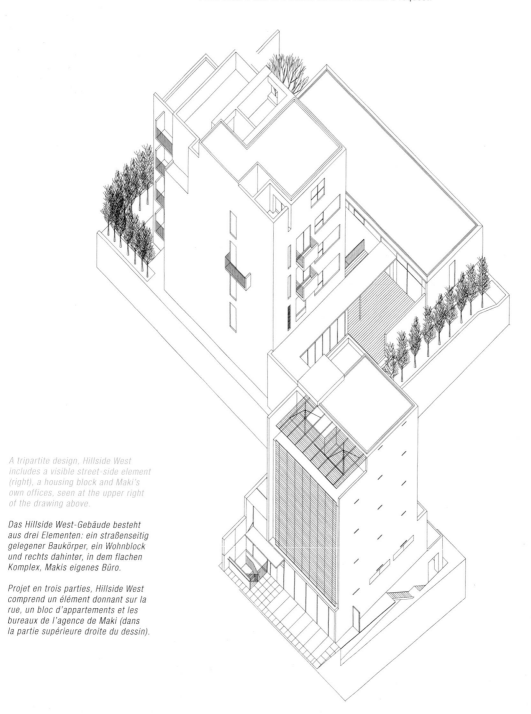

A tripartite design, Hillside West
includes a visible street-side element
(right), a housing block and Maki's
own offices, seen at the upper right
of the drawing above.

Das Hillside West-Gebäude besteht
aus drei Elementen: ein straßenseitig
gelegener Baukörper, ein Wohnblock
und rechts dahinter, in dem flachen
Komplex, Makis eigenes Büro.

Projet en trois parties, Hillside West
comprend un élément donnant sur la
rue, un bloc d'appartements et les
bureaux de l'agence de Maki (dans
la partie supérieure droite du dessin).

Fumihiko Maki has been building along Old Yamate Street in the Shibuya district of Tokyo since 1967. This building complex, known as Hillside Terrace, is exemplary in its constancy, and contributes to the district's pleasant, urban atmosphere. In 1993, Maki was awarded the Third Prince of Wales Prize in Urban Design for the Hillside Terrace Complex. His most recent addition to the area, **HILLSIDE WEST,** has a total floor area of 2958 m² and is situated down the street from the other buildings on an odd-shaped sloping lot that Maki has transformed into housing, office space (including his own) and an exhibition area. From its most visible facade on Old Yamate Street, shielded with a subtle, perforated aluminum screen, to the interior walkway leading toward his offices, this building is a testimony not only to Maki's talent as an architect, but also to his ability to evoke a civilized understanding of urban life in the midst of Tokyo's sprawling complexity.

Fumihiko Maki arbeitet schon seit 1967 an der Old Yamate Street im Tokioter Shibuya Distrikt. Der Hillside Terrace genannte Gebäudekomplex, für den Maki 1993 mit dem Third Prince of Wales Prize in Urban Design ausgezeichnet wurde, ist exemplarisch in seiner Konsistenz und trägt zu der urbanen Atmosphäre des Stadtviertels bei. Sein zuletzt hinzugefügter Teil, das **HILLSIDE WEST**-Gebäude, hat eine Gesamtnutzfläche von 2958 m². Es wurde ein Stück entfernt von den anderen Gebäuden auf einem unregelmäßig geformten Hanggrundstück errichtet und enthält Wohnungen, Büros (darunter das des Architekten) sowie einen Ausstellungsbereich. Von der mit einem zarten Aluminiumgitter abgeschirmten sichtbaren Front an der Old Yamate Street bis zu dem Gehweg, der zu Makis Büros führt, zeugt dieses Bauwerk nicht nur von Makis Talent als Architekt, sondern ebenso von seiner Fähigkeit, inmitten des ausufernden Stadtgebietes von Tokio den Geist einer kultivierten Urbanität aufleben zu lassen.

Depuis 1967, Fumihiko Maki est responsable d'un long chantier en bordure de la vieille rue Yamate dans le quartier Shibuya de Tokyo. Cet ensemble de bâtiments, appelé Hillside Terrace, est exemplaire par sa continuité et contribue à l'agrément urbain du quartier. En 1993, Maki a obtenu le Third Prince of Wales Prize in Urban Design pour ce projet. **HILLSIDE WEST**, sa plus récente réalisation, a une surface brute de 2958 m². Construite dans la même rue, en contrebas des immeubles déjà achevés, elle se situe sur une parcelle en pente et de forme complexe. Maki a édifié là des logements, des bureaux (dont celui de son agence) et un espace d'exposition. Que ce soit par sa façade sur la rue protégée par un subtil écran d'aluminium perforé, ou ses allées intérieures qui conduisent aux bureaux de l'architecte, cet immeuble témoigne du talent de Maki et de sa capacité de concrétiser une demarche personelle et une certaine idee de l'urbanisme au cœur de l'envahissant désordre de Tokyo.

Right: The passageway, neither fully interior nor fully exterior, leading to Maki's offices.

Rechts: Der überdachte Durchgang zu Makis Büro changiert zwischen Innen- und Außenraum.

Le passage couvert (à droite) qui conduit aux bureaux de Maki n'est ni intérieur ni vraiment extérieur.

TOYAMA INTERNATIONAL CONVENTION CENTER

Toyama, Japan, 1996-99

*Planning: 4/96-3/97. Completion: 6/99. Client: Toyama City and Toyama Prefecture.
Floor area: 13 273 m². Costs: 6 787 167 000 ¥.*

Described as a convention facility, **INTERNATIONAL CONFERENCE HALL** and hotel annex, this complex is intended to increase the public presence of the city of Toyama. The 13 273-m² building, a structural steel design with steel-reinforced concrete, contains a public atrium, a gallery, conference rooms and the main hall, seating 825 people. Situated in Castle Park in central Toyama, the building features a metal and glass curtain wall with a wooden lattice screen made of solid maple. As he has in his other work, such as the well-known Tepia Building, Fumihiko Maki again demonstrates his ability to distill Japanese tradition in a modern setting. He uses the idea of the screen to provide softness and warmth in an otherwise cooler setting, at the same time maintaining the connection between the interior and the exterior environment.

Das als **INTERNATIONALES KONGRESSZENTRUM** und Versammlungshalle mit angeschlossenem Hotel beschriebene Projekt soll zum internationalen Ansehen der japanischen Stadt Toyama beitragen. Der 13 273 m² umfassende Stahlbetonbau enthält einen großen Saal mit 825 Sitzen, ein Atrium, eine Ausstellungsgalerie und einen Konferenzsaal. Der Bau im Castle Park in der Innenstadt von Toyama hat eine Curtain-Wall-Fassade aus Stahl und Glas mit einer Gitterwand aus massivem Ahorn. Ebenso wie in seinen anderen Bauten, so dem bekannten Tepia-Gebäude in Tokio, zeigt sich auch in diesem Projekt Makis Fähigkeit, japanische Traditionen in ein modernes Baugefüge einfließen zu lassen. Mit der Gitterwand aus Ahornholz greift er die Idee des Paravents auf, um in einem sonst eher kühlen Ambiente für Weichheit und Wärme zu sorgen und schafft gleichzeitig die Verbindung zwischen der inneren und der äußeren Umgebung.

CENTRE INTERNATIONAL DE CONFÉRENCES et hôtel, cet ensemble en structures d'acie et béton armé a pour objectif de renforcer l'image de la ville de Toyama. Sur 13 273 m², il abrite un vaste hall principal, un atrium, une galerie, une salle de conférences et une salle principale de 825 places. Situé dans le Parc du château, au centre de Toyama, le bâtiment est clos par un mur-rideau de métal et de verre et un écran en lattis de bois d'érable massif. Comme dans ses autres réalisations, en particulier le célèbre Tepia-Building, Fumihiko Maki fait une fois de plus preuve de sa capacité à évoquer la tradition japonaise dans un cadre résolument moderne. Il se sert du concept d'écran pour apporter douceur et chaleur dans un cadre par ailleurs assez froid, tout en maintenant le lien entre l'intérieur et l'environnement extérieur.

In the generous sophistication of the foyer, Maki succeeds in translating into a large scale, the mastery of details that is so evident in his work on a smaller scale.

Mit der großzügigen Eleganz des Foyers ist es Maki gelungen, seine meisterliche Beherrschung der Details, die bei seinen kleineren Arbeiten so ins Auge fällt, auf ein Großprojekt zu übertragen.

Grâce au raffinement de ce généreux foyer, Maki réussit à appliquer à grande échelle la maîtrise du détail si évidente dans ses réalisations de dimensions moins ambitieuses.

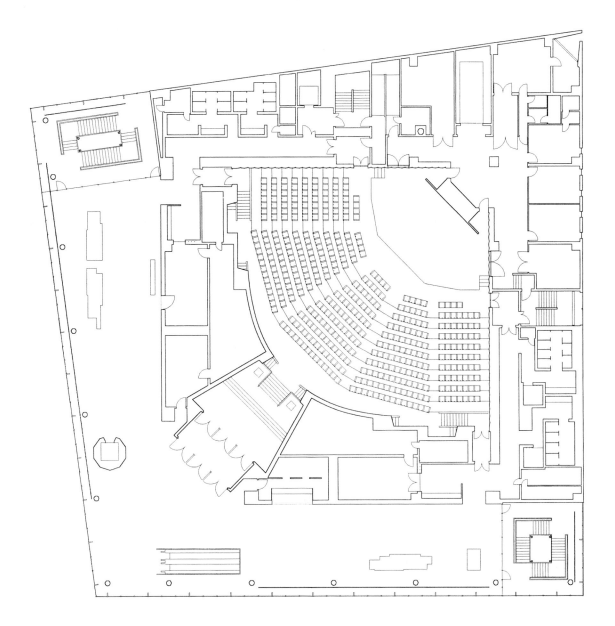

Left: Calling on the tradition of the
Japanese Shoji screen, Maki filters
the light coming into the foyer.

Links: Auf die Tradition der Shoji-
Wandschirme zurückgreifend, filtert
Maki das ins Foyer einfallende
Tageslicht, indem er eine Gitter-
wand aus Ahornholz vor die Fenster
setzt.

A gauche : En reprenant la tradition
de l'écran Shoji japonais, Maki filtre
la lumière qui arrive dans le foyer.

MARMOL RADZINER

Marmol Radziner + Associates AIA
architecture + construction
2902 Nebraska Avenue
Santa Monica, California 90404
United States

Tel.: + 1 310 264 1814
Fax: + 1 310 264 1817
Web: www.marmol-radziner.com

Restored Kaufmann House

LEONARDO MARMOL, the Managing Principal of Marmol Radziner received his B.Arch. degree from Cal Poly San Luis Obispo in 1987. He has worked as the head of consulting teams on projects for the Los Angeles Unified School District and the LA Department of Airports. Aside from the restoration of the Kaufmann House, he oversaw the restoration of the Raymond Loewy House by Albert Frey, also located in Palm Springs. **RONALD RADZINER** received his M.Arch degree from the University of Colorado in 1986. He is the Design Principal of the firm, created in 1989. He is currently working on the design of the San Francisco Offices of TBWA/Chiat/Day, and the Accelerated School in South Central Los Angeles. Marmol Radziner has approximately 50 employees. Their work on the Kaufmann House earned them two AIA California Council awards for historic preservation, a National AIA Honor Award, and an Honor Award from the California Preservation Foundation.

LEONARDO MARMOL, Geschäftsführer von Marmol Radziner, erwarb 1987 seinen Bachelor of Architecture an der Cal Poly San Luis Obispo. Er war als leitender Berater für Bauprojekte der Schul- und der Flughafenverwaltung von Los Angeles tätig und beaufsichtigte die Renovierungsarbeiten am Haus Kaufmann und am Haus Raymond Loewy von Albert Frey, beide in Palm Springs. **RONALD RADZINER** machte 1986 seinen Master of Architecture an der University of Colorado und ist heute Planungschef der 1989 gegründeten Firma. Derzeit arbeitet er an der Gestaltung einer Niederlassung von TBWA/Chiat/Day in San Francisco und der Schule für Hochbegabte in South Central Los Angeles. Das Büro Marmol Radziner hat ungefähr 50 Angestellte. Für ihre Arbeit am Haus Kaufmann erhielten sie zwei Preise für die Erhaltung historisch wertvoller Bauwerke des AIA California Council, den National AIA Honor Award und den Ehrenpreis der California Preservation Foundation.

LEONARDO MARMOL, directeur de l'agence Marmol Radziner est Bachelor of Architecture de Cal Poly San Luis Obispo (1987). Il a été responsable d'équipes de consultants pour des projets du Los Angeles Unified School District et pour le département des aéroports de Los Angeles. Hormis la restauration de Kaufmann House, il a supervisé la restauration par Albert Frey de la maison de Raymond Loewy, également à Palm Springs. **RONALD RADZINER,** Master of Architecture de l'Université du Colorado (1986), dirige l'agence créée en 1989. Il travaille actuellement au projet des bureaux de San Francisco de l'agence de publicité TBWA/Chiat/Day et de l'Accelerated School de South Central Los Angeles. Marmol Radziner emploient environ 50 personnes. Leur intervention sur la Kaufmann House leur a valu deux prix du Conseil de Californie de l'AIA pour la préservation de monuments historiques, un prix d'honneur national de l'AIA et un prix d'honneur de la California Preservation Foundation.

KAUFMANN HOUSE RESTORATION

Palm Springs, California, USA, 1994-98

Planning: 1993-94. Construction: 1994-98. Client: Brent and Beth Harris.
Floor area: 474m² before restoration, 297m² after restoration.

Originally designed in 1946 by the architect Richard Neutra, the **KAUFMANN HOUSE** was built for the same client who commissioned Frank Lloyd Wright to design Falling Water. Because successive owners since its original construction had significantly modified the house, the owners decided to return it to its original state. Originally 297 m² in size, the house had been expanded to almost 474 m². The architects removed the later additions, basing the restoration on Julius Shulman's famous photographs of the house, taken in 1947. The architects decided to return the garden to the indigenous desert landscape that existed in Neutra's time. A discreet heating, ventilation and air conditioning system was added, as was a new pool house, named the Harris Pool House.

Das 1946 von dem Architekten Richard Neutra entworfene **KAUFMANN HOUSE** wurde ursprünglich für denselben Bauherrn gebaut, der Frank Lloyd Wright mit dem Bau von Falling Water beauftragt hatte. Da das Haus von den nachfolgenden Eigentümern stark verändert worden war, beschlossen die Eigentümer, es in seinen Originalzustand zurückzuversetzen. Ursprünglich 297 m² groß, war das Gebäude auf fast 474 m² erweitert worden. Bei ihrer Restauration entfernten die Architekten diese späteren Anbauten, wobei sie sich an Julius Shulmans berühmten Photographien des Hauses von 1947 orientierten. Außerdem entschieden sie sich, den Garten in jene Wüstenlandschaft zurückzuverwandeln, die das Haus zu Neutras Zeiten umgeben hatte. Neu hinzugefügt wurden eine unauffällige Heizungs-, Belüftungs- und Klimaanlage sowie ein neues Schwimmbad, Harris Pool House genannt.

Œuvre de Richard Neutra (1946), la **KAUFMANN HOUSE** avait été édifiée pour le même client éclairé qui avait commandé Falling Water à Frank Lloyd Wright. Depuis sa construction, les propriétaires successifs avaient fortement modifié la maison. Ils ont décidé de revenir à son état premier, même si la surface d'origine de 297 m² a gagné 177 m². Marmol Radziner ont supprimé certaines extensions tardives en s'appuyant sur des photos prises en 1947 par Julius Shulman. De plus, ils ont entrepris de rendre au jardin l'aspect désertique qu'il avait du temps de Neutra. Un système discret de chauffage, de ventilation et de conditionnement de l'air a été ajouté, ainsi qu'un nouveau pavillon de piscine, appelé la Harris Pool House.

As Julius Shulman's well-known 1947 photograph (below) of the house shows, the restoration (right) of the Kaufmann House has been faithful to the spirit of Neutra.

Wie Julius Shulmans bekannte Photographie des Hauses von 1947 (unten) zeigt, haben die Architekten bei ihrer Restauration (rechts) den Geist von Richard Neutras Werk bewahrt.

Comme le montre la célèbre photographie de Julius Shulman (ci-dessous) prise en 1947, la restauration de la Kaufmann House (à droite) a été fidèle a l'esprit de Neutra.

The clear, powerful lines of Neutra's design permit an ample degree of openness toward the exterior landscapes.

Neutras Entwurf mit seinen klaren, kraftvollen Linien schafft ein hohes Maß an Offenheit gegenüber der umgebenden Landschaft.

Les lignes simples et fortes imaginées par Neutra permettent une ample ouverture de la maison sur le paysage.

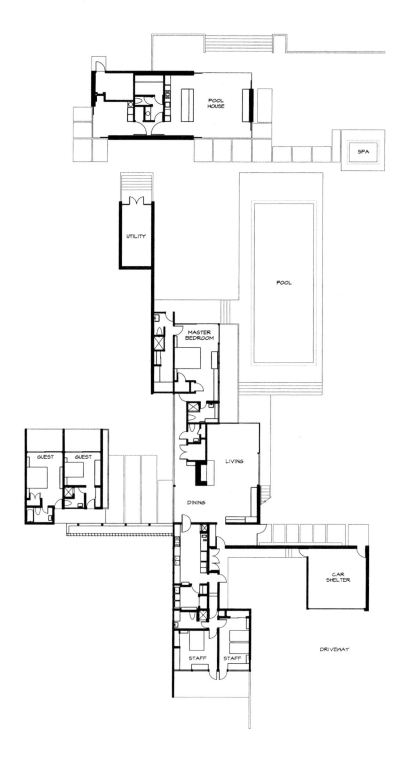

POOL
HOUSE

SPA

UTILITY

POOL

MASTER
BEDROOM

GUEST   GUEST

LIVING

DINING

CAR
SHELTER

STAFF   STAFF

DRIVEWAY

0'   10'   20'

The minimalist simplicity of the
Kaufmann House honors Neutra's
clairvoyance and the quality of the
restoration carried out by Marmol
Radziner.

Minimalistische Schlichtheit zeichnet
sowohl Neutras wegweisende Gestaltung des Kaufmann House als auch
die sehr gelungene Renovierung von
Marmol Radziner aus.

La qualité de la restauration conduite
par Marmol Radziner est un hommage
à la simplicité minimaliste de la Kaufmann House et à la vision d'avant-
garde de Neutra.

RICHARD MEIER

Richard Meier & Partners
475 Tenth Avenue
New York, NY 10018
United States

Tel: +1 212 967 6060
Fax: +1 212 967 3207
e-mail: rmp@richardmeier.com
Web: www.richardmeier.com

Neugebauer House

Born in Newark, New Jersey, in 1934, **RICHARD MEIER** received his architectural training at Cornell University, Ithaca, New York and worked in the office of Marcel Breuer (1960-63) before establishing his own practice in 1963. He won the Pritzker Prize, 1984, and the Royal Gold Medal, 1988. Notable buildings include The Atheneum (New Harmony, Indiana, 1975-79), Museum for the Decorative Arts (Frankfurt, Germany, 1979-85), High Museum of Art (Atlanta, Georgia, 1980-83), Canal+ Headquarters (Paris, France, 1988-92), City Hall and Library (The Hague, 1990-95), Barcelona Museum of Contemporary Art (1988-95), and the Getty Center (Los Angeles, California, 1984-97). Current work includes a US Courthouse and Federal Building, Phoenix, Arizona (1995-2000).

RICHARD MEIER, geboren 1934 in Newark, New Jersey, studierte Architektur an der Cornell University und arbeitete bei Marcel Breuer (1960-63), bevor er 1963 sein eigenes Büro eröffnete. Er wurde 1984 mit dem Pritzker Prize und 1988 mit der Royal Gold Medal ausgezeichnet. Zu seinen bedeutendsten Bauten gehören das Athenäum in New Harmony, Indiana (1975-79), das Museum für Kunsthandwerk in Frankfurt am Main (1979-85), das High Museum of Art, Atlanta (1980-83), die Hauptverwaltung von Canal+ in Paris (1988-92), Rathaus und Bibliothek, Den Haag (1990-95), das Museum für Zeitgenössische Kunst, Barcelona (1988-95) und das Getty Center in Los Angeles (1984-97). Zu seinen jüngsten Projekten gehört das U. S. Courthouse and Federal Building in Phoenix, Arizona (1995-2000).

Né à Newark (New Jersey), en 1934, **RICHARD MEIER** étudie à Cornell University et travaille dans l'agence de Marcel Breuer (1960-63) avant de se mettre à son compte en 1963. Prix Pritzker 1984, Royal Gold Medal, 1988. Principales réalisations : The Athenaeum, New Harmony (Indiana, 1975-79), Musée des Arts Décoratifs de Francfort-sur-le-Main (1979-1984), High Museum of Art (Atlanta, Géorgie, 1980-83), siège de Canal+ (Paris, 1988-91), hôtel de ville et bibliothèque (La Haye, 1990-95), Musée d'Art Contemporain de Barcelone (1988-95), Getty Center (Los Angeles, Californie, 1984-96). Il achève actuellement un tribunal fédéral et un immeuble de l'administration fédérale à Phoenix (Arizona, 1995-2000).

NEUGEBAUER HOUSE

Naples, Florida, USA, 1995-98

Planning: 1995-96. Construction: 1996-98.
Client: Klaus and Ursula Neugebauer. Floor area: 697 m².

Richard Meier's most recent house, the **NEUGEBAUER HOUSE**, is also one of his finest. Located on the Bay of Doubloon, the house has an unusual V-shaped roof. Meier explains that local building regulations required a slanted roof, but did not indicate the direction of the slant. Using 3cm-thick glass for heat insulation, he devised a complex system of brise-soleils. The house's horizontal, shed-like design represents a change in the architect's design options, which are usually more complex, articulated geometric forms, as is the case in another waterfront home, the Ackerberg House in California, but he certainly retains his preference for a white, light-filled architecture.

Richard Meiers jüngstes Haus, das **NEUGEBAUER HOUSE**, ist gleichzeitig eines seiner besten. Es ist an der Bucht von Doubloon gelegen und hat ein ungewöhnliches, V-förmiges Dach. Meier erklärt dazu, dass in den örtlichen Bauvorschriften ein schräges Dach vorgeschrieben, aber nicht die Richtung der Schräge angegeben war. Unter Verwendung einer Wärmedämmung aus 3 cm dickem Glas entwarf er ein komplexes System aus »Brisesoleils« (Sonnenschutz an der Außenseite der Fenster). Die langgestreckte, schuppenartige Form des Hauses ist eine Erweiterung der Gestaltungsmöglichkeiten des Architekten, der bislang meist mit komplex gegliederten geometrischen Formen gearbeitet hat. Dies war auch bei einem anderen Strandhaus, dem Ackerberg House in Kalifornien, der Fall. Seine Vorliebe für eine weiße, lichterfüllte Architektur behielt Meier jedoch auch in der Gestaltung dieses Hauses bei.

En bordure de la baie de Doubloon, la dernière maison de Richard Meier, la **MAISON NEUGEBAUER**, est l'une de ses créations les plus raffinées. Elle se caractérise par un étonnant toit en V. Meier explique que la réglementation locale exigeait un toit en pente, sans en indiquer l'orientation. Il a mis au point un système complexe de brise-soleil en verre de 3 cm d'épaisseur qui isole de la chaleur. L'horizontalité et la simplicité du plan représentent un changement pour l'architecte qui, jusqu'alors, mettait plutôt en œuvre des formes géométriques complexes, comme pour Ackerberg House, une villa construite au bord de l'océan, en Californie. Il conserve néanmoins son goût pour une architecture lumineuse et un blanc immaculé.

Richard Meier quite simply turned the slanted roof required by local zoning restrictions upside down, to allow the house to open out onto the water in a spectacular way.

Durch das »auf den Kopf stellen« des von den örtlichen Bauvorschriften geforderten Satteldachs öffnet sich das Haus auf ganz ungewöhnliche Weise zum Meer.

Richard Meier a tout simplement inversé le toit à deux pentes exigé par la réglementation d'urbanisme locale, permettant ainsi à la maison de s'ouvrir sur l'océan.

In typical fashion, Richard Meier uses the white luminosity of his spaces to their best advantage, particularly in this near tropical climate.

In charakteristischer Weise setzt Richard Meier in seiner Innenraumgestaltung Licht und weiße Farbe ein, was die Räume, besonders in dieser fast tropischen Umgebung, optimal zur Geltung bringt.

L'une des caractéristiques de Richard Meier est de savoir tirer le meilleur parti de la lumineuse blancheur d'espaces situés à proximité des tropiques.

JOSÉ RAFAEL MONEO

José Rafael Moneo
Cinca 5
28002 Madrid
Spain

Tel: +34 91 564 2257
Fax: +34 91 563 5217

JOSÉ RAFAEL MONEO was born in Tudela, Navarra (Spain), in 1937. He graduated from the Escuela Técnica Superior de Arquitectura (ETSA) in Madrid in 1961. The following year, he went to work with Jørn Utzon in Denmark. Rafael Moneo has taught extensively, including at the ETSA in Madrid and Barcelona. He was chairman of the Department of Architecture at the Graduate School of Design at Harvard from 1985 to 1990. Moneo received the Pritzker Prize in 1996. His recent work includes the National Museum of Roman Art (Mérida, Spain, 1980-86); San Pablo Airport (Seville, 1987-92), built for Expo '92; Atocha Railway Station (Madrid, 1985-92); Pilar and Joan Miró Foundation (Palma de Mallorca, 1987-92); transformation of the Villahermosa Palace in Madrid into a museum for the Thyssen-Bornemisza Collection (1989-92); the Davis Art Museum at Wellesley College (Wellesley, Massachusetts, 1990-93); Hyatt Hotel; and an office building (Berlin, 1993-98); the Auditorium (Barcelona, 1989-99); and an Auditorium and Cultural Center in San Sebastián (1991-99).

JOSÉ RAFAEL MONEO, 1937 in Tudela, Navarra (Spanien) geboren, schloß 1961 sein Studium an der Escuela Técnica Superior de Arquitectura (ETSA) in Madrid ab. Im darauffolgenden Jahr ging er nach Dänemark, um dort mit Jørn Utzon zu arbeiten. Rafael Moneo hat an zahlreichen Architekturschulen gelehrt, so an der ETSA in Madrid und in Barcelona. Von 1985 bis 1990 war er Leiter des Department of Architecture der Graduate School of Design (GSD) in Harvard. 1996 erhielt er den Pritzker Prize. Zu Moneos neueren Bauten gehören das Nationalmuseum für Römische Kunst in Mérida, Spanien (1980-86), der für die Expo '92 gebaute Flughafen San Pablo in Sevilla (1989-91), der Bahnhof Atocha in Madrid (1991), die Stiftung Pilar und Joan Miró in Palma de Mallorca (1987-92), die Umgestaltung des Villahermosa-Palasts in Madrid für die Sammlung Thyssen-Bornemisza (1992), das Davis Art Museum am Wellesley College in Wellesley, Massachusetts (1990-93), das Hyatt Hotel und ein Bürogebäude am Potsdamer Platz in Berlin (1993-98) sowie ein Auditorium in Barcelona (1999) und das hier vorgestellte Kursaal/Kulturzentrum im baskischen San Sebastián (1991-99).

JOSÉ RAFAEL MONEO naît à Tuleda, province de Navarre, Espagne, en 1937. Il est diplômé de l'Escuela Tecnica de Arquitectura de Madrid en 1961. En 1962, il part au Danemark pour travailler avec Jørn Utzon. Il enseigne beaucoup, y compris aux ETSA de Madrid et de Barcelone. Président du département d'architecture de la Graduate School of Design de Harvard de 1985 à 1990. Il obtient le Prix Pritzker en 1996. Parmi ses réalisations récentes : le Musée national d'art romain (Merida, Espagne, 1980-86), le terminal de l'aéroport de San Pablo (Séville, 1989-91) édifié pour Expo '92, la gare d'Atocha (Madrid, 1991), la Fondation Pilar et Joan Miró (Palma de Mallorca, 1987-1992), la transformation du Palais Villahermosa à Madrid pour la Collection Thyssen-Bornemisza (1992), le Davis Art Museum du Wellesley College (Wellesley, Massachusetts, 1993), l'hôtel Hyatt et un immeuble de bureaux, Potsdamer Platz (Berlin, 1993-98), un auditorium à Barcelone (1999) et l' auditorium du Kursaal et centre culturel de San Sebastián, Pays basque, Espagne (1991-99).

MURCIA TOWN HALL ANNEX

Murcia, Spain, 1991-98

Planning: 1991-95. Construction: 1995-98. Client: Municipal Government of Murcia.
Floor area: 3 000 m². Costs: Ptas 500 million.

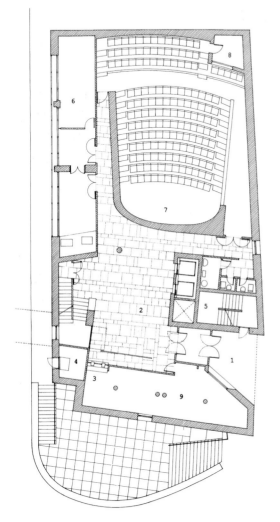

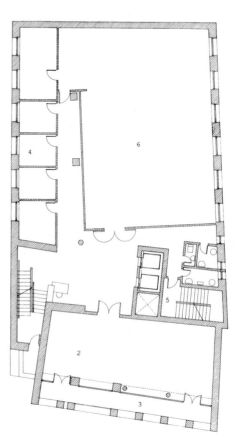

Ground floor	Erdgeschoss	Rez-de-chaussée
1 - Entrance hall	1 - Eingangshalle	1 - Entrée
2 - Vestibule/Information	2 - Vorhalle/Information	2 - Accueil, information
3 - Cashier	3 - Kasse	3 - Caisse
4 - Garbage room	4 - Abstellraum	4 - Local pour les poubelles
5 - Emergency stair	5 - Feuertreppe	5 - Escalier de secours
6 - Office	6 - Büro	6 - Bureau
7 - Lecture hall	7 - Vorlesungssaal	7 - Salle de lecture
8 - Projection room	8 - Projektionsraum	8 - Salle de projections
9 - General office	9 - Verwaltung	9 - Administration centrale

First floor	1. Etage	Premier étage
1 - Vestibule/Information	1 - Vorhalle/Information	1 - Accueil, information
2 - Reception room	2 - Empfang	2 - Accueil
3 - Gallery	3 - Galerie	3 - Galerie
4 - Office	4 - Büro	4 - Bureau
5 - Emergency stair	5 - Feuertreppe	5 - Escalier de secours
6 - General offices	6 - Verwaltung	6 - Administration centrale

Situated on Plaza Cardenal Belluga, near the cathedral and the Cardinal's Palace, the **MURCIA TOWN HALL ANNEX** presented Rafael Moneo with the difficult task of designing a building that neither challenged the architectural power of the older structures nor timidly denied contemporary municipal power. The reinforced concrete town hall is clad in local sandstone and brick. The interior finishes are plaster and wood paneling, with stone and wood floors. The building specifications required space for the municipal offices, a tourist and information center, a lecture hall, a reception room and a cafeteria. As Rafael Moneo says, "The facade/retable is organized like a musical score, numerically accepting the horizontal levels of the floor slabs. It resists symmetries, and offers, as the key element, the balcony of the gallery that rests on exactly the same horizontal plane as the central balcony of the piano nobile of the Palace, both at the same height."

Der 3 000 m² umfassende, an der Plaza del Cardenal Belluga nahe der Kathedrale und dem Kardinalspalast gelegene **MURCIA RATHAUS ANNEX** stellte Rafael Moneo vor die schwierige Aufgabe, ein Gebäude zu entwerfen, das weder die architektonische Kraft der alten Bauwerke schmälert, noch schüchtern die Vitalität der modernen Provinzhauptstadt leugnet. Das neue Rathaus ist aus Stahlbeton erbaut und mit örtlichem Sandstein verkleidet. Die Innenraumausstattung besteht aus Gipsputz und Holztäfelung sowie Stein- und Holzfußböden. Der Bauplan verlangte Büros für die Stadtverwaltung, ein Fremdenverkehrsamt, einen Hörsaal, einen Empfangsraum und ein Café. Rafael Moneo erläutert seinen Entwurf: »Die vorgelegte Fassade ist wie eine Partitur angelegt, wobei sich die Anzahl der Geschosse zahlenmäßig an der Fassade wiederspiegelt. Entgegen jeder Symmetrie gestaltet, bietet sie als beherrschendes Bauelement den Balkon der Galerie, der auf derselben horizontalen Ebene ruht wie der zentrale Balkon im Hauptgeschoß (piano nobile) des Kardinalspalasts.«

Situé Plaza del Cardenal Belluga près de la cathédrale et du palais du Cardinal, le nouveau l'**ANNEX D'HÔTEL DE VILLE DE MURCIE** de 3 000 m² représentait pour l'architecte un défi délicat : comment respecter la forte présence des bâtiments anciens sans nuire, par timidité, à l'autorité que représente la municipalité moderne. Construit en béton armé, l'hôtel de ville est paré de grès local. Les murs intérieurs sont en plâtre ou en lambris, les sols en bois ou pierre. Le programme comprenait des bureaux administratifs, un centre d'information pour les touristes, une salle de conférence, un salon de réception et une cafétéria. Comme Rafael Moneo le précise : « la façade-retable est organisée à la manière d'une partition musicale, et laisse s'affirmer la présence horizontale des dalles de niveau. Contrairement aux principes de symétrie, l'élément majeur, le balcon de la galerie, est aligné sur le même plan que le balcon central (piano nobile) du palais. »

Rafael Moneo has met the challenge of integrating a decidedly modern structure into a tight, traditional urban environment. A view from the inside of a balcony shows the proximity to the older buildings of the city.

José Rafael Moneo ist es gelungen, ein sehr modernes Gebäude in eine dichtbebaute, traditionelle Umgebung zu integrieren. Oben: Der Ausblick vom Balkon macht die Nähe der alten Bauwerke deutlich.

Rafael Moneo relève ici le défi d'intégrer une construction résolument moderne dans un tissu urbain traditionnel et serré. Une vue de l'intérieur d'un balcon montre la proximité des bâtiments anciens.

KURSAAL AUDITORIUM AND CULTURAL CENTER

San Sebastián, Guipuzcoa, Spain, 1990-99

Planning: 3/1990-11/1993. Construction: 6/1995-8/1999.
Total floor area: 60 440 m². Usable floor area: 49 908 m².
Client: Centro Kursaal – Kursaal Elkargunea, S. A. Costs: Ptas 9 000 million.

One major objective of Rafael Moneo's design for this complex was to integrate as intact as possible much of the natural setting of the mouth of the Urumea River by placing the **KURSAAL AUDITORIUM AND CULTURAL CENTER** like "two gigantic rocks stranded at the river mouth that are part of the landscape, not the city." The "rock" containing the 1 806-seat Auditorium is a 65 x 46 x 22-m prismatic volume, inclined toward the sea. The other 43 x 32 x 20-m independent prism, which is also inclined, is a Chamber Music Hall. The unusual wall surfaces, made up of a metal structure with flat glass on the interior and curved glass on the exterior, permit adequate resistance to high winds. This system provides a certain transparency during the day, and permits a glowing, overall lighting effect at night. Other facilities are located in the base of the complex. Set near the water, the Center is at once an abstract composition and, at the same time, a discreet homage to its geographic and urban setting. With its purity of line and dynamic inclinations, the Kursaal Auditorium would appear to be one of Rafael Moneo's most successful recent buildings.

Eines der Hauptziele von Rafael Moneos Entwurf bestand darin, die natürliche Umgebung an der Mündung des Urumea Flusses so weit wie möglich in die Gestaltung der Anlage zu integrieren. Die Formen des **KURSAAL AUDITORIUM UND KULTURZENTRUMS** erinnern an »zwei gigantische, ans Flussufer angeschwemmte Felsbrocken, die mehr Teil der Landschaft als der Stadt sind.« Der das Auditorium mit 1 806 Sitzen enthaltende »Fels« ist ein zum Meer hin abfallender, prismenförmiger Baukörper mit den Maßen 65 x 46 x 22 m. Der andere, 43 x 32 x 20 m große, ebenfalls prismenförmige Bauteil mit schrägen Wänden beherbergt eine Konzerthalle. Im Fundament der Anlage sind die Serviceeinrichtungen untergebracht. Die Oberflächen der Wände, die eine angemessene Windfestigkeit bieten sollen, sind ungewöhnlich: die Innenwände sind mit einem Metallgefüge und Tafelglas verkleidet, die Außenfassaden bestehen aus gewölbtem Glas. Darüber hinaus wird durch diese Konstruktion tagsüber eine gewisse Transparenz erreicht, nachts leuchtet der Baukörper weithin sichtbar. Der gesamte Komplex ist eine abstrakte Komposition und eine diskrete Huldigung an die geographische und urbane Umgebung zugleich. Mit seinen klaren Linien und dynamischen Schrägen lässt sich das Kursaal-Auditorium als eines von Rafael Moneos erfolgreichsten Bauwerken bezeichnen.

L'un des principaux objectifs du projet de Rafael Moneo était, si possible, d'intégrer l'**AUDITORIUM DU KURSAAL ET LE CENTRE CULTUREL**, dans le cadre naturel de l'embouchure de l'Urumea en disposant les bâtiments à la manière de « deux gigantesques rochers échoués sur les berges du fleuve et faisant partie du paysage, et non de la ville. » Le « rocher » qui contient l'auditorium de 1 806 places est un parallélépipède de 65 x 46 x 22 m, incliné vers la mer. Le second de 43 x 32 x 20 m, également un parallélépipède indépendant et incliné, sert de salle de musique de chambre. Les curieuses parois extérieures sont constituées d'une structure métallique recouverte de verre plat à l'intérieur et bombé à l'extérieur pour renforcer la résistance aux vents. Ce principe permet une certaine transparence de jour et crée un effet lumineux en nocturne. D'autres installations sont implantées à la base du complexe. Au bord de l'océan, le Centre est à la fois une composition abstraite et un hommage discret à son cadre géographique et urbain. Par sa pureté de lignes et sa dynamique due à son inclinaison, ce Kursaal est l'une des récentes réalisations de Rafael Moneo les plus réussies.

Above right: As seen in its urban context the Kursaal Auditorium and Cultural Center affirms a geometric presence whose angling gives a certain dynamism to forms that might have threatened to be too static otherwise.

Oben rechts: Im städtebaulichen Kontext fällt das Kursaal-Auditorium und Kulturzentrum deutlich durch seine geometrischen Anlage auf. Unten rechts: Die schräg gestellten Fassaden verleihen den sonst sehr statisch wirkenden Gebäudeformen eine gewisse Dynamik.

Ci-dessus à droite : Dans son contexte urbain, l'Auditorium et centre culturel affirment la forte présence de leur géométrie. L'inclinaison donne un certain dynamisme à des formes qui auraient pu être statiques.

Right: Rafael Moneo shows a surprising capacity to renew his architectural
vocabulary according to the circumstances, though he does tend to favor
rather closed structures, preferring to
modulate internal lighting conditions
in a more intimate way.

Rechts: Moneo besitzt die ungewöhnliche Fähigkeit, seine Formensprache
den jeweiligen Umständen entsprechend zu erneuern. Grundsätzlich ten-
diert er zu eher geschlossenen
Baukörpern und einer intimen Gestaltung der Lichtverhältnisse im Inneren.

A droite : Rafael Moneo fait preuve
d'une étonnante capacité à renouve-
ler son vocabulaire architectural
selon les circonstances, même s'il
préfère toujours les structures assez
fermées dont il peut moduler l'éclairage intérieur de façon plus intime.

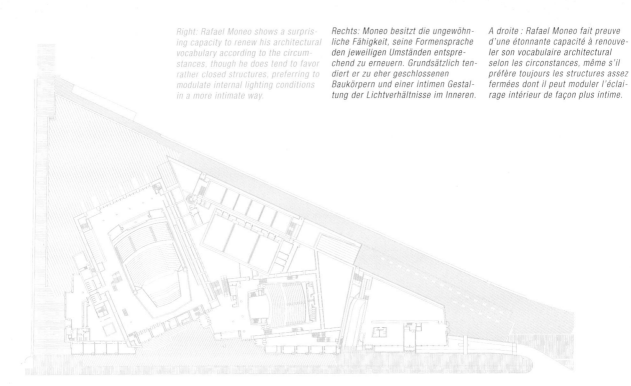

Stairways and facades present an
intricate arrangement of opaque and
translucent surfaces. The articulation
of the stairways gives an impression
that solid slabs of stone or metal are
hovering in space.

Treppenaufgänge und Fassaden bilden
ein ausgeklügeltes System lichtundurchlässiger und durchscheinen-
der Oberflächen. Die Anordnung der
Treppen erweckt den Eindruck, als
schwebten die massiven Körper aus
Stein- und Metallplatten im Raum.

Les escaliers et les façades s'imbriquent de façon à produire un étonnante composition de surfaces
opaques et transparentes. L'articulation des escaliers donne l'impression
que les dalles de pierre ou de métal
sont en suspension dans l'espace.

TOSHIKO MORI

Toshiko Mori Architect
145 Hudson Street, 4th Floor
New York, NY 10013
United States

Tel: +1 212 274 8687
Fax: +1 212 274 9043
e-mail: TMoriArch@AOL.com

Woven Inhabitation

TOSHIKO MORI attended the Cooper Union School of Art and School of Architecture, New York (1970-76) and received an Honorary Master of Architecture degree from the Harvard School of Design in 1996. She is currently a Professor at Harvard. She has worked on numerous retail stores, such as Comme des Garçons (New York, 1998) and Kyoto Arts & Fashions (New York, 1989), as well as corporate offices such as Sony Research Laboratories (New York, 1996) and Nigel French International (New York, 1991). She completed the Issey Miyake Pleats Please Boutique with Gwenael Nicolas in Soho, New York in 1998.

TOSHIKO MORI studierte von 1970 bis 1976 an der Cooper Union in New York und erhielt 1996 den Honorary Master of Architecture an der Harvard School of Design, wo sie zur Zeit eine Professur innehat. Sie hat zahlreiche Ladeninterieus gestaltet, so etwa Comme des Garçons (1998) und Kyoto Arts & Fashions (1989), beide in New York. Außerdem entwarf sie Bürobauten wie die Sony Research Laboratories (1996) und Nigel French International (1991), ebenfalls in New York. In Zusammenarbeit mit Gwenael Nicolas führte sie 1998 die Pleats Please-Boutique von Issey Miyake in Soho, New York, aus.

TOSHIKO MORI a étudié à la Cooper Union School of Art and School of Architecture (1970-76) elle a obtenu un Honorary Master of Architecture de la Harvard School of Design en 1996. Elle est actuellement Professeur à Harvard. Elle a travaillé sur de nombreux projets de magasins dont Comme des Garçons (New York, 1998) et Kyoto Arts and Fashions (New York, 1989), ainsi que pour des sièges sociaux de sociétés comme Sony Research Laboratories (New York, 1996) ou Nigel French International (New York, 1991). Elle vient d'achever une nouvelle boutique Issey Miyake Pleats Please avec Gwenael Nicolas, dans le quartier de Soho à New York.

WOVEN INHABITATION

New York, NY, USA, 1999

Exhibition: 20/11/99-15/1/2000, Artists Space. Selection: Claudia Gould.
Curator: Jenelle Porter. Materials: Polar fleece and Goretex remnant, rope, chicken wire (among others).

Japanese-born architect Toshiko Mori has challenged the barriers that divide art from architecture, or perhaps architecture from the real world. Her **WOVEN INHABITATION**, presented at the Artists Space in New York in 1999, seeks to offer a simple, elegant solution to the vast problem of providing temporary housing to refugees or victims of natural disasters. Her concept is to make use of "the woven remnants of revolutionary industrial fabrics already utilized by the aerospace, medical and fashion industries but never before developed as architectural building products." Mori proposes an elegant, inexpensive solution to a vast problem.

Die in Japan geborene Architektin Toshiko Mori hat mit ihrer Arbeit die Grenzen zwischen Kunst und Architektur, oder auch zwischen Architektur und dem »wirklichen Leben« durchlässig gemacht. Ihre Arbeit **WOVEN INHABITATION,** 1999 im New Yorker Artists Space präsentiert, ist der Versuch, eine einfache, kostengünstige und dabei elegante Lösung für das enorme Problem zu finden, Flüchtlingen oder Opfern von Naturkatastrophen eine vorübergehende Unterkunft zu bieten. Ihr Konzept besteht in der Nutzbarmachung »der Reste neuartiger Industriegewebe, die bereits von der Raumfahrt-, der Pharma- und der Modeindustrie verwendet, aber noch nie zuvor als Baumaterial eingesetzt wurden.«

L'architecte japonaise Toshiko Mori remet en question les barrières qui séparent l'art de l'architecture, et peut-être l'architecture du monde réel. Son **WOVEN INHABITATION** présentée à l'Artists Space à New York en 1999, cherche à offrir une solution simple et élégante au vaste problème du logement temporaire des réfugiés et victimes de catastrophes naturelles. Son idée est d'utiliser « les déchets de tissus industriels révolutionnaires, déjà utilisés en aéronautique, dans la mode et dans le secteur de la santé, que personne n'a jamais pensé employer comme matériaux de construction. » Mori propose une solution élégante et économique à un vaste problème.

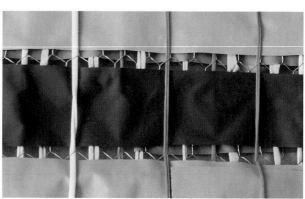

Obviously, new materials open unexpected horizons in construction, and Toshiko Mori aims to make the most of those.

Neue Materialien, die Toshiko Mori optimal nutzen möchte, eröffnen unerwartete Möglichkeiten für die Architektur.

De nouveaux matériaux ouvrent à l'architecture de nouveaux horizons que Toshiko Mori a l'intention d'explorer.

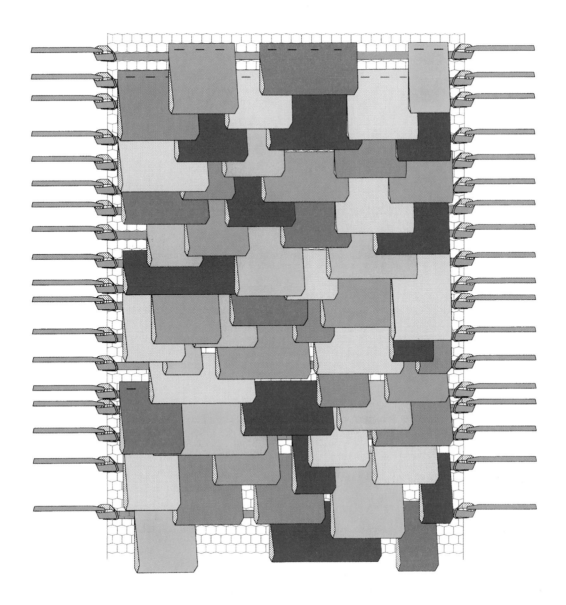

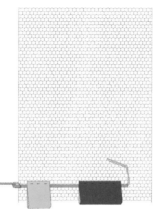

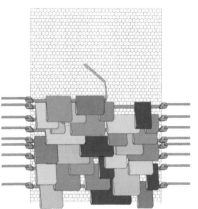

The Woven Inhabitation is more experimental and thoughtful than it is a
fully elaborated plan for construction.

Die Woven Inhabitation ist eher
ein Gedankenexperiment als ein
voll ausgearbeiteter Entwurf.

Woven Inhabitation est plus un objet
expérimental de réflexion qu'un
projet élaboré.

MORPHOSIS

Morphosis
2041 Colorado Avenue
Santa Monica, California 90404
United States

Tel: +1 310 453 2247
Fax: +1 310 829 3270
e-mail: studio@morphosis.net

MORPHOSIS principal Thom Mayne, born in Connecticut in 1944, received his B.Arch. degree in 1968 at the University of Southern California, and his M.Arch. degree at Harvard in 1978. He created Morphosis in 1979 with Michael Rotondi, who has since established his own firm, RoTo. He has taught at the University of California, Los Angeles, Harvard, Yale, and the Southern California Institute of Architecture (SCI-Arc), of which he was a founding Board Member. Based in Santa Monica, California, some of the main buildings of Morphosis are the Lawrence House (1981), Kate Mantilini Restaurant (1986), and Cedar's Sinai Comprehensive Cancer Care Center (1987) at Beverly Hills, California; Crawford Residence (Montecito, California, 1987-92); Yuzen Vintage Car Museum (project, West Hollywood, California, 1992), as well as the Blades Residence (Santa Barbara, California, 1992-97), and the International Elementary School (Long Beach, California, 1995-98) published here.

Der 1944 in Connecticut geborene Leiter von **MORPHOSIS**, Thom Mayne, erwarb 1968 den Bachelor of Architecture an der University of Southern California (USC) und 1978 den Master of Architecture in Harvard. 1979 gründete er Morphosis in Partnerschaft mit Michael Rotondi, der heute seine eigene Firma, RoTo, besitzt. Mayne lehrte an der University of California, Los Angeles (UCLA), in Harvard und Yale sowie am Southern California Institute of Architecture (SCI-Arc), wo er ein Gründungsmitglied des Vorstands war. Zu den wichtigsten Bauten des im kalifornischen Santa Monica ansässigen Büros Morphosis gehören das Haus Lawrence (1981), das Restaurant Kate Mantilini (1986) und das Cedar's Sinai Comprehensive Cancer Care Center (1987) in Beverly Hills, Kalifornien, die Villa Crawford in Montecito, Kalifornien (1987-92), die Planung des Yuzen Vintage Car Museum in West Hollywood, Kalifornien (1992) sowie das Wohnhaus Blades in Santa Barbara, Kalifornien (1992-97) und die hier vorgestellte International Elementary School in Long Beach (1995-98).

Associé principal de **MORPHOSIS,** Thom Mayne, né dans le Connecticut en 1944 est Bachelor of Architecture de l'University of Southern California, USC (1968) et Master of Architecture de Harvard (1978). Il fonde Morphosis en 1971 et s'associe en 1980 à Michael Rotondi qui a depuis créé sa propre agence, RoTo. Il a enseigné à UCLA, Harvard, Yale, et au SCI-Arc, dont il est l'un des fondateurs. Morphosis est basé à Santa Monica, Californie. Parmi ses principales réalisations : Lawrence House (1981), Kate Mantilini Restaurant (1986) et le Cedar's Sinai Comprehensive Cancer Care Center (1987), toutes à Beverly Hills, Californie ; puis viennent la Crawford Residence (Montecito, Californie, 1987-92), le Yuzen Vintage Car Museum (projet, West Hollywood, 1992) ainsi que la Baldes Residence (Santa Barbara, 1992-97) et l'International Elementary School (Long Beach, Californie, 1995-98), publiée ici.

INTERNATIONAL ELEMENTARY SCHOOL

Long Beach, California, USA, 1995-98

*Planning: 1995-96. Construction: 7/97-12/98. Client: Long Beach Unified School District.
Floor area: 8 547 m². Costs: $14 000 000.*

The design specifications for the **INTERNATIONAL ELEMENTARY SCHOOL** called for 34 classrooms, administrative offices, a library, a multi-purpose room, and parking space. A vertical layering of the space, placing play areas above the classrooms, for example, made it possible to lower the costs. The building uses one third less land than other comparable schools in the Los Angeles area. Set on a 2.5-hectare site, the school's total floor area is 8 547 m² and the cost was US$14 million. Although the school presents a relatively closed facade, it is entirely open within its grounds, which comprise a series of terraced courtyards. Parking, the kindergarten, courtyards and the library are on the ground floor; classrooms are concentrated in one three-story block, and a large playground is on the second level.

Vorgaben beim Bau dieser **INTERNATIONALEN GRUNDSCHULE** waren die Unterbringung von 34 Unterrichtsräumen, Verwaltungsbüros, einer Bibliothek, eines Mehrzweckraums und einer Parkgarage. Eine vertikale Schichtung, in der etwa der Schulhof über den Klassenzimmern angelegt wurde, ermöglichte eine Reduzierung der Baukosten. Darüber hinaus nimmt das Gebäude nun ein Drittel weniger Grundfläche ein als andere vergleichbare Schulen in der Umgebung von Los Angeles. Auf einem 2,5 ha großen Grundstück gelegen, verfügt die Schule über eine Gesamtnutzfläche von 8 547 m², die Baukosten betrugen 14 Millionen US$. Im Gegensatz zu seiner relativ geschlossenen Fassade, ist das Gebäude nach innen durch eine Reihe terrassenförmig abgestufter Höfe völlig offen strukturiert. Garage, Kindergarten, Innenhöfe und Bibliothek befinden sich im Erdgeschoß, die Unterrichtsräume sind in einem dreistöckigen Block konzentriert und im zweiten Obergeschoß liegt der große Schulhof.

Le programme de **L'INTERNATIONAL ELEMENTARY SCHOOL** comprenait 34 salles de classe, des bureaux administratifs, une bibliothèque, une salle polyvalente, et des parkings. L'étagement des espaces – avec par exemple l'implantation des aires de jeux au dessus des classes – a permis de diminuer les coûts. L'ensemble occupe un tiers de surface au sol de moins que les écoles comparables de la région de Los Angeles. Implantée sur un terrain de 2,5 ha, il offre 8 547 m² de planchers pour un budget de $14 millions. Bien que relativement fermée vue de l'extérieur ; à l'intérieur, l'école est entièrement ouverte sur des cours en terrasse. Le parking, le jardin d'enfants, les cours et la bibliothèque se trouvent au rez-de-chaussée ; les salles de classe sont concentrées dans un bloc de trois niveaux, doté d'une vaste aire de jeux au deuxième niveau.

Larger than much of the earlier work of Morphosis, this school nonetheless calls on the variety of construction materials and the volumetric variations that Thom Mayne's office is known for.

Auch wenn diese Schule größer ist als die meisten früheren Arbeiten von Morphosis, weist sie dieselbe Vielfalt in den Baumaterialien und der Raumeinteilung auf, für die Thom Maynes Architekturbüro bekannt ist.

De dimensions plus vastes que les précédentes réalisations de Morphosis, cette école fait appel à des matériaux très divers et aux ruptures volumétriques caractéristiques de l'agence de Tom Mayne.

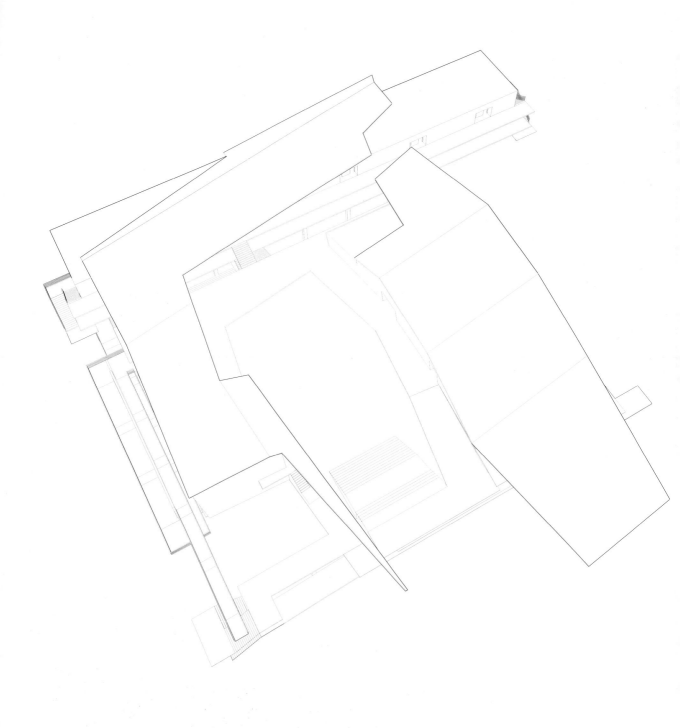

Complex forms are used both to solve the programmatic requirements and to offer a large variety of spatial perceptions. This is not the kind of building that can be understood by looking at one facade only.

Die komplexen Formen des Gebäudes entsprechen nicht nur den differenzierten Anforderungen, sondern ermöglichen auch ganz verschiedenartige räumliche Wahrnehmungen. Deshalb reicht es zum Verständnis dieses Bauwerks nicht aus, nur eine seiner Außenfassaden zu betrachten.

La complexité des formes suscite une grande variété de perceptions spatiales tout en répondant aux spécifications du programme. La vision d'une seule façade ne suffit pas à comprendre le fonctionnement de l'ensemble du bâtiment.

ERIC OWEN MOSS

Eric Owen Moss Architects
8557 Higuera Street
Culver City, California 90232
United States

Tel: +1 310 839 1199
Fax: +1 310 839 7922
e-mail: ericmoss@ix.netcom.com
Web: www.ericowenmoss.com

The Umbrella

Born in Los Angeles, California, in 1943, **ERIC OWEN MOSS** received his B.A. degree from the University of California, Los Angeles in 1965, and his M.Arch. from the University of California at Berkeley in 1968. He also received a M.Arch. degree from Harvard in 1972. He founded Eric Owen Moss Architects in 1973. He has been a Professor of Design at the Southern California Institute of Architecture (SCI-Arc) since 1974. His built work includes the Central Housing Office, University of California at Irvine (1986-89), Lindblade Tower (1987-89), Paramount Laundry (1987-89), Gary Group (1988-90), The Box (1990-94), I. R. S. Building (1993-94), and Samitaur (1994-96), all in Culver City. Current work includes high-rise towers in Los Angeles and a residential project in Hollywood, as well as ongoing designs in Culver City.

ERIC OWEN MOSS, geboren 1943 in Kalifornien, erwarb 1965 den Bachelor of Arts an der University of California, Los Angeles (UCLA) und 1968 den Master of Architecture an der University of California at Berkeley. 1972 erwarb er einen weiteren Master of Architecture in Harvard und gründete ein Jahr später das Büro Eric Owen Moss Architecture. Seit 1974 hat er eine Professur für Design am Southern California Institute of Architecture (SCI-Arc) inne. Zu seinen Bauten zählen das Central Housing Office an der University of California in Irvine (1986-89), der Lindblade Tower (1987-89), die Paramount Laundry (1987-89), Gary Group (1988-90), The Box (1990-94), das I. R. S-Gebäude (1993-94) und Samitaur (1994-96), alle in Culver City. Zu seinen jüngsten Projekten gehören Hochhaustürme in Los Angeles und ein Wohnhaus in Hollywood, sowie seine laufenden Planungsarbeiten in Culver City.

Né en 1943 à Los Angeles, **ERIC OWEN MOSS** est diplômé en architecture de University of California, Los Angeles (Bachelor of Arts, 1965) et titulaire de deux masters : University of California at Berkeley (1968) et de Harvard (1972). Il crée Eric Owen Moss Architects en 1973 et enseigne la conception architecturale au Southern California Institute of Architecture (SCI-Arc) depuis 1974. Il fonde sa propre agence à Culver City, Californie, en 1976. Parmi ses réalisations aux Etats-Unis : Central Housing Office, University of California at Irvine (Irvine, 1986-89), à Culver City : Lindblade Tower (1987-89), Paramount Laundry (1987-89), Gary Group (1988-90), The Box (1990-94), l'I. R. S. Building (1993-94) et Samitaur (1994-96). Il travaille actuellement sur un projet de tours de grande hauteur à Los Angeles, sur une résidence à Hollywood ainsi qu'à de nouvelles réalisations à Culver City.

THE UMBRELLA

Culver City, California, USA, 1998-99

Completion: 12/99. Client: Samitaur Constructs.
Floor area: 1 468 m².

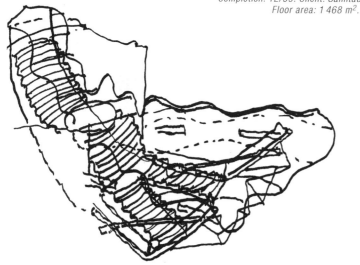

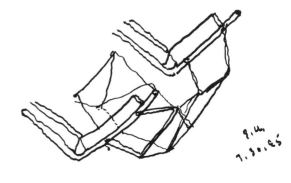

As he has done in other buildings in Culver City, Eric Owen Moss here adds a spectacular sculptural element to the outside of the corner of this structure.

Wie schon bei seinen anderen Bauprojekten in Culver City fügte Moss auch der Fassade dieses Gebäudes ein spektakulär gestaltetes plastisches Element hinzu.

Comme il l'a fait précédemment pour d'autres projets à Culver City, Eric Owen Moss greffe un élément sculptural spectaculaire à l'angle extérieur d'un bâtiment.

Part of the architect's ongoing effort to renovate industrial buildings in Culver City, sponsored by a promoter who owns the Hayden Tract in this district in Los Angeles, **THE UMBRELLA** is a 1 468-m² project undertaken at a cost of $ 1 185 000. It consists of two contiguous warehouses built in the 1940s and renovated to provide 20 private office spaces, two conference areas and large open workspaces. According to Moss, the name "Umbrella" derives from "an experimental piece of construction." "It is a conceptual bowl," says the architect, "an arena the slope of which is determined by the curving top chord of two inverted wood trusses salvaged from the demolition of an adjacent project and inserted here." Like most of his Culver City projects, this renovation does not fundamentally alter the exterior forms of the existing structures but rather adds a sculptural element whose origin is linked to the spaces. It is this added piece that gives an unusual identity to the completed building.

Als Teil der laufenden Renovierungsarbeiten des Architekten an den Industriebauten in Culver City und gesponsert von einem Veranstalter, dem der Hayden Tract in diesem Distrikt von Los Angeles gehört, ist **THE UMBRELLA** (der Regenschirm) ein 1 468 m² umfassendes Projekt, das für 1 850 000 $ realisiert wurde. Es besteht aus zwei aneinander grenzenden Lagerhäusern aus den 1940er-Jahren, die nun zur Unterbringung von 20 Privatbüros, zwei Konferenzsälen und einigen großflächigen, offenen Arbeitsräumen umgebaut wurden. Laut Moss bezieht sich der Name »Umbrella« auf ein experimentelles Bauteil, das der Architekt so beschreibt: »Es beruht auf der Grundidee einer Schüssel und stellt eine Arena dar. Deren Schräge wird von der oberen gekrümmten Spannweite zweier nach innen gekehrter Balken vorgegeben, die beim Abriss eines benachbarten Gebäudes geborgen und hier eingesetzt wurden.« Wie bei den meisten seiner Bauprojekte in Culver City verändert Moss bei dieser Renovierung die äußeren Formen der bestehenden Gebäude nicht grundlegend, sondern fügt lediglich ein plastisch gestaltetes Element hinzu, das sich auf die ursprünglichen Gebäude bezieht. Auch bei The Umbrella ist es dieses zusätzliche Element, das dem fertigen Gebäude seine Individualität verleiht.

Dans le cadre d'un programme permanent de rénovation de bâtiments industriels à Culver City financé par le promoteur propriétaire du Hayden Tract, **THE UMBRELLA** (le parapluie) est un projet de $1 485 000 pour une surface de 1 468 m². Il se compose de deux entrepôts contigus édifiés dans les années 1940 puis transformés par Moss en 20 bureaux indépendants, deux salles de conférence et de vastes plateaux ouverts. Selon l'architecte, le nom de « Umbrella » désigne « une construction expérimentale. Un ‹ bol › conceptuel, une arène, dont la pente est déterminée par la courbe supérieure de deux fermes de bois récupérées dans la démolition d'un projet voisin… » Comme pour la plupart de ses réalisations à Culver City, cette rénovation ne modifie pas fondamentalement les formes extérieures des constructions existantes, mais leur ajoute un élément sculptural lié à la nature de chaque espace. C'est cet ajout qui confère à chaque bâtiment son identité originale.

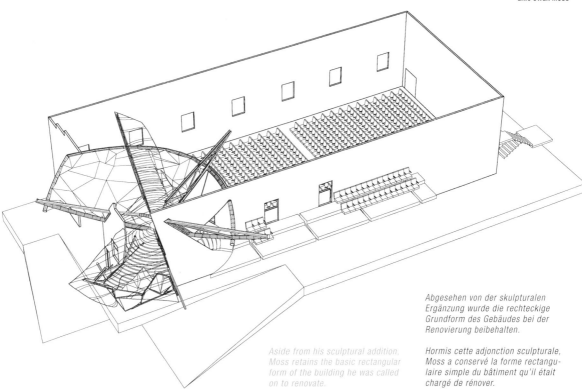

Abgesehen von der skulpturalen Ergänzung wurde die rechteckige Grundform des Gebäudes bei der Renovierung beibehalten.

Aside from his sculptural addition, Moss retains the basic rectangular form of the building he was called on to renovate.

Hormis cette adjonction sculpturale, Moss a conservé la forme rectangulaire simple du bâtiment qu'il était chargé de rénover.

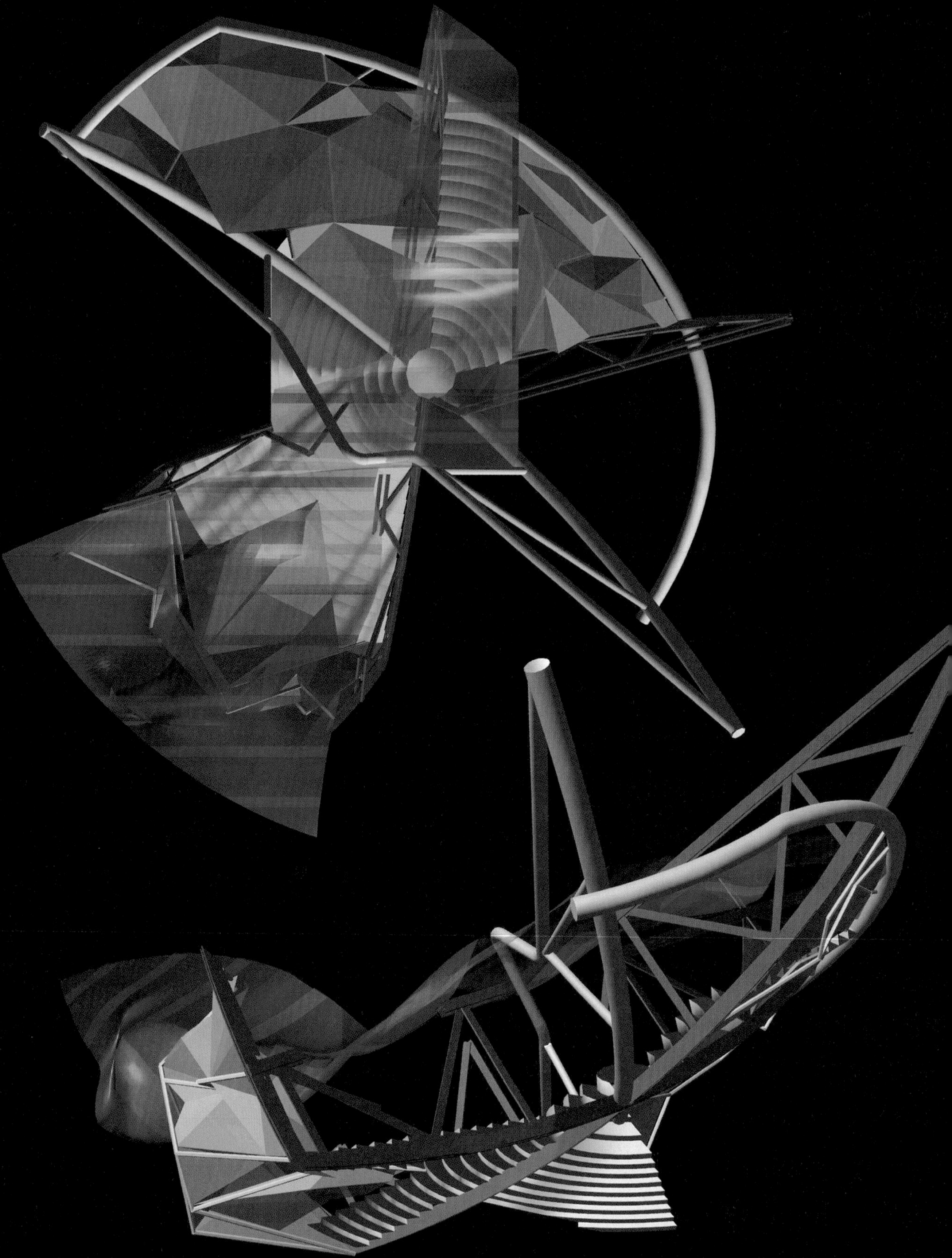

Inside the building, Moss uses his sense of materials and complex spaces to enliven the visitor's experience. Thus a run-down warehouse is transformed into a up-to-date office.

Im Inneren steigert Moss das Raumgefühl mit dem ihm eigenen Gespür für Materialien und komplexe Räume und verwandelt ein baufälliges Lagerhaus in ein modernes Büro.

Moss use de son sens des matériaux et des espaces complexes pour créer un univers stimulant. Un entrepôt abandonné se transforme en bureaux d'avant-garde.

GLENN MURCUTT

Glenn Murcutt Architect
Sydney
Australia

The Arthur and Yvonne Boyd Education Centre

GLENN MURCUTT was born in London in 1936 of Australian parents. He received his Diploma of Architecture from the Sydney Technical College (UNSW) in 1961 and joined Ancher Mortlock Murray & Woolley Architects, Sydney from 1964 to 1969 before he established his own practice in 1969. He has taught at numerous universities, among them the University of Pennsylvania, Philadelphia, USA (1990/91/95); University of Technology, Sydney (1990/92/95); University of Arizona, Tucson, USA (1991); University of Technology, Helsinki, Finland (1994); University of Hawaii, Honolulu, USA (1996); University of Texas at Austin, USA (1997); University of Virginia, Charlottesville, USA (1997); School of Architecture, Aarhus, Denmark (1999); and is presently holding the William Henry Bishop Chair at Yale University. He was honored with national and international awards such as the Alvar Aalto medal (1992), Royal Australian Institute of Architects Gold Medal (1992), and the Thomas Jefferson Medal for Architecture (2001). He has traveled extensively in Europe and the United States. His built work in Australia includes numerous private houses, such as the Magney House (Bingi Point, NSW, 1982-84), the Meagher House (Bowral, NSW, 1988-92), or the Marika-Alderton House (Yirrkala, Northern Territory, 1991-94), a private residence (Mount Wilson, NSW, 1989-94), the Museum of Local History and the Tourism Office (Kempsey, NSW, 1979-82, 1986-88), a restaurant (Berowra Waters, Sydney, 1977-78, 1982-83), and The Arthur and Yvonne Boyd Education Centre, West Cambewarra, NSW, Australia (1995-98).

GLENN MURCUTT wurde 1936 als Sohn australischer Eltern in London geboren. Sein Studium am Sydney Technical College der University of New South Wales schloss er 1961 mit dem Diplom ab. Von 1964 bis 1969 arbeitete er für Ancher Mortlock Murray & Woolley Architects, Sydney. 1969 gründete er sein eigenes Büro. Er lehrte an zahlreichen Universitäten, u.a. an der University of Pennsylvania, Philadelphia, USA (1990/91/95), University of Technology, Sydney (1990/92/95), University of Arizona, Tucson, USA (1991), University of Technology, Helsinki, Finnland (1994), University of Hawaii, Honolulu, USA (1996), University of Texas at Austin, USA (1997), University of Virginia, Charlottesville, USA (1997), School of Architecture, Aarhus, Dänemark (1999), und hat zur Zeit den William Henry Bishop-Lehrstuhl an der Yale University inne. Er unternahm ausgedehnte Reisen nach Europa und in die Vereinigten Staaten. Er wurde u.a. mit folgenden nationalen und internationalen Preisen ausgezeichnet: Alvar Aalto Medal (1992), Royal Australian Institute of Architects Gold Medal (1992), und der Thomas Jefferson Medal for Architecture (2001). Sein Werk umfaßt zahlreiche Privathäuser: Haus Magney in Bingi Point, NSW (1982-84), Haus Meagher in Bowral, NSW (1988-92) und Haus Marika-Alderton in Yirrkala, Northern Territory (1991-94). Außerdem entwarf er das lokalgeschichtliche Museum und Fremdenverkehrsamt in Kempsey, NSW (1979-82, 1986-88), das Restaurant Berowra Waters in Sydney (1977-78, 1982-83) und das Arthur and Yvonne Boyd Education Centre »Riversdale«, West Cambewarra, NSW, Australien.

GLENN MURCUTT naît à Londres en 1936 de parents australiens. Il étudie au Sydney Technical College de l'Université de Galles du Sud, dont il obtient le diplôme d'architecte en 1961. De 1964 à 1969 il travaille pour Ancher Mortlock Murray & Wooley architectes à Sydney et crée sa propre agence en 1969. Il a enseigné dans de nombreuses universités parmi lesquelles : University of Pennsylvania, Philadelphia, USA (1990/91/95), University of Technology, Sydney (1990/92/95), University of Arizona, Tucson, USA (1991), University of Technology, Helsinki, Finlande (1994), University of Hawaii, Honolulu, USA (1996), University of Texas at Austin, USA (1997), University of Virginia, Charlottesville, USA (1997), School of Architecture, Aarhus, Danemark (1999), et est actuellement professeur à l'université de Yale. Il a beaucoup voyagé en Europe et aux Etats-Unis. Il a obtenu des prix nationaux et internationaux dont l'Alvar Aalto Medal (1992), la Royal Australian Institute of Architects Gold Medal (1992), et le Thomas Jefferson Medal for Architecture (2001). Parmi ses réalisations en Australie : de nombreuses maisons privées dont la Magney House (Bingi Point, NSW, 1982-84), la Meagher House (Bowral, NSW, 1988-92), ou la Marika-Alderton House (Yirrkala, Northern Territory, 1991-94), ainsi que le musée d'histoire locale et l'office du tourisme de Kempsey, NSW, (1979-82, 1986-88), le restaurant Berowra Waters à Sydney, (1977-78, 1982-83) et le centre d'éducation « Riversdale », West Cambewarra, NSW, Australie.

THE ARTHUR AND YVONNE BOYD EDUCATION CENTRE

West Cambewarra, New South Wales, Australia, 1995-98

Planning: 17 months. Construction: 13 months. Client: Bundanon Trust.
Costs: A$ 2 379 000.

Seen from certain angles, the Boyd Centre is different from Glenn Murcutt's previous work. This results possibly from the larger scale, but also from the collaboration with Wendy Lewin and Reg Lark.

Das Boyd Centre unterscheidet sich von Murcutts früheren Arbeiten. Das liegt einerseits am deutlich größeren Maßstab, andererseits an der Zusammenarbeit mit Wendy Lewin und Reg Lark.

Le Boyd Centre se différencie des précédents ouvrages. Cela résulte probablement de la dimension plus importante mais également de la collaboration avec Wendy Lewin et Reg Lark.

Set on the ranch of the late artist Arthur Boyd, 180 km south of Sydney, this A$2.38 million **ART EDUCATION CENTER** is designed in association with the architects Wendy Lewin and Reg Lark (Sydney) for resident artists and 32 young students from both Australia and round the world, providing facilities for art, musical and theatrical events in the middle of the country side. With concrete floors and walls, the center has a roof made of recycled timbers and steel under a corrugated galvanized iron roof sheet. Glenn Murcutt is proud of the fact that the modest construction cost included "on-site water supply and waste treatment, external works, landscaping, and the demolition of existing buildings." The design for the complex includes a multipurpose hall, kitchen, dormitory area, and an outdoor amphitheater, which have not yet been realized. Despite its rough materials, the Arthur and Yvonne Boyd Education Centre seems to mark a more formal approach than many of the architect's earlier houses. This building received the 1999 Sir Zelman Cowen Award for Public Buildings, the Royal Australian Institute of Architects (RAIA) most prestigious Federal Award and The Kenneth F. Brown Asia Pacific Culture and Architecture Design Award 2001.

Die in Zusammenarbeit mit den Architekten Wendy Lewin und Reg Lark (Sydney) für 2,38 Millionen A$ erbaute **KUNSTSCHULE** befindet sich 180 km südlich von Sydney auf dem abgelegenen Landgut des verstorbenen australischen Malers und Bildhauers Arthur Boyd. Sie ist für Stipendiaten sowie 32 junge Kunststudenten aus aller Welt konzipiert und enthält Einrichtungen für bildende Kunst, Musik- und Theaterveranstaltungen. Böden und Wände des Gebäudes sind aus Beton, das Dach besteht aus recycelten Holzbalken und Stahl unter Dachplatten aus gewelltem Eisenblech. Glenn Murcutt ist stolz darauf, dass in den bescheidenen Baukosten die Ausgaben für »eine eigene Wasserversorung und Abfallbeseitigung, externe Arbeiten, die Landschaftsgestaltung und der Abriss bestehender Gebäude« enthalten sind. Der Entwurf für den Komplex sieht außerdem eine Mehrzweckhalle, einen Wohnbereich mit Küche und ein Freiluft-Amphitheater vor, welche noch nicht realisiert wurden. Trotz der groben Baumaterialien scheint das Arthur and Yvonne Boyd Education Centre durch einen formelleren Zugang gekennzeichnet zu sein als viele der früheren Projekte des Architekten. Für dieses Gebäude wurden die Architekten 1999 mit dem Sir Zelman Cowen Award for Public Buildings ausgezeichnet, dem renommiertesten vom Royal Australian Institute of Architects (RAIA) vergebenen Staatspreis und dem Kenneth F. Brown Asia Pacific Culture and Architecture Design Award 2001.

Edifié en association avec les architectes Wendy Lewin et Reg Lark (Sydney) à 180 km au sud de Sydney, sur le ranch d'Arthur Boyd, artiste décédé, ce **CENTRE D'ÉDUCATION ARTISTIQUE** de A$2,38 millions a été conçu pour accueillir des artistes résidents et 32 jeunes étudiants d'Australie et d'ailleurs. Il offre les équipements nécessaires à l'exercice d'activités artistiques diverses dont la musique et le théâtre en pleine campagne. Si les murs et les sols sont en béton, le toit est en bois recyclé et en acier protégé par une feuille de métal ondulé galvanisé. Glenn Murcutt est fier d'avoir réussi à inclure dans le modeste budget dont il disposait « l'approvisionnement en eau sur place, le traitement des déchets, les travaux extérieurs, les aménagements paysagers et la démolition de bâtiments existants ». Ce projet comprend également une salle polyvalente, une cuisine, un dortoir et un amphithéâtre en plein air qui n'a pas encore été construit. Même s'il fait appel à des matériaux bruts, ce Centre semble annoncer une approche plus formaliste que les réalisations antérieures de l'architecte. En 1999, il a obtenu le prix Sir Zelman Cowen pour les bâtiments publics, la plus prestigieuse récompense décernée par le Royal Australian Institute of Architects (RAIA) et le Kenneth F. Brown Asia Pacific Culture and Architecture Design Award 2001.

Extruding panels provide a high degree of articulation to the facade of the residential space as well as a degree of privacy.

Die vorstehenden Platten an der Fassade des Wohntrakts gliedern das Gebäude und schaffen mehr Privatsphäre für die einzelnen Wohnungen.

Un jeu de panneaux projetés vers l'avant accentue l'articulation de la façade, tout en renforçant l'intimité des pièces.

An imaginative observer might well
see a reference to temple architecture
in these views, whether they are of
the antique, Western variety or of the
lighter, more ephemeral Asian type.

Die Kunstschule erinnert sowohl an
Tempelbauten der abendländisch-
antiken als auch an solche der leich-
teren, fast vergänglich wirkenden,
asiatischen Architektur.

L'observateur peut trouver dans ces
vues une référence à l'architecture
de temples de l'antiquité occidentale
et même aux modèles asiatiques
plus éphémères.

MVRDV

MVRDV
Postbus 63136
3002 JC Rotterdam
Netherlands

Tel: +31 10 477 2860
Fax: +31 10 477 3627
e-mail: office@mvrdv.nl
Web: www.mvrdv.nl

MetaCITY/DATATOWN

Winy Maas, Jacob van Rijs and Nathalie de Vries created **MVRDV** in 1991. The name of the firm is made up of the initials of the surnames of the partners. Born in 1959, Maas, like his two partners (van Rijs born in 1964, de Vries born in 1965), studied at the Technical University in Delft. Both Maas and van Rijs worked for the Office for Metropolitan Architecture (OMA). De Vries worked in the office of Mecanoo and van Rijs in the office of Ben van Berkel before founding MVRDV. Aside from the Villa VPRO (Hilversum, 1993-97), their work includes the RVU Building (Hilversum, 1994-97), a Double House (Utrecht, 1995-97), WoZoCo, 100 apartments for elderly people (Amsterdam-Osdorp, 1997), all in the Netherlands, and the Dutch Pavilion for Expo 2000 (Hanover, Germany). They have also worked on urban development schemes such as their Ypenburg project (1998), or the Masterplan for Parklane Airport, Eindhoven, Netherlands.

Winy Maas, Jacob van Rijs und Nathalie de Vries gründeten **MVRDV** im Jahre 1991; der Name des Büros ist aus den Initialen ihrer Nachnamen gebildet. Maas (geboren 1959), van Rijs (geboren 1964) und de Vries (1965 geboren) studierten an der Technischen Universität Delft. Vor der Gründung von MVRDV arbeiteten Maas und van Rijs für das Office for Metropolitan Architecture (OMA), de Vries bei Mecanoo und van Rijs bei Ben van Berkel. Zu ihren Werken gehören die Villa VPRO in Hilversum (1993-97), das RVU-Gebäude in Hilversum (1994-97), ein Doppelhaus in Utrecht (1995-97) sowie WoZoCo, ein Komplex mit 100 Seniorenwohnungen in Amsterdam-Osdorp (1997) und der Niederländische Pavillon für die Expo 2000 in Hannover. Darüber hinaus haben sie Stadtentwicklungsplanungen wie das Projekt Ypenburg (1998) oder den Masterplan für den Flughafen Parklane in Eindhoven erarbeitet.

Winy Maas, Jacob van Rijs et Nathalie de Vries fondent en 1991 l'agence **MVRDV** dont le sigle se compose des initiales de leurs prénoms. Né en 1959, Maas, comme ses deux autres associés (van Rijs né en 1964, de Vries née en 1965) étudie à l'Université Polytechnique de Delft. Maas et van Rijs ont travaillé pour l'Office for Metropolitan Architecture (OMA), de Vries a travaillé pour Mecanoo et van Rijs dans l'agence de Ben van Berkel avant de créer MVRDV. Outre la Villa VPRO (Hilversum, 1993-97), ils ont réalisé l'immeuble RVU (Hilversum, 1994-97), une maison double (Amsterdam-Osdorp, 1997), WoZoCo, 100 logements pour personnes âgées (Amsterdam-Osdorp, 1997) et le Pavillon Néerlandais à Expo 2000, Hanovre. Ils ont également travaillé sur des projets de rénovation urbaine comme « Ypenburg » (1998) ou le plan directeur de l'aéroport Parklane à Eindhoven, Pays-Bas.

METACITY/DATATOWN

1998-

Research project conceived by Winy Maas which resulted in a video installation
developed by Winy Maas, Jan van Grunsven and Arno van der Mark
in collaboration with Stroom and a book produced by MVRDV.

Based on a video installation produced by MVRDV for the Stroom Center for the Visual Arts in The Hague at the end of 1998, **METACITY/DATATOWN** is essentially an exhibition that has been shown in such locations as Galerie Aedes (Berlin) and Venice Biennale. "Datatown," say the architects, "is based only upon data. It is a city that wants to be described by information; a city that knows no given topography, no prescribed ideology, no representation, no context." Extrapolating from the rapid expansion of urban centers, based on methods of transportation and communication, MVRDV concludes that the Datatown of the future will measure some 400 x 400 km (roughly the distance from Tokyo to Osaka), and that it will have an extremely high population density (1 477 inhabitants per km^2), which would imply a city population of 241 million people. A cross between computer games such as SimCity and genuine urban development ideas, MetaCITY/Datatown is also an aesthetic environment that reflects the design concepts of this influential Dutch firm, even if the world may not be quite ready for the 376 Datatowns they project (i.e. a world urban population of more than 88 billion people).

METACITY/DATATOWN basiert auf einer 1998 von MVRDV für das Stroom Center for the Visual Arts in Den Haag produzierten Video-Installation. Es ist im Wesentlichen als Ausstellung konzipiert, die unter anderem in der Galerie Aedes (Berlin) und auf der Biennale in Venedig gezeigt wurde. Die Architekten beschreiben ihr Projekt so: »Datatown beruht nur auf Daten. Es ist eine Stadt, die allein durch Information beschrieben wird. Sie kennt keine festgelegte Topographie, keine vorgeschriebene Ideologie, keine Repräsentation und keinen Kontext.« Ausgehend von der rasanten Ausdehnung urbaner Zentren und den neuen Transport- und Kommunikationsmethoden, stellt MVRDV folgende Hochrechnung an: Die Datatown der Zukunft wird circa 400 km^2 (in etwa die Entfernung von Tokio nach Osaka) messen und über eine extrem hohe Bevölkerungsdichte verfügen, nämlich 1 477 Einwohner pro km^2, was einer Einwohnerzahl von knapp 241 Millionen Menschen entspricht. MetaCITY/Datatown stellt eine Mischung aus Computerspielen wie SimCity und ernstzunehmenden Ideen für zukünftige Möglichkeiten der Stadtentwicklung dar. Darüber hinaus bildet das Projekt einen ästhetischen Rahmen für die Präsentation der Designkonzepte dieser einflussreichen holländischen Architektengruppe, auch wenn die Welt noch nicht reif sein mag für ihre projektierten 376 Datatowns (d. h. eine Weltbevölkerungszahl von annähernd 88 Milliarden Menschen).

Inspirée d'une installation vidéo produite par MVRDV pour le Centre Stroom d'arts plastiques de la Haye fin 1998, **METACITY/DATATOWN** est essentiellement une exposition présentée dans des lieux comme la Galerie Aedes (Berlin) et la Biennale de Venise. « Datatown », expliquent les architectes « repose uniquement sur les données informatiques. C'est une ville qui se décrit par l'information, une ville sans topographie, sans idéologie prescrite, sans représentation, sans contexte. » Partant de la rapide expansion des centres urbains et de méthodes de transport et de communication, MVRDV conclut que la Datatown du futur mesurera quelques 400 km^2 (sur à peu près la distance de Tokyo à Osaka) et connaîtra une densité de population extrêmement élevée (1 477 habitants au km^2) soit 241 millions de personnes. Au croisement de jeux d'ordinateur comme SimCity et de concepts urbanistiques, MetaCITY/Datatown possède par ailleurs une qualité esthétique qui reflète la pensée de cette influente agence néerlandaise, même si le monde n'est peut-être pas encore prêt pour les 376 « datatowns » qu'elle imagine (soit une population de plus de 88 milliards d'habitants).

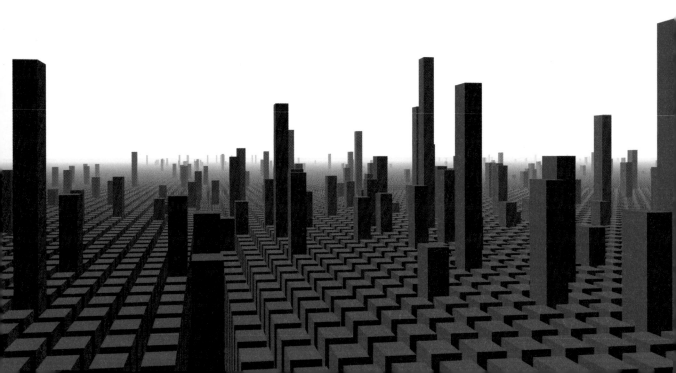

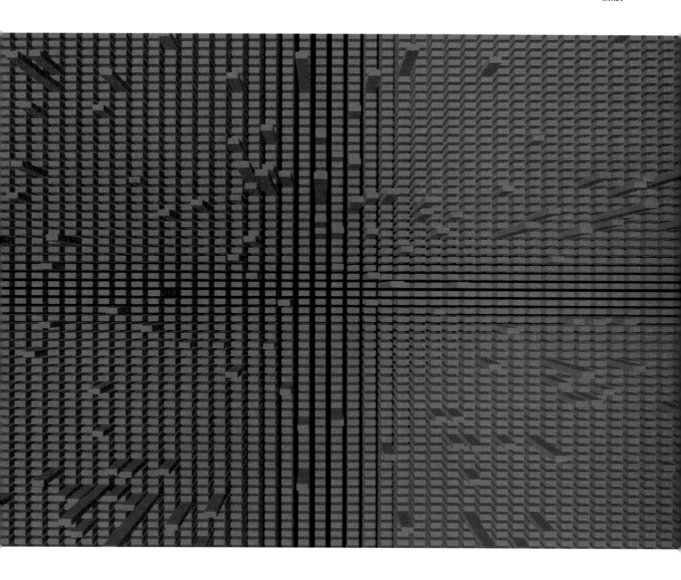

Each part of the MVRDV plan is divided by function. Here, the Living Sector, assuming a given population density, as it would appear if it were to be spread evenly over the entire zone.

Der Entwurf von MVRDV ist in einzelne Funktionsbereiche aufgeteilt. Der hier abgebildete »Sector Living« (Lebenssektor) geht von einer gleichmäßig über das gesamte Gebiet verteilten Bevölkerungsdichte aus.

Le plan est divisé en fonctions. Ici, le Secteur de vie, conçu pour une densité démographique précise, tel qu'il apparaîtrait s'il devait couvrir toute la zone.

The Agricultural Sector consists of millions of individual farming plots. Above: Assuming that there would be no meat consumption, it would be possible to subtract 81 876 km² for the production of animal fodder crops.

Der Agrarsektor besteht aus Millionen einzelner Ackerflächen. Oben: Sollte kein Fleisch mehr verzehrt werden, könnten die für den Anbau von Viehfutter vorgesehenen 81 876 km² abgezogen werden.

Le Secteur agricole consiste en plusieurs millions de parcelles individuelles cultivables.
Ci-dessus : si la ville était végétarienne, il serait possible d'économiser les 81 876 km² prévus pour la production d'aliments pour le bétail.

Above: The total area required for agriculture is 814 215 km², i.e. five times the total area of Datatown. Below: "Lamb consumption per capita." The sector is divided according to its functions into different zones, lamb consumption being one of them.

Oben: Die für die landwirtschaftliche Nutzung erforderliche Gesamtfläche (814 215 km²) entspricht der fünf-fachen Größe von Datatown. Unten: Lammkonsum pro Kopf – eine der verschiedenen Zonen im Sektor.

Ci-dessus : comme le montre cette image, la surface agricole prévue est de 814 215 km² soit cinq fois celle de Datatown. Ci-dessous : « Consommation d'agneau par tête. » Le secteur est divisés en différentes zones, la production d'agneau étant l'une d'entre elles.

Data Town's CO$_2$-Sector or Forest Sector. Above left: The Industry Sector is compared to a "stacked Ruhr Valley." A series of forests, 3 834 stories high, reaching a height of more than 100 km, are located within the boundaries of the Industry Sector. As the architects claim, this massive CO$_2$-machine of forest-towers "monumentalizes economy and ecology."

Der CO$_2$-Sektor (Wald) von Datatown. Oben links: Der Industriesektor als »aufgestapeltes Ruhrgebiet«, inner-halb dessen sich ein 3 834-geschos-siger Wald befindet, der eine Höhe von mehr als 100 km erreicht (unten links). Diese gewaltige CO$_2$-Maschine (oben rechts) setzt den Waldtürmen der Ökonomie und Ökologie (unten rechts) ein Denkmal.

Le secteur forestier de Datatown. Les architectes comparent le secteur industriel à une « vallée de la Ruhr empilée. » Une série de forêts de 3 834 étages, hautes de plus de 100 km sont implantées dans les limites de ce secteur. Cette énorme machinerie d'absorption de CO_2 « monumentalise l'économie d'énergie et l'écologie. »

The Energy Sector: Assuming that all of Datatown's energy would be produced by windmills, the city would need a windmill park totalling 77 860 km², or half the size of Datatown.

Der Energiesektor: Davon ausgehend, die gesamte Energieversorgung von Datatown erfolge durch Windmühlen, wäre ein Gebiet von insgesamt 77 860 km² nötig, das entspricht der Hälfte der Fläche von Datatown.

Le secteur de l'énergie : si toute l'énergie de Datatown était fournie par des moulins à vent, la ville aurait besoin d'un parc éolien de 77 860 km², soit la moitié de sa surface.

Below: The Water Sector: Assuming that Datatown's drinking water is stored in a water-storage-sector totalling 23.1 km³ the water column would reach a height of 500 m.

Unten: Der Wassersektor: Das für Datatown benötigte Trinkwasser würde, in einem Wasser-Speicher-Sektor von 23,1 km³ aufbewahrt, eine 500 m hohe Wassersäule ergeben.

Ci-dessous: Le secteur de l'eau: si l'eau potable de Datatown était réservé dans un réservoir de 23,1 km³, la colonne de l'eau aurait une hauteur du 500 m.

The Waste Sector: Each day Datatown produces 315 864 t of waste, yielding a hill with a volume of 1 525 906 m³ and a height of 73 m.

Above left and right: Anticipating future developments of waste disposal areas, MVRDV writes, "If we stay within the current boundaries of the sector, after 150 years the Waste Sector will become a dolomitic landscape."

Below right: According to the architects, "After a million years, Datatown becomes an alpine mountain range."

Der Abfallsektor: Die von Datatown täglich produzierte Müllmenge von 315 864 t ergibt einen Berg mit einem Volumen von 1 525 906 m³ und einer Höhe von 73 m.

Oben links und rechts: Die zukünftige Entwicklung der Abfallbeseitigung vorwegnehmend schreibt MVRDV: »Wenn wir innerhalb der jetzigen Grenzen des Sektors bleiben, entwickelt sich der Abfallsektor nach 150 Jahren zu einer Gebirgslandschaft.«

Unten rechts: Nach einer Million Jahren wird ganz Datatown zu einer Gebirgskette.

Le secteur des déchets : chaque jour, Datatown produit 315 864 t de déchets, soit l'équivalent d'une volume de 1 526 000 m³ pour une hauteur de 73 m.

En haut à gauche et à droite : anticipant le développements des zones de déchets, MVRDV précise : « Si nous nous contentons de ce secteur, en 150 ans, il aura pris l'aspect d'un paysage dolomitique. »

Ci-dessous à droite : selon les architectes : « Au bout d'un million d'années, Datatown ressemblera à une chaîne de montagnes. »

TAKEHIKO NAGAKURA

Takehiko Nagakura
Associate Professor of Design and Computation
Department of Architecture
Massachusetts Institute of Technology
77 Massachusetts Avenue, 10-472M
Cambridge, Massachusetts 02139
United States

Tel: +1 617 253 0781
Fax: +1 627 253 9407
e-mail: takehiko@mit.edu

TAKEHIKO NAGAKURA is an architect from Tokyo. He received undergraduate education in architectural design under Professor Fumihiko Maki at the University of Tokyo and was a Ishizaka Memorial Foundation Scholar (1985-87) while he studied in the M.Arch. program at the Harvard University Graduate School of Design (GSD). Currently, he is an Associate Professor of Design and Computation at the Department of Architecture of the Massachusetts Institute of Technology (MIT). After graduation from GSD, Nagakura established a design practice in Japan, where he is a registered architect and engaged in building projects in Tokyo and Okinawa. His recent project for the Gushikawa Orchid Center was selected for the SD Review Award in 1998, and is currently under construction in Okinawa. He heads Team Unbuilt, with research scientist Kent Larson, which is developing computer graphics visualizations of significant unbuilt projects of early Modernism.

All following images were originally developed at the Massachusetts Institute of Technology by Team Unbuilt, sponsored by the Takenaka Corporation of Japan under supervision of Takehiko Nagakura and Kent Larson.

TAKEHIKO NAGAKURA wurde in Tokio geboren. Er studierte Architekturdesign bei Professor Fumihiko Maki an der Universität Tokio und von 1985 bis 1987 als Stipendiat der Ishizaka Memorial Foundation an der Harvard University's Graduate School of Design (GSD), wo er den Master of Architecture erwarb. Gegenwärtig ist er als außerordentlicher Professor für Design und Computerisierung am Fachbereich Architektur des Massachusetts Institute of Technology (MIT) tätig. Nach seinem Abschluss an der GSD eröffnete Nagakura ein Planungsbüro in Japan, wo er mehrere Bauprojekte in Tokio und Okinawa ausführte. Sein Entwurf für das Gushikawa Orchid Center wurde 1998 für den SD Review Award nominiert und wird derzeit in Okinawa realisiert. Nagakura leitet zusammen mit dem Forscher Kent Larson das Team Unbuilt, das Computergrafiken zur Veranschaulichung bedeutender, aber unrealisiert gebliebener Architekturentwürfe der frühen Moderne entwickelt.

Die folgenden Bilder wurden mit finanzieller Unterstützung der Takenaka Corporation of Japan unter Leitung von Takehiko Nagakura und Kent Larson vom Team Unbuilt am Massachusetts Institute of Technology (MIT) entwickelt.

TAKEHIKO NAGAKURA est un architect basé à Tokyo. Il étudie la conception architecturale auprès du Professeur Fumihiko Maki à l'Université de Tokyo, et obtient une bourse de la Fondation mémoriale Ishikaza (1985-87) pour son Master of Architecture de la Graduate School of Design de l'Université de Harvard. Il est actuellement professeur assistant de conception et d'informatique au département d'architecture du Massachusetts Institute of Technology. Actif au Japon, il travaille sur des projets à Tokyo et Okinawa. Son récent projet pour le centre de l'orchidée Gushikawa, actuellement en chantier à Okinawa, a été sélectionné pour le prix de la revue SD (1998). En compagnie du chercheur Kent Larson, il dirige le Team Unbuilt qui se propose de visualiser par des moyens informatiques d'importants projets modernistes jamais réalisés.

Toutes les images publiées ici ont été développées au Massachusetts Institute of Technology par Team Unbuilt, financé par la Takenaka Corporation of Japan, et supervisé par Takehiko Nagakura et de Kent Larson.

MONUMENT TO THE THIRD INTERNATIONAL

Petrograd, Soviet Union, 1919/1998

Computer Graphics Visualization Project. Producer/Director: Takehiko Nagakura.
Computer graphics: Andrzej Zarzycki, Takehiko Nagakura, Dan Brick, Mark Sich.
Production period: 1997-98. Film length: 3 min. 10 sec.
Funding support: Takenaka Corporation.

Vladimir Tatlin's Constructivist project for a **MONUMENT TO THE THIRD INTERNATIONAL** was a machine in which the various sections would rotate within an exposed steel armature. Because of Stalin's dislike of modern architecture, the tower was never completed. Its foundation was later used for an outdoor swimming pool. "Tatlin was a sculptor," says Nagakura, "and his project was a wildly shaped 400-m tower in the middle of the great classic city of St. Petersburg (then Petrograd). The computer graphics (by Takehiko Nagakura, Andrzej Zarzycki, Dan Brick, and Mark Sich) attempt to show the visual effect that this jarring addition would have today, with its 'double-spiral form, rusting iron materiality and enormous out-scaled size, none of which had any precedents in the context of the old Russian city."

Vladimir Tatlins konstruktivistischer Entwurf für das **MONUMENT DER DRITTEN INTERNATIONALE** war eine Maschine, deren verschiedene Teile innerhalb einer freiliegenden Stahlkonstruktion rotieren sollten. Wegen Stalins Abneigung gegen moderne Architektur wurde dieser Turm jedoch nie realisiert. Sein Fundament wurde später für ein Freibad genutzt. »Tatlin war Bildhauer«, erklärt Nagakura, »und sein Projekt war ein kühn geformter 400 m hoher Turm, der mitten im klassizistischen Zentrum von Petrograd, dem heutigen St. Petersburg, stehen sollte. Die Computergrafiken (von Takehiko Nagakura, Andrzej Zarzycki, Dan Brick und Mark Sich) versuchen deutlich zu machen, welche optische Wirkung dieses Bauwerk heute haben würde: mit seiner Gestalt in Form einer Doppelspirale, der Massivität des rostigen Stahls und seiner enormen Größe verkörpert es Eigenschaften, für die es in dieser alten russischen Stadt keinerlei Vorläufer gab.«

Le projet constructiviste de **MONUMENT À LA IIIᵉ INTERNATIONALE** proposé par Vladimir Tatline était en fait une machine dont les diverses sections devaient tourner à l'intérieur d'une armature d'acier. Staline n'appréciant pas l'architecture moderne, la tour ne fut jamais achevée. Par la suite, ses fondations servirent à la construction d'une piscine en plein air. « Tatline était un sculpteur », explique Nagakura, « et son projet était celui d'une incroyable tour au milieu de cette grande cité néo-classique qu'est Saint-Pétersbourg. » Le traitement en image de synthèse (par Takehiko Nagakura, Andrzej Zarzycki, Dan Brick et Mark Sich) tente de montrer l'effet visuel que cette provocante incursion exercerait aujourd'hui, avec sa double spirale, son aspect de fer rouillé et ses gigantesques dimensions, sans précédent dans le contexte de l'ancienne capitale impériale. »

Takehiko Nagakura and his Team Unbuilt group at MIT chose to give their computer perspectives of Tatlin's Monument to the Third International the look and feeling of an aging structure, as though the monument had actually been built in 1919.

Takehiko und seine Gruppe am MIT, Team Unbuilt, gaben ihren Computeransichten von Tatlins Monument der Dritten Internationale das Aussehen und die Aura eines gealterten Bauwerks, um den Eindruck zu erzeugen, es sei tatsächlich 1919 erbaut worden.

Takehiko Nagakura et son équipe Team Unbuilt du MIT ont choisi de traiter en image de synthèse le Monument à la troisième Internationale de Tatline, en vieillissant artificiellement la construction, comme si elle avait été réalisée.

PALACE OF THE SOVIETS

Moscow, Soviet Union, 1931/98

Computer Graphics Visualization Project. Producer/Director: Takehiko Nagakura.
Computer graphics: Shinsuke Baba. Production period: 1997-98. Film length: 5 min. 20 sec.
Funding support: Takenaka Corporation.
(Unrealized project by Le Corbusier, graphic interpretation by responsibility of the author.)

During a trip to Moscow, Le Corbusier came into contact with the Constructivists. As Takehiko Nagakura says, "In 1931, Le Corbusier participated in and lost the competition for the **PALACE OF THE SOVIETS**. Corbusier's entry comprised two symmetric structures: a roof suspended by a giant arch, and another folded roof, along the riverside of Moscow. Corbusier's exterior model for this project has been well published in the architectural media, but its interior space had existed only in the mind of the architect. The computer graphics (by Shinsuke Baba) attempt here to put viewers at the foot of the giant arch and to let the visitor proceed inside of this widely acknowledged modern masterpiece for the first time."

Während einer Reise nach Moskau kam Le Corbusier mit den russischen Konstruktivisten in Kontakt. Takehiko Nagakura meint: »1931 nahm Le Corbusier am Wettbewerb für den **PALAST DER SOWJETS** teil, den er jedoch verlor. Sein Beitrag bestand aus zwei symmetrischen Strukturen: einem Dach, das an einem riesigen Bogen aufgehängt, und einem weiteren Faltdach, das zum Flussufer ausgerichtet war. Le Corbusiers Modell vom Äußeren des Baus wurde in zahlreichen Architekturzeitschriften veröffentlicht, während die Innenraumgestaltung bislang nur in der Vorstellung des Architekten existierte. Die Computergrafiken (von Shinsuke Baba) führen nun den Besucher zum ersten Mal vom Fuß des riesigen Bogens in das Innere dieses berühmten Meisterwerks der Moderne.«

Lors d'un voyage à Moscou, Le Corbusier entra en contact avec les constructivistes russes. Comme le fait remarquer Takehiko Nagakura, «En 1931, Le Corbusier avait participé au concours pour le **PALAIS DES SOVIETS** qu'il avait perdu. Son projet comprenait deux constructions symétriques : un toit suspendu à une arche géante et un toit replié le long de la Moscova. La maquette de l'extérieur de ce projet a été amplement publiée dans la presse architecturale, mais l'intérieur n'existait que dans l'esprit de Le Corbusier. Les images de synthèse (de Shinsuke Baba) placent le visiteur au pied de l'arche géante et, pour la première fois, le font pénétrer à l'intérieur de ce chef d'œuvre reconnu de l'architecture moderne.

Using their knowledge of the original architectural plans and software capable of modeling light patterns, Nagakura and Team Unbuilt virtually resurrected this essentially unknown masterpiece.

In Kenntnis der Originalentwürfe und einer Software, die selbst die Wirkung des Lichteinfalls veranschaulichen kann, erweckten Nagakura und sein Team Unbuilt dieses fast unbekannte Meisterwerk zu virtuellem Leben.

A partir de leur connaissance des plans d'origine et de leur maîtrise du traitement de la lumière par ordinateur, Nagakura et Team Unbuilt ont littéralement donné vie à ce chef d'œuvre en grande partie inconnu.

CHURCH IN ALTSTETTEN

Zurich, Switzerland, 1967/2000

Computer Graphics Visualization Project. Producer/Director: Takehiko Nagakura.
Computer graphics: Andrzej Zarzycki. Production period: 1998-2000.
Funding support: Takenaka Corporation.

Takehiko Nagakura and his Team Unbuilt group at MIT chose this competition entry for a **CHURCH IN ALTSTETTEN** by Alvar Aalto as an example of their efforts to shed light on unbuilt works of modern masters. As Nagakura says, "With the same technology Hollywood uses for their special effects, I believe computer graphics can replicate a certain level of reality. Computer graphics are the only way of getting close to the real sensation of spatial experience in the case of these unbuilt works. The process of computer graphics is usually very laborious and time consuming. However, it is rewarding. It brings about an excitement of the space and it is often very different from and much more than what I imagined. What great architecture provides is quite often concealed. A rigorous computer graphics visualization work lets us take a glimpse at this wonderful secret."

Takehiko Nagakura und sein »Team Unbuilt« am MIT wählten Alvar Aaltos Wettbewerbsbeitrag für eine **KIRCHE IN ALTSTETTEN** als weiteres Beispiel für ihre Bemühungen, nicht realisierte Werke der Meister der Moderne sichtbar werden zu lassen. Nagakura erläutert das Projekt so: »Ich glaube, dass Computergrafiken mit Hilfe der gleichen Technologie, die in Hollywood-Filmen für Spezialeffekte verwendet wird, ein gewisses Maß an Wirklichkeitsnähe hervorbringen können. Im Fall dieser nicht realisierten Bauten bieten Computergrafiken die einzige Möglichkeit, sich einem authentischen Raumerlebnis anzunähern. Der Prozess der Computerisierung ist in der Regel sehr mühsam und zeitaufwändig. Es ist jedoch auch ein sehr befriedigender und spannender Prozess, der häufig ganz anders und lohnender verläuft, als ich es mir vorgestellt hatte. Was große Architektur an Potential bereithält, bleibt häufig verborgen. Eine konsequente computergrafische Visualisierungsarbeit gewährt uns jedoch einen Einblick in dieses wundervolle Geheimnis.«

Takehiko Nagakura et son groupe de Team Unbuilt du MIT ont choisi ce projet de concours pour une **ÉGLISE À ALTSTETTEN** d'Alvar Aalto pour illustrer l'éclairage nouveau qu'il veulent apporter à des œuvres de maîtres modernes jamais réalisées. Comme le précise T. Nagakura : «Avec la même technologie qu'utilise Hollywood pour ses effets spéciaux, je pense que l'image de synthèse peut nous permettre d'accéder à un certain niveau de réalité. L'image de synthèse est la seule façon d'approcher les sensations d'espace données par des œuvres restées sur le papier. Le processus de synthèse est généralement très laborieux et requiert beaucoup de temps. Cependant, l'expérience est enrichissante. Elle apporte toute l'excitation de la découverte d'un volume qui est souvent très différent et beaucoup plus intéressant que ce que j'avais imaginé. Ce qu'apporte une grande architecture reste souvent dissimulé. Une rigoureuse visualisation en images de synthèse nous fait entr'apercevoir ce merveilleux secret. »

Using the most sophisticated available technology, Nagakura's team will soon succeed in giving a photo-realistic impression of the interior and exterior of unbuilt structures.

Unter Verwendung modernster Computer-Technologie vermittelt Nagakuras Team einen photo-realistischen Eindruck vom Inneren und Äußeren nicht realisierter Bauten, wie hier von Alvar Aaltos Kirche in Altstetten.

A l'aide des technologies les plus avancées, l'équipe de Nagakura a réussi à créer une impression photographique de l'intérieur et de l'extérieur de projets jamais réalisés.

NEUTELINGS RIEDIJK

Neutelings Riedijk Architecten BV
Scheepmakersstraat 13
3011 VH Rotterdam
Netherlands

Tel: +31 10 404 6677
Fax: +31 10 414 2712

Minnaert Building

WILLEM JAN NEUTELINGS was born in 1959 in Bergen op Zoom, Netherlands. He studied at the Technical University in Delft (1977-86) before working in the Office for Metropolitan Architecture with Rem Koolhaas (1981-86). He has taught at the Academy of Architecture in Rotterdam and at the Berlage Institute in Amsterdam (1990-99). MICHIEL RIEDIJK was born in Geldrop, Netherlands in 1964. He attended the Technical University in Delft (1983-89) before working with Juliette Bekkering in Amsterdam. He has taught at the Technical University in Delft and Eindhoven and at the Academies of Architecture in Amsterdam, Rotterdam and Maastricht. Neutelings and Riedijk started collaborating in 1991. Their built work includes the Prinsenhoek Residential Complex (Sittard, 1992-95), Tilburg Housing (1993-96), Borneo Sporenburg Housing (Amsterdam, 1994-97), Lakeshore Housing, first phase (Hulzen, 1994-96), and the Building for Veenman Printers (Ede, 1995-97), all in the Netherlands, as well as Hollainhof Social Housing (Ghent, Belgium, 1993-98).

WILLEM JAN NEUTELINGS wurde 1959 in Bergen op Zoom, Niederlande, geboren. Er studierte von 1977 bis 1986 an der Technischen Universität in Delft und arbeitete anschließend im Office for Metropolitan Architecture bei Rem Koolhaas. Von 1990 bis 1999 lehrte er an der Akademie für Architektur in Rotterdam und am Berlage-Institut in Amsterdam. MICHIEL RIEDIJK, geboren 1964 im niederländischen Geldrop, studierte an der Technischen Universität in Delft (1983-1989), bevor er bei J. D. Bekkering in Amsterdam arbeitete. Er lehrte an den Technischen Universitäten in Delft und Eindhoven sowie an den Akademien für Architektur in Amsterdam, Rotterdam und Maastricht. Zu den Bauten von Neutelings Riedijk gehören der Wohnkomplex Prinsenhoek in Sittard (1992-95), die Wohnanlagen Tilburg (1993-96) und Borneo Sporenburg in Amsterdam (1994-97), Lakeshore, Phase I in Hulzen (1994-96) und das Veenman Drukkers-Gebäude in Ede (1995-97), alle in den Niederlanden, sowie die Sozialwohnanlage Hollainhof in Gent, Belgien (1993-98).

WILLEM JAN NEUTELINGS, né en 1959 à Bergen op Zoom, Pays-Bas, étudie à l'Université Technique de Delft (1977-86) avant de travailler pour l'Office for Metropolitan Architecture auprès de Rem Koolhaas. Il a enseigné à l'Académie d'architecture de Rotterdam et au Berlage Institute d'Amsterdam (1990-99). MICHIEL RIEDIJK, né à Geldrop, Pays-Bas, en 1964, étudie à l'Université Technique de Delft (1983-89) avant de travailler pour J. D. Bekkering à Amsterdam. Il a enseigné à l'Université Technique de Delft, d'Eindhoven et aux Académies d'architecture d'Amsterdam, Rotterdam et Maastricht. Parmi leurs réalisations : le complexe résidentiel de Prinsenhoek (Sittard, 1992-95), un immeuble d'appartement à Tilburg (1993-96), l'immeuble résidentiel Borneo Sporenburg (Amsterdam, 1994-97), les logements de Lakeshore (Hulzen, 1994-96) et l'immeuble de Veenman Drukkers (Ede, 1995-97), toutes aux Pays-Bas, ainsi que les logements sociaux de Hollainhof (Gand, Belgique, 1993-98).

MINNAERT BUILDING

Utrecht, Netherlands, 1994-97

Planning: 1994-96. Construction: 1996-97.
Client: University Utrecht. Floor area: ca. 9 000 m².

Located on the campus of Uithof University, the **MINNAERT BUILDING** includes three main components – a restaurant, classrooms and laboratories, and work-space. Characterized by its sienna pigmented undulating skin of sprayed concrete, the building includes a 50 x 10-m pond that collects rainwater and is situated in a main hall. The water is pumped in and out of the building by the roof for cooling purposes. Water falls into the basin during rainy periods, adding the element of sound to a composition that intends to evoke the five senses. Large-scale letters spelling the name Minnaert replace columns on part of the south elevation, making the building immediately recognizable to passersby.

Das **MINNAERT-GEBÄUDE** liegt auf dem Uithof-Campus der Universität Utrecht und besteht aus drei Bauteilen, in denen ein Restaurant, Klassen- und Arbeitsräume sowie Laboratorien untergebracht sind. Das durch seine ockerfarben pigmentierte und gewellte Haut aus gespritztem Beton gekennzeichnete Gebäude besitzt in der Haupthalle einen 50 x 10 m großen Brunnen, in dem Regenwasser aufgefangen wird. Zum Zweck der Kühlung wird das Wasser vom Dach aus in das Gebäude hinein und wieder heraus gepumpt. Wenn es regnet, fällt Wasser in das Becken, was der Komposition, die alle Sinne ansprechen will, das akustische Element hinzufügt. Auf der Süd-seite ruht der Bau auf Stützen in Form von großformatigen Buchstaben. Diese ergeben den Namen Minnaert, wodurch das Gebäude für Passanten sofort kenntlich ge-macht wird.

Situé sur le campus de l'Université Uithof, ce bâtiment se compose de trois parties principales : un restaurant, des salles de cours et des laboratoires. Caractérisé par sa peau externe ondulée en béton projeté de couleur terre de Sienne, il possède un bassin de 50 x 10 m dans le hall principal qui récupère les eaux de pluie ; cet élé-ment sonore enrichit une composition qui évoque les cinq sens. L'eau est pompée ou rejetée sur le toit en fonction de la température. Les énormes lettres qui composent le nom de **MINNAERT** remplacent les colonnes sur la façade sud et rendent le bâtiment facilement identifiable.

As the drawing (below right) shows, the architects share a typical Dutch concern for the environmental effi-ciency of their building, this in spite of the rather massive appearance of the structure.

Das Minnaert-Gebäude ist nach umweltfreundlichen Gesichtspunkten konzipiert (unten rechts). Diese ener-giesparende Bauweise, die in den Niederlanden mittlerweile Tradition hat, ist an den eher massiv und geschlossen wirkenden Oberflächen nicht ablesbar.

Le dessin de droite montre que les architectes ont conçu le bâtiment dans un souci de respect de l'envi-ronnement traditionnel aux Pays-Bas, préoccupation qui ne transparaît pas dans l'aspect massif de sa strucutre.

The rather heavy feeling of the interior spaces is somewhat alleviated by the use of some bright colors. The angled ceilings and walls are typical of the architects.

Die eher schweren Innenräume werden durch einige helle Farbtöne aufgelockert. Charakteristisch für den Stil des Büros sind die schrägen Decken und Wände.

Une certaine lourdeur perçue dans les espaces intérieurs est allégée par le recours à des couleurs vives. Les plafonds et les murs inclinés sont typiques du style des architectes.

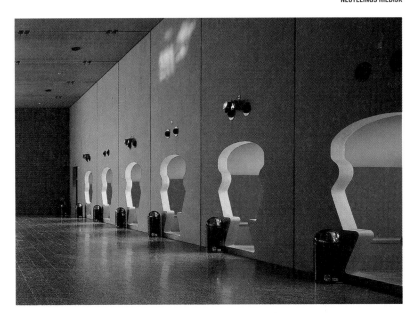

FIRE STATION

Maastricht, Netherlands, 1996-99

Planning: 1996-98. Construction: 1998-99. Landscape: West-8 Landscape Architects, Rotterdam.
Client: Gemeente Maastricht. Floor area: ca. 4 000 m².

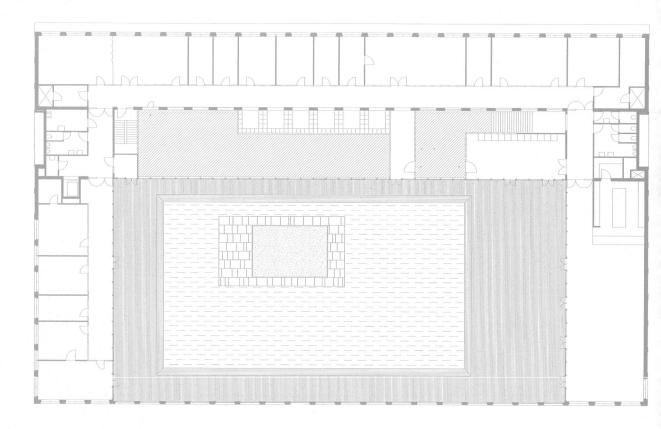

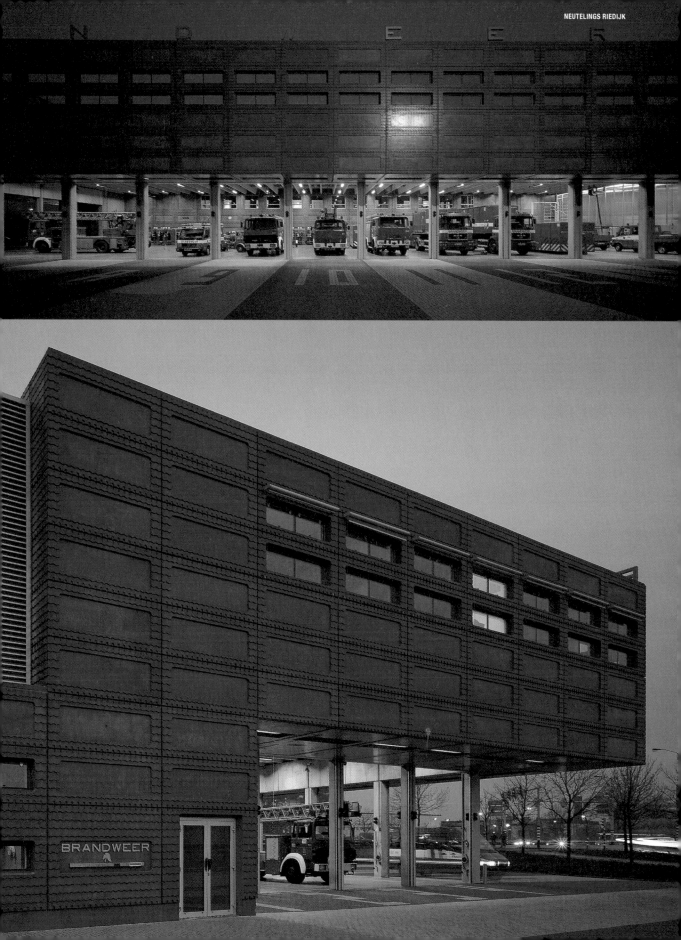

Situated at the northern, industrial periphery of the southern Dutch city of Maastricht, this **FIRE STATION** includes a garage with a workshop and storage area, living and sleeping quarters for the firemen, and offices. A double-height hall with ample natural light gives a different impression than the relatively harsh, gray concrete paneling of the exterior might lead one to believe. The patterning seems to have been inspired by truck tires. The unit cantilevered over the garage entrances gives the entire structure a sense of movement not unlike that obtained by the architects in their Minnaert Building. In the interior, large areas near the central hall painted in red brighten the rather severe gray tonality of the whole. A roof garden with a pond, designed to catch rainwater, also adds a more natural element to the composition.

Dieses **FEUERWEHRHAUS** liegt in einem Gewerbegebiet am Nordrand der niederländischen Stadt Maastricht. Es beherbergt eine Garage mit Werkstatt und Lagerhalle, Wohn- und Schlafräume für die Feuerwehrmänner sowie Büros. Die von natürlichem Licht durchflutete doppelgeschossige Halle vermittelt einen anderen Eindruck als die relativ abweisende graue Betonverkleidung der Außenwände erwarten lässt. Ihre Gestaltung scheint von Lastwagenreifen inspiriert zu sein. Der über den Garageneinfahrten auskragende Bauteil gibt dem gesamten Bau eine Ausstrahlung von Lebendigkeit und Bewegung, die an das Minnaert-Gebäude erinnert. Im Inneren hellen große rot gestrichene Bereiche die etwas streng wirkende graue Farbgebung des Ganzen auf, und auch der Dachgarten mit einem Teich, der zum Auffangen von Regenwasser dient, verleiht dem Bauwerk eine natürliche und aufgelockerte Note.

En pleine banlieue industrielle au nord de Maastricht (Sud des Pays-Bas), ce **CASERNE DE POMPIERS** comprend un garage, un atelier, un entrepôt et des bureaux. Un hall double-hauteur baigné de lumière donne une impression différente de ce que l'austère revêtement extérieur en panneaux de béton gris laisse supposer. Le motif semble avoir été inspiré par des pneus de camions. La partie en porte-à-faux au-dessus des entrées du garage donne à l'ensemble un mouvement assez proche de celui créé par les architectes pour l'immeuble Minnaert. A l'intérieur, à proximité du hall central, de vastes plans peints en rouge animent la tonalité grise assez sévère de l'ensemble. Un toit-terrasse traité en jardin, conçu pour récupérer l'eau de pluie, ajoute un élément naturel à la composition.

There is a kind of solid efficiency in the interior volumes of this fire station. As in the Minnaert Building, the design approach seems to be based on a quest for durability.

Die Innenräume des Feuerwehrhauses sind von wuchtiger Funktionalität gekennzeichnet. Wie im Minnaert-Gebäude drückt der Entwurf das Streben nach Dauerhaftigkeit aus.

Efficacité lourdement soulignée dans les volumes de cette caserne de pompiers. Comme dans l'immeuble Minnaert, l'approche semble axée sur une recherche de durabilité.

A rainwater-collecting pond serves both to make the building more environmentally friendly, and to play on the fire/water opposition that is inscribed in the function of the station.

Ein Auffangbecken für Regenwasser auf dem Dach basiert auf umweltfreundlichen Aspekten und ist gleichzeitig ein spielerischer Hinweis auf den Gegensatz zwischen Feuer und Wasser, der in der Funktion eines Feuerwehrhauses angelegt ist.

Le bassin de collecte des eaux pluviales sert à des fins écologiques tout en jouant sur l'opposition feu-eau inscrite dans la raison d'être de la caserne.

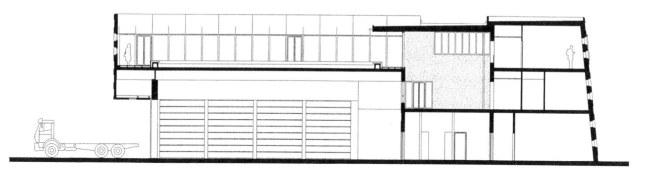

FIRE STATION

Breda, Netherlands, 1996-99

Planning: 1996-97. Construction: 1997-99.
Client: City of Breda. Floor area: ca. 6 000 m².

The almost blank brick walls of the station as seen from certain angles give it an enigmatic presence, more like a factory than a fire station.

Die fast ungegliederten Backstein-wände erinnern eher an eine Fabrik als an ein Feuerwehrhaus und verlei-hen dem Gebäude etwas Geheimnis-volles.

Les murs de brique en partie aveugles renforcent l'aspect énigmatique de cette caserne qui fait presque penser à une usine.

The **BREDA FIRE STATION** is placed into an essentially oval site near the former ramparts of the city. Patterned bricks cover most of the exterior of the building, whose sliced and cantilevered volumes make it appear less severe than the fire station in Maastricht. It is divided into four zones for training, workshops, garage and sport. A central hall and inner courtyard bring light and air to the interior of the complex, defying its rather closed exterior appearance. The architects point out the elevated "brow" of the building as the recognizable design element on this site near a major road leading into the city. A raked metal roof and checkered garage doors form strong architectural elements.

Das **FEUERWEHRHAUS** von Breda liegt auf einem annähernd ovalen Grundstück in der Nähe der ehemaligen Befestigungsanlagen der Stadt. In einem dekorativen Muster angeordnete Backsteine bedecken den Großteil der Außenwände des Gebäudes, dessen angeschnittene und überhängende Bauteile der Feuerwache ihre Strenge nehmen. Der Komplex ist in vier Bereiche für Ausbildung, Werkstätten, Garage und Sport unterteilt. Einen Kontrast zu dem sehr geschlossen wirkenden Äußeren bilden die zentrale Eingangshalle und ein Innenhof, die Licht und Luft in das Gebäudeinnere lassen. Die Architekten weisen auf die »hochgezogene Augenbraue« des Gebäudes hin, die an diesem Standort nahe einer der Haupteinfallstraßen als Erkennungszeichen dienen soll. Eine geneigte Metallfläche und die schachbrettartig gemusterten Garagentore sind weitere ausdrucksstarke Gestaltungsmittel.

Sur un terrain presque ovale, près des remparts de la ville, l'extérieur de cette **CASERNE DE POMPIERS** est agrémenté d'un parement de briques formant un motif décoratif. La répartition des différents parties en strates et en porte-à-faux la rendent moins sévère que celle de Maastricht. Elle est divisée en quatre zones pour l'entraînement, les ateliers, les garages et le sport. Un hall central et une cour intérieure contrastant avec l'aspect fermé de l'extérieur, font entrer air et lumière au sein de l'edifice. Le « sourcil » relevé du bâtiment lui donne une identité qui le fait remarquer du grand axe de circulation qui passe à proximité. Un plan de métal gratté et des portes de garage à carreaux constituent également des éléments architecturaux forts.

Hanging volumes and angled ceilings or ramps are recurring elements in the design vocabulary of Neutelings Riedijk, as is a sense of efficiency.

Überhängende Bauteile und schräge Decken oder Rampen sind immer wiederkehrende Elemente in der Formensprache von Neutelings Riedijk.

Les volumes suspendus, les plafonds en pente, les rampes et le fonctionnalisme sont des éléments récurrents du vocabulaire architectural de Neutelings Riedijk.

As seen from this angle, the station takes on a more dynamic profile, with its long slanted roof and protruding cantilevered volume. Even from this angle, the function of the structure is not at all evident, except in the name "Brandweer."

Das langgestreckte Schrägdach und der weit vorkragende Bauteil verleihen dem Feuerwehrhaus eine gewisse Dynamik, verschleiern aber auch seine eigentliche Funktion, die nur noch durch den Schriftzug »Brandweer« erkennbar bleibt.

Sous cet angle, la caserne retrouve un profil plus dynamique grâce à son vaste toit à pente unique et à son volume en porte-à-faux. Seule l'enseigne « Brandweer » permet d'identifier la fonction du bâtiment.

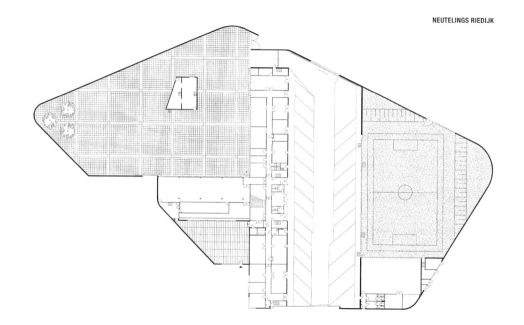

JEAN NOUVEL

Architectures Jean Nouvel
10, Cité d'Angoulême
75011 Paris
France

Tel: +33 1 4923 8383
Fax: +33 1 4314 8110

Born in 1945 in Fumel, France, **JEAN NOUVEL** was admitted to the École des Beaux-Arts in Bordeaux in 1964. In 1970, he created his first office with François Seigneur. His first widely noticed project was the Institut du Monde Arabe (Paris, 1981-87, with Architecture Studio). Other works include his Nemausus housing (Nîmes, 1985-87), offices for the CLM/BBDO advertising firm (Issy-les Moulineaux, 1988-92), Lyon's Opera House (1986-93), Vinci International Conference Center (Tours, 1989-93), Euralille Shopping Center (Lille, 1991-94), Fondation Cartier (Paris, 1991-95), and Galeries Lafayette (Berlin, 1992-96). Among his unbuilt projects are the "Tours sans fins" (La Défense, Paris, 1989), Grand Stade for the 1998 World Cup (Paris, 1994), and Tenaga National Tower (Kuala Lumpur, Malaysia, 1995). His largest recent project is the Music and Conference Center in Lucerne, Switzerland (1992-99). He won both the competition for the Musée du Quai Branly, Paris (1999-2004) and the competition for the refurbishment of the Reina Sofia Art Center, Madrid, in 1999.

JEAN NOUVEL, geboren 1945 in Fumel, Frankreich, studierte ab 1964 an der École des Beaux-Arts in Bordeaux. 1970 gründete er zusammen mit François Seigneur sein erstes Büro. Weithin bekannt wurde Nouvel mit seinem Institut du Monde Arabe in Paris (1981-87), bei dem er mit Architecture Studio zusammenarbeitete. Weitere herausragende Werke sind die Wohnanlage Nemausus in Nîmes (1985-87), die Büros der Werbeagentur CLM/BBDO in Issy-les-Moulineaux (1988-92), das Opernhaus in Lyon (1986-93), das internationale Kongresszentrum Vinci in Tours (1989-93), das Einkaufszentrum Euralille in Lille (1991-94) und die Fondation Cartier in Paris (1991-95). Außerdem baute Nouvel die Galeries Lafayette in Berlin (1992-96) und plante die 400 m hohe »Tour sans fins« in La Défense, Paris (1989), das Grand Stade für die Fußball-Weltmeisterschaft von 1998 in Paris (1994) und den Tenaga National Tower in Kuala Lumpur, Malaysia (1995), die aber alle nicht realisiert wurden. 1999 gewann er den Wettbewerb für das Musée de Quai Branly in Paris und für die Modernisierung des Reina Sofia Zentrums in Madrid, 1999.

Né en 1945 à Fumel, **JEAN NOUVEL** est admis à l'Ecole des Beaux-Arts de Bordeaux en 1964. En 1970, il crée une première agence avec François Seigneur. Son premier projet vraiment remarqué est l'Institut du Monde Arabe, à Paris (1981-87, avec Architecture Studio). Parmi ses autres réalisations : les immeubles d'habitation Nemausus, à Nîmes (1985-87), les bureaux de l'agence de publicité CLM/BBDO (Issy-les-Moulineaux, 1988-92), l'Opéra de Lyon (1986-93), le Vinci Centre International de Congrès (Tours, 1989-93), le centre commercial Euralille (Lille, 1991-94), la Fondation Cartier (Paris, 1991-95), les Galeries Lafayette (Berlin, 1992-96). Parmi ses projets non réalisés : une tour de 400 m (« Tour sans fin », La Défense, Paris, 1989), le Grand Stade de la Coupe du Monde de football 1998, (Paris, 1994), la Tenaga National Tower (Kuala Lumpur, Malaisie, 1995). Son dernier grand projet est le Centre de Congrès et de Musique de Lucerne (Suisse, 1992-99). En 1999, il a remporté le concours du Musée des Arts et Civilisations (Paris) et le concours pour la restructuration-extension du Centre Reina Sofia (Madrid, 1999).

LAW COURTS
Nantes, France, 1997-2000

Planning: 2/1995-6/97. Construction: 7/1997-6/2000.
Client: Ministère de la Justice. Total floor area: 20 000 m².
Usable floor area: 15 000 m². Budget: FF 230 000 000.

Set on a very visible site across from the old town of Nantes on the banks of the Loire River, Jean Nouvel's **LAW COURTS** are both ample and impressive. Part of a large effort to renovate the French courts that has led to buildings being designed in Bordeaux by Richard Rogers, and in Grasse by Christian de Portzamparc, the Nantes building covers a floor area of 15 000 m² and had a budget of 230 million FF. A sloping area paved with cobblestones leads up to the high black structure, whose most prominent feature is a public entrance hall 113 m long and 15 m high. The highly polished Zimbabwean black granite floor reflects the sky and even the city opposite, but does not really relieve the impression of gravity or even severity intended by Nouvel. The courtrooms are set in three 12 m-high black cubes, whose reddish and slightly claustrophobic interiors allude to the significance of the judicial process. A footbridge designed by the architects Barto & Barto is scheduled to be completed in June 2001, making the largely undeveloped site more accessible, in view of further construction, to include a planned school of architecture nearby.

Der weitläufig angelegte **GERICHTSHOF,** der weithin sichtbar gegenüber der Altstadt von Nantes am Ufer der Loire liegt, ist eindrucksvoll gestaltet. Er ist Teil eines umfassenden Programms zur Erneuerung französischer Gerichtsgebäude, in dessen Rahmen bereits Richard Rogers in Bordeaux und Christian de Portzamparc in Grasse tätig waren. Das Gerichtsgebäude in Nantes hat eine Nutzfläche von 15 000 m² und wurde mit einem Budget von 230 Millionen FF errichtet. Über einen leicht ansteigenden, mit Kopfstein gepflasterten Weg gelangt man in eine 113 m lange und 15 m hohe Eingangshalle, die das hohe, in schwarz gehaltene Bauwerk beherrscht. In ihrem Boden aus hochglanzpoliertem schwarzem Simbabwe-Granit spiegeln sich der Himmel und die Silhouette der gegenüberliegende Stadt, was jedoch den von Nouvel beabsichtigten Eindruck von Ernst und Strenge kaum mildert. Die Gerichtssäle wurden in drei 12 m hohe, dunkle kubische Räume verlegt, deren rötlich schimmerndes und leicht klaustrophobisch wirkendes Interieur auf die Bedeutung des Gerichtsprozesses anspielt. Eine von den Architekten Barto & Barto entworfene Fußgängerbrücke, die vorraussichtlich im Juni 2001 fertiggestellt wird, soll das zur Zeit größtenteils noch unbebaute, angrenzende Gelände, für das weitere Gebäude wie eine Architekturschule geplant sind, erschließen.

Implanté sur un terrain très exposé en bordure de Loire, face au vieux centre ville, ce **PALAIS DE JUSTICE** est à la fois vaste et impressionnant. Dans le cadre d'un important programme de rénovation des bâtiments judiciaires auquel ont participé Richard Rogers à Bordeaux ou Christian de Portzamparc à Grasse, le bâtiment nantais de 15 000 m² a été édifié pour un coût de 230 millions de F. Un plan incliné en galets conduit au bâtiment intégralement noir dont l'élément le plus caractéristique est un hall d'entrée de 113 m de long et 15 de haut. Le sol en granit noir poli du Zimbabwe reflète le ciel et même la ville, sans pour autant atténuer l'impression de gravité ou même de sévérité voulue par Nouvel. Les salles des tribunaux sont installées dans des cubes noir de 12 m de haut, dont l'intérieur rougeâtre et l'atmosphère claustrale illustrent le processus de la justice. Une passerelle dessinée par les architectes Barto et Barto devrait être achevée en juin 2001 pour rendre plus accessible le site qui devrait bientôt compter une école d'architecture.

Nouvel's Law Courts are intended to give a rather severe impression of the judiciary system. Black, a favorite color of the architect, dominates the vast entrance hall (right).

Wie von Nouvel beabsichtigt, vermittelt das Gerichtsgebäude einen Eindruck von der Strenge des Justizsystems. In der riesigen Eingangshalle (rechts) dominiert Schwarz, die Lieblingsfarbe des Architekten.

Le Palais de justice de Nouvel donne une impression plutôt sévère du système judiciaire. Le noir, couleur favorite de l'architecte, domine le vaste hall d'entrée (à droite).

The courtrooms are housed in three cubical volumes set at the rear of the cavernous black entrance hall. A rigorous grid system is used to determine all of the dimensions of the structure.

Die Gerichtssäle sind in drei kubischen Baukörpern untergebracht, die sich auf der Rückseite der höhlenartigen, in schwarz gehaltenen Eingangshalle (rechts) befinden.

Les salles des tribunaux sont logées dans trois volumes cubiques au fond du hall d'entrée dont le noir évoque une caverne. La trame rigoureuse s'impose à l'ensemble de la construction.

MUSÉE DU QUAI BRANLY

Paris, France, 2001-04

Planning: 1/2000-5/2001. Construction: 5/2001-2004.
Client: Établissement Public du Musée du Quai Branly.
Total floor area: 39 760 m². Usable floor area: 30 228 m².
Budget: Euro 79 550 000 (c. FF 525 000 000).

Set along the banks of the Seine, the future museum will feature glass screens near the river and a freely designed garden conceived by Gilles Clément.

Am Seine-Ufer gelegen, soll das Museum auf der dem Fluss zugewandten Seite eine Glasfront und einen von Gilles Clément entworfenen Garten erhalten.

En bordure de Seine, le futur musée donnera sur le fleuve grâce à des écrans de verre et un jardin informel signé Gilles Clément.

Jean Nouvel was the winner of the international competition for the **MUSÉE DU QUAI BRANLY** after the 15 original participants, including Tadao Ando, MVRDV, and Rem Koolhaas were narrowed down to three (Jean Nouvel, Renzo Piano and Peter Eisenman) early in December 1999. Working with the noted landscape architect Gilles Clément and the lighting expert Yann Kersalé, Nouvel proposed a 7 500-m² complex including the garden on the 2.5 hectare lot. The main building will be 200 m long, and will be set 12 m off the ground. Two smaller structures will house logistic facilities and a media center. Collaborating with Françoise Raynaud on this project, Nouvel intends to pay careful attention to ecological concerns, using materials that can be recycled. The total budget is 79 550 000 Euro. The museum will house collections on loan from the Musée de l'Homme and the Musée des Arts d'Afrique et d'Océanie.

Jean Nouvel gewann Anfang Dezember 1999 den internationalen Wettbewerb für das **MUSÉE DU QUAI BRANLY**, an dem insgesamt 15 Architekten, einschließlich Tadao Ando, Peter Eisenman, Rem Koolhaas, MVRDV und Renzo Piano teilnahmen. In Zusammenarbeit mit dem bekannten Landschaftsarchitekten Gilles Clément und dem Lichtdesigner Yann Kersalé entwarf Nouvel für das 2,5 ha große Grundstück einen 7 500 m² umfassenden Komplex mit Gartenanlage. Das Hauptgebäude hat eine Länge von 200 m und ist 12 m vom Erdboden abgehoben. Zwei kleinere Bauten enthalten logistische Einrichtungen und ein Medienzentrum. Unter besonderer Berücksichtigung ökologischer Kriterien verwendet Nouvel in Zusammenarbeit mit Françoise Raynaud bei diesem Projekt recycelbare Baumaterialien. Das mit Baukosten von 79 500 000 Euro kalkulierte Museum wird nach seiner Fertigstellung Exponate aus dem Musée de l'Homme und dem Musée des Arts d'Afrique et d'Océanie vereinigen.

En décembre 1999, Jean Nouvel a remporté le concours international pour le **MUSÉE DU QUAI BRANLY** auquel participaient 15 architectes, dont Tadao Ando, MVRDV et Rem Koolhaas, puis en en phase finale devant Renzo Piano et Peter Eisenmann. Dans ce projet auquel ont collaboré le célèbre architecte paysagiste Gilles Clément et l'expert en éclairage Yann Kersalé, Nouvel propose de créer un jardin de 7 500 m² sur un terrain de 2,5 ha. Le bâtiment principal fera 200 m de long et sera surélevé à 12 m du sol. Deux constructions moins importantes abriteront la logistique et un centre pour les médias. Avec sa collaboratrice Françoise Raynaud, Nouvel prévoit de porter une grande attention aux préoccupations écologiques et de recourir à des matériaux recyclables. Pour un budget de 79 500 000 Euro, le musée accueillera, entre autres, des collections prêtées par le Musée de l'Homme et par le Musée des Arts d'Afrique et d'Océanie.

In Nouvel's computer generated images, the natural or garden element becomes a major factor in the exterior perception of the building.

Nouvels Computergrafiken geben einen Eindruck davon, welche Bedeutung den Gartenanlagen im äußeren Erscheinungsbild des Gebäudes zukommt.

Cette image de synthèse martie que le jardin joue un rôle prépondérant pour la perception du bâtiment.

DOMINIQUE PERRAULT

Dominique Perrault, Architecte
26/34, rue Bruneseau
75629 Paris cedex 13
France

Tel: +33 1 4406 0000
Fax: +33 1 4406 0001
e-mail: dparchi@club-internet.fr

Olympic Swimming Pool

DOMINIQUE PERRAULT was born in 1953 in Clermont-Ferrand, France. He received his diploma as an architect from the École des Beaux-Arts (UP 6) in Paris in 1978. He also received a degree in urbanism from the École nationale des Ponts et Chaussées, Paris in 1979. He created his own firm in 1981 in Paris. Recent and current work includes the Engineering School (ESIEE) (Marne-la-Vallée, 1984-87), the Hôtel industriel Jean-Baptiste Berlier (Paris, 1986-90), Hôtel du département de la Meuse (Bar-le-Duc, 1988-94), his best-known project, the Bibliothèque Nationale de France (Paris, 1989-97), all in France, and the Olympic Velodrome, Swimming and Diving Pool (Berlin, 1992-97/99), and a large-scale study of the urbanism of Bordeaux (1992-2000).

DOMINIQUE PERRAULT, geboren 1953 in Clermont-Ferrand, erwarb 1978 sein Architekturdiplom an der Beaux-Arts in Paris und 1979 ein Diplom in städtebaulicher Planung an der École nationale des Ponts et Chaussées in Paris. 1981 gründete er in Paris seine eigene Firma, 1992 und 1998 zwei weitere in Berlin und Luxembrug. Zu seinen jüngsten Projekten gehören die Ingenieurschule (ESIEE) in Marne-la-Vallée (1984-87), das Hôtel industriel Jean-Baptiste Berlier in Paris (1986-90), das Hôtel du département de la Meuse in Bar-le-Duc (1988-94), sein bekanntestes Werk, die Bibliothèque Nationale de France in Paris (1989-97), die Olympische Radsporthalle und Schwimmsporthalle in Berlin (1992-97/99) sowie eine groß angelegte Studie der Stadtentwicklung von Bordeaux (1992-2000).

DOMINIQUE PERRAULT naît en 1953 à Clermont-Ferrand, France. Il est diplômé d'architecture de l'Ecole des Beaux-Arts de Paris (UP 6) en 1978 et diplômé en urbanisme de l'Ecole nationale des Ponts et Chaussées, Paris (1979). Il crée son agence en 1981 à Paris. Parmi ses réalisations : l'Ecole d'ingénieurs ESIEE (Marne-la-Vallée, 1984-87), l'hôtel industriel Jean-Baptiste Berlier (Paris, 1986-90), l'hôtel du département de la Meuse (Bar-le-Duc, France, 1988-94), la Bibliothèque Nationale de France (Paris, 1989-97) qui est son œuvre la plus connue, le vélodrome et la piscine olympiques (Berlin, 1992-97/99) et une étude urbanistique de fond sur la ville de Bordeaux (1992-2000).

OLYMPIC SWIMMING POOL

Berlin, Germany, 1992-99

*Completion: 11/99. Client: City of Berlin, Department for Construction and Housing, represented by
Olympia 2000 Sportstättenbau GmbH. Landscape: Landschaft Planen & Bauen, Berlin.
Floor area: 28 490 m². Capacity: 1 600 seats.
Costs: DM 400 000 000 (total including the Velodrome).*

Originally intended as an element of Berlin's proposal for the 2000 Olympic Games, the **SWIMMING POOL** is located next to the Velodrome conceived by Perrault (in collaboration with Rolf Reichert and Hans Jürgen Schmidt) for the same event. Echoing the low-lying geometric circle traced in the ground for the Velodrome, Perrault here uses a strict rectangle, set deeply into a surrounding orchard of 450 apple trees. Trying to avoid the heavy-handed symbolism that characterized the 1936 Olympic Games, Perrault opted for a minimalist discretion, a digging into the earth that is atypical of modernist designs. Although the idea of placing a major part of the structure below ground level initially necessitated higher construction costs, it will ensure the thermal stability of the complex, and reduce the building's energy consumption. The 28 490m² complex was built at a cost of 270 million DM.

Ursprünglich für die Bewerbung Berlins um den Austragungsort der Olympischen Spiele 2000 geplant, befindet sich diese **SCHWIMMSPORTHALLE** neben der von Perrault (in Zusammenarbeit mit Rolf Reichert und Hns Jürgen Schmidt) für das gleiche Ereignis entworfenen Radsporthalle. Sowohl das tieferliegende kreisförmige Velodrom als auch die rechteckig angelegte Schwimmsporthalle sind in einen Obstgarten mit 450 Apfelbäumen eingebettet. Um den plumpen Symbolismus, der die Olympischen Spiele von 1936 kennzeichnete, zu vermeiden, entschied sich der Architekt für eine minimalistische Zurückhaltung, die für zeitgenössische Bauten ungewöhnlich ist. Zwar mag die Idee, einen Großteil des Gebäudes unter die Erde zu verlegen, höhere Baukosten verursacht haben, dadurch wird aber andererseits die Wärmestabilität gewährleistet und so letztendlich der Energieverbrauch reduziert. Der 28 490 m² große Komplex wurde für 270 Millionen DM erbaut.

Projetée à l'occasion de la candidature de Berlin aux Jeux Olympiques 2000, cette **PISCINE** est située à côté du vélodrome olympique, réalisation de Perrault (en collaboration avec Rolf Reichert et Hans Jürgen Schmidt) s'inscrivant dans le même contexte, le vélodrome olympique. En opposition au cercle surbaissé du vélodrome, il utilise ici un forme strictement rectangulaire entourée d'un verger de 450 pommiers. Pour éviter le lourd symbolisme des Jeux Olympiques de 1936, l'architecte a opté pour une discrétion minimaliste atypique des projets contemporains. Bien que l'idée d'implanter la plus grande partie du bâtiment sous le niveau du sol ait entraîné des coûts de construction plus élevés, elle permet d'assurer une meilleure stabilité thermique et de réduire la consommation énergétique. Cet ensemble de 28 490 m² a coûté 270 millions de DM.

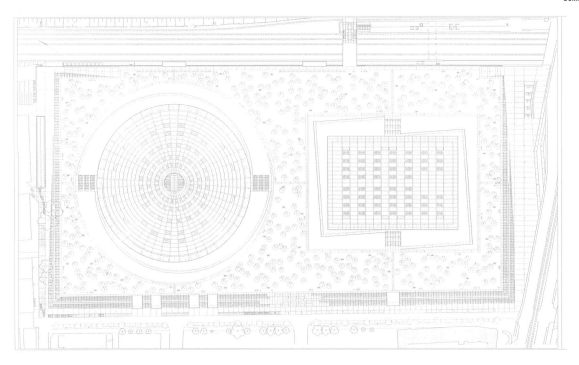

Like the neighboring Velodrome, the Olympic Swimming Pool is recessed into the site, making its size and volume much less evident than they might have been.

Die Schwimmhalle wurde ebenso wie die benachbarte Radrennbahn zum Teil unter Bodenniveau angelegt, was den Bauten trotz ihrer Grösse die Massivität nimmt.

De même que son voisin, le vélodrome, la piscine olympique est en partie enterrée, ce qui réduit d'autant son volume apparent.

Using the kind of strong minimalist vocabulary with an insistence on hard surfaces that he demonstrated in the Bibliothèque de France in Paris, Dominique Perrault created a strict, efficient swimming facility.

Die kraftvoll-minimalistische Formensprache, die er bei der Bibliothèque de France demonstrierte, bestimmt auch Perraults strenge, funktionalistische Schwimmhalle.

A partir d'un vocabulaire minimaliste vigoureux et du goût pour les surfaces dures telles que celles de la Bibliothèque de France à Paris, Dominique Perrault a créé un centre de natation sobre et fonctionnel.

POLSHEK PARTNERSHIP

Polshek Partnership Architects, UP
320 West 13th Street
New York, NY 10014-1278
United States

Tel.: +1 212 807 7171
Fax: +1 212 807 5917
Email: info@polshek.com
Web: www.polshek.com

JAMES STEWART POLSHEK was born in Akron, Ohio, in 1930. He attended Case Western Reserve University (Cleveland, Ohio), graduating in 1951. He received his M.Arch. degree from Yale in 1955 and established his own practice in New York in 1963. Recent projects include the renovation of Carnegie Hall (New York), the Center for the Arts Theater at Yerba Buena Gardens (San Francisco, 1993), a Government Office Building (Chambery-le Haut, France, 1994), the Skirball Institute for Biomolecular Medicine and Residence Tower at New York University Medical Center (1993), the Seamen's Church Institute in the South Street Seaport Historic District (New York, 1991) and the renovation and expansion of the Brooklyn Museum of Art (New York). Recent projects include the Rose Center for Earth and Space, American Museum of Natural History (1997-2000) with his co-Design Principal on this project **TODD H. SCHLIEMANN**, the Cooper Hewitt National Design Museum renovation, and the Manhattan Supreme Court Criminal Courts Building, all in New York, and the National Museum of the American Indian Cultural Resources Center in Suitland, Maryland. James Stewart Polshek was Dean of the Graduate School of Architecture, Columbia University, New York (1972-1987) until Bernard Tschumi succeeded him in that post.

JAMES STEWART POLSHEK, geboren 1930 in Akron, Ohio, schloss 1951 sein Studium an der Case Western Reserve University in Cleveland ab. 1955 erwarb er seinen Master of Architecture an der Yale University und gründete 1963 sein eigenes Architekturbüro in New York. Zu Polsheks neueren Projekten zählen die Renovierung der Carnegie Hall in New York, das Center for the Arts Theater in den Yerba Buena Gardens in San Francisco (1993), ein Regierungsgebäude im französischen Chambery-le Haut (1994), das Skirball Institute for Biomolecular Medicine und ein Wohnturm im New York University Medical Center (1993), das Seamen's Church Institute im South Street Seaport Historic District in New York (1991) sowie die Renovierung und Erweiterung des Brooklyn Museum of Art in New York. Zu seinen jüngsten Arbeiten gehören das hier vorgestellte Rose Center for Earth and Space am American Museum of Natural History (1997-2000), zusammen mit **TODD H. SCHLIEMANN**, die Modernisierung des Cooper Hewitt National Design Museum und das Manhattan Supreme Court Criminal Courts Building alle in New York, sowie das National Museum of the American Indian Cultural Resources Center in Suitland, Maryland. Von 1971 bis 1987 war James Stewart Polshek Dekan der Graduate School of Architecture an der Columbia University in New York, bis Bernard Tschumi ihm auf diesem Posten nachfolgte.

JAMES STEWART POLSHEK naît à Akron, Ohio, en 1930. Il suit les cours de la Case Western Reserve University (Cleveland, Ohio) dont il est diplômé en 1951. Il passe son Master en architecture à Yale (1955) et crée sa propre agence à New York en 1963. Parmi ses réalisations : la rénovation de Carnegie Hall (New York), le Center for the Arts en Yerba Buena Gardens (San Francisco, 1993), un immeuble administratif en France (Chambéry-le-Haut, 1994), le Skirball Institute for Biomolecular Medicine and Residence Tower à la New York University Medical Center (1993), le Seamen's Church Institute du South Street Seaport Historic District (New York, 1991), la rénovation et l'extension du Brooklyn Museum of Art (New York). Plus récemment, il a réalisé avec **TODD H. SCHLIEMANN** le Rose Center for Earth and Space, American Museum of Natural History (1997-2000), la rénovation du Cooper Hewitt National Design Museum et le Manhattan Supreme Court Criminal Courts Building à New York, le National Museum of the American Indian Cultural Resources Center à Suitland, Maryland. James Stewart Polshek a été doyen de la Graduate School of Architecture, Columbia University, New York (1972-87), poste dont Bernard Tschumi a pris la succession.

ROSE CENTER FOR EARTH AND SPACE

*Frederick Phineas and Sandra Priest Rose Center for
Earth and Space, American Museum of Natural History
New York, NY, USA, 1997-2000*

*Client: American Museum of Natural History. Floor area of the sphere: 3 045 m².
Volume of the cube: c. 53 930 m³. Costs: $210 million.*

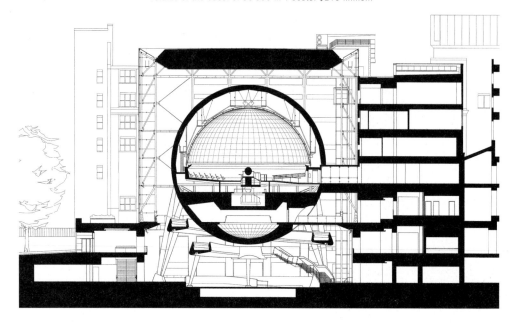

Located on the Upper West Side of Manhattan, at the northern extremity of the **AMERICAN MUSEUM OF NATURAL HISTORY, THE ROSE CENTER** is a seven-story complex of 30 000 m², built at a cost of $210 million. Set near Central Park on 81st Street, the spectacular 29 m-high glass building encloses the 27 m-diameter sphere housing the Hayden Planetarium. The original Hayden Planetarium, built in 1935, was considered a historic landmark by New Yorkers, and Polshek's plan to "blow it up and build a planetarium for the 21st century" caused initial opposition. The building's spherical form brings to mind historical precedents such as Etienne-Louis Boullée's cenotaph to Isaak Newton, or Claude-Nicolas Ledoux's Maison des gardes agricoles and his cemetery of the Saline de Chaux. More recently, Itsuko Hasegawa's Shonandai Cultural Center (Fujisawa, Kanagawa, 1987-90), and Adrien Fainsilber's Géode at La Villette in Paris. The new Rose Center, calling on the most sophisticated technology of astronomy and architecture, brings the public experience of the universe up to date in a most spectacular manner and, at that, in the heart of New York.

Das **ROSE CENTER** liegt an der Upper West Side von Manhattan, am nördlichen Ende des **AMERICAN MUSEUM OF NATURAL HISTORY** und ist ein siebengeschossiger, insgesamt 30 000 m² umfassender Komplex, der für 210 Millionen Dollar erbaut wurde. Das nahe dem Central Park in der 81. Straße errichtete spektakuläre Gebäude ist 29 m hoch und schließt eine Kugel mit einem Durchmesser von 27 m ein, die das Hayden Planetarium beherbergt. Dieses Planetarium wurde 1935 erbaut und gilt unter New Yorkern als historisches Baudenkmal, weshalb Polsheks Plan, »es in die Luft zu jagen und ein Planetarium für das 21. Jahrhundert zu errichten« für Widerstand sorgte. Die Kugelform des Gebäudes erinnert an historische Vorläufer wie Étienne-Louis Boullées Kenotaph für Isaac Newton oder das Maison des Gardes Agricoles und den Friedhof von Saline de Chaux von Claude-Nicolas Ledoux. Jüngere Beispiele für die Verwendung dieser geometrischen Grundform sind Itsuko Hasegawas Shonandai Cultural Center in Fujisawa, Kanagawa (1987-90) oder Adrien Fainsilbers Géode im Pariser La Villette. Das neue, mit modernster astronomischer und architektonischer Technologie konzipierte Rose Center bringt der Öffentlichkeit auf beeindruckende Weise das Erlebnis des Universums nahe, und das im Herzen von New York.

Situé dans le quartier de l'Upper West Side à Manhattan, à l'extrémité nord du **MUSEUM D'HISTOIRE NATURELLE, LE ROSE CENTER** est un complexe de sept niveaux et de 30 000 m² édifié pour un budget de $210 millions. Sur 81st Street, en bordure de Central Park, ce spectaculaire bâtiment de verre de 296 m de haut enferme une sphère de 27 m de diamètre qui abrite le Hayden Planetarium. Le Hayden Planetarium d'origine, construit en 1935, était considéré comme un monument par les New-yorkais, c'est porquoi l'intention de Polshek de « l'exploser et de construire un planétarium pour le XXIᵉ siècle » rencontra d'abord une vive opposition. La forme sphérique du bâtiment rappelle des projets comme le cénotaphe pour Isaak Newton de Etienne-Louis Boullée ou la maison des gardes agricoles et le cimetière des Salines de Chaux de Claude-Nicolas Ledoux, ainsi que plus récemment, le centre culturel Shonandai de Itsuko Hasegawa (Fujisawa, Kanagawa, 1987-90) ou la géode d'Adrien Fainsilber à la Cité des Sciences de la Villette à Paris. Le nouveau Rose Center qui fait appel aux technologies les plus sophistiquées en matière d'astronomie et d'architecture, il propose au public une des plus spectaculaires expérimentations de l'univers à ce jour, et ce en plein cœur de New York.

Where Santiago Calatrava chose the image of an eye for his Planetarium in Valencia, Polshek has preferred to use the sphere as a metaphor for the earth or other celestial bodies.

Während Santiago Calatrava die Form eines Auges für sein Planetarium in Valencia wählte, zog Polshek die Kugel als Metapher für die Erde und andere Himmelskörper vor.

Alors que Calatrava choisissait la forme d'un œil pour son Planétarium de Valence, Polshek a préféré celle de la sphère, métaphore de la terre et des planètes.

INEAS & SANDRA PRIEST ROSE CENTER FOR EARTH

The external envelope reveals the inner sphere, if not the full complexity of the structure as seen in the drawing above left.

Die äußere Hülle gibt die Sicht auf den inneren Baukörper frei. Die Komplexität des Gebäudes wird erst im Aufriß (oben links) deutlich.

L'enveloppe externe révèle la sphère intérieure, mais non la complexité de la structure que montre le dessin ci-dessus à gauche.

WATER MOLEC

THE SPECTRUM OF LIGHT

Light is radiant energy. It moves in waves through space at 300,000 kilometers (186,000 miles) per second. Light comes in many wavelengths. Humans see only the visible band of light, containing the familiar colors of the rainbow. Many other bands, however, ...beyond the visible spectrum. Radio waves, x-rays, and other types of light ...are the...

Around the central sphere, the theme of the solar system is carried through to areas efficiently designed to receive the very large number of daily visitors drawn to the building.

Das Thema des Sonnensystems wird in allen Bereichen aufgegriffen und diese so gestaltet, dass sie die großen Besuchermengen gut bewältigen können.

Autour de la sphère centrale, le thème du système solaire se poursuit à travers les halls et les circulations conçus pour un grand nombre de visiteurs.

CHRISTIAN DE PORTZAMPARC

Atelier Christian de Portzamparc
1, rue de l'Aude
75014 Paris
France

Tel: +33 1 4064 8000
Fax: +33 1 4327 7479
e-mail: studio@chdeportzamparc.com

CHRISTIAN DE PORTZAMPARC was born in Casablanca, Morocco in 1944. He studied at the École des Beaux-Arts, Paris (1962-69). Built projects include a Water Tower (Marne-la-Vallée, 1971-74), Les Hautes Formes public housing, (Paris, 1975-79), Nexus World housing (Fukuoka, Japan, 1989-91), extension for the Bourdelle Museum (Paris, 1988-92), the Cité de la Musique (Paris, 1984-95), the housing complex ZAC Bercy (Paris, 1991-94), and the Crédit Lyonnais Tower (Euralille, Lille, France, 1991-95, built over the new Lille-Europe railway station). He was awarded the 1994 Pritzker Prize. Recent work includes the LVMH Tower on 57th Street in New York (1996-99) published here, an extension to the Palais des Congrès Porte Maillot in Paris (1994-99), a tower for the Bandai Toy Company in Tokyo (1995-), a courthouse for Grasse in southern France (1993-2000), and the French Embassy in Berlin, due to be completed in 2002.

CHRISTIAN DE PORTZAMPARC, geboren 1944 in Casablanca, Marokko, studierte von 1962 bis 1969 an der École des Beaux-Arts in Paris. Zu seinen realisierten Projekten gehören der Water Tower in Marne-la-Vallée (1971-74), die Wohnanlage Les Hautes Formes in Paris (1975-79), die Nexus World-Wohnanlage im japanischen Fukuoka (1989-91), die Erweiterung des Museums Bourdelle in Paris (1988-92), die Cité de la Musique in Paris (1984-95), die ZAC Bercy-Wohnsiedlung in Paris (1991-94) und der über dem neuen Euralille-Bahnhof errichtete Crédit Lyonnais Tower in Lille (1991-1995). 1994 wurde Portzamparc mit dem Pritzker Prize ausgezeichnet. Zu seinen jüngsten Arbeiten zählen der hier vorgestellte LVMH Tower in New York (1996-99), ein Anbau für den Palais des Congrès Porte Maillot in Paris (1994-99), ein seit 1995 im Bau befindlicher Turm für die Spielzeugfabrik Bandai in Tokio, ein Gerichtsgebäude im südfranzösischen Grasse sowie die Französische Botschaft in Berlin, deren Fertigstellung für 2002 geplant ist.

Né à Casablanca en 1944, **CHRISTIAN DE PORTZAMPARC** étudie à l'Ecole des Beaux-Arts de Paris (1962-69). Parmi ses réalisations : un château d'eau (Marne-la-Vallée, 1971-74), l'immeuble de logements économiques Les Hautes Formes (Paris, 1975-79), un immeuble d'appartement, Nexus World (Fukuoka, Japon, 1989-91), l'extension du Musée Bourdelle (Paris, 1988-92), la Cité de la Musique (Paris, 1984-95), un immeuble d'habitation dans la ZAC de Bercy (Paris, 1991-94) et la tour du Crédit Lyonnais (Euralille, Lille, 1991-95), au-dessus de la gare de Lille-Europe. Il obtient en 1994 le Pritzker Prize. Il a récemment réalisé la tour LVMH, 57th Street, à New York (1996-99) publiée ici, l'extension du Palais des Congrès Porte Maillot (Paris, 1994-99), le Palais de justice de Grasse, France (1993-2000), une tour pour la Bandai Toy Company à Tokyo (1995-) et l'ambassade de France à Berlin, qui devrait être achevée en 2002.

LVMH TOWER

New York, NY, USA, 1995-99

*Planning: 1995-97. Construction: 1997-99. Client: LVMH Corporation.
Floor area: 8 683 m². Costs: withheld.*

By using New York City zoning regulations very efficiently, the architect managed to translate the setbacks in the facade into extra height – used for the three-story "Magic Room" at the top of the structure.

In sehr geschickter Umsetzung der New Yorker Bauvorschriften gelang es dem Architekten durch das Zurückstufen der Fassade (rechts) zusätzliche Höhe zu gewinnen, die er für die Anlage des dreistöckigen »Magic Room« (oben) als Bekrönung des Gebäudes nutzte.

Par une interprétation habile de la réglementation du zoning new-yorkais, l'architecte a mis à profit des retraits pour augmenter la hauteur de la tour et créer sa "Magic Room" de trois étages de haut, au sommet de l'édifice.

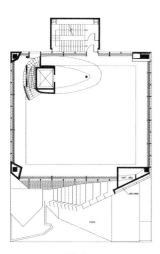

23th floor

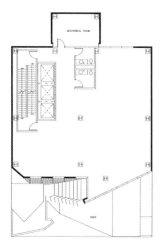

19th floor

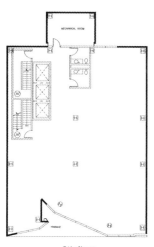

3th floor

Set near the corner of 57th Street and Madison Avenue, the **LVMH TOWER** represents a shift in the design of tall buildings. Rather than the more common un-differentiated facade generally seen in Manhattan, this 23-story office building represents a complex Saint Gobain glass facade designed to avoid direct reflections of the black IBM Tower just across 57th Street. By carefully studying New York's complex zoning laws after a series of setbacks, the architect managed, through the use of a sophisticated design, to increase the overall height of his building, even edging out the neighboring Chanel Tower. This gave him the possibility of creating the so-called "Magic Room" atop the tower – a spectacular three-story room with views on three sides onto 57th Street, and toward Central Park. Portzamparc's contribution to the tower is in good part limited to this room and the facade, since the design of the offices, and of the boutiques on the ground floor, is the work of other architects. A sophisticated lighting system inserted into a "fault" line running up the facade gives the building a real night-time identity in the cityscape.

Der nahe der Kreuzung von 57. Straße und Madison Avenue gelegene 23-geschossige **LVMH TOWER** stellt mit seiner komplexen Fassade aus Saint Gobain-Glas eine Neuerung in der Hochhausarchitektur dar. Die Fassade, die sich deutlich vom üblichen Erscheinungsbild der Hochhäuser in Manhatten absetzt, ist so strukturiert, dass eine direkte Spiegelung des genau gegenüberliegenden schwarzen IBM-Turms vermieden wird. In Umgehung der komplizierten New Yorker Baugesetze durch den Einsatz eines raffinierten Entwurfs, ist es dem Architekten gelungen, die Gesamthöhe seines Bürogebäudes so zu vergrößern, dass es nun sogar den benachbarten Chanel Tower überragt. Dies gab Portzamparc die Möglichkeit, den sogenannten »Magic Room« an die Turmspitze zu setzen – einen spektakulären dreigeschossigen Raum mit freiem, dreiseitigem Ausblick auf die 57. Straße und den Central Park. Portzamparcs Beitrag zur Gestaltung des Hochhauses beschränkt sich im Wesentlichen auf diesen Raum und die Fassade, die Büros und die im Erdgeschoß befindlichen Geschäfte wurden von anderen Architekten entworfen und ausgeführt. Eine kunstvolle Beleuchtung, die in einer an der Fassade verlaufenden »Bruchlinie« eingesetzt wurde, verleiht dem Gebäude auch bei Nacht eine unverkennbare Identität.

Dressée presque à l'angle de la 57th Street et de Madison Avenue, la **TOUR LVMH** marque une évolution dans la conception des immeubles de grande hauteur. Au lieu de ces façades plus ou moins différenciées que l'on voit d'habitude à Manhattan, cette tour de bureaux de 23 étages arbore une complexe façade en verre de Saint Gobain conçue pour éviter la réflexion directe de l'énorme tour noire d'IBM qui se dresse de l'autre côté de la rue. Après avoir étudié attentivement la réglementation compliquée du zoning de la ville de New York, Portzamparc a réussi, au moyen d'une série d'habiles retraits, à augmenter la hauteur totale de l'immeuble, jusqu'à dépasser sa voisine, la Tour Chanel. Ceci lui a permis de créer, au sommet, la « Magic-Room », une spectaculaire salle de trois étages de haut qui offre des vues sur trois côtés et sur Central Park. La contribution de l'architecte s'est pour une bonne part limitée à la façade et à cette salle, car l'aménagement des bureaux et des boutiques a été confiée à d'autres intervenants. Un système sophistiqué d'éclairage a été inséré dans une « faille » qui court verticalement sur la façade ce qui, la nuit, confère à l'immeuble sa forte identité.

Christian de Portzamparc concentrated his efforts on the facade, and the Magic Room. His responsibility did not extend to interior decoration or to the ground level Christian Dior boutique designed by Peter Marino.

Christian de Portzamparc konzentrierte sich in seiner Gestaltung auf die Fassade und den »Magic Room«. Er war weder für die Innenraumausstattung noch für die im Erdgeschoss liegende und von Peter Marino entworfene Christian Dior Boutique zuständig.

Christian de Portzamparc a concentré ses efforts sur la façade et la "Magic Room". Il n'a été chargé ni des aménagements intérieurs ni du magasin Christian Dior du rez-de-chaussée, œuvre de Peter Marino.

Christian Dior

ELIZABETH DE PORTZAMPARC

Elizabeth de Portzamparc
Architecte d'Intérieurs-Mobilier
77/79, rue du Cherche Midi
75006 Paris
France

Tel: + 33 1 5363 3232
Fax: + 33 1 5363 3239
e-mail: elizabeth.deportzamparc@wanadoo.fr
web: www.elizabethdeportzamparc.com

Born in Brazil, **ELIZABETH DE PORTZAMPARC** has been active in design and architecture in Paris since 1975, when she did a study of the urban development of the Elancourt-Maurepas area of Saint-Quentin en Yvelines. She was Director of the Urban Planning Atelier of the city of Antony from 1977 to 1980. From 1988 to 1992, she created and directed the design gallery Mostra in Paris. She worked on the interior design of the Grasse Law Courts (1996-99), and is presently designing the interiors of the future French Embassy in Berlin (with Christian de Portzamparc). She was selected to design the station stops for the new Bordeaux tramway line, and is creating not only the interior design and furniture for The Munt, a multiple-screen movie theater in Amsterdam, but also the interiors for the Musée de la Bretagne in Rennes. She completed the Espionne boutique at the Palais des Congrès in Paris (1999), and the Café de la Musique, also in Paris (1995), as well as numerous apartments.

Die in Brasilien geborene **ELIZABETH DE PORTZAMPARC** ist seit ihrer 1975 entstandenen Studie über die Stadtentwicklung des Elancourt-Maurepas Bezirks von Saint-Quentin en Yveline als Designerin und Architektin in Paris tätig. Von 1977 bis 1980 war sie Leiterin des Ateliers für Stadtplanung der Stadt Antony und von 1988 bis 1992 gestaltete und leitete sie die Design Galerie Mostra in Paris. Sie entwarf die Innenausstattung des Gerichtsgebäudes in Grasse (1996-99) und arbeitet derzeit zusammen mit ihrem Mann Christian de Portzamparc an der Innenarchitektur der zukünftigen Französischen Botschaft in Berlin. Aktuell ist sie mit der Gestaltung der Haltestellen für eine neue Straßenbahnlinie in Bordeaux beauftragt und entwirft die Innenraumgestaltung und Einrichtung für The Munt (ein Multiplex-Kino in Amsterdam) und die Interieurs des Musée de la Bretagne in Rennes. Abgeschlossene Projekte sind die Boutique Espionne im Palais des Congrès in Paris (1999), das ebenfalls in Paris liegende Café de la Musique (1995) sowie zahlreiche Privatwohnungen.

Née au Brésil, **ELIZABETH DE PORTZAMPARC** est active dans les domaines de l'architecture et du design à Paris depuis 1975, date de son étude sur le développement de la zone d'Elancourt-Maurepas à Saint-Quentin-en-Yvelines. Elle dirige l'atelier d'urbanisme de la ville d'Antony de 1977 à 1980. De 1988 à 1992, elle a créé et animé la galerie de design Mostra à Paris. Elle conçoit les aménagements intérieurs du palais de justice de Grasse (1996-99) et l'intérieur de la future ambassade de France à Berlin (avec Christian de Portzamparc). Elle a été sélectionnée pour les arrêts de la nouvelle ligne de tramway de Bordeaux, les aménagements intérieurs et le mobilier de De Munt (une salle de cinéma multiplex à Amsterdam) et ceux du Musée de la Bretagne à Rennes. Elle a réalisé la boutique Espionne au Palais des Congrès de Paris (1999), le Café de la Musique, toujours à Paris (1995), ainsi que de nombreux appartements.

LES GRANDES MARCHES RESTAURANT

Paris, France, 2000

Planning: 11/1999-4/2000. Construction: 06-09/2000. Client: FLO Prestige.
Floor area: 1000 m². Costs: FF 13 million (not including the kitchen).

In the large, deep volume of the ground floor, Elizabeth de Portzamparc has installed a spectacular spiraling staircase. She specifically designed the furniture for this restaurant as well.

Elizabeth de Portzamparc setzte eine spektakulär geschwungene Treppe in das sich weiträumig in die Tiefe erstreckende Erdgeschoss. Sie hat auch die Möbel speziell für dieses Restaurant entworfen.

Dans le vaste et profond rez-de-chaussée, Elisabeth de Portzamparc a implanté un spectaculaire escalier en spirale. Elle a également dessiné l'ensemble du mobilier de ce restaurant.

Built in the ground floor of an annex of the Bastille Opera in Paris (designed by Carlos Ott), **LES GRANDES MARCHES RESTAURANT** is set in a space whose previous decor was truly banal. Elizabeth de Portzamparc reworked the ground and first floor of the space (a total of 1 000 m², with 650 m² open to the public) around a sweeping new monumental staircase, whose steps are referred to in the restaurant's name. The upper level offers carefully framed views of the Bastille Square. The facility, which can seat 220 people, was built in just three months (June 5 to September 6, 2000). Many of the curving, sensuous wall surfaces have a metallic appearance achieved through the use of sprayed titanium particles. Elizabeth de Portzamparc designed not only the basic volumes of the restaurant, but also its furniture, and facilities such as the bar or toilets, giving a sense of coherence to the whole that is rarely achieved in a chain restaurant (Les Grandes Marches belongs to the Flo brasserie chain). Christian de Portzamparc designed a glazed structure for the restaurant's terrace, but the interior is very much in the spirit of his wife's work, in particular her Café de la Musique in the Villette area of Paris.

Das im Erdgeschoss eines von Carlos Ott entworfenen Anbaus der Pariser Opéra de la Bastille gelegene **RESTAURANT LES GRANDES MARCHES** entstand als Umbau von ursprünglich eher unspektakulär gestalteten Räumlichkeiten. Das Zentrum der Räume im Erdgeschoss und dem ersten Stock (mit einer Gesamtnutzfläche von 1 000 m², von denen 650 m² der Öffentlichkeit zugänglich sind) bildet eine monumentale, weit ausschwingende Treppe, die dem Restaurant seinen Namen gab. Im oberen Stockwerk bieten sich dem Besucher sorgfältig gerahmte Ausblicke auf den Place de la Bastille. Das Restaurant mit 220 Sitzplätzen wurde in nur drei Monaten, von Juni bis September 2000, fertiggestellt. Die sinnlich gewölbten Wandoberflächen sind teilweise mit Titanpartikeln besprüht, was ihnen eine metallische Wirkung verleiht. Elizabeth de Portzamparc ist nicht nur für die Innenarchitektur des Restaurants verantwortlich, sondern entwarf auch die Möbel sowie verschiedene Nebenräume wie die Bar und die Toiletten. Dies verleiht dem Ganzen einen in sich stimmigen Eindruck, der in zu einer Kette gehörenden Restaurants (Les Grandes Marches gehört zur Flo Brasserie-Gruppe) selten anzutreffen ist. Das Restaurant-Interieur ist ein charakteristisches Beispiel für den Stil von Elizabeth de Portzamparc, der auch in anderen ihrer Arbeiten, insbesondere im Café de la Musique im Pariser Viertel Villette, zum Ausdruck kommt. Der verglaste Bauteil für die Restaurant-Terrasse stammt von ihrem Mann Christian de Portzamparc.

Aménagé au rez-de-chaussée d'un bâtiment annexe de l'Opéra Bastille de Paris (Carlos Ott), le **RESTAURANT LES GRANDES MARCHES** est implanté dans un volume dont le décor était banal. Elisabeth de Portzamparc a retravaillé ses deux niveaux (1 000 m², dont 650 ouverts au public) autour d'un nouvel escalier monumental en courbe, dont les marches évoquent le nom de l'établissement. Le niveau supérieur donne sur la place de la Bastille avec des vues soigneusement cadrées. L'ensemble de 220 places a été réalisé en trois mois (5 juin-6 septembre 2000). Les courbes sensuelles des murs présentent un aspect métallique dû à la projection de particules de titane. Elisabeth de Portzamparc a conçu à la fois les volumes, le mobilier et les équipements, comme le bar ou les toilettes, pour arriver à une cohérence que l'on trouve rarement dans un restaurant de chaîne (Flo en l'occurrence). Pour la terrasse, Christian de Portzamparc a dessiné une structure de métal et de verre, dans l'esprit du travail de son épouse, qui avait déjà créé le café de la Musique à la Villette.

A view of the restaurant area (above) and the bar (right) on the upper level of the Grandes Marches Restaurant. Views toward the Place de la Bastille are combined here with a refinement in both color schemes and lighting patterns.

Blick in den Restaurantbereich (oben) und die Bar (rechts) in der oberen Etage des Grandes Marches Restaurants. Die Aussicht auf den Place de la Bastille wird hier mit einer raffinierten Farbzusammenstellung und Lichtgestaltung kombiniert.

Vue de la salle de restaurant (en haut) et du bar (à droite) à l'étage du Restaurant des Grandes Marches. Les vues sur la place de la Bastille participent au raffinement des propositions chromatiques et de l'éclairage.

RICHARD ROGERS

Richard Rogers Partnership
Thames Wharf
Rainville Road
London W6 9HA
England

Tel: +44 207 385 1235
Fax: +44 207 385 8409
e-mail: enquiries@richardrogers.co.uk
Web: www.richardrogers.co.uk

Born in 1933 in Florence, Italy, of British parents, **RICHARD ROGERS** studied at the Architectural Association in London (1954-59). He received his M.Arch. degree from the Yale University School of Architecture in 1962, and created partnerships with his wife Su Rogers, Norman and Wendy Foster (Team 4, London, 1964-66), and with Renzo Piano in London, Paris and Genoa (1971-77). In 1977, he founded Richard Rogers Partnership in London. He has taught at Yale, and has been Chairman of the Trustees of the Tate Gallery, London (1981-89). His main buildings include the Centre Georges Pompidou (Paris, with Renzo Piano, 1971-77), the Lloyd's of London Headquarters (1978-86), Channel 4 Television Headquarters (London, 1990-94), the European Court of Human Rights (Strasbourg, France, 1989-95), the Daimler Benz Offices and Housing (Potsdamer Platz, Berlin, 1994-98), and the Law Courts (Bordeaux, France, 1993-98).

RICHARD ROGERS, 1933 als Sohn britischer Eltern in Florenz geboren, studierte von 1954 bis 1959 an der Architectural Association in London. Seinen Master of Architecture erwarb er 1962 an der Yale University School of Architecture. Mit seiner Frau Su sowie Norman und Wendy Foster gründete er 1964 in London das Büro Team 4, das bis 1966 bestand. Von 1971 bis 1977 arbeitete er in Partnerschaft mit Renzo Piano in London, Paris und Genua. 1977 gründete er Richard Rogers Partnership in London. Rogers hat in Yale gelehrt und war von 1981 bis 1989 Vorstand des Kuratoriums der Tate Gallery in London. Zu seinen wichtigsten Bauten gehören das Centre Georges Pompidou in Paris (mit Renzo Piano, 1971-77), die Hauptverwaltung von Lloyd's of London (1978-86), die Zentrale von Channel 4 in London (1990-94), der Europäische Gerichtshof für Menschenrechte in Straßburg (1989-95), die Büros und Wohnungen für Daimler-Benz am Potsdamer Platz in Berlin (1994-98) sowie das Palais de Justice in Bordeaux (1993-98).

Né à Florence, Italie, en 1933 de parents britanniques, **RICHARD ROGERS** étudie à l'Architectural Association de Londres (1954-59). Diplômé d'architecture de la Yale University School of Architecture en 1962, il fonde une agence avec son épouse Su Rogers, Norman and Wendy Foster (Team 4, Londres, 1964-66), puis avec Renzo Piano à Londres, Paris et Gènes (1971-77). Il crée Richard Rogers Partnership à Londres en 1977. Il a enseigné à Yale et a été président du Conseil d'administration de la Tate Gallery, (Londres, 1981-89). Parmi ses principales réalisations : le Centre Georges Pompidou (Paris, avec Renzo Piano, 1971-77), le siège des Lloyd's of London (Londres, 1978-86), le siège de Channel 4 (Londres, 1990-94), la Cour européenne des droits de l'homme (Strasbourg, France, 1989-95), le Palais de justice de Bordeaux (1993-98), ainsi que des bureaux et des logements pour Daimler Benz (Potsdamer Platz, Berlin, 1994-98).

MILLENNIUM DOME

London, England, 1996-99

Competition: 2/96. Planning: 5/96-5/97. Construction: 6/97-9/99.
Client: The New Millennium Experience Company Limited. Total floor area: 250 000 m².
Costs: £43 000 000.

The structure of Richard Rogers' **MILLENNIUM DOME** is based on a network of cable netting suspended from twelve 100-m masts, covered by a 100,000-m² canopy of PTFE-coated glass fiber. This project is by any definition massive; the site structures and associated infrastructure cost no less than £43 million. Despite its size, the Millennium Dome appears in a sense as little more than a large tent. At that, its overall height gives visitors the impression that the structure is in fact less imposing than it really is. The interior pavilions have very little to do with the design of the dome itself, since they are each the work of other architects. Rogers' technological approach is evident in the masts and the freestanding blocks that provide climatic control or electrical power for the complex. Heavily criticized for its cost and infrastructure failures, the Dome nonetheless marked the turn of the century more clearly than any other building erected elsewhere in the world.

Richard Rogers' **MILLENNIUM DOME** besteht aus einem an zwölf 100 m hohen Masten aufgehängten Stahlkabelgeflecht, das von einem 100 000 m² großen Schutzdach mit Teflon PTFE (Polytetrafluorethylen) beschichteter Glasfaser überdeckt wird. Dieses in jeder Hinsicht riesige Projekt hat alles in allem die Summe von 43 Millionen Pfund verschlungen. Trotz seiner enormen Größe wirkt der Millennium Dome eher wie ein überdimensionales Zelt, und auch seine Gesamthöhe macht auf ankommende Besucher einen weitaus weniger imposanten Eindruck als erwartet. Die im Inneren verteilten Ausstellungspavillons haben sehr wenig mit der Gestaltung des Bauwerks selbst zu tun, da sie alle von unterschiedlichen Architekten ausgeführt wurden. Rogers sehr technisch geprägter Entwurf zeigt sich an den Masten und freistehenden Baukörpern, die zur Regulierung von Temperatur und Luftfeuchtigkeit bzw. der Stromversorgung dienen. Obgleich der Millennium Dome wegen seiner Kosten und aufgetretener infrastruktureller Pannen heftig kritisiert wurde, markierte er die Jahrhundertwende eindrucksvoller als jedes andere Bauwerk.

La structure du **DOME DU MILLÉNAIRE** de Richard Rogers est tenue par un réseau de câbles suspendus partant de 12 mâts de 100 m de haut. Elle est recouverte d'une toile de 100 000 m² en fibre de verre enduite de PTFE. Ce projet est gigantesque à tous égards. Rien que les aménagements du site et les infrastructures ont coûté £43 millions. Malgré sa taille, le dôme n'est guère plus imposant qu'une immense tente. Vu de loin, sa hauteur relativement faible par rapport à sa circonférence donne aux visiteurs l'impression qu'il est moins gigantesque qu'en réalité. Les pavillons intérieurs ont peu de rapport avec le dôme lui-même, puisque chacun d'entre eux a été confié à un architecte différent. L'approche technologique de Rogers se reconnaît aux mâts et aux blocs techniques indépendants qui conditionnent l'air et fournissent l'électricité à l'ensemble. Très critiqué pour son coût et les problèmes posés par certains défauts d'infrastructures, le dôme néanmoins a marqué davantage le changement de millénaire que n'importe quel bâtiment érigé à cette occasion dans le monde.

Seen from almost any angle, the Dome does not give a real sense of its immensity, because of the flat curve of the roof.

Die flache Wölbung des Daches verschleiert die eigentliche Größe des Millennium Dome.

La courbe aplatie du toit empêche de percevoir l'immensité du dôme, quel que soit l'angle de vue.

The carnival or circus atmosphere beneath the Dome was of course not at all the architect's responsibility, but the Dome itself remains tainted in England by the failure of its attractions.

Obwohl der Architekt für die zirkusartige Atmosphäre im Inneren des Doms nicht verantwortlich war, hat sein Gebäude auch wegen des Misserfolgs seiner Attraktionen in England erheblich an Ansehen verloren.

L'atmosphère de carnaval ou de cirque de l'intérieur du dôme ne doit rien à l'architecte. L'échec du projet tient au manque d'attractivité de son contenu.

SCHMIDT, HAMMER & LASSEN

Schmidt, Hammer & Lassen K/S
Mønsgade 8
Postbox 13
8000 Århus C
Denmark

Tel: +45 86 201900
Fax: +45 86 184513
e-mail: info@shl.dk
Web: www.shl.dk

Extension of the Royal Library of Denmark ▶

MORTEN SCHMIDT was born in 1956. Joint Managing Director of SHL, he graduated from the School of Architecture in Århus (1982). He is in charge of the company's international projects. **BJARNE HAMMER** was born in 1955, and is also a Joint Managing Director of the firm. He graduated from the Århus School of Architecture in 1982, and is in charge of projects for the Danish government, municipalities and service businesses. **JOHN F. LASSEN,** born in 1953, also graduated from the Århus School (1983) ,and is in charge of housing projects for SHL. The fourth Joint Managing Director is **KIM HOLST JENSEN**, born in 1964. Current work for the firm includes a new headquarters for NCC Denmark (under construction), new headquarters for Andersen Consulting near the Copenhagen Harbor (1998-2001), and 700 housing units for NCC Polska in Warsaw, currently under construction.

MORTEN SCHMIDT, geboren 1956, schloß 1982 sein Studium an der Architekturschule in Århus ab. Gegenwärtig ist er als Kodirektor von SHL für die Durchführung der internationalen Firmenprojekte verantwortlich. **BJARNE HAMMER** wurde 1955 geboren und machte ebenfalls 1982 seinen Abschluß an der Architekturschule in Århus. Auch er ist Kodirektor von SHL; sein Aufgabengebiet umfaßt die Betreuung von Projekten für die dänische Regierung sowie für Stadtbehörden und Dienstleistungsunternehmen. **JOHN LASSEN**, geboren 1953, studierte bis 1983 an der Architekturschule in Århus und betreut derzeit die Wohnbauprojekte von SHL. Vierter Kodirektor der Firma ist der 1964 geborene **KIM HOLST JENSEN**. Zu den jüngsten Projekten von SHL gehören neue Hauptverwaltungen für NCC Dänemark (im Bau) und für Andersen Consulting in der Nähe des Kopenhagener Hafens (1998-2001) sowie die derzeit im Bau befindlichen 900 Wohneinheiten für NCC Polska in Warschau.

Né en 1956, **MORTEN SCHMIDT** est codirecteur de l'agence SHL et chargé des projets internationaux. Il est diplômé de l'Ecole d'architecture de Århus (1982). **BJARNE HAMMER**, né en 1955 et également codirecteur, est chargé des projets pour l'Etat danois, les municipalités et les entreprises de service. Il est diplômé de l'Ecole d'architecture de Århus (1982). **JOHN LASSEN**, né en 1953, a fait ses études au même endroit (diplômé en 1983), il est responsable de projets pour les secteur du logement. Le quatrième codirecteur est **KIM HOLST JENSEN**, né en 1964. Parmi leurs projets en cours : le nouveau siège de NCC Danemark, le siège de Andersen Consulting, près du port de Copenhague (1999-2001) et 900 appartements pour NCC Polska à Varsovie, actuellement en construction.

EXTENSION OF THE ROYAL LIBRARY OF DENMARK

Copenhagen, Denmark, 1993-99

Planning: 1993-95. Construction: 1995-99. Client: The Danish Ministry of Culture/The Royal Library.
Floor area: new building ca. 21 000 m², rebuilding ca 6 500 m². Costs: DKK 370 000 000.

This **EXTENSION OF THE ROYAL LIBRARY OF DENMARK** founded in 1653 on the island of Slotsholmen in historical Copenhagen, near the Christiansborg Palace and the Copenhagen Stock Exchange, adds to the space 21 000 m² and increases its shelf capacity on open shelving to 200 000 volumes. A slanted seven-story black granite cube, the new building includes five exhibition galleries, a restaurant and a cafe, a store, an auditorium seating 600 people, and space for the National Folklore Archives, a Danish Literature Information Center and other cultural facilities. A dramatic sandstone-clad atrium looks out on the water, and escalators lead up to the first-floor reading rooms. The architects write that the atrium is "the organic interior of the building. The wavy design of the walls refers to the human, the body and the inner world of the soul." A transparent 18 m-long bridge connects to the original building above Christians Brygge from the main (C level) floor, emphasizing the proximity of the old city and underlining the openness of the new structure in contrast to its apparently closed black facades.

Der **ERWEITERUNGSBAU DER KÖNIGLICHEN BIBLIOTHEK VON DÄNEMARK** befindet sich in der Nähe des Christiansborg Palasts und der Kopenhagener Börse. Er fügt der Fläche der 1653 auf der Insel Slotsholmen im historischen Kopenhagen gegründeten Bibliothek etwa 21 000 m² hinzu und vergrößert die Regalfläche auf ein Fassungsvermögen von 200 000 Bände. Das neue Gebäude besteht aus einem siebengeschossigen Kubus aus schwarzem Granitstein und enthält fünf Ausstellungsräume, ein Restaurant und Café, ein Geschäft, ein Auditorium mit 600 Sitzen sowie Räume für das Nationale Volkskundearchiv, ein Informationszentrum zum Thema dänische Literatur und andere kulturelle Einrichtungen. Ein dramatisch wirkendes, mit Sandstein verkleidetes Atrium ist zum Wasser hin ausgerichtet, Rolltreppen führen zu den Lesesälen im ersten Stock. Die Architekten schreiben: »Das Atrium ist das organische Zentrum des Gebäudes. Das wellenförmig verlaufende Muster der Wände soll den Menschen, seinen Körper und die Innenwelt seiner Seele symbolisieren.« Durch eine transparente, 18 m lange Brücke, die das neue mit dem alten Gebäude verbindet, wird die Nähe der Altstadt spürbar und die Offenheit des neuen Bauteils im Kontrast zu seiner scheinbar geschlossenen schwarzen Außenfassade unterstrichen.

L'EXTENSION DE LA BIBLIOTHÈQUE ROYALE DU DANEMARK fondée en 1653 sur l'île de Slotsholmen dans le Copenhague historique, à proximité du palais de Christianborg et de la Bourse, augmente la surface jusqu'alors disponible de 210 000 m² et la capacité de stockage de 200 000 volumes. Un cube incliné, en granit s'élève sur 7 étages contenant cinq galeries d'exposition, un restaurant, une cafétéria, une boutique, un auditorium de 600 places, un espace pour les archives du folklore national, un centre d'information sur la littérature danoise et d'autres équipements culturels. Un spectaculaire atrium habillé de grès donne sur un plan d'eau. De là, des escaliers mécaniques conduisent aux salles de lecture du premier étage. Les architectes expliquent que l'atrium «est le cœur organique du bâtiment. En forme de vague, le dessin des murs renvoie à l'être humain, au corps et au monde intérieur de l'âme.» Une passerelle transparente de 18 de long au-dessus de Christians Brygge relie l'extension au niveau principal (C) du bâtiment historique, ce qui renforce le lien avec la vieille ville et fait ressortir le caractère ouvert de cette nouvelle construction, qui contraste avec ses façades noires apparemment fermées.

Like Moneo's Kursaal Auditorium, the extension of the Royal Library has an angled, geometric monolithic quality that does not immediately identify any specific function.

Der Erweiterungsbau der Königlichen Bibliothek besitzt, ebenso wie Moneos Kursaal-Auditorium, schräge, streng-monolithisch wirkende Fassaden, die zunächst keine bestimmte Funktion erkennen lassen.

Comme dans le Kursaal de Moneo, l'extension de la Royal Library se présente sous forme d'un monolithe incliné qui n'exprime pas directement sa fonction spécifique.

Openings and passageways permit
visitors both to penetrate into the
monolith and to move about its inner
space more freely than might be
expected on the basis of the rather
austere facade.
Here, the mystery gives way to
an inner light, like a closed book
opening to its reader.

Zahlreiche Öffnungen und Durchgän-
ge erlauben den Besuchern, sich im
Inneren des Bauwerks freier zu bewegen (links), als es seine eher strenge,
geschlossene Außenfassade (oben)
erwarten lässt. Hier weicht das ge-
heimnisvolle Dunkel einer inneren
Helligkeit, wie bei einem Buch, das
sich seinem Leser öffnet.

Des ouvertures et des passages permettent aux visiteurs de pénétrer
dans le bâtiment monolithique et de
se déplacer à l'intérieur plus aisé-
ment que son austère façade ne le
laisse supposer. Le mystère fait place
à une sorte de lumière intérieure,
comme un livre fermé s'ouvrant sous
les yeux d'un lecteur.

The basic fragility of the book is here contrasted with the powerful materiality of a dark solid block of matter. Although some technical elements are visible, on the whole priority has been given to volume and movement over exposure of the workings of the building.

Die Fragilität des Buchs kontrastiert mit dem kraftvollen Materialcharakter der dunklen, massiven Stein- und Metallblöcke. Obwohl einige technische Details sichtbar sind, besaßen die Raumwirkung und Offenheit insgesamt Priorität vor einer funktionalen Ausdrucksweise.

La fragilité intrinsèque du livre contraste ici avec la puissante présence de ce bloc massif. Bien que certains éléments techniques restent visibles, dans l'ensemble, la priorité a été donnée aux espaces et au mouvement plutôt qu'à la mise en valeur de la structure du bâtiment.

Overlapping passageways and stairs give an almost Piranesian quality to this interior view (left), while a view of the same space from a different angle (right) emphasizes the opening toward the light and water of the exterior.

Einander überschneidende Übergänge und Treppen verleihen der Innenansicht eine an Piranesis Phantasiearchitektur erinnernde Raumwirkung (links). Dagegen wird in der Ansicht desselben Raums aus einem anderen Blickwinkel (rechts) die Öffnung nach außen, hin zu Licht und Wasser deutlich.

Des passages couverts et des escaliers superposés confèrent une qualité quasi piranèsienne à cette vue intérieure (à gauche), tandis qu'une vue du même espace sous un angle différent (à droite) met en valeur l'ouverture vers la lumière et l'eau, à l'extérieur.

ÁLVARO SIZA

Álvaro Siza – Arquitecto, LDA.
Rua do Aleixo, 53-2°
4150-043 Porto
Portugal

Tel: +351 22 616 7270
Fax: +351 22 616 7279

Serralves Foundation ◖

Born in Matosinhos, Portugal, in 1933, **ÁLVARO SIZA** studied at the University of Porto School of Architecture (1949-55). He created his own practice in 1954, and worked with Fernando Tavora from 1955 to 1958. Since 1976 he has been Professor of Construction at the University of Porto, receiving the European Mies van der Rohe Prize in 1988, and the Pritzker Prize in 1992. He built a large number of small-scale projects in Portugal, and more recently has worked on the reconstruction of the Chiado (Lisbon, Portugal, since 1989), the Meteorology Center (Barcelona, Spain, 1989-92), the Vitra Furniture Factory (Weil am Rhein, Germany, 1991-94), the Porto School of Architecture at Porto University (1986-95), and the University of Aveiro Library (Aveiro, Portugal, 1988-95). His latest projects are the Portuguese Pavilion for Expo '98 (Lisbon, 1998), and the Serralves Foundation (Porto, 1996-99) published here.

ÁLVARO SIZA, geboren 1933 in Matosinhos, Portugal, studierte von 1949 bis 1955 Architektur an der Universität Porto. 1954 gründete er sein eigenes Büro, in dem er von 1955 bis 1958 mit Fernando Tavora zusammenarbeitete. Seit 1976 lehrt Siza als Professor für Bauwesen an der Universität Porto. 1988 wurde ihm der Mies-van-der-Rohe-Preis der Europäischen Gemeinschaft verliehen, 1992 erhielt er den Pritzker Prize. In Portugal hat er viele kleinere Bauten ausgeführt, und seit 1989 arbeitet er am Wiederaufbau des Lissabonner Chiado-Viertels. Neuere Bauten sind das Meteorologische Zentrum in Barcelona (1989-92), die Möbelfabrik Vitra in Weil am Rhein (1991-94), die Architekturschule der Universität Porto (1986-95) und die Bibliothek der Universität Aveiro (1988-95). Seine jüngsten Projekte sind der Portugiesische Pavillon für die Expo '98 in Lissabon (1998) und die hier vorgestellte Stiftung Serralves in Porto (1996-99).

Né à Matosinhos, Portugal, en 1933, **ALVARO SIZA** étudie à l'Ecole d'architecture de l'Université de Porto (1949-55). Il crée sa propre agence en 1954 puis collabore avec Fernando Tavora de 1955 à 1958. Il est professeur de construction à l'Université de Porto depuis 1976. Il obtient le Prix Mies van der Rohe de la Communauté Européenne en 1988 et le Prix Pritzker en 1992. Il réalise un grand nombre de projets de petites dimensions au Portugal, puis travaille à la restructuration du quartier du Chiado, à Lisbonne (1989-). Réalisations récentes : le centre de météorologie, Barcelone, Espagne (1989-92) ; l'usine de meubles Vitra, Weil-am-Rhein, Allemagne (1991-94) ; l'Ecole d'architecture de Porto, Université de Porto (1986-95) ; la bibliothèque de l'Université d'Aveiro, Portugal (1988-95). Parmi ses derniers projets : le pavillon portugais pour Expo '98 à Lisbonne (1998) et la Fondation Serralves (Porto, 1996-99), publiée dans ces pages.

SERRALVES FOUNDATION

Porto, Portugal, 1991-99

Planning: 1991-99. Construction: 1996-99. Client: Serralves Foundation.
Landscape: Global – João Gomes da Silva and Erika Skabar. Floor area: 15 000 m².

The **SERRALVES FOUNDATION,** specializing in contemporary art, was created through a joint venture of the Portuguese government and 50 private investors. Established in the Quinta de Serralves, a large property including the main house built in the 1930s, it is located not far from the center of Porto. Siza's new structure, located in the park of the Foundation, is both substantial in size and ambitious in scope. Using a suspended ceiling system similar to the one he devised for the Galician Center of Contemporary Art, Siza created a number of large, flexible galleries, intended for temporary art shows. Interior courtyards and numerous windows permit the visitor to remain in contact with the attractive park environment (of which Siza designed three hectares).

Die auf zeitgenössische Kunst spezialisierte **STIFTUNG SERRALVES** wurde durch die Zusammenarbeit der portugiesischen Regierung mit 50 Investoren aus der Privatwirtschaft begründet. Ihr in der Quinta de Serralves gelegener Sitz mit dem in den 1930er Jahren erbauten Haupthaus befindet sich auf einem großen Gelände unweit des Zentrums von Porto. Sizas neues Gebäude, das in dem zur Stiftung gehörenden Park errichtet wurde, ist sowohl von seiner Größe als auch seinem Anspruch her ein großangelegtes Unternehmen. Der Architekt schuf unter Verwendung einer Hängedeckenkonstruktion, wie er sie in ähnlicher Form bereits für das Galicische Zentrum für Zeitgenössische Kunst entworfen hat, eine Reihe großer, flexibler Galerien, in denen Wechselausstellungen gezeigt werden sollen. Innenhöfe und zahlreiche Fenster erlauben dem Besucher einen ständigen Ausblick auf die reizvolle, umgebende Parklandschaft (von der Siza 3 ha gestaltet hat).

La **FONDATION SERRALVES** d'art contemporain est née d'un partenariat entre l'Etat portugais et 50 mécènes privés. Installée dans la Quinta de Serralves, vaste propriété où se trouvait déjà une belle demeure des années 1930, elle est située à proximité du centre de Porto. Le nouveau bâtiment de Siza, édifié dans le parc de la Fondation, est de taille et de propos ambitieux. A partir d'un système de plafonds suspendus ressemblant à celui mis au point pour le Centre d'art contemporain de Galice, Siza a créé plusieurs vastes galeries d'expositions temporaires. Des cours intérieures et de nombreuses ouvertures permettent au visiteur de conserver le contact avec un parc magnifique (dont 3 ha ont été conçus par Siza).

Set at some distance from the old city of Porto, the new building of the Serralves Foundation does not give a very open impression from the exterior (above) but its complex forms allow ample light into the appropriate galleries, as well as views out toward the park (right).

Das neue Gebäude der unweit der Altstadt von Porto gelegenen Stiftung Serralves macht von außen einen eher abweisenden Eindruck (oben). Seine komplexen Formen lassen jedoch viel natürliches Licht in die einzelnen Ausstellungsräume und geben immer wieder Ausblicke auf den Park frei (rechts).

Non loin de la vieille ville de Porto, le nouveau bâtiment de la Fondation Serralves semble très peu ouvert sur l'extérieur (ci-dessus), mais ses formes complexes laissent pénétrer une généreuse lumière dans ses galeries, et découvrir des perspectives sur le parc (à droite).

Siza is a master of the subtle
manipulation of light and materials,
here to the benefit of the art works
that are placed in spaces whose
architecture and lighting can be
modified to accommodate specific
types of installation.

Siza ist ein Meister der subtilen
Gestaltung mit Licht und Material.
Im Vordergrund stehen dabei die
Kunstwerke, die in Räumen präsentiert werden, deren Innenausstattung
und Lichtdesign je nach Art der Ausstellung verändert werden können.

Siza est un des maîtres de la manipulation subtile de la lumière et des
matériaux, ici au bénéfice d'œuvres
d'art disposées dans des espaces
dont l'architecture et l'éclairage peuvent être modifiés selon les types de
présentations.

PORTUGUESE PAVILION

Expo 2000, Hanover, Germany, 1999-2000

Planning: 3/99-9/99. Construction: 9/99-3/2000. Client: Portugal 2001, S.A.
Floor area: 1 375 m². Costs: ca. DM 7 500 000.

Working with his colleague Souto de Moura, Álvaro Siza uses a variety of materials for the external cladding of the structure, maintaining the austere geometry that he is well known for, especially in his native Portugal.

Für die Außenverkleidung des Portugisischen Pavillons, der in Zusammenarbeit mit seinem Kollegen Eduardo Souto de Moura entstand, verwendete Siza unterschiedliche Materialien. Dabei bleibt die nüchterne Geometrie gewahrt, für die er, besonders in seiner Heimat Portugal, bekannt ist.

En collaboration avec son confrère Souto Moura, Alvaro Siza utilise divers matériaux pour le bardage externe de la structure qui renforce l'austérité géométrique (et contraste avec les arbres noueux) qui ont fait sa notoriété, en particulier dans son Portugal natal.

Like the **PORTUGUESE PAVILION** at the Lisbon Fair this elegant, minimalist design, clad in limestone, tile and cork, was the result of a collaboration between Álvaro Siza and Eduardo Souto de Moura. Within, a white plaster exhibition hall houses a film screen and a small presentation of Portuguese products. Merging tradition and modernity that is a hallmark of today's Portugal. The use of 150 mm-thick cork panels as a cladding material is just one clear indication of the use of a traditional local product in an innovative manner. The small cork oaks planted in front of the structure recall a familiar element of the Portuguese landscape. Aware of the problems caused by permanent structures in the context of such fairs, the architects designed the building so that it could be dismantled at the end of Expo 2000 and reassembled in Portugal.

Der **PORTUGIESISCHE PAVILLON** für die Expo 2000 in Hannover ist ebenso wie der für die Expo '98 in Lissabon eine Zusammenarbeit zwischen Álvaro Siza und Eduardo Souto de Moura. Mit seiner Verkleidung aus Kalkstein, Fliesen und Kork hob sich das elegante, minimalistische Design von den übrigen Bauten ab. In dem schlichten, mit weißem Gips verputzten Innenraum wurden Filme über Portugal gezeigt und landestypische Produkte ausgestellt, eine Verschmelzung von Tradition und Moderne, die für das heutige Portugal typisch ist. Ein Beispiel für den innovativen Umgang mit traditionellen lokalen Materialien ist die Verwendung von 150 mm dicken Korkplatten für die Außenverkleidung. Die vor dem Gebäude eingepflanzten Korkeichen sind ein typisches Element der portugiesischen Landschaft. Zweifellos waren sich die beiden Architekten der besonderen Anforderung an die Gestaltung temporärer Bauten im Kontext von Weltausstellungen bewusst, weshalb sie ihr Gebäude so konzipierten, dass es nach dem Ende der Expo 2000 demontiert und in Portugal wieder zusammengebaut werden konnte.

Comme le **PORTUGUESE PAVILION** pour la foire internationale de Lisbonne, ce projet est né d'une collaboration entre Alvaro Siza et Eduardo Souto de Moura. Revêtue de grès, de carrelage et de liège, cette élégante réalisation minimaliste se détache au milieu de l'ambiance événementielle de l'Expo. A l'intérieur, un hall d'exposition aux murs de plâtre blanc abrite un écran de projection et une petite présentation de produits portugais. L'idée centrale de ce projet est le mariage de la tradition et de la modernité, image du Portugal d'aujourd'hui. L'utilisation de panneaux de liège de 15 cm d'épaisseur comme matériau d'habillage montre qu'un matériau local et traditionnel peut être traité de façon novatrice. Les petits chênes-lièges plantés devant la construction évoquent un élément familier des paysages portugais. Conscient des problèmes des constructions de ce genre de manifestation, les architectes ont voulu que le bâtiment soit démontable pour être réassemblé au Portugal.

As in many other designs by Álvaro Siza the cork oaks outside the building offer a sharp contrast to the rigorous modernity of the building itself.

Wie bei anderen Entwürfen Sizas stehen die Korkeichen vor dem Pavillon in scharfem Kontrast zu der strengen Modernität des Gebäudes selbst.

Comme dans beaucoup d'autres projets de Siza, le puissant contraste entre les chênes-lièges et la modernité rigoureuse du bâtiment est bien calculé.

Eduardo Souto de Moura and
Álvaro Siza share a sense of complex minimalism, where the unexpected is more the rule than any
predictable geometric progression.

Eduardo Souto de Moura und Álvaro
Siza haben die gleiche Vorliebe für
einen »komplexen Minimalismus«,
bei dem eher das Unerwartete die
Regel ist als eine vorhersehbare
geometrische Abfolge von Formen.

Souto Moura et Siza partagent un
sens de minimalisme complexe,
où l'inattendu est plus fréquent
qu'une succession de séquences
géometriques prévisibles.

SKIDMORE, OWINGS & MERRILL

Skidmore, Owings & Merrill LLP
224 South Michigan Avenue, Suite 1000
Chicago, Illinois 60604
United States

Tel: +1 312 554 9090
Fax: +1 312 360 4545
Web: www.som.com

7 South Dearborn ▶

Created in 1936, **SOM** has built in more than 50 countries. With offices in Chicago, New York, Miami, San Francisco, Los Angeles, London, and Hong Kong, the firm is one of the largest of its type in the world. SOM has considerable experience in the area of tall buildings since the completion of the famous Lever House Tower on Park Avenue (New York, 1954). The Sears Tower (1974) and the John Hancock Center (1970) in Chicago as well as the more recent Jin Mao Tower in Shanghai (completed in 1999) are all the work of SOM. The Design Partner for the 7 South Dearborn project is Adrian D. Smith (left), who joined SOM in 1969, and worked recently on the Jin Mao Tower as well as a number of other skyscrapers. William F. Baker (right) is the Structural Engineering Partner, Raymond J. Clark (center left) is the Mechanical and Electrical Engineering Partner, and Richard F. Tomlinson (center right) is the Project Partner for 7 South Dearborn.

Seit seiner Gründung im Jahr 1936 hat das Büro **SKIDMORE, OWINGS & MERRILL (SOM)** Bauprojekte in mehr als 50 Ländern durchgeführt. Mit Niederlassungen in Chicago, New York, Miami, San Francisco, Los Angeles, London und Hongkong ist SOM eines der größten Architekturbüros der Welt. Seit der Fertigstellung des berühmten Lever House-Turms auf der New Yorker Park Avenue (1954) hat SOM beachtliche Leistungen auf dem Gebiet der Hochhausarchitektur vollbracht, so mit dem Sears Tower (1974) und dem John Hancock Center (1970) in Chicago sowie dem 1999 fertiggestellten Jin Mao Tower in Shanghai. Leitender Konstrukteur für das Projekt 7 South Dearborn ist Adrian D. Smith (links), der 1969 in die Firma eintrat. In jüngerer Zeit hat er sowohl am Jin Mao Tower als auch an einer Reihe anderer Wolkenkratzer gearbeitet. Für 7 South Dearborn sind verantwortlich: William F. Baker (rechts) als leitender Bauingenieur, Raymond J. Clark (Mitte links) als leitender Maschinenbau- und Elektroingenieur sowie Richard F. Tomlinson (Mitte rechts) als Projektleiter.

Fondée en 1936, l'agence **SOM** a construit dans plus de 50 pays. Installée à Chicago, New York, Miami, San Francisco, Los Angeles, Londres et Hongkong, c'est l'une des plus grandes agences du monde. Elle possède une expérience considérable dans les immeubles de grande hauteur depuis la célèbre Lever House de Park Avenue (New York, 1954), la Sears Tower (1974) et le John Hancock Center (1970) à Chicago et la Tour Jin Mao à Shanghai (achevée en 1999). L'associé responsable de la conception du projet de 7 South Dearborn est Adrian D. Smith (à gauche), entrée chez SOM en 1969. Récemment, Smith a travaillé sur le projet de la Tour Jin Mao ainsi que sur d'autres gratte-ciel. William F. Baker (à droite) est associé en charge de l'ingénierie structurelle, Raymond J. Clark (au centre à gauche) de l'ingéniérie mécanique et électrique tandis que Richard F. Tomlinson (au centre à droite) est chef de projet.

7 SOUTH DEARBORN

Chicago, Illinois, USA, 2000-03

*Construction: 2000-03 (scheduled). Client: European American Realty Ltd.
Floor area: ca. 176 514 m². Costs: estimated US$500 million.*

Intended to be the world's tallest building, **7 SOUTH DEARBORN** will rise to a height of 473 m and 108 stories. It will include 32 floors of office space, 360 residential units located on 40 floors, with communications facilities for digital television on the top 13 floors. The exterior facade will be covered with aluminum and stainless steel with lightly tinted glazing on the lower floors. The upper residential floors (the highest in the world are situated on the 92nd floor) will be cantilevered from a concrete core, making it possible to have no columns on the exterior walls. Expected to cost about US$500 million, the building will be topped by twin digital television transmission towers that will reach a height of no less than 610 m above street level.

Der nach seiner Adresse **7 SOUTH DEARBORN** genannte Wolkenkratzer soll mit einer Höhe von 473 m und 108 Geschossen das höchste Gebäude der Welt werden. Er wird 32 Geschosse mit Büroräumen, 360 Privatwohnungen auf 40 Stockwerken und auf den oberen 13 Etagen Kommunikationseinrichtungen beherbergen. Die Außenfassade wird mit Aluminium und Edelstahl und in den unteren Geschossen mit leicht getöntem Glas verkleidet. Weil die oberen Wohngeschosse (von denen sich die weltweit höchsten auf dem 92. Stockwerk befinden werden) von einem Betonkern auskragen, kann an den Außenwänden auf Stützen verzichtet werden. Die Baukosten sind mit 500 Millionen US$ kalkuliert. An der Spitze des Gebäudes sollen sich zwei Leitungsmasten für Digitalfernsehen zu einer Höhe von 610 m über Straßenniveau erheben.

Avec ses 473 m et 108 niveaux, le **7 SOUTH DEARBORN** sera sans doute le plus haut gratte-ciel du monde. Il comprendra 32 étages de bureaux, et 360 appartements, locatifs répartis dans 40 étages, tandis que les 13 niveaux supérieurs seront réservés à des equipements de communication. La façade extérieure sera recouverte d'aluminium, d'acier inoxydable et de verre légèrement teinté pour les étages inférieurs. Les niveaux résidentiels (les appartements les plus hauts du monde se trouveront au 92ème étage) seront en porte-à-faux par rapport au noyau de béton, pour éviter la présence de colonnes sur les murs extérieurs. Pour un budget estimé à $500 millions, l'immeuble sera surmonté de deux antennes jumelles de télévision qui s'élèveront à 610 m au-dessus du niveau du sol.

With its twin television towers, 7 South Dearborn will stand out against the Chicago skyline, despite the fact that the city is already home to some of the tallest office buildings in the world.

Mit seinen beiden Fernsehmasten wird der Wolkenkratzer 7 South Dearborn aus der Skyline von Chicago hervorstechen, obwohl die Stadt bereits einige der höchsten Bürogebäude der Welt beherbergt.

Avec ses pylônes de télévision jumeaux, 7 South Dearborn, ne manquera pas d'être remarqué dans le panorama urbain de Chicago, ville qui compte déjà quelques unes des plus hautes tours de bureaux du monde.

EDUARDO SOUTO DE MOURA

Souto Moura Arquitectos Lda
Rua do Aleixo, 53-1°A
4150-043 Porto
Portugal

Tel: +351 2 618 7547
Fax: +351 2 610 8092
e-mail: souto.moura@mail.telepac.pt

EDUARDO SOUTO DE MOURA was born in Porto, Portugal, in 1952. He graduated from the School of Architecture of Porto in 1980. He was an Assistant Professor at the Faculty of Architecture in Porto from 1981 to 1991. From 1974 to 1979 he worked in the office of Álvaro Siza and established his own practice the following year. Recent work includes row houses in the Rua Lugarinho (Porto, Portugal, 1996), the renovation of the Municipal Market in Braga (1997), the Silo Norte Shopping building published here, a house and wine cellar (Valladolid, Spain, 1999), and the Portuguese Pavilion, Expo 2000 (Hanover, Germany, with Álvaro Siza, 1999). Current work includes the conversion of the building of the Carvoeira da Foz (Porto) and a project for the Braga Stadium.

EDUARDO SOUTO DE MOURA, geboren 1952 im portugiesischen Porto, schloß 1980 sein Studium an der Architekturschule der Universität Porto ab. Von 1981 bis 1991 lehrte er am Fachbereich Architektur der Universität Porto. Bevor er sich 1980 mit einem eigenen Büro selbständig machte, arbeitete er von 1974 bis 1979 im Büro von Álvaro Siza. Zu seinen neueren Projekten gehören eine Reihenhausanlage in der Rua Lugarinho in Porto (1996), die Modernisierung des städtischen Marktplatzes in Braga (1997) und das hier vorgestellte Gebäude im Einkaufszentrum Silo Norte in Portugal, ein Wohnhaus und Weinkeller in Valladolid, Spanien (1999) und, in Zusammenarbeit mit Álvaro Siza, der Portugiesische Pavillon für die Expo 2000 in Hannover (1999). Gegenwärtig arbeitet er am Umbau des Gebäudes der Carvoeira da Foz in Porto und an einem Projekt für das Stadion in Braga.

Né à Porto, Portugal, en 1952, **EDUARDO SOUTO DE MOURA** est diplômé de l'Ecole d'architecture de Porto (ESBAP, 1980). Il a été Professeur assistant à la faculté d'architecture de Porto (FAUP) de 1981 à 1991. Après avoir travaillé auprès d'Álvaro Siza de 1974 à 1979, il a fondé sa propre agence en 1980. Parmi ses réalisations récentes : une succession de maisons rua Lugarinho (Porto, 1996), la rénovation du marché municipal de Braga (1997), le centre commercial de Silo Norte publié ici, une maison et un chais (Valladolid, Espagne, 1999) et le projet du pavillon portugais d'Expo 2000 (Hanovre, Allemagne, avec Álvaro Siza, 1999). Il travaille actuellement à la reconversion de l'immeuble de la Carvoeira da Foz (Porto) et à un projet de stade à Braga, au Portugal.

SILO NORTE SHOPPING

Matosinhos, Portugal, 1998

Planning and construction: 1998. Client: IMOR-R.
Floor area: 226 m². Costs: withheld.

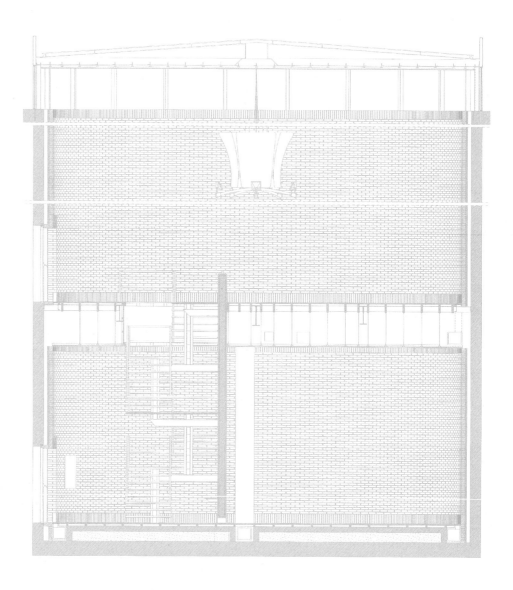

Located in the rather ugly, industrial Porto suburb of Matosinhos, birthplace of Álvaro Siza, this facility demonstrates the architect's ability to reuse a very specific building type for an entirely different purpose.

Dieser Bau, der in dem tristen Industrievorort von Porto, Matosinhos, gelegen ist, demonstriert Souto de Mouras Talent, einen spezifischen Bautyp für einen vollkommen anderen Zweck zu adaptieren.

Situé dans l'assez laide banlieue industrielle de Matosinhos, lieu de naissance d'Alvaro Siza, cette intervention montre la capacité de l'architecte à réutiliser un type de bâtiment destiné à un autre usage.

The architect was asked to create an exhibition gallery and an auditorium inside a spiral ramp that gives access to a parking area. The available space was thus defined in terms of a 22 m-high, 12 m-diameter cylinder, with the auditorium placed on the ground level. The architect lined the cylinder with adobe brick to reduce reverberations, and placed the gallery space above the auditorium to obtain some natural light. With its wooden floors and street lamps used for internal night lighting, the space reflects the sober, powerful style of Souto de Moura. Although **SILO NORTE SHOPPING** was a difficult space to work with, the architect succeeded in making it seem coherent with the relatively elegant external concrete spiral of the parking access ramp.

Eduardo Souto de Moura wurde beauftragt, innerhalb einer spiralförmig verlaufenden Rampe, die den Zugang zu einem Parkkomplex bildet, eine Kunstgalerie und ein Auditorium zu entwerfen. Der verfügbare Raum ist als 22 m hoher Zylinder mit einem Durchmesser von 12 m definiert, in dessen Erdgeschoss das Auditorium untergebracht wurde. Um den Widerhall zu vermindern, kleidete der Architekt den Zylinder mit Lehmziegeln aus. Die Galerie wurde zur Nutzung der natürlichen Lichtverhältnisse über dem Auditorium angelegt. Sowohl die Straßenlaternen, die für eine Innenbeleuchtung bei Nacht sorgen, als auch die Holzböden spiegeln den nüchternen, kraftvollen Stil von Souto de Moura. Obwohl **SILO NORTE SHOPPING** als Raum schwierig zu gestalten war, gelang dem Architekten ein harmonisches Zusammenspiel von Innenraum und äußerer Betonspirale.

Le problème posé était de concevoir une galerie d'exposition et un auditorium à l'intérieur d'une rampe en spirale donnant accès à un parking. Le volume disponible consistait donc en un cylindre de 12 m de diamètre et 22 de haut, l'auditorium étant implanté en sous-sol. Souto de Moura a doublé le cylindre de briques de terre pour réduire la réverbération du bruit et place la galerie au-dessus de l'auditorium pour bénéficier de la lumière naturelle. Avec ses sols en bois et son éclairage de type urbain, l'espace créé incarne le style sobre et puissant de l'architecte. Dans cet espace de **SILO NORTE SHOPPING** difficile à traiter, l'architecte a réussi à trouver une cohérence entre l'intérieur et l'élégante spirale en béton.

Souto de Moura typically suspends an apparently solid wall on a sliced I-beam, raising some doubt as to where solidity and weight actually lie in this structure.

Charakteristisch für Souto de Moura ist das Einhängen einer scheinbar massiven Wand in Doppel-T-Träger, was den Betrachter im Unklaren darüber lässt, wo bei dieser Konstruktion die Masse und das Gewicht liegen.

A sa manière très personnelle, Souto de Moura fait reposer un mur apparemment massif sur une IPN, si bien que le visiteur se démande ce qui porte le poids et la masse de la construction.

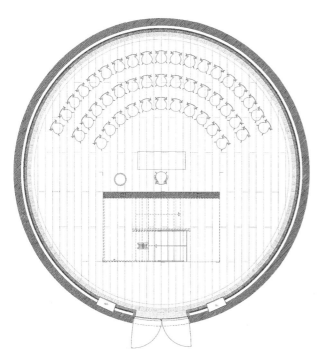

Creating architectural surprise inside such a restricted volume is a measure of the designer's ability to redefine existing space.

Architektonische Überraschungen dieser Art in einem so begrenzten Baukörper sind ein Maßstab für die Fähigkeit des Architekten, einen bestehenden Raum neu zu definieren.

La création de surprises architecturales dans un volume aussi réduit donne la mesure du talent de ce concepteur qui redéfinit admirablement un espace existant.

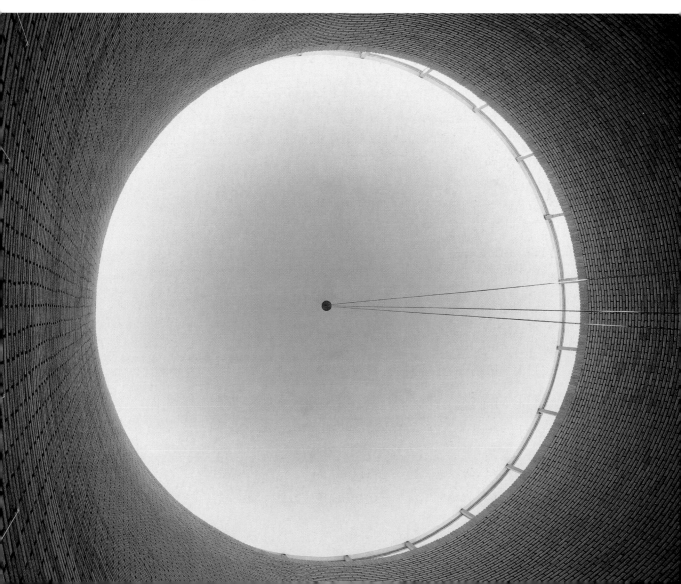

PHILIPPE STARCK

Philippe Starck
27, rue Pierre Poli
92130 Issy-les-Moulineaux
France

Tel: +33 1 4108 8282
Fax: +33 1 4108 9665

PHILIPPE STARCK was born in Paris in 1949, and attended the École Nissim de Camondo there. He is of course best known as a designer of objects such as chairs or lamps. He has always had an interest in architecture, however. His architectural and interior design projects include the Café Costes (Paris, 1984), the Royalton Hotel (New York, 1988), the Laguiole Knife Factory (France, 1988), the Paramount Hotel (New York, 1990), the Nani Nani Building (Tokyo, 1989), the Asahi Beer Building (Tōkyō, 1989), the Teatriz Restaurant (Madrid, 1990), and his Baron Vert Building in Osaka, Japan (1990). He has worked on a number of hotels with Ian Schrager, including the St. Martin's Lane Hotel published here and the Sanderson Hotel, both in London.

PHILIPPE STARCK, geboren 1949 in Paris, studierte an der École Nissim de Camondo in Paris. Obwohl er vor allem als Designer von Einrichtungsgegenständen bekannt geworden ist, zeigte er immer auch ein aktives Interesse an Architektur. Zu seinen baulichen und innenarchitektonischen Projekten gehören das Café Costes in Paris (1984), das Royalton Hotel (1988) und das Paramount Hotel (1990), beide in New York, die Messerfabrik in Laguiole, Frankreich (1988), das Nani Nani-Gebäude (1989) und das Gebäude der Asahi-Brauerei (1989), beide in Tokio, das Restaurant Teatriz in Madrid (1990) sowie das Baron Vert Building in Osaka (1990). Darüber hinaus hat Starck in Zusammenarbeit mit Ian Schrager eine Reihe von Hotels gestaltet, so das hier vorgestellte St. Martin's Lane Hotel und das ebenfalls in London befindliche Sanderson Hotel.

PHILIPPE STARCK, né à Paris en 1949, suit les cours de l'Ecole Camondo. Il est surtout connu comme designer d'objets (sièges, luminaires, etc.) mais s'est toujours intéressé à l'architecture. Parmi ses projets d'architecture et d'aménagements intérieurs : le café Costes (Paris, 1984), le Royalton Hotel (New York, 1988), l'usine de coutellerie (Laguiole, France, 1988), le Paramount Hotel (New York, 1990), l'immeuble Nani Nani (Tokyo, 1989), l'immeuble de la brasserie Asahi (Tokyo, 1989), le restaurant Teatriz (Madrid, 1990) et l'immeuble Baron vert (Osaka, Japon, 1990). Il est intervenu sur plusieurs hôtels pour Ian Schrager, dont le récent St. Martin's Lane Hotel, publié ici, et le Sanderson Hotel, tous deux à Londres.

ST. MARTIN'S LANE HOTEL

London, England, 1999

Opening date: September 1999. Client: Ian Schrager London Limited.

Set on St. Martin's Lane not far from Trafalgar Square, the first **HOTEL** to be opened in London by the American Ian Schrager, in collaboration with the French designer Philippe Starck, is nothing if not a success. Starck's unexpected combinations of giant flower vases, outsized chess pieces, Louis XV-style armchairs, and stools shaped like golden molars combined with Schrager's marketing talent are what is required to bring the rich and the fashionable together in one place. The place is a revamped modernist office building whose facade remains remarkably uncluttered by such inconvenient items as the hotel's name. Clearly, you don't belong in this hotel if you don't know that you have arrived. This is a successful combination of a renovated modernist architecture with Starck's theatrical sense of space and design.

Das in der St. Martin's Lane unweit des Trafalgar Square gelegene, von dem Amerikaner Ian Schrager eröffnete und in Zusammenarbeit mit dem französischen Designer Philippe Starck gestaltete **HOTEL** ist zweifellos ein Erfolg. Starcks ungewöhnliche Kombinationen von riesigen Blumenvasen, überdimensionalen Schachfiguren, Sesseln im Louis XV-Stil und Stühlen in Form goldener Backenzähne, ergeben zusammen mit Schragers Marketing-Talent die erforderlichen Zutaten, um die Hautevolee anzuziehen. Das Haus ist ein renoviertes modernes Bürogebäude, dessen Fassade auffallend frei ist von Banalitäten wie dem Namenszug des Hotels. Alles in allem stellt dieses Projekt eine gelungene Mischung aus moderner Architektur und Starcks theatralischer Auffassung von Raum und Form dar.

En bordure de St. Martin's Lane, non loin de Trafalgar Square, ce premier **HÔTEL** ouvert à Londres par l'Américain Ian Schrager en collaboration avec le designer français Philippe Starck est un grand succès. Le bizarre assemblage starckien de vases pour fleurs géants, de pièces d'échec surdimensionnées, de fauteuils de style Louis XV et de tabourets dorés en forme de molaires ainsi que le vigoureux marketing de Schrager correspondent aux attentes d'une clientèle riche et sensible à la mode. Il s'agit en fait de la restructuration d'un immeuble de bureaux moderniste dont la façade se passe de toute enseigne : vous ne méritez pas de descendre ici si vous n'en connaissez pas l'adresse. Combinaison réussie d'architecture moderniste revisitée et d'un sens théâtral de l'espace et du design à la Starck.

The enormous revolving doors on St. Martin's Lane lead to the entrance foyer, which opens out into a bar and restaurant.

Die riesige Drehtür auf der an der St. Martin's Lane gelegenen Gebäudeseite führt in die Hotelhalle, die sich zu einer Bar und einem Restaurant erweitert.

Les énormes portes pivotantes qui donnent sur St. Martin's Lane conduisent au hall d'entrée qui s'ouvre à son tour sur un bar et un restaurant.

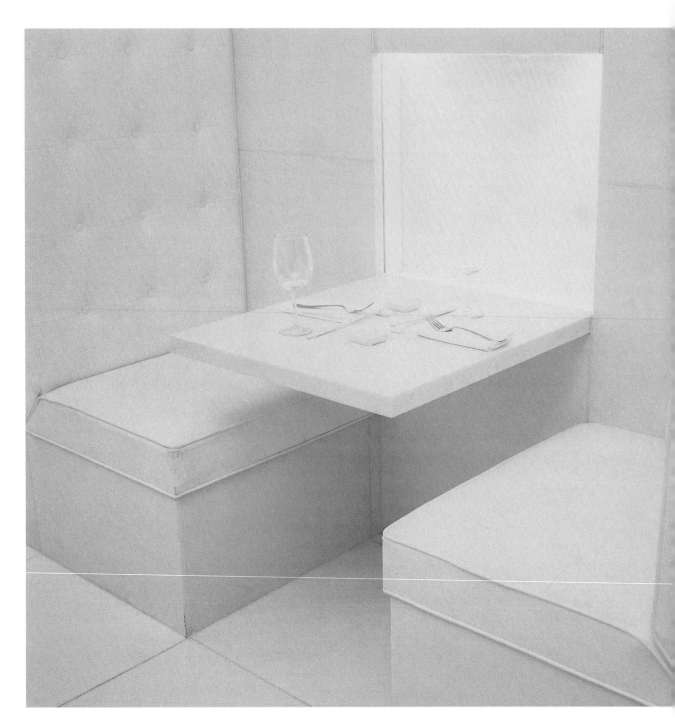

A view of the dining room.

Ansicht des Restaurants.

Vue de la salle-à-manger.

The ground-level bar, located at the rear of the entrance foyer, features these small vertical tables. Well suited to bar use, they, typically for Philippe Starck, challenge existing furniture typology.

Die Bar an der Rückseite der Hotelhalle ist mit kleinen, auf überproportional langen Beinen stehenden Tischen ausgestattet, die auf eine für Starck charakteristische Weise die bestehende Typologie für Einrichtungsgegenstände in Frage stellt.

Le bar du rez-de-chaussée, situé à l'arrière du hall d'entrée, est équipé de petites tables perchées. Bien adaptées à l'utilisation dans un bar, elles sont fideles aux principes de Starck qui remet en question la typologie classique du mobilier.

P 538.539

YOSHIO TANIGUCHI

Taniguchi and Associates
Yamakatsu Building
4-1-40 Toranomon, Minato-ku
Tokyo 105-0001
Japan

Tel: +81 3 3438 1506
Fax: +81 3 3438 1248

YOSHIO TANIGUCHI was born in Tokyo in 1937. He received a Bachelor's degree in Mechanical Engineering from Keio University in 1960 and his M.Arch. degree from the Harvard Graduate School of Design in 1964. He worked in the practice of Kenzo Tange from 1964 to 1972. In 1979 he established Taniguchi and Associates. His built work in Japan includes the Tokyo Sea Life Park (Tokyo, 1989), the Marugame Genichiro-Inokuma Museum of Contemporary Art, and the Marugame City Library (Marugame, Japan, 1991), the Toyota Municipal Museum of Art (Toyota City, 1995), the Tokyo Kasai Rinkai Park View Point Visitors Center (Tokyo, 1995), and the Tokyo National Museum Gallery of Horyuji Treasures (Tokyo, 1997-99) published here. Yoshio Taniguchi is currently working on the complete renovation and expansion of the Museum of Modern Art in New York.

YOSHIO TANIGUCHI, geboren 1937 in Tokio, erwarb 1960 sein Diplom in Maschinenbau an der Keio-Universität und 1964 seinen Master of Architecture an der Harvard Graduate School of Design (GSD). Von 1964 bis 1972 arbeitete er im Büro von Kenzo Tange. 1979 gründete er Taniguchi and Associates. Zu seinen Bauten in Japan gehören der Sea Life Park in Tokio (1989), das Genichiro-Inokuma Museum für zeitgenössische Kunst in Marugame und die Stadtbibliothek von Marugame (1991), das Städtische Museum für Kunst in Toyota City (1995), das Kansai Rinkai Park View Point Visitors Center in Tokio (1995) und die hier vorgestellten Ausstellungsräume der Horyuji Schatzkammern im Nationalmuseum in Tokio (1997-99). Gegenwärtig arbeitet Taniguchi an der Renovierung und Erweiterung des Museum of Modern Art in New York.

Né à Tokyo en 1937, **YOSHIO TANIGUCHI** est diplômé d'ingénierie mécanique de l'Université Keio (1960) et Master of Architecture de la Harvard Graduate School of Design (1964). Il travaille dans l'agence de Kenzo Tange de 1964 à 1972, et crée Taniguchi et Associés en 1979. Parmi ses réalisations au Japon : le parc marin de Tokyo (Tokyo, 1989), le Musée d'art contemporain Genichiro-Inokuma et la bibliothèque municipale de Marugame (Japon, 1991), le Musée d'art municipal Toyota (Toyota City, 1995), le Centre d'accueil des visiteurs du parc de Kasai Rinkai (Tokyo, 1995) et la galerie des Trésors Horyuji du Musée national (Tokyo, 1997-99), publié ici. Il travaille actuellement à la rénovation intégrale et à l'extension du Museum of Modern Art de New York.

TOKYO NATIONAL MUSEUM, GALLERY OF HORYUJI TREASURES

Tokyo, Japan, 1994-99

Planning: 4/1994-3/95. Construction: 4/1995-3/99.
Client: Ministry of Education and Ministry of Construction.
Total floor area: 4 031 m².

Set in the grounds of the **TOKYO NATIONAL MUSEUM** in Ueno Park in Tokyo, this new structure by Taniguchi was designed to house a number of treasures from the Horyuji Temple in Nara. The building covers an area of 1 934 m² and has a total floor area of 4 031 m². It is a four-story structure built of reinforced concrete with a steel frame. Inspired by the wooden boxes used to protect precious art objects in Japan, the design includes a high metal canopy, a glazed entrance area and a completely darkened exhibition area in the interior. Open on two sides to the garden environment with a shallow basin marking the entrance area, the building's construction has a jewel-like precision. It is a masterpiece in itself, worthy of one of the finest architects currently working in Japan.

Yoshio Taniguchi entwarf für das **TOKIOTER NATIONAL MUSEUM** in Ueno Park einen Bau zur Präsentation von Kunstwerken, die ursprünglich dem Horyuji Tempel in Nara gehörten. Die viergeschossige Stahlbetonkonstruktion – ein mit Stahlbeton ummanteltes Stahlskelett – hat eine Grundfläche von 1 934 m² und eine Gesamtnutzfläche von 4 031 m². Inspiriert von den in Schichten aufgebauten Holzkisten, die im alten Japan zum Schutz kostbarer Kunstgegenstände verwendet wurden, beinhaltet die Gestaltung ein hohes, überhängendes Schutzdach aus Metall, einen verglasten Eingangsbereich und einen vollständig abgedunkelten Ausstellungsbereich. Im Eingangsbereich ist das Gebäude nach zwei Seiten zum umgebenden Garten und einem flachen Wasserbecken hin geöffnet. Mit seinen präzisen und kostbaren Formen kann dieser Bau mit Recht ein Meisterwerk genannt werden, würdig eines der besten japanischen Architekten unserer Tage.

Sur les terrains du **MUSÉE NATIONAL DE TOKYO**, dans le parc Ueno, cette nouvelle réalisation de Taniguchi a été spécialement construite pour recevoir un certain nombre d'œuvres qui se trouvaient à l'origine dans le temple Horyuji de Nara. Pour une surface au sol de 1 934 m², le musée dispose de 4 031 m² de planchers sur quatre niveaux. Il est en béton armé sur ossature d'acier. Inspiré des boîtes en bois qui servaient à protéger les objets précieux au Japon, il possède un auvent en métal surplombant, une zone d'entrée vitrée entourée d'un bassin et une aire d'exposition centrale sans ouverture. Donnant de deux côtés sur le parc, il a été construit avec une précision d'horloger. Ce chef d'œuvre est à l'image du travail de Taniguchi, l'un des architectes le plus raffinés travaillant actuellement au Japon.

The extreme rigor and geometric clarity of Taniguchi's architecture is visible in these images of the main approach path to the museum (left) and in the entrance foyer (below).

Der Hauptzugangsweg zum Museum (links) und das Foyer (unten) machen die extreme Strenge und geometrische Klarheit von Taniguchis Baukunst augenfällig.

La rigueur extrême et la pureté géométrique du travail de Taniguchi sont évidentes dans ces vues de l'accès principal du musée (à gauche) et du foyer d'entrée (ci-dessous).

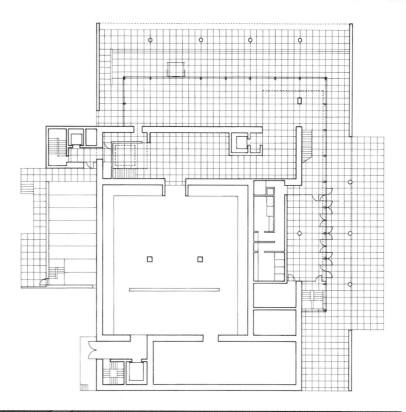

The visitor progresses from the light entrance areas to the almost total darkness of the main exhibition hall, where the extraordinary Buddhist relics of the Temple are displayed.

Die Besucher gelangen von dem hellen Eingangsbereich in den abgedunkelten Ausstellungssaal, wo die kostbaren Reliquien des Tempels präsentiert werden.

Partant de la zone d'entrée très lumineuse, le visiteur pénètre dans l'obscurité quasi totale de la principale salle d'exposition où sont présentées d'extraordinaires reliques du temple.

BERNARD TSCHUMI

Bernard Tschumi Architects
227 West 17th Street
New York, NY 10011
United States

Tel: +1 212 807 6340
Fax: +1 212 242 3693
e-mail: nyc@tschumi.com
Web: www.tschumi.com

7 rue Pecquay
75004 Paris
France
Tel: +33 1 5301 9070
Fax: +33 1 5301 9079
e-mail: bernard.tschumi.architectes@wanadoo.fr

BERNARD TSCHUMI was born in Lausanne, Switzerland, in 1944. He studied in Paris and at the ETH, Zurich. He taught at the Architectural Association, London (1970-79), and at Princeton (1976 and 1980). He has been Dean of the Graduate School of Architecture, Planning and Preservation of Columbia University in New York since 1988. He opened his own office, Bernard Tschumi Architects (Paris, New York), in 1981. Major projects include: Parc de la Villette (Paris, France, 1982-98), second prize in the Kansai International Airport Competition (1988), Glass Video Gallery (Groningen, Netherlands, 1990, recently made part of the Groninger Museum, the Fresnoy National Center for the Contemporary Arts (Tourcoing, France, 1991-98), Lerner Hall Student Center, Columbia University (New York, 1994-99), School of Architecture (first phase, Marne-la-Vallée, France, 1994-99) published here, and the Interface Flon Transport System in Lausanne, Switzerland (1988-2001).

BERNARD TSCHUMI, geboren 1944 in Lausanne in der Schweiz, studierte in Paris und an der Eidgenössischen Technischen Hochschule in Zürich. Von 1970 bis 1979 lehrte er an der Architectural Association in London und von 1976 bis 1980 in Princeton. Seit 1988 ist er Dekan der Graduate School of Architecture, Planning and Preservation der Columbia University in New York. 1981 eröffnete er sein eigenes Büro, Bernard Tschumi Architects, mit Niederlassungen in Paris und New York. Zu seinen wichtigsten Projekten gehören: der Parc de la Villette in Paris (1982-98), ein Wettbewerbsbeitrag für den internationalen Flughafen Kansai (1988), der den zweiten Preis erhielt, die Glass Video Galerie in Groningen, Niederlande, die kürzlich in das Groninger Museum eingegliedert wurde (1990), das staatliche Zentrum für zeitgenössische Kunst Le Fresnoy in Tourcoing, Frankreich (1991-98) sowie das Interface Flon Transport System in Lausanne (1988-2001). Das Lerner Hall Student Center der Columbia University in New York (1994-99) und die Architekturschule in Marne-la-Vallée (erster Bauabschnitt 1994-99) werden beide hier vorgestellt.

Né à Lausanne, Suisse, en 1944, **BERNARD TSCHUMI** étudie à Paris et à l'Institut fédéral de technologie de Zurich (ETH). Il enseigne à l'Architectural Association (Londres, 1970-79) et à Princeton (1976 et 1980). Il est doyen de la Graduate School of Architecture, Planning and Preservation de Columbia University, New York, depuis 1988. Il a ouvert son agence, Bernard Tschumi Architects en 1981 (New York et Paris). Parmi ses principaux projets : le Parc de la Villette (Paris, 1982-98), le second prix du concours pour l'aéroport international de Kansai (1988), la Glass Video Gallery (Groningue, Pays-Bas, 1990 ; récemment intégrée au Musée de Groningue), le Centre National pour les Arts contemporains du Fresnoy (Tourcoing, France, 1991-98), le Lerner Hall Student Center, Columbia University (New York, 1994-99) et l'Ecole d'Architecture de Marne-la-Vallée, (1ère phase, 1994-99), publiée dans ces pages, ainsi que l'Interface Flon Transport System à Lausanne (1988-2001).

LERNER HALL STUDENT CENTER

Columbia University, New York, NY, USA, 1994-99

Planning: 1994-95. Construction: Fall 1996 – Summer 1999.
Client: Columbia University. Floor area: 20 903 m². Costs: $85 000 000.

The $85 million 20 903-m² **LERNER HALL STUDENT CENTER** is built (in collaboration with Gruzen Samton Architects) in large part of precast concrete, brick and cast-stone masonry with cast-in-place concrete columns. One of its most surprising features is the bank of ramps set just behind a structural glass wall on the side of the building facing the campus. This skewed space is used incidentally to house some 6 000 student mailboxes, but it is also a device to bring students together into a common space, while solving the structural questions related to the uneven terrain of the site. Indeed, the glass facade of the building stands out as being surprisingly different than the opposite (Broadway) side of the building, which had to fit into the plan for the campus alignments and building design of McKim, Mead and White of 1890. As Dean of the Columbia School of Architecture, Bernard Tschumi thus leaves a lasting mark on the university.

Das für 85 Millionen $ in Zusammenarbeit mit Gruzen Samton Architects erbaute, 20 903 m² große Alfred **LERNER HALL STUDENT CENTER** besteht überwiegend aus Betonfertigteilen, einer Kombination von Ziegel- und Kunststeinmauerwerk, Aluminium, Glas und vor Ort gegossenen Betonstützen. Um die Unebenheiten des Geländes auf der dem Campus zugewandten Gebäudeseite auszugleichen, wurden im mittleren Bauteil hinter einer Fassade aus Glas Rampen angelegt. Diese verbinden die auf unterschiedlicher Höhe liegenden Geschosse der angrenzenden Bauten, darüber hinaus wird der Bereich hinter der Fassade als Treffpunkt und zur Unterbringung von fast 6 000 Briefkästen für die Studenten genutzt. Die Glasfassade unterscheidet sich stark von der am Broadway liegenden Seite des Gebäudes, die sich in den Generalplan für den Campus einfügen musste, den McKim, Mead and White 1890 entwickelt hatte. Damit hat Bernard Tschumi, Dekan der Columbia School of Architecture, eine bleibende Spur an seiner Universität hinterlassen.

Le **LERNER HALL STUDENT CENTER** de 20 903 m² (budget : $85 millions) est en grande partie construit (en collaboration avec Gruzen Samton Architects) en éléments de béton préfabriqués, brique et pierre moulée. L'une de ses caractéristiques les plus surprenantes est la succession de rampes implantée juste derrière une façade en verre donnant sur le campus. Cet espace « en biais » sert éventuellement à abriter les quelques 6 000 boîtes aux lettres des étudiants, mais correspond aussi à la volonté de réunir les étudiants dans un espace commun tout en résolvant les problèmes de structure posés par un terrain inégal. Cette façade de verre est étonnamment différente de celle qui donne sur Broadway contrainte de respecter l'alignement et le plan de masse de McKim, Mead and White de 1890. Doyen de la Columbia School of Architecture, Bernard Tschumi aura laissé une marque durable sur son université.

The architect approached the problem of the difference in levels of the street and campus sides of the building by using a system of inclined ramps.

Der Architekt löste das Problem der unterschiedlichen Höhe von Campus und straßenseitigen Gebäudeteilen durch ein System geneigter Rampen.

L'architecte a traité la différence de niveaux entre la rue et le campus au moyen d'un système de rampes inclinées.

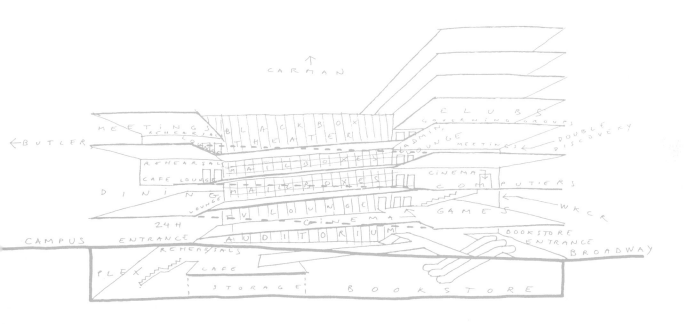

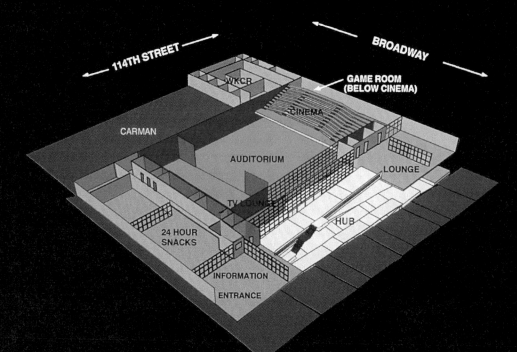

114TH STREET

BROADWAY

WKCR

GAME ROOM
(BELOW CINEMA)

CINEMA

CARMAN

AUDITORIUM

LOUNGE

TV LOUNGE

24 HOUR
SNACKS

HUB

INFORMATION

ENTRANCE

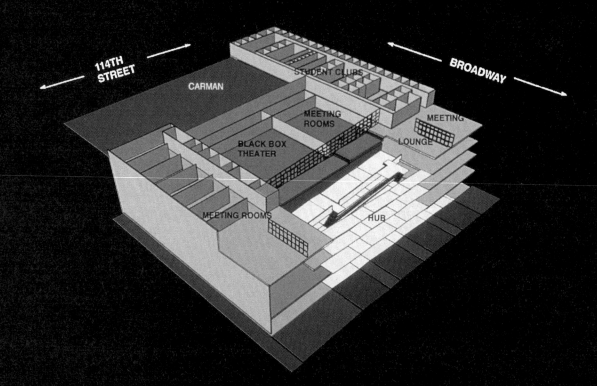

114TH
STREET

BROADWAY

CARMAN

STUDENT CLUBS

MEETING
ROOMS

MEETING

BLACK BOX
THEATER

LOUNGE

MEETING ROOMS

HUB

The tilting of the access ramps gives an unexpected image of a building that is fundamentally very practical and intended for use by large numbers of students.

Die geneigten Erschließungsrampen verleihen dem sehr funktional gestalteten Gebäude, das von einer großen Zahl von Studenten genutzt wird, eine überraschende Note.

L'inclinaison des rampes d'accès donne une image étrange à ce bâtiment très pratique, conçu pour être utilisé par un grand nombre d'étudiants.

SCHOOL OF ARCHITECTURE

Marne-la-Vallée, France, 1994-99

*Competition: 1994. Planning: 1994-96. Construction: Summer 1998 – Fall 1999 (1st phase),
expansion to be completed by 2001. Client: French Ministry of Culture.
Floor area: 14 864 m² (1st phase), 25 548 m² (total). Total costs: $26 000 000 (both phases).
Cross square footage: 148 643 m² (1st phase)*

Tschumi's work is characterized by an intelligent adaptation of essentially industrial forms to varying contexts, here the teaching of architecture in an open environment that consciously eschews the "Beaux-Arts" tradition.

Typisch für Tschumis Arbeitsweise ist die durchdachte Verwendung industrieller Formen in verschiedenen Kontexten. Der in eine offene Umgebung verlegte Unterricht vermeidet bewusst jede Anlehnung an vergangene Traditionen.

L'œuvre de Tschumi se caractérise par l'adaptation raffinée de formes essentiellement industrielles à des contextes variés. Ici, on enseigne l'architecture dans un environnement ouvert qui renonce consciemment à toute tradition « Beaux-Arts ».

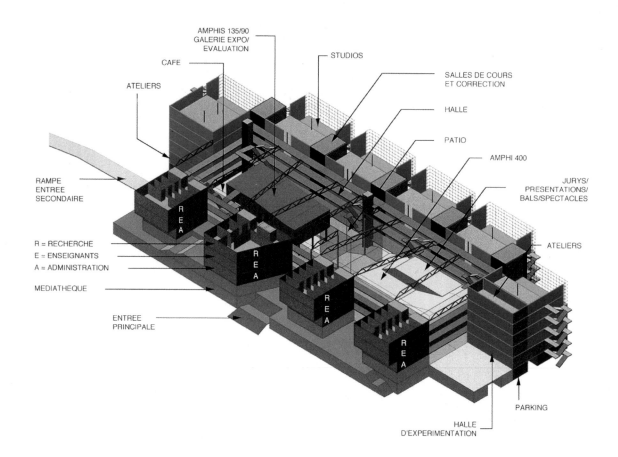

AMPHIS 135/90
GALERIE EXPO/
EVALUATION

STUDIOS

CAFE

SALLES DE COURS
ET CORRECTION

ATELIERS

HALLE

PATIO

AMPHI 400

RAMPE
ENTREE
SECONDAIRE

JURYS/
PRESENTATIONS/
BALS/SPECTACLES

ATELIERS

R = RECHERCHE
E = ENSEIGNANTS
A = ADMINISTRATION

MEDIATHEQUE

ENTREE
PRINCIPALE

PARKING

HALLE
D'EXPERIMENTATION

The first phase of the two-phase **SCHOOL OF ARCHITECTURE** project is a 14 864-m² building made of cast-in-place concrete, precast concrete, steel panels, structural glass and glass curtain walls. A 25 x 100-m "event-oriented" central space with no specific programmatic use contrasts intentionally with rigorously defined studios, faculty offices, jury spaces and the 400-seat auditorium. Tschumi specifically sought to avoid creating a structure inspired by the École des Beaux-Arts, the Bauhaus or even American universities. Set in the middle of a new "technological" campus area, Tschumi's building undoubtedly seeks to propose a new model for university buildings. As in the case of the Lerner Hall, the architect places great emphasis on the transparency and ease of circulation within the building. He clearly counts on these factors to facilitate relations between students and faculty, and to stimulate the learning process.

Der erste Bau dieses zweiteiligen Projekts für die **SCHOOL OF ARCHITECTURE** ist ein 14 864 m² umfassendes Gebäude aus vor Ort gegossenem Beton, Betonfertigteilen, Stahltafeln sowie Quer- und Vorhangwänden aus Glas. Ein 25 x 100 m messender zentraler Raum, der außer der Nutzung für »Events« keine spezielle programmatische Funktion hat, kontrastiert mit den streng definierten Ateliers, Räumen für Lehrkörper und Wettbewerbsjuroren und einem Auditorium mit 400 Sitzen. Tschumi hat bei seiner Gestaltung ganz bewusst eine Anlehnung an die École des Beaux-Arts-Tradition, das Bauhaus oder auch an amerikanische Universitätsbauten vermieden. Sein in die Mitte eines neuen »technologischen« Campusbereichs gesetzter Bau ist der Versuch, neue Maßstäbe für die Planung von Universitätsgebäuden zu setzen. Ebenso wie bei seiner Lerner Hall legt der Architekt großen Wert auf Transparenz und Leichtigkeit in der Nutzung des Gebäudes. Er betrachtet diese Faktoren als wesentlich für optimale Kommunikationsstrukturen zwischen Studenten und Lehrenden und für eine Stimulierung des Lernprozesses.

La première phase de cette **ECOLE D'ARCHITECTURE**, qui en compte deux, est un bâtiment de 14 864 m² construit en béton préfabriqué, béton coulé sur place, panneaux d'acier, verre structurel et murs-rideaux en verre. Un espace central de 25 x 100 m « prévu pour des manifestations mais sans affectation précise contraste volontairement avec les volumes rigoureusement définis réservés aux ateliers, bureaux des enseignants, salles de jurys ou de l'auditorium de 400 places ». Tschumi a pris soin d'éviter de recréer une structure ressemblant à l'Ecole des Beaux-Arts, au Bauhaus ou même aux universités américaines. Au centre d'un nouveau campus « technologique », sa création propose un nouveau modèle de bâtiment universitaire. Comme pour le Lerner Hall, il a mis l'accent sur la transparence et les facilités de circulation intérieure. Il compte sur ces facteurs pour faciliter les relations entre les étudiants et le corps enseignant et stimuler le processus d'apprentissage.

Making frequent use of computer-assisted design, Bernard Tschumi bends and folds spaces, making their perception and use an aesthetic and intellectual experience.

Die Nutzung von CAD-Programmen erlaubt Tschumi, seine Räume so zu gestalten, dass ihre Wahrnehmung und Nutzung zu einer ästhetischen und intellektuellen Erfahrung werden.

Utilisant beaucoup la CAO, Bernard Tschumi plie et déplie ses espaces, faisant de leur perception et de leur usage une expérience à la fois esthétique et intellectuelle.

UN STUDIO

UN Studio Van Berkel & Bos BV
Stadhouderskade 113
1073 AX Amsterdam
Netherlands

Tel: +31 20 570 2040
Fax: +31 20 570 2041
e-mail: info@unstudio.com
web: www.unstudio.com

Bascule Bridge and Bridgemaster's House ▶

BEN VAN BERKEL was born in Utrecht in 1957, and studied at the Rietveld Academie in Amsterdam and at the Architectural Association (AA) in London, receiving the AA Diploma with honors in 1987. After working briefly in the office of Santiago Calatrava, he established his practice in Amsterdam with **CAROLINE BOS** in 1988. He was visiting professor at Columbia University, New York, and visiting critic at Harvard University (1994). Diploma Unit Master, AA, London (1994-95). UN Studio Van Berkel & Bos has built the Karbouw (1990-92) and ACOM office buildings (1989-93), and the REMU electricity station (1989-93), all in Amersfoort, housing projects and the Aedes East Gallery for Kristin Feireiss (now Director of the Netherlands Architecture Institute, Rotterdam) in Berlin, as well as the Erasmus Bridge in Rotterdam (inaugurated in 1996). More recent projects in the Netherlands include the Möbius House ('t Gooi, 1993-97), the Museum Het Valkhof (Nijmegen, 1995-99), and renovation and extension of Rijksmuseum Twente (Enschede, 1992-96). Current work includes the MuMuTh Music Theater (Graz, 1998-2002), and the electrical substation Umspannwerk Mitte (Innsbruck, 1996-2000), both in Austria.

BEN VAN BERKEL, geboren 1957 in Utrecht, studierte an der Rietveld-Akademie in Amsterdam und an der Architectural Association (AA) in London, wo er 1987 sein Diplom mit Auszeichnung erwarb. Nach kurzer Tätigkeit bei Santiago Calatrava gründete er 1988 mit **CAROLINE BOS** ein eigenes Büro in Amsterdam. 1994 war van Berkel Gastprofessor an der Columbia University in New York und Gastkritiker in Harvard, von 1994 bis 1995 erwarb er das Diploma Unit Master an der AA in London. Außer der 1996 eröffneten Erasmus-Brücke in Rotterdam hat das Architekturbüro UN Studio Van Berkel & Bos die Bürogebäude Karbouw (1990-92) und ACOM (1989-93) sowie das Elektrizitätswerk REMU (1989-93), alle im niederländischen Amersfoort, ausgeführt. In Berlin entstanden Wohnbauten und die Galerie Aedes East für Kristin Feireiss (der jetzigen Leiterin des Niederländischen Architekturinstituts in Rotterdam). Zu den jüngsten Projekten in den Niederlanden gehören das Möbius-Haus in 't Gooi (1993-97), das Museum Het Valkhof in Nijmegen (1995-99) und die Modernisierung und Erweiterung des Rijksmuseum Twente in Enschede (1992-96). UN Studio realisiert derzeit zwei Bauten in Österreich: das Musiktheater MuMuTh in Graz (1998-2002) und das Umspannwerk Mitte in Innsbruck (1996-2000).

BEN VAN BERKEL naît à Utrecht en 1957. Il étudie à la Rietveld Academie d'Amsterdam et à l'Architectural Association (AA) de Londres, dont il sort diplômé avec mention en 1987. Après avoir brièvement travaillé dans l'agence de Santiago Calatrava en 1988, il ouvre son agence à Amsterdam, et s'associe avec **CAROLINE BOS**. En 1994, il est professeur invité à la Columbia University, New York, et critique invité à Harvard puis Diploma Unit Master à l'AA, Londres en 1994-95. Outre le pont Erasme à Rotterdam (inauguré en 1996), UN Studio Van Berkel & Bos a construit les immeubles de bureaux Karbouw (1990-92), ACOM (1989-93) et la centrale électrique REMU (1989-93), tous à Amersfoort en Pays-Bas, ainsi que des projets de logements et la galerie Aedes East à Berlin pour Kristin Feireiss (actuellement directrice de l'Institut néerlandais d'architecture de Rotterdam). Parmi leurs projets les plus récents, la maison Möbius ('t Gooi, 1993-97) ; le musée Het Valkhof (Nimègue, 1995-99) ; la rénovation et l'extension du Rijksmuseum Twente (Enschede, 1992-96) toutes dans les Pays-Bas; le complexe consacré à la musique MuMuTh (Graz, Autriche, 1998-2002) et le Umspannwerk Mitte (Innsbruck, Autriche, 1996-2000)

BASCULE BRIDGE AND BRIDGEMASTER'S HOUSE

Purmerend, Netherlands, 1995-98

Planning: 4/95-4/96. Construction: 12/96-3/98. Client: City of Purmerend.
Floor area ground floor bridgemaster's house: 36 m². Costs: ca. Hfl 14 000 000.

Ben van Berkel often works at the border between industry, architecture and engineering, as his Electrical Substation in Amersfoort or the Erasmus Bridge in Rotterdam prove. In what he calls "bridge for an ordinary place" in the north of the Netherlands, the three decks of the **BASCULE BRIDGE** open and close asynchronously "imitating the movement of playing fingers." A 12-m-high **BRIDGEMASTER'S HOUSE** controls the movement of the bridge. A concrete core covered with perforated steel plates reveals some of its inner workings, but also gives a mysterious appearance to this unique object. As van Berkel points out, redesigning such apparently banal elements requires new "non-hierarchical relationships between architects and engineers."

Ben van Berkels Entwürfe bewegen sich häufig an der Grenze zwischen Industrie, Architektur und Maschinenbaukunst, wie sein Elektrizitätswerk in Amersfoort oder seine Erasmus-Brücke in Rotterdam beweisen. Bei der im Norden Hollands gelegenen **HEBEBRÜCKE**, die van Berkel als »Brücke für einen alltäglichen Ort« bezeichnet, öffnen und schließen sich drei Plattformen auf asynchrone Weise, wodurch sie »die Bewegung spielender Finger nachahmen«. Von dem 12 m hohen Gebäude der **BRÜCKENWACHT** werden die Aktivitäten der Hebebrücke gesteuert. Ein mit perforierten Stahlplatten umhüllter Betonkern lässt einen Teil seiner inneren Mechanik sichtbar werden und verleiht diesem einzigartigen Bauwerk gleichzeitig ein geheimnisvolles Aussehen. Wie van Berkel betont, erfordert die Gestaltung solch scheinbar alltäglicher Gebäude neue »nicht-hierarchical Formen der Zusammenarbeit zwischen Architekten und Ingenieuren«.

Ben van Berkel travaille souvent aux frontières de l'industrie, de l'architecture et de l'ingénierie, comme le montrent sa station électrique d'Amersfoort, Pays-Bas (1994) ou le pont Erasme à Rotterdam. L'ouvrage qu'il qualifie de « pont pour un lieu ordinaire », au Nord des Pays-Bas présente trois tabliers du **PONT BASCULANT** qui s'ouvrent et se ferment de façon asynchrone « reprenant le mouvement de doigts qui pianotent. » Un petit bâtiment de 12 m de haut sert de **POSTE DE CONTRÔLE**. Le noyau de béton, couvert de plaques d'acier perforé révèle une partie des mécanismes intérieurs, mais donne également un aspect mystérieux à cet objet architectural original. Comme le fait remarquer van Berkel, concevoir des éléments apparemment aussi banalisés demande d'inventer de nouvelles « relations non hiérarchiques entre les architectes et les ingénieurs. »

Using unusual surface treatments and skewed building forms, Ben van Berkel challenges the very staid model of the traditional bridgemaster's house, adding an element of movement and transparency.

Mit ungewöhnlicher Oberflächenbehandlung und schrägen Flächen stellt van Berkel der traditionellen Bauweise von Brückenwachtgebäuden mit eher statischer Wirkung hier Bewegung und Transparenz entgegen.

A partir de formes inclinées et de surfaces inhabituelles, Ben van Berkel remet en question la forme classique du poste de contrôle de batellerie et l'enrichit d'un élément de mouvement et de transparence.

The angled form of the bridge-master's house recalls the movement of the bridge itself, as the image below clearly demonstrates.

Die schräge Form der Brückenwacht nimmt Bezug auf die Bewegungsabläufe der Hebebrücke.

L'inclinaison de la forme penchée rappelle le mouvement et le profil du pont lui-même, comme le montre la vue ci-dessous.

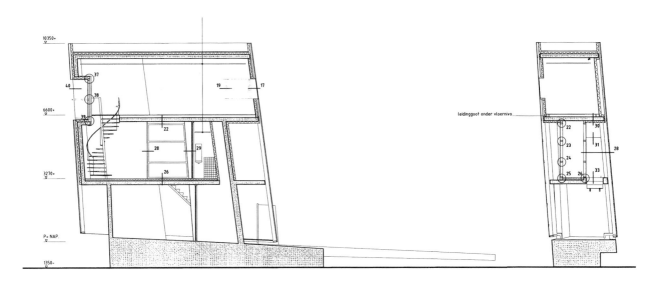

MUSEUM HET VALKHOF

Nijmegen, Netherlands, 1995-98

*Planning: 1995. Completion: 1998. Client: Stichting Museum Het Valkhof.
Floor area: ca. 6 100 m². Costs: Hfl 13 000 000.*

*The strong horizontal form and
cladding of the museum obviously
contrast with the small traditional
buildings located nearby.*

*Die streng horizontale Form und die
kraftvolle Fassadengestaltung des
Museums bilden einen auffallenden
Kontrast zu den kleinen Häusern der
Nachbarschaft.*

*Le volume horizontal et puissant du
musée contraste avec l'alignement
des petites maisons voisines.*

Part of an urban renewal program in this eastern Dutch city, the **MUSEUM HET VALKHOF** combines the Provinciaal Museum G. M. Kam and the Nijmeegs Museum Commanderie van Sint-Jan. The former is known for its extensive collection of Roman art, while the latter houses antiques, prints, and other works of art. Situated on a market square near Hunner Park, the building is clad in transparent greenish-blue and translucent glass. Although Studio Dumbar and WAAC from Rotterdam handled the interior design of the building, Ben van Berkel designed the basic structures. He points out that, by his estimate, there are no less than 88 different ways to visit the exhibitions that basically describe the history of the city at the same time offering a certain view of art.

Teil eines im ostholländischen Nijmegen durchgeführten Stadterneuerungsprogramms ist das **MUSEUM HET VALKHOF**, das die Bestände des Provinciaal Museum G. M. Kam und des Nijmeegs Museum Commanderie van Sint-Jan in sich vereint. Ersteres ist bekannt für seine umfangreiche Sammlung römischer Kunst, während letzteres Antiquitäten, Stiche und andere Kunstwerke beheimatet. An einem Marktplatz in der Nähe des Hunner Parks gelegen, ist das Gebäude mit grünlich-blauem Glas verkleidet. Obgleich das Studio Dumbar und WAAC aus Rotterdam die Innenausstattung des Bauwerks ausführten, entwarf Ben van Berkel die Grundelemente. Er weist darauf hin, dass es seiner Schätzung nach nicht weniger als 88 verschiedene Möglichkeiten gebe, die Ausstellungsräume zu besichtigen, in denen im Wesentlichen die Geschichte der Stadt und zugleich ein besonderer Blickwinkel auf die Kunst vermittelt werden.

Elément d'un programme de rénovation urbaine au centre d'une ville du Sud-Est des Pays-Bas, le **MUSÉE HET VALKHOF** regroupe le Provinciaal Museum G. M. Kam et le Nijmeegs Museum Commanderie van Sint-Jan. Le premier est connu pour son importante collection d'antiquités romaines, le second pour ses antiquités, gravures et autres œuvres d'art. Situé sur une place de marché près du Hunner Park, le bâtiment est habillé de verre bleu vert translucide. Le Studio Dumbar et WAAC de Rotterdam ont été chargés des aménagements intérieurs. Van Berkel fait remarquer qu'il n'existe pas moins de 88 façons de parcourir les salles d'exposition qui décrivent l'histoire de la ville tout en offrant une vision spécifique de l'histoire de l'art.

Ben van Berkel's approach is to offer an unusual degree of freedom to the visitor. Unlike many museum architects he prefers not to dictate a specific path, but rather to allow many different points of view to be expressed, including perspectives out onto the neighboring park.

Ben van Berkels Entwurf bietet den Museumsbesuchern ein ungewöhnliches Maß an Freiheit, indem er keinen bestimmten Weg durch die Räume vorgibt, sondern den Besuchern verschiedene Möglichkeiten lässt, zu denen auch Ausblicke in die umliegende Parklandschaft gehören.

La démarche de van Berkel consiste à offrir au visiteur un degré de liberté rarement atteint. A la différence de beaucoup de ses confrères, il préfère ne pas dicter un cheminement, et favorise une multiplicité de points de vue, y compris des échappées sur le parc environnant.

Though its rectilinear shape is specifically modern and non-organic, the museum's design gives it a direct relationship to its natural setting.

Trotz seiner modern und unorganisch-geradlinigen Form tritt das Museum durch seine Gestaltung in direkte Verbindung mit der Umgebung.

En dépit de ses lignes modernes et anorganiques, le musée entretient un lien direct avec son cadre naturel.

Rifkind House ▶

WILLIAMS AND TSIEN

Tod Williams Billie Tsien and Associates
222 Central Park South
New York, NY 10019
United States

Tel.: +1 212 582 2385
Fax: +1 212 245 1984
e-mail: twbta@network.net

TOD WILLIAMS was born in Detroit in 1943. He gained his B.A. degree (1965) and his M.F.A. degree (1967) from Princeton University. After six years as associate architect with Richard Meier in New York, he began his own practice there in 1974. He taught at Cooper Union for more than 15 years, as well as at Harvard, Yale, the University of Virginia, and the Southern California Institute of Architecture (SCI-Arc). He won the Prix de Rome in 1983. **BILLIE TSIEN,** born in Ithaca, New York, in 1949, gained her B.A. degree from Yale, and her M.Arch. from the University of California, Los Angeles (1977). A painter and graphic designer (1971-75), she has taught at Parsons School of Design, SCI-Arc, Harvard and Yale. Their built work includes the Feinberg Hall at Princeton University (New Jersey, 1986), the New College of the University of Virginia (Charlottesville, Virginia, 1992), and the renovation and extension of the Museum of Fine Arts in Phoenix, Arizona (1996). Current projects include an aquatic center for the Cranbrook Schools in Michigan, the Museum of American Folk Art in New York, and an amphitheater seating 25 000 in Guadalajara, Mexico.

TOD WILLIAMS, geboren 1943 in Detroit, erwarb 1965 den Bachelor of Arts und 1967 den Master of Fine Arts an der Princeton University. Nach sechsjähriger Mitarbeit im Büro von Richard Meier machte er sich 1974 in New York selbständig. Er lehrte an der Cooper Union, in Harvard und Yale, an der University of Virginia und am Southern California Institute of Architecture (SCI-Arc). 1983 wurde ihm der Prix de Rome verliehen. **BILLIE TSIEN**, geboren 1949 in Ithaca, New York, erwarb den Bachelor of Arts an der Yale University und 1977 den Master of Architecture an der University of California, Los Angeles. Von 1971 bis 1975 arbeitete sie als Malerin und Grafikerin. Außerdem lehrte sie an der Parsons School of Design, am SCI-Arc, in Harvard und Yale. Wichtige Bauten von Williams und Tsien sind die Feinberg Hall in Princeton, New Jersey (1986), das New College der University of Virginia in Charlottesville (1992), sowie der Umbau des Museum of Fine Arts in Phoenix, Arizona (1996). Zu ihren jüngsten Projekten gehören ein Zentrum für Wassersport für die Cranbrook Schulen in Michigan, das Museum of American Folk Art in New York und ein Amphitheater mit 25 000 Plätzen in Guadalajara, Mexiko.

TOD WILLIAMS, né à Detroit en 1943, Bachelor of Arts en 1965, Master of Fine Arts, 1967, Princeton University. Après six ans d'exercice comme architecte associé dans l'agence de Richard Meier (1967-73), il crée son agence à New York en 1974. Il enseigne pendant plus de 15 ans à la Cooper Union, à Harvard, Yale, à l'Université de Virginie et au Southern California Institute of Architecture (SCI-Arc). Prix de Rome en 1983. **BILLIE TSIEN**, née à Ithaca, New York, en 1949, Bachelor of Arts, Yale, Master of Architecture, UCLA, 1977. Elle a été peintre et graphiste de 1971 à 1975. Enseigne à la Parsons School of Design, SCI-Arc, à Harvard et à Yale. Parmi leurs réalisations : Feinberg Hall (Princeton, New Jersey, 1986), New College, University of Virginia (Charlottesville, Virginia, 1992) ; restauration complète et extension du Museum of Fine Arts de Phoenix, Arizona (1996). Parmi leurs projets actuels : un centre aquatique pour les Cranbrook Schools (Michigan), le Museum of American Folk Art (New York) et un amphithéâtre de 25 000 places à Guadalajara (Mexique).

RIFKIND HOUSE

Georgica Pond, Long Island, New York, USA, 1997-98

Construction: 1997-98. Client: Robert and Arleen Rifkind.
Floor area: 465 m² Costs: withheld

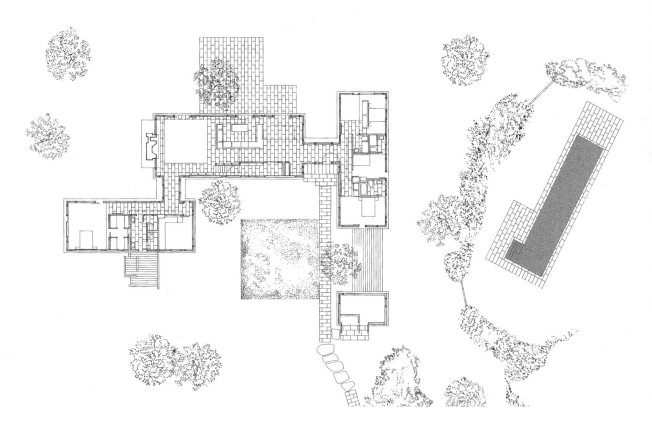

Set on a 1.5-hectare site on the edge of a large pond within view of the ocean, the **RIFKIND HOUSE** was intended to satisfy the client's specifications for "quiet serenity, an openness to the landscape and a sense of spaciousness without monumentality." It is, except for the slightly higher living room area, only about 3 m in height. It comprises four units – a planting and storage shed, a three-bedroom guest wing, a master bedroom area, and a "public" section. A wood-frame structure with cedar-siding, the house has ample glazing set in mahogany window frames, while inside floors are covered with Douglas fir and New York bluestone. Bookshelves, beds, dressers and furniture, also designed by the architects, are made of American cherry.

Das **RIFKIND HOUSE** ist auf einem 1,5 ha großen Grundstück mit Blick auf den Atlantik am Rand eines Teichs gelegen. Es sollte auf Wunsch des Bauherrn von »gelassener Heiterkeit, einer Offenheit für die Landschaft und einem Gefühl von Geräumigkeit ohne Monumentalität« geprägt sein. Das gesamte Gebäude ist, mit Ausnahme des leicht erhöhten Wohnraums, nur ca. 3 m hoch und setzt sich aus vier Einheiten zusammen: einer Kombination von Gewächshaus und Lagerschuppen, einem Gästetrakt mit drei Zimmern, einem großen Schlafraum und einem »öffentlichen« Bereich. Die aus einem mit Zedernholz verkleideten Holzgerüst bestehende Außenfassade des Hauses wird von großen Glasflächen mit Mahagoniholzrahmen durchbrochen, während die Böden im Inneren mit Douglasie und blauem Tonsandstein aus dem Hudsongebiet bedeckt sind. Die ebenfalls von den Architekten entworfenen Bücherregale, Betten, Kommoden und auch die anderen Möbel sind aus amerikanischem Kirschbaum gefertigt.

Située au bord d'un étang sur un terrain de 1,5 ha, la **MAISON RIFKIND** répond au souhait du client qui recherchait la « sérénité naturelle, l'ouverture sur le paysage et une impression d'espace sans monumentalité ». A l'exception du séjour, légèrement surélevé, la maison ne dépasse pas 3 m de hauteur. Elle se compose de quatre éléments – un hangar de stockage et de jardinage, une aile pour invités avec trois chambres, une partie réservée à la chambre du maître de maison et une zone « publique ». La structure en bois est bardée de cèdre. Les ouvertures en acajou sont vastes et les sols en pin de Douglas ou pierre bleue de New York. Les rayonnages pour les livres, les lits, les commodes et le mobilier sont en cerisier américain et ont été dessinés par les architectes.

Seen from two different angles, the house appears to be quite closed, with its horizontal cedar siding, or alternatively quite open, with the large vertical glass panels allowing views out toward the wooded site.

Während die mit Zedernholz verkleideten Wände auf der einen Seite des Gebäudes einen eher geschlossen Charakter vermitteln, wirken die großen Glasflächen, die den Blick auf das bewaldete Grundstück freigeben, sehr offen.

Selon les angles de vue, la maison semble plutôt fermée derrière son habillage de cèdre ou très ouverte par ses hauts panneaux de verre qui donnent sur le terrain boisé.

INDEX OF PLACES

CREDITS

PHOTO CREDITS

PHOTOGRAPHER CONTACTS

LUIS FERREIRA ALVES Rua de Algeria, Parque Habitacional do Lima, Entrada 29–Habitação 3A, P–4200 Porto / **TOM BONNER PHOTOGRAPHY** 1201 Abbot Kinney Boulevard, USA–Venice, CA 90291, Tel: +1 310 396 7125, Fax: +1 310 396 4792 / **NICOLAS BOREL** 237, rue Saint Denis, F–75002 Paris, Tel: +33 1 4026 4355, Fax: +33 1 4026 4336 / **ANTOINE BUONOMO** 36, rue des Pommiers, F–93500 Pantin, Tel: +33 1 4171 0064, Fax: +33 1 4171 0065 / **GITTY DARUGAR** Via Noseda 4, CH–6977 Ruvigliana, Tel/Fax: +41 91 972 1076 / **RICHARD DAVIES** Tel: +44 20 7722 3032, Fax +44 20 7483 1432, e-mail: richarddavies@easynet.co.uk / **ESTO PHOTOGRAPHICS INC.** 222 Valley Place, USA–Mamaroneck, NY 10543, Tel: +1 914 698 4060, Fax: +1 914 698 1033, e-mail: esto@esto.com / **DAVID GLOMB** 71340 Estellita Drive, USA–Rancho Mirage, CA 92270, Tel: +1 760 340 4455, Fax: +1 960 779 1872, e-mail: d.glomb@worldnet.att.net / **JEANNINE GOVAERS** Ruyschstraat 39", NL–1091 BS Amsterdam, Tel: +31 20 665 2332, Fax: +31 20 692 7760, e-mail: jgovaers@wxs.nl / **HEDRICH BLESSING** 11 West Illinois Street, USA–Chicago, IL 60610, Tel: +1 312 321 1151, Fax: +1 312 321 1165, e-mail: hb@hedrichblessing.com / **HEINRICH HELFENSTEIN** Böcklinstr. 17, CH–8032 Zurich, Tel: +41 1 380 2877, Fax: +41 1 252 5849, Mobile: +41 079 5752424 / **HIROYUKI HIRAI** 12-16-201 2-chome Aobadai, Japan–Meguro-ku, Tokyo 153-0042, Tel: +81 3 3462 5504, Fax: +81 3 3462 5535, e-mail: hiraiphoto@mug.biglobe.ne.jp / **TIMOTHY HURSLEY** The Arkansas Office, 1911 West Markham, USA–Little Rock, AR 72205, Tel: +1 501 3720 640, Fax: +1 510 372 3366, e-mail: tharkoff@aol.com / **TOSHIHARU KITAJIMA** NF Maison Interface, 23-102 Araki-cho, Japan–Shinjuku-ku, Tokyo 160, Tel: +81 3 3354 2203, Fax: +81 3 3354 2203 / **HERVÉ LANGLAIS** 118 rue Monge, F–75005 Paris, Tel: +33 1 4331 7896, e-mail: hervé.langlais@cybercable.fr / **MAURIZIO MARCATO** Via Apollo XI, 5-7, I–37050 S. Maria di Zevio (Vr), Tel: +39 045 6050601, Fax: +39 045 6050146, web: www.mauriziomarcato.com / **PAUL MAURER** 10, rue Jean Bouton, F–75012 Paris, Tel/Fax: +33 1 4342 3272, Mobile: +33 6 8090 3236, e-mail: pmaurer@cybercable.fr / **NORMAN MCGRATH** 164 West 79th Street, USA–New York, NY 100124, Tel: +1 212 799 6422, Fax: +1 212 799 1285, e-mail: mcgrath@gte.net / **MICHAEL MORAN** 245 Mulberry Street, No. 14, USA–New York, NY 10012, Tel: +1 212 334 4543, Fax: +1 212 334 3854 / **PALLADIUM PHOTODESIGN** Barbara Burg / Oliver Schuh, Leyendeckerstrasse 27, D–50825 Köln, Tel: +49 221 954 1424, Fax: +49 221 954 1425, e-mail: info@palladium.de, web: www.palladium.de / **JEAN-PIERRE PORCHER** 9, avenue Parmentier, F–75011 Paris, Tel: +33 6 1510 0606, Fax: +33 1 4493 7665 / **UNDINE PRÖHL** 1930 Ocean Avenue # 302, USA–Santa Monica, CA 90405, Tel/Fax: +1 310 399 503, e-mail: uprohl@aol.com / **CHRISTIAN RICHTERS** Dettenstrasse 1, D–48147 Münster, Tel: +49 251 277 447, Fax: +49 251 274 388 / **PHILIPPE RUAULT** (Nouvel-Koolhas-Fuksas-Lacaton-Vassel-Ricciotti-Rudy), 23bis, rue Jean-Jaures, F–4400 Nantes, Tel: +33 6 0760 9606, Fax: +33 2 4008 2596 / **EIICHIRO SAKATA** 1-33-33-201 Ebisu Nishi, Japan–Shibuya-ku, Tokyo 150-0021, Tel: +81 3 3780 0329, Fax: +81 3 3780 0849 / **JULIUS SHULMAN** 7875 Woodrow Wilson Drive, USA–Los Angeles, CA 90046, Tel: +1 323 654 0877, Fax: +1 323 654 1047, e-mail: mckee@silcom.com / **J. SCOTT SMITH** USA–Santa Monica, CA 90405, Tel/Fax: +1 310 392 1300, e-mail: jssp@tstonramp.com / **MARGHERITA SPILUTTINI** Schoenlaterngasse 8, A–1010 Vienna, Tel/Fax: +43 1 512 5908, web: www.spiluttini.com / **JAN STALLER** 161 Charles Street, USA New York, NY 10014, e-mail: StallCo@aol.com, web: www.janstaller.net / **DAN STEVENS** Woodstock Studios, 36 Woodstock Grove, UK–London W12 8LE, Tel: +44 20 8749 4045, Fax: +44 20 8749 9950, e-mail: dan@danstevens.co.uk / **TIM STREET PORTER** 2074 Watsona Terrace, USA–Los Angeles, CA 90068, Tel: +1 323 874 4278, Fax: +1 323 876 8795 / **HISAO SUZUKI** Torrent del Fondo, 8, E–08338 Premià de Dalt (Barcelona), Tel: +34 93 752 1559, Fax: +34 93 751 7825, e-mail: hisao.suzuki@teleline.es / **LUCA VIGNELLI** 475 Tenth Avenue, USA–New York, NY 10018, Tel: +1 212 675 6457, Fax: +1 212 675 6457 / **PAUL WARCHOL PHOTOGRAPH** 224 Centre St. 5th fl, USA–New York, NY 10013, Tel: +1 212 431 3461, Fax: +1 212 274 1953, e-mail: pw@warcholphotography.com / **ANDREW WARD** 73 Gartmoor Gardens, UK–London SW19 6NX, Tel/Fax: +44 20 8789 4415, Mobile: +44 0780 1278540, e-mail: andward@wards.u-net.com / **GASTON WICKY** Freie Strasse 17, CH–8028 Zurich, Tel: +41 1 261 6863, Fax: +41 1 261 6896 / **REINHARD ZIMMERMANN** Grubenstrasse 45, CH–8045 Zurich, Tel: +41 1 461 5544, Fax: +41 1 461 5545